healing
foods

healing foods

Over 300 delicious recipes
for special diets

Consultant Editor
Jill Scott

HERMES
HOUSE

This edition is published by Hermes House

Hermes House is an imprint of
Anness Publishing Limited
Hermes House
88–89 Blackfriars Road
London SE1 8HA

A CIP catalogue record for this book is available from the British Library.

Publisher: Joanna Lorenz
Executive Editor: Linda Fraser
Project Editor: Susannah Blake
Designer: Ian Sandom
Reader: Kate Sillence
Production Controller: Ben Worley
Photographers: Karl Adamson, Edward Allwright, Steve Baxter, Nicki Dowey, James Duncan, Ian Garlick,
Michelle Garrett, Amanda Heywood, Janine Hosegood, Dave Jordan, Dave King, Don Last,
William Lingwood, Patrick McLeavey, Michael Michaels, Tom Odulate, Peter Reilly, Sam Stowell
Recipes: Catherine Atkinson, Angela Boggiano, Carla Capalbo, Jacqueline Clarke, Carole Clements,
Kit Chan, Trish Davies, Roz Denny, Nicola Diggins, Matthew Drennan, Sarah Edmonds, Joanna Farrow,
Christine France, Silvana Franco, Shirley Gill, Carole Handslip, Christine Ingram, Manisha Kanani,
Lesley Mackley, Norma Macmillan, Sue Maggs, Kathy Mann, Norma Miller, Sallie Morris, Annie Nichols,
Maggie Pannell, Jennie Shapter, Anne Sheasby, Laura Washburn, Stephen Wheeler, Kate Whiteman,
Elizabeth Wolf-Cohen, Jeni Wright

Previously published in nine separate volumes, *The Allergy-free Cookbook, The Arthritis Cookbook, The Cancer Prevention Cookbook,*
The Dairy-free Cookbook, The Diabetic Cookbook, The Gluten-free Cookbook, The Healthy Heart Cookbook,
The Low Cholesterol Cookbook and *The Low-salt Cookbook.*

1 3 5 7 9 10 8 6 4 2

NOTES
For all recipes, quantities are given in both metric and imperial
measures and, where appropriate, measures are also given in standard
cups and spoons. Follow one set, but not a mixture, because they
are not interchangeable.

Soy sauce contains wheat flour and is unsuitable for wheat or gluten-free
diets. As a substitute, use tamari, which is also made from soya beans
but is rice based. It is readily available from health-food shops.

Many commercial stock cubes contain MSG (monosodium glutamate), which
can be made from wheat starch, and are therefore unsuitable for wheat- or
gluten-free diets. If there is no time to make your own stock, look for
bouillon cubes or powders that are labelled "gluten-free" or use chilled stocks,
which are available from larger supermarkets. Always read the ingredients
list on any food product to check that it is "safe" to eat for any special diet.

Medium eggs are used unless otherwise stated.

ALLERGY-FREE RECIPES
The recipes in this book have an at-a-glance guide to the foods
that each is free from:

Gluten-free   Wheat-free   Corn-free   Dairy-free   Nut-free

Fish and
Shellfish-free   Egg-free   Yeast-free   Soya-free

CONTENTS

PREFACE

The way we live our lives today, in a fast-moving world of technology, means we often have less time to look after ourselves properly. Most people are less active than they should be. They eat diets that are too high in fat and too low in fruit and vegetables, and live busy and stressful lives. As a consequence, there is a greater risk of heart disease and other serious illnesses, as well as weight problems and even obesity. But the good news is that we can do something about it.

Choosing to follow a healthy lifestyle can help you to live longer and make the most of your life. The main focus of this book is on the dietary aspects involved, but to attain the real benefits, it is important to look carefully at your life as a whole.

Working towards leading a healthier lifestyle means not only eating well but also being more physically active, not smoking and taking "time out" for relaxation. You can have the healthiest diet possible, but the benefits will be reduced if you smoke cigarettes or rarely take exercise.

Even apparently small changes in your daily lifestyle can make a noticeable difference to your overall health and help to improve your energy levels and general quality of life.

THE BENEFITS OF A HEALTHY LIFESTYLE

Taking care of yourself by trying to change your habits and live more healthily will help you to:
• Gain confidence in how you look and feel.
• Manage your weight better.
• Lower your risk of developing serious illnesses such as heart disease, high blood pressure, diabetes, obesity and some forms of cancer.
• Achieve a positive outlook and feeling of well-being.

LIFESTYLE GUIDELINES

Scientists and nutrition experts recommend the following five key guidelines for a healthy lifestyle:
• Be active in your daily life.
• Make sure your leisure time is varied and stimulating.
• Aim for five or more servings of fruit and vegetables a day.

• Base meals around starchy foods, such as rice and pasta.
• Choose low-fat or lower-fat foods whenever possible.

Below: Enjoying active leisure time, such as a walk in the countryside or in a city park, can help you on your way to achieving a healthy lifestyle.

THE LINK BETWEEN DIET AND HEALTH

There is no doubt that what we eat affects our health, and there are now proven links between diet and disease. Diseases that are known to be linked to diet include heart disease, osteoporosis, cancer, diverticular disease, constipation and other digestive disorders.

OBESITY

Throughout the developed world, evidence suggests that the number of people who are overweight or obese continues to rise. Both dietary factors and physical inactivity are linked to the development of obesity. Being overweight can be detrimental to good health and is associated with an increase in cardiovascular disease risk factors, such as high blood pressure (hypertension), high blood cholesterol levels and diabetes. Being overweight and obese can also aggravate other existing problems that are otherwise unrelated, such as osteoarthritis.

Scientists agree that dietary change is essential if we are to see a reduction in the prevalence of heart disease, strokes and certain types of cancer. Recommendations have been made about specific dietary changes, in particular the reduction of fat, especially saturated fat. Many people consume more than the recommended daily intake of fat, which should be no more than 35 per cent of dietary energy, and most people would benefit from switching to lower-fat options.

Right: Foods that are high in saturated fats can increase your risk of heart disease.

CARDIOVASCULAR DISEASE

A diet high in saturated fat is known to be one of several risk factors in the development of cardiovascular disease, which includes heart disease and strokes, and which accounts for a huge number of deaths every year. Nutrients such as those contained in fish oils, the anti-oxidants found in fruit and vegetables, and possibly dietary fibre, are all believed to help in protecting against the development of heart disease.

CANCER

It is estimated that, worldwide, some 7.6 million people will develop cancer and 5 million will die of the disease every year. Diet is believed to be linked to 10–70 per cent of all cancers. This compares with estimates of 30 per cent for smoking, 3 per cent for alcohol, about 4 per cent for occupation and 10 per cent for infections. Dietary factors are particularly associated with colo–rectal cancer, stomach cancer, and possibly oral and oesophageal cancer.

Left: Foods such as oily fish, fruit and vegetables are believed to protect against many diseases, such as cancer.

HEALING FOODS AND SPECIAL DIETS

We all need food for life. It provides us with the nutrients we need to stay healthy. Some foods are healthier than others, and can help to lower our risk of developing certain diseases, such as some cancers and other degenerative disorders.

Fresh fruit and vegetables, for example, are packed with health-giving nutrients, such as antioxidants, flavenoids and phytochemicals, as well as many other important constituents, which can have a protective effect on our health.

Sometimes, changes to the diet are needed to treat or manage a diagnosed condition, such as a food allergy or diabetes. In other words, it may be necessary to follow a special diet in which the healthy eating guidelines are adapted to suit individual needs.

Whatever your condition or food sensitivity, it is vital that your diet continues to provide the essential nutrients that your body needs. Careful substitution of one food or group of foods can be achieved with a little thought and planning. For example, if milk and dairy foods are excluded from the diet, it is essential that you continue to include foods that will provide sufficient calcium, because dairy foods are the richest dietary source of calcium.

Thankfully there is now a good range of alternatives to dairy foods, mainly in the form of soya, such as soya milk and soya desserts, so it can be quite easy to substitute one product for another. Try to opt for the calcium-fortified varieties, because soya is not naturally a good source of calcium. This will help to boost your daily calcium intake. The section on cow's milk intolerance offers more practical advice about which foods can be included in the diet to ensure a healthy calcium intake.

The more restricted a diet is, the more difficult it will be to meet all of your body's nutritional requirements. This is because variety is the key to a healthy, balanced diet and eating a variety of different foods every day is the easiest way of ensuring a healthy diet. If the variety of foods that you can eat is restricted, particularly if several different groups of food are avoided, more care is needed when planning your diet. If you find this very difficult, then a dietary supplement may be needed to boost your intake of essential vitamins and minerals.

There might be other reasons why someone decides to change his or her diet. The healthy eating guidelines outlined in each section form the foundation of a well-balanced diet, but you may choose to fine tune these to suit your own needs, or to include foods that you believe will reduce your risk of developing other diseases, such as cancer or heart disease.

There is certainly good scientific evidence that the antioxidant nutrients, particularly vitamin A, in the form of betacarotene, vitamin C and vitamin E, can help prevent the build up of

Left: A diet that is rich in fruit and vegetables is essential for good health. Aim to eat five or more portions of fruit and vegetables a day.

compounds called free radicals, which are thought to be responsible for triggering cellular damage, resulting in the development of serious illness.

Betacarotene and vitamin C in particular are associated with protection against the development of certain cancers. Good sources of betacarotene include yellow or orange fruits and vegetables, such as carrots, tomatoes, pumpkin, red peppers, apricots and peaches, as well as green leafy vegetables, such as broccoli and spinach. Rich supplies of vitamin C can be found in citrus fruits and juices, kiwi fruit, blackcurrants, strawberries and tomatoes.

Vitamin E is associated with protection against heart disease. Good food sources of vitamin E include vegetable oils, particularly sunflower oil; almonds; wholegrain breakfast cereals and bread; eggs; avocados; dairy products; margarines and spreads.

One of the best ways of increasing your intake of these valuable health-giving nutrients is to eat five or more portions of fruit and vegetables each day. In parts of the world where people eat lots of fresh fruit and vegetables, such as Mediterranean countries, the incidence of both heart disease and cancers is much lower.

Above: Eating can be one of the greatest pleasures in life, so take time out to enjoy meals in a calm and relaxing environment with your friends and family.

THE PLEASURES OF EATING

In all the discussions around what to eat and what to watch out for, it is important not to forget that eating is also a very enjoyable everyday activity. It is important that food is eaten not just for health but also for taste, and – sometimes – for pure indulgence. Even on a very restricted diet, try not to cut out all of your favourite foods, and enjoy them occasionally as a treat.

ALLERGY-FREE EATING

If you have ever developed a bad migraine or an irritating skin rash,

it may be that the condition was caused not by illness but by

something to which you are allergic or sensitive. The idea of changing

your eating habits and cutting out certain foods that you are used to

eating may seem like a daunting task. This chapter provides all the

practical advice you will need, from recognizing an allergic reaction

to isolating the culprit and maintaining a healthy diet.

INTRODUCTION

Allergic reactions, intolerances and sensitivities can take many different forms, and can prove difficult to pinpoint. Although they are not thought of as illnesses, they can sometimes make the sufferer feel extremely unwell, as anyone with asthma or hayfever will tell you. Depending on the nature and severity of your symptoms, the problem can be either a mild, short-term nuisance or a more serious, long-term condition, such as asthma or coeliac disease.

The potential causes of an allergic reaction are numerous and can be difficult to identify. The aim of this chapter is to help you discover if something that you are eating or drinking could be the cause of your symptoms. Once you've tracked down the cause, this chapter has helpful advice on how to adapt your diet to be nutritionally balanced while excluding anything to which you're sensitive. By investigating your symptoms and excluding suspect foods from your diet, you can discover those responsible for the reaction and use the delicious and easily prepared recipes in the second part of the book to help you enjoy a healthy, allergy-free life.

CAUSES AND REACTIONS

An allergy is a reaction that occurs when the body's immune (defence) system overreacts to a normally harmless substance, causing irritation, disability and sometimes even fatality. A substance that causes an allergy is called an allergen and can be anything in the environment – whether it's something ingested, inhaled or that touches the skin – that causes an adverse reaction. Among the most commonly found allergens are pollen, house-dust mites, pet hair, insect stings, chemicals or food and drink.

Our immune system usually protects us from harmful foreign invaders, such as viruses and bacteria, that might otherwise cause illness. In the allergic person, however, the system believes that the allergen is damaging and reacts to it accordingly. A special type of anti-body, called IgE (immunoglobulin E), is produced to fend off the threatening substance. This in turn leads the special "mast" cells in our bodies to release further chemicals, the best known being histamine, which join the IgE antibodies in attacking the invading material. The result is an allergic reaction, with its associated symptoms. The site of the reaction will depend on where the mast cells are located, and is often in such places as the nose, skin, lungs or intestines. Typical allergic reactions and their symptoms include vomiting and diarrhoea; hayfever; asthma (coughing, wheezing and breathlessness); perennial rhinitis (blocked or runny nose); urticaria or hives (skin rash); and eczema (mild to severe dry skin condition).

Below: Pet hair may cause an allergic reaction that results in irritation to the eyes, nose and skin, and difficulty in breathing.

How Common are Allergies?

It is not known just how common allergies are because the potential causes are numerous and can be difficult to identify. It is not even known exactly how many people react badly to certain substances, since many cases are mild enough to be undetected or may be misdiagnosed.

Allergies (particularly asthma and hayfever) appear to be on the increase and this may be a consequence of aspects of contemporary living, such as increased air pollution and more use of chemicals and pesticides.

It has also been suggested that because modern medicine has reduced our risk of infection from "naturally" harmful foreign invaders, such as bacteria, our immune systems are now insufficiently challenged, leading to a reaction, in genetically susceptible people, to ordinarily harmless substances. Greater awareness and recognition of allergies may also be a factor in our perception of the problem: it is important not to use the term indiscriminately as a convenient scapegoat for all kinds of ailments and complaints that have never been proved to be the result of an allergic reaction.

Surprisingly, the onset of an allergy or intolerance can occur at any age and the substance causing it may be something that has previously been tolerated. Equally, sensitivity can be outgrown, and troublesome symptoms can completely disappear.

Susceptibility to Allergic Disease

There is a strong genetic link with the development of allergies. If someone in your family – a parent, for example – has an allergy to something, it is quite likely that this susceptibility may be passed on. It is also thought that some people have a susceptible immune system, particularly if they have increased levels of the IgE antibody (immunoglobulin E). Children with

high levels of blood IgE often suffer from asthma and hayfever, and may also be allergic to some foods.

The Difference Between Allergy, Intolerance and Sensitivity

Strictly speaking, the word "allergy" should only be used to describe a specific response caused by an over-reaction of the immune system. An intolerance, however, is a broader term describing any unpleasant reaction to an offending substance. Hyper-sensitivity can be used as a general description covering both allergy and intolerance, although none of these should be confused with food aversion, which has psychological roots.

There are many different causes of food intolerance, which may be linked to the behaviour of various enzymes or bacteria in the body. Lactose (milk sugar) intolerance, for example, is not an allergic reaction but occurs because a person has insufficient lactase

Above: Eggs, citrus fruits, peanuts and shellfish pose a problem for many people.

enzyme, which is needed for the digestion of lactose.

There are also a number of substances in food that can cause a reaction in some people. Caffeine in tea, coffee, chocolate and cola, for instance, can bring on palpitations and restless behaviour, while amines found in red wine, chocolate and cheese can trigger a migraine. These are not true allergic reactions, although the term is frequently used loosely for describing all sorts of food intolerance.

Non-food Allergens

Discover the cause of your allergy, then take action to avoid the substance or to minimize your exposure to it. Could one of these allergens be to blame?
House-dust mites Modern homes often have fitted carpets, double glazing, central heating and poor ventilation, providing ideal conditions

for house mites to thrive. You should vacuum regularly, wet-wipe surfaces, consider wood, lino or other hard flooring rather than carpets, and blinds rather than curtains. Open windows as often as possible.

Bee and Wasp Stings These may cause pain and swelling and can even occasionally cause anaphylactic shock.

Jewellery Metal allergy (especially to nickel) can cause skin irritation.

Medicines Aspirin and penicillin and other antibiotics can cause an allergic rash. Aspirin may cause asthma.

Pets Both fur and feathers can be responsible for allergic rhinitis, asthma and eczema.

Pollen Hayfever is a very common allergy. It causes itchy eyes, sneezing and a blocked nose, especially when the sufferer ventures outdoors, and particularly in early summer. To reduce the symptoms, it is best to avoid over-exposure by closing windows and wearing sunglasses.

Toiletries and Cosmetics Some perfumed products can be a problem so try changing to a pure formulation or using non-allergenic make-up.

Above: Beauty preparations and soaps with non-allergenic formulae are now widely available and popular for their purity.

COMMON ALLERGIES AND THEIR SYMPTOMS

Allergic Disease	Allergen	Typical Symptoms
Hayfever (seasonal)	Pollen	Sneezing, streaming eyes, blocked nose
Asthma wheezing, breathlessness	Dust mites, animal hair, pollen	Coughing,
Allergic Rhinitis (perennial)	Dust mites, animal hair	Sneezing, runny nose, itchy eyes
Urticaria (skin rash)	Food, medicines	Itchy rash, characterized by the eruption of weals or "hives"

FOOD ALLERGIES

Allergic Disease	Allergen	Typical Symptoms
Coeliac Disease	Gluten (protein found in wheat, barley, rye and oats)	Poor growth, weight loss through vomiting and diarrhoea, tiredness
Peanut Allergy	Peanuts (and possibly other nuts and seeds)	Can cause a massive, potentially fatal reaction called anaphylactic shock, where the victim finds it hard to breathe, turns blue around the lips and faints or loses consciousness
Wheat Allergy	Wheat and wheat products	Asthma, itchy skin, diarrhoea
Egg Allergy	Eggs and egg products	Eczema or urticaria
Fish Allergy	Fish and shellfish	Urticaria in mild cases, but can lead to anaphylactic shock in severe cases
Milk Allergy	Milk protein	Eczema, asthma, perennial rhinitis, intestinal upsets

A small minority of people may also be allergic to food additives, both natural and artificial, such as food colours like tartrazine and anatto and preservatives such as benzoate. However, as the chart shows,

TRACKING DOWN THE PROBLEM

The first step in investigating any potential food allergy or intolerance is to speak to your family doctor, who should initially make sure that your symptoms are not due to any other illness. He or she will try to diagnose the problem by asking questions about your diet and lifestyle and whether you've noticed if symptoms are worse at any particular time. The medical profession varies in its attitude and approach to the treatment of allergies. You may be referred to a special hospital unit or clinic for further investigation or you could be advised to see a dietician, if dietary changes are to be considered. Many clinics offer allergy testing by a variety of methods, which are described below. While these may prove useful, not all of these methods are recognized by the medical profession as providing reliable results.

IS AN ALLERGIC REACTION LIKELY TO BE IMMEDIATE?

In cases of severe, acute allergy (which susceptible individuals may experience after eating peanuts, fish, eggs or sesame seeds) reaction is immediate and can be life threatening. After a first attack, those affected will be well aware of their allergy. It is vital that they avoid the offending food and always carry appropriate treatment, such as steroid inhalers, antihistamine tablets or emergency adrenaline (for anaphylaxis/anaphylactic shock).

Acute reactions to milk (and wheat) tend to be less severe and are often delayed (12–48 hours after ingesting the trigger food). In infants, severe acute reaction can occur, but as the diet is limited, the offending trigger is usually obvious – as when formula milk is introduced after breastfeeding. Recurring headaches, skin complaints, sinus or digestive problems are likely to be caused by something environmental or something eaten regularly, which is why milk or wheat is often suspected.

Above: If you suspect that you or someone in your family may be suffering from an allergy, the first thing to do is make an appointment with your doctor.

WHAT METHODS ARE USED TO TEST FOR ALLERGIES OR INTOLERANCES?

The RAST (Radio Allergo Sorbent Test) This test can be used for identifying acute allergies when there is an immediate reaction, by measuring IgE (immunoglobulin E) antibody levels in the blood.

The Skin Prick Test A few drops of the suspect allergen (prepared to a standardized concentration) are put on the skin, which is then pricked, so that the allergen seeps underneath. After a brief delay, the allergist looks for signs of a reaction. The test is quite successful for detecting environmental allergies, such as pollen or cat hair, which exhibit immediate sensitivity, but may be less useful for food intolerances, which are often delayed. However, extreme allergic disorders, such as anaphylaxis, do usually give a positive skin prick test.

The Vega Test In this test, an electrode is placed on an acupuncture point or held in the hand. It is said to detect whether a substance placed on the machine causes you to react, but again tests may not be reliable.

Lactose intolerance in infants may be diagnosed by checking stools for acidity (lactic acid is a by-product of undigested lactose).

Exclusion and Challenge Diets These provide the most accurate and effective means of discovering a food intolerance. The sufferer excludes suspect foods, waits to see whether there is an improvement in symptoms, then gradually reintroduces them. For more information, see "Testing for Food Allergies".

TESTING FOR FOOD ALLERGIES

Diet investigation is often used to try and discover the cause of food sensitivities. Depending on which food(s) are suspected, the diet may be relatively simple or involve the dieter in a substantial amount of thought and commitment.

In cases of multiple food intolerance, it is far more difficult to discover the whole problem and, because psychological factors may influence a person's perception of how a food affects them, blind testing may be advised so that an accurate diagnosis can be obtained.

Food intolerances are often not lifelong sensitivities. People find that after a rest period the offending food can be reintroduced gradually. However, the food should only be eaten infrequently; eating too much or too often may trigger a repeat of the previous symptoms.

Different clinics and specialists will vary in their approach towards dietary testing, so follow the advice given by your own dietician. Whatever the diet, it is essential that you stick to it rigidly as any lapses will affect the validity of your results.

SIMPLE EXCLUSION DIET

If you have a fairly good idea about which single food is causing you a problem, it is a simple matter to exclude it from your diet and see if the symptoms disappear or improve. It is quite easy to avoid some foods, such as cheese, red wine and citrus fruits, but if a major food group, such as dairy products or wheat is suspected, you will need to take professional advice from a dietician on how to modify your diet safely without missing out on important nutrients. After avoiding the suspect food for a few weeks, try eating it again and see if the symptoms return. If you have experienced a severe allergic reaction to a particular food, such as peanuts, don't attempt to try the food again. You already know the cause of the problem and are strongly advised not to risk repeating the reaction.

Below: Common trigger foods that cause food intolerances and allergies include dairy products such as milk and yogurt, wheat, nuts, citrus fruits and citrus drinks, coffee, chocolate, eggs and shellfish.

ELIMINATION DIET TIPS AND GUIDELINES

- Don't choose a busy time, whether at work or at home, to undertake an elimination diet; you need to be stress-free.
- Prepare and plan ahead, so that you don't run out of suitable foods and can easily cater for other members of the family.
- Do not skip meals.
- Try to base your diet on fresh foods as much as possible.
- Stick to plain cooked dishes because using a lot of ingredients in recipes will make detection all the more difficult.
- Avoid eating out, or if you do, choose plainly cooked dishes.
- Make a note of the ingredients used in any manufactured foods.
- Plan some non-food treats for yourself, such as a trip to the hairdresser, a manicure or a sauna, so that you don't focus all your attention on your diet.

MULTIPLE FOOD EXCLUSION DIET

If it's suspected that there is a dietary cause for your symptoms but the offending food is not known, it may be suggested that you cut out common trigger foods, which are known to cause problems most frequently. These foods include milk and dairy products, eggs, shellfish, wheat, citrus fruits, nuts, coffee, chocolate and azo dyes, and also possibly corn, yeast and soya.

You will need to follow this diet for two to three weeks to see if any improvement occurs. If symptoms ease or disappear, the excluded foods should

Below: A strict elimination diet permits only foods that rarely cause allergy problems, such as lamb, turkey, rice, potatoes, broccoli, cauliflower and pears.

then be reintroduced individually, allowing an interval of several days between each. If the symptoms reappear, you have your answer – although several repeat exercises may be necessary to be sure of the diagnosis.

If there is no improvement while following the diet, either some other food could be responsible (and you may be advised to try the simple exclusion diet) or you will need to investigate other, non-dietary causes.

STRICT ELIMINATION DIET

This very strict diet consists of only a few basic foods that are rarely known to cause a reaction. Because it severely limits the food selection, a strict elimination diet is only advised in extreme cases where medication does not provide any relief. Foods that are commonly allowed include lamb or turkey, potatoes, rice, pears, cauliflower or broccoli (and sometimes other vegetables), sunflower or olive oil and bottled water. The exact range of permitted foods may vary at the discretion of your consultant.

The diet is followed strictly for two to three weeks. Foods are reintroduced one by one, and any change of symptoms observed.

RARE FOODS DIET

This is basically the same as the strict elimination diet, except that some more unusual foods, such as exotic fruits and unusual vegetables and meats, are allowed. The theory behind this diet is that people are less likely to react to foods that they have not eaten (or rarely eaten) before. If symptoms still persist on this diet, then the likely diagnosis is that the person is not food-sensitive and that some other factor is responsible, or that the person has an undiagnosed medical condition.

FASTING

This is a drastic measure that is not generally advised because of the risk of severe nutritional disorders that may

---

FOOD DIARY

Date : *Monday 24th*

Meal	Food / Drink	Time taken	Symptoms
Breakfast	*orange juice* *2 slices of toast* *spread with butter* *& marmalade* *cup of tea*	*7.45am*	
Mid-morning	*cup of coffee* *chocolate biscuit*	*10.30am*	
Lunch	*cheese sandwich* *packet of crisps* *strawberry yogurt*	*12.30pm*	*Migraine about 2.00pm*
Mid-afternoon	*cup of tea* *jam doughnut*	*3.00pm*	
Evening meal	*grilled fish* *new potatoes and peas* *glass of white wine*	*7.00pm*	

Additional Notes
Difficult day at work – felt very stressed and tired.
Might be starting a cold, sneezing a lot and felt rather blocked up.

---

affect the balance of your health. It is not advisable to attempt such an extreme regime, whether for intolerance testing, weight loss or any other dietary reason.

KEEPING A FOOD DIARY

This is a useful exercise, both as an initial reminder of which foods you eat and when you eat them, and in order to find out whether you are achieving a healthy, balanced diet. It is also advisable when you are following an exclusion or elimination diet.

The food diary can help you discover if you really do have a true food intolerance or sensitivity, or whether your symptoms may have other, non food-related causes. Stress, tiredness and even the menstrual cycle

can all aggravate a condition. Write down everything that you eat and drink, any symptoms that appear, and when or if they worsen.

A detailed food diary will also be a helpful aid for your doctor or dietician when they are trying to reach a diagnosis and may help them see where to make any dietary adjustments. Remember that symptoms may not appear immediately after eating an offending food. Any reaction may happen hours – or even days – later. You can't presume that the culprit is something you ate at your last meal. In addition, a sensitivity reaction to food may be worse one day than another. All this makes the detection process quite difficult so you will need to be both vigilant and patient.

THE HEALTHY DIET

Eating a healthy, well-balanced diet can help us to feel more energetic and improve both our short-term and long-term health. Before deciding to cut out foods from your diet because of a food allergy or intolerance, it is important to check that you have been eating a healthy diet. Sometimes, symptoms that are thought to be due to allergies clear up when the overall diet is improved.

Healthy eating doesn't just mean cutting down on foods that are high in fat, sugar or salt. A healthy diet is all about balance and variety. Foods can be grouped according to the essential nutrients they contain. To provide the body with the essential nutrients it needs, eat a variety of foods from each of these food groups, in appropriate amounts, every day. This is an easy way of making sure you are eating a healthy, well-balanced diet. For most people, this means eating more fruit and vegetables and cutting down on foods containing fat and foods containing sugar.

FRUIT AND VEGETABLES
Foods in this group include fresh, frozen and canned fruit and vegetables, dried fruits and fruit and vegetable juices. These foods provide a rich supply of nutrients, such as vitamins, betacarotene, folate and fibre.

Try to eat five or more portions of fruit and vegetables a day. In places where large amounts of fruit and vegetables are eaten every day, such as Mediterranean countries, the incidence of heart disease, cancer and other degenerative diseases is relatively low. Fruit and vegetables are believed to help protect against these diseases.

Above: Starchy foods, such as plantain, yam, sweet potatoes and potatoes, should be included in every meal.

STARCHY FOODS
Foods in this group include bread, potatoes, pasta, rice, noodles, couscous, oats, polenta and breakfast cereals (especially wholegrain varieties). These foods provide vitamins, especially B vitamins; nutrients and minerals, such as calcium and iron; fibre, particularly from wholegrain foods; and energy. Try to include a food from this group at every meal, choosing wholegrain varieties whenever possible.

MILK AND DAIRY FOODS
Foods in this group include milk, cheese, yogurt and fromage frais. They are rich in vitamins B_{12}, A and D; calcium; and protein. Try to include two to three portions of dairy products every day, choosing lower-fat varieties whenever possible. Low-fat varieties contain just as much calcium.

Left: Fruit and vegetables are a valuable source of vitamins and essential nutrients.

HOW TO BOOST YOUR DAILY INTAKE OF FRUIT AND VEGETABLES

Try adding an extra portion to your daily diet and gradually build up to a target of five or more portions a day.

BREAKFAST
- Add fresh or dried fruit to breakfast cereal, e.g. sliced banana, raisins or apricots.
- Have half a grapefruit or canned grapefruit segments in fruit juice.
- Include a glass of fruit juice with your breakfast.
- For a cooked breakfast, try grilled mushrooms on toast.

MAIN MEALS
- Try to include at least two different lightly cooked vegetables with main meals.
- Add frozen vegetables, such as peas, sweetcorn or mixed vegetables to rice or pasta, while it is cooking.
- Add vegetables or fruit (such as dried apricots or apple) to stews or casseroles.

SNACK MEALS
- Always add salad or other vegetables to sandwiches.
- Fresh fruit is the perfect convenient snack – enjoy it on its own or add to other foods, such as plain or fruit yogurt.
- Fingers of raw vegetables, such as peppers, celery and carrots, make a tasty snack when served with a salsa, yogurt or cheese dip.

MEAT, FISH AND ALTERNATIVES

Foods in this group include meat, fish, poultry, eggs, nuts, beans and pulses. These foods provide a good supply of B vitamins, especially B_{12}, iron, magnesium, zinc, and protein. Try to eat two to three portions of foods from this group every day. Choose lean meat, poultry and game and opt for healthy, low-fat cooking methods, such as grilling, steaming and stir-frying. Try to eat oily fish at least twice a week. Beans, such as canned baked beans and peas and lentils, are all low in fat, and have the added advantage of being high in fibre, so try to include some of these foods as often as you can.

FATS AND OILS

This group includes foods such as vegetable oils and fat spreads. These can be included in small amounts every day to provide fat-soluble vitamins and some essential fats which your body cannot make. However, these foods are high in calories, so limit your intake.

FATTY AND SUGARY FOODS

Foods in this group include cakes, biscuits, commercial savoury snacks, sweets, salad dressings and soft drinks. Your consumption of these foods should be limited, as they are usually high in fat, sugar and calories and tend to be less nourishing than other foods. Consider these as "occasional" foods that should be eaten in moderation.

Above: Milk and dairy foods are rich in certain vitamins and minerals but can also have very high levels of saturated fat.

Above: Meat and fish provide a good supply of B vitamins, iron, magnesium and protein.

THE BENEFITS OF EATING FIVE OR MORE PORTIONS OF FRUIT AND VEGETABLES A DAY

- Eating a variety of different fruits and vegetables every day will help you get maximum nutritional benefit.
- They are low in fat and calories so you needn't worry about your weight.
- These foods are packed full of essential vitamins and minerals.
- Brightly coloured vegetables and fruits, and dark green vegetables, are our main source of antioxidants: compounds which help protect us from heart disease and some cancers.
- They are an excellent source of dietary fibre – essential for a healthy digestive system.
- Fruits and vegetables of all varieties add flavour, texture, colour and taste to almost any meal or snack.

TIPS TO STOP VITAMINS BEING LOST FROM FRUIT AND VEGETABLES

- Prepare fruit and vegetables as near to the time for cooking and serving as possible.
- Avoid preparing vegetables in advance and leaving them to soak in water.
- Steam, microwave or lightly boil vegetables in just enough water to cover them, and then serve immediately.
- Keep vegetables in the fridge when possible.
- Try to serve raw fruit and vegetables on a regular basis.
- Where possible, eat fruit and vegetables with the skins on.

THE BENEFITS OF EATING A HEALTHY, WHOLEFOOD DIET

- Eating well will help you to get the most out of life.
- You will gain better control of your weight, without having to diet or count calories.
- There is a lower risk of developing degenerative diseases, such as heart disease and some types of cancer.
- The risk of developing various bowel disorders and osteoporosis is also reduced.
- Tooth decay and gum disease should be less of a problem.
- You will feel more energetic and feel and look more vibrant.

ORGANIC FOODS

These are foods that have been produced without the use of chemicals or artificial fertilizers. There are strict rules governing the production of organic foods, and these are monitored by certification bodies to ensure that manufacturers and farmers comply.

Organic foods are more costly to produce, so are more expensive to buy. However, in recent years there has been a rapid growth in this sector of the market as consumer interest and demand have increased. This has meant greater availability and choice in some supermarkets, which should result in more competitive prices. The range of organic produce has expanded from fruit and vegetables to include meat, dairy products (especially milk), cereal products, wines and beers.

The trend for organic products appears to be continuing to grow, as people become more aware of the health implications surrounding the way in which foods are produced.

Left: With an increased demand for organic produce, supermarkets are now offering a wider range of organic foods.

MAINTAINING A HEALTHY BALANCE

If you are embarking on a diet which potentially cuts out some of the major food groups, and therefore the nutrients they provide, it is important that you include alternative dietary sources, so that the nutritional quality of your diet is maintained.

For example, if milk and dairy foods – the major source of calcium in the diet – are to be avoided, suitable alternatives must be included to ensure the body receives enough calcium for good health. Thankfully, there are alternatives, particularly in the form of calcium-fortified soya milks and foods made from these, which are becoming increasingly popular and are found in major supermarkets. People with coeliac disease sometimes worry that, because they are unable to eat wheat and wheat bran, they may not be getting enough fibre in their diet. Once again, alternatives need to be included, for example wholegrain rice, beans and pulses, and plenty of fresh fruit and vegetables, with the skins on. Commercially produced high-fibre, gluten-free foods are also available.

Cutting out eggs or fish from the diet is less of a problem nutritionally, because these foods can easily be replaced. However, it can be quite difficult to establish which processed foods contain egg.

It is usually possible, therefore, to maintain a healthy, well-balanced diet, even when some staple foods are excluded. Clearly, the more restricted you are in terms of which foods you can eat, the harder it is to ensure a proper nutritional balance, and the more planning and effort it will take to ensure a healthy diet. This book will provide all the advice and information you may need about various special diets, along with a huge choice of delicious recipes to suit your needs.

Below: If you have to cut out certain foods from your diet, it is important to include a wide range of foods to maintain a healthy balance of nutrients.

GLUTEN AND COELIAC DISEASE

If you are reading this chapter, the chances are that you, or someone close to you, has been advised to follow a gluten-free diet. The most likely reason for this is a diagnosis of coeliac disease, but you may have a wheat allergy or a relatively rare skin condition. Whatever the reason, being faced with following a diet for life may seem rather daunting. The good news is that gluten is not particularly difficult to avoid: a huge range of delicious foods remains open to you and you won't need to be singled out from family or friends as everything you eat can be enjoyed by them, too.

WHAT IS GLUTEN?

Gluten is a protein that occurs naturally in wheat and rye and is closely related to similar proteins in oats and barley. When the grain is milled, it is the gluten that gives the flour its strength and elasticity. Most people ingest gluten without any difficulty, but in some individuals, it can cause problems.

COELIAC DISEASE

This lifelong condition, caused by a sensitivity to gluten, affects about one in 1,000 to one in 1,500 people worldwide. Coeliac disease was once thought of as a disease exclusive to childhood, but while the condition is present from birth, the symptoms may not appear until much later in life. Nowadays, far more adults than children have the condition; the majority of newly diagnosed coeliacs are aged between 30 and 45, with a significant number falling in the over-60s category.

The condition is known to run in families, and some coeliacs without obvious symptoms are detected when their relatives are being studied. It is suspected that many cases of coeliac disease remain undiagnosed, so the number of cases may in fact be higher.

Coeliac disease was first recognized by the Greeks in the 2nd century AD; the word "coeliac" is derived from the Greek word "koiliakos", meaning "suffering in the bowels", an apt description of a condition that affects the gastrointestinal tract.

In a person with a healthy digestive system, food that has been broken down in the stomach and duodenum passes through the small intestine, where thread-like projections called villi absorb essential nutrients.

SYMPTOMS

The symptoms of coeliac disease vary widely, and can be attributable to other medical conditions, so it is vital to seek a proper diagnosis before starting a gluten-free diet.

An adult with coeliac disease may be chronically tired (often due to anaemia resulting from poor iron and folic acid absorption). Mouth ulcers are common, as is abdominal discomfort, often with a feeling of fullness or bloating. Sufferers can be very ill indeed, with vomiting, diarrhoea and severe weight loss. There may be a long history of stomach upsets, or the onset may have been sudden.

The symptoms of coeliac disease may become apparent at any age. In a baby, for instance, the first sign of a problem is usually about three months, when the child is being weaned. If a child who previously enjoyed his or her feeds becomes miserable at mealtimes, refuses foods and stops gaining weight, medical advice should be sought.

If undiagnosed and untreated, a baby with the coeliac condition will lose weight, become listless and irritable and develop a swollen pot-belly. The stools will be unusually pale, with an offensive odour, and there may be diarrhoea and vomiting. If the condition persists, the child will eventually become seriously ill.

Left: Seek medical advice before you or one of your family starts a gluten-free diet.

When someone who suffers from coeliac disease eats food containing gluten, the intestine responds to the food as if it were a foreign body. There is an immune response: the lining of the intestine becomes inflamed and this causes the villi to become flattened. As a result, the surface area is reduced and the gut is no longer able to absorb nutrients efficiently. Over time, weight loss and wasting can occur, leading to malnutrition.

Precisely how or why gluten is harmful to the small intestine is not known, but the only cure for the diagnosed coeliac is to follow a strict gluten-free diet for life. Once gluten is withdrawn from the diet, the flattened villi in the lining of the small intestine will gradually return to normal. Gluten can never be reintroduced, however; once the body has become sensitized to gluten, it will always be affected by it. The occasional minor slip-up may only have a minimal effect, but if the diet is not followed strictly and even small quantities of foods containing gluten are eaten regularly, the unpleasant symptoms will return, causing severe discomfort as well as further damage to the delicate intestine.

If you are uncertain as to whether a given food contains gluten, avoid it. It is simply not worth taking the risk.

When an individual embarks upon a gluten-free diet, the results are sometimes dramatic, but more often he or she will see a gradual but continuing improvement. It takes time for the lining of the small intestine to grow again.

Some coeliacs find that very fatty foods irritate their stomachs; these are often best avoided, particularly in the early stages of the diet. However, it is important not to lose sight of the fact that everyone suffers from illness at some time and a coeliac who feels under the weather may simply have succumbed to a bug that is doing the rounds; before jumping to conclusions, consult a doctor.

WHEAT ALLERGY OR WHEAT INTOLERANCE AND DERMATITIS HERPETIFORMIS

A strict gluten-free diet may also prove beneficial to people who suffer from an allergy or intolerance to wheat, as well as anyone suffering from the rare and irritating skin complaint known as dermatitis herpetiformis.

Wheat allergy or intolerance can cause a wide range of symptoms including aches and pains in the joints and muscles, coughing, sneezing, runny nose, watery and itchy eyes, skin rashes, eczema, faintness and dizziness. The sufferer may have a swollen throat or tongue and find it difficult to swallow. Chest pains, palpitations, nausea, vomiting, diarrhoea, tiredness, lethargy, depression and mood swings have also been reported. Of course, all of these symptoms can be indicative of a range of conditions, and sufferers should always seek sound medical advice before assuming that wheat is the culprit.

If the sufferer's suspicions are confirmed, however, he or she should exclude all sources of wheat, including wheat protein and wheat starch. Some sufferers may also have an allergic reaction to other grains, such as rye, corn and barley, but unlike coeliacs, many people who are allergic to wheat can still tolerate oats.

A product labelled as being gluten-free may also be wheat-free, but this is not inevitable; there may certainly be no gluten present, but the product may contain wheat starch. Always check the packaging or seek more information.

Dermatitis herpetiformis – also caused by a sensitivity to gluten – is a rare skin condition that causes an extremely itchy skin rash that consists of red raised patches and small blisters, appearing most often on the elbows, buttocks and knees. The first appearance of the skin rash most often occurs in people who are aged between 15 and 40. The condition is rare in children, although the symptoms can appear at any age.

Dermatitis herpetiformis affects about 1 in 20,000 people (slightly more males than females) and must be diagnosed by a specialist in skin diseases.

Because gluten is implicated, people who suffer from dermatitis herpetiformis may also have coeliac disease, although in these people the symptoms will usually be quite mild. A permanent gluten-free diet will alleviate both the skin condition and the mild version of coeliac disease, although it may take some time for the skin rash to disappear entirely.

DIAGNOSIS

Whether the sufferer is an adult or a child, it is vital that the coeliac condition is properly diagnosed by a doctor before a gluten-free diet is embarked upon.

Diagnosis is by a standard test – a jejunal biopsy – performed under light sedation in the outpatient department of a hospital. A gastroenterologist will remove a small piece of the villi from the lining of the small intestine. Microscopic examination will reveal whether or not the coeliac condition is present.

If the diagnosis is positive, all the patient needs to do to restore the intestine to health is to adhere strictly to a full and varied gluten-free diet. In the short term, the doctor may decide to prescribe a course of vitamins or mineral supplements.

WHICH FOODS CONTAIN GLUTEN?

A gluten-free diet excludes all foods containing any form of wheat, barley, rye and oats. (Some coeliacs can tolerate oats with no adverse effects, but many cannot, so it is a wise precaution to exclude it.) Items such as bread, cakes, biscuits, pasta and pastries made from wheat flour are obvious sources of gluten, but it is also essential to be aware of less obvious sources, as when wheat flour has been used to coat or dust foods or thicken soups, stews, gravies and puddings. Breadcrumbs, for instance, are used in stuffings and coatings or as a filler in foods such as sausages and hamburgers.

FOODS THAT ARE NATURALLY GLUTEN-FREE

- Fresh or frozen plain meat, fish or poultry, without stuffing or a crumb coating; canned or pre-packed plain cooked meats, such as corned beef or ham (without any coating); smoked and cured pure meats; fresh, frozen or cured plain fish or shellfish; fish canned in oil, brine or water.

Above: Anchovies canned in oil, smoked mackerel and cooked prawns, are all naturally gluten-free.

- Fresh or frozen plain vegetables or fruit, dried fruit and vegetables (including pulses), plain canned fruit in syrup or juice, vegetables canned in brine, water or juice, plain vegetables pickled in vinegar, potato crisps.
- Eggs (but not Scotch eggs).
- Nuts and seeds of all types, provided they are plain; also peanut butter.
- Gelatine and agar agar.
- Dairy produce including all plain cheeses (but not spreads or processed cheese), milk, dairy cream, natural yogurt, fromage frais; also plain dried milk, evaporated and condensed milk.
- Fats and oils, including pure vegetable oils, such as olive, sunflower and rapeseed; butter, margarine (as long as it does not contain wheatgerm oil), reduced-fat and low-fat spreads.
- Sugar in all its forms, including pure honey, syrup, molasses and treacle.
- Fruit conserves, jam and marmalade.
- Flavourings, seasonings, herbs and spices, including salt, freshly ground black pepper, black peppercorns, cider vinegar and wine vinegar, pure whole or ground spices, tomato purée and garlic purée, pure food flavourings, such as vanilla and almond essences, pure food colourings.
- Breakfast cereals, such as rice crispies, puffed rice, some cornflakes.

Above: Breakfast need not be a problem for coeliacs. Eggs, jam or marmalade, milk and rice- and corn-based cereals, such as rice crispies and some cornflakes, are all gluten-free. Serve them with gluten-free toast.

Above: Add flavour and colour to your meals using black peppercorns, tomato purée, red wine vinegar, pure ground cinnamon, pure food flavourings and colourings.

- Grains, whether whole or ground, including buckwheat flakes and flour, carob flour, cornflour, gram flour (from ground chick-peas), maize flour, millet flour, potato flour, sorghum flour, soya flour, sweet chestnut flour, teff flour, yam flour, yellow split pea flour, arrowroot, rice (all types including wild rice; also ground rice and rice flour), hominy grits, millet (also millet flakes and millet seeds), polenta, quinoa grains, sago and tapioca.
- Good quality plain chocolate.
- Yeast (and yeast extract).
- Pure rice noodles, pure corn, rice and millet pasta, pure buckwheat pasta – check that pastas do not contain added wheat flour, starch or binders.
- Drinks, such as tea, coffee, fruit squashes (except barley water), pure fruit juices (preferably unsweetened); also cider, wine, sherry, brandy, port.

MANUFACTURED FOODS THAT ARE GLUTEN-FREE

A wide range of specially manufactured gluten-free foods is also available. The list includes breads, cakes, biscuits, crackers and crispbreads, plus flours, flour mixes, bread and cake mixes, muesli, pastas and rusks. Talk to your doctor, as in certain countries, such as the UK, you may be able to obtain some of these products on prescription. Others can be purchased from chemists or health food shops, or by mail order, although they can be costly.

Manufactured foods that have been specifically made for the market by reputable companies are very useful. They look like the wheat-flour products they are intended to replace, so will go unremarked at occasions such as children's parties.

Many everyday canned and packaged foods are also gluten-free.

When using products, such as gluten-free flours or bread or cake mixes for the first time, always follow the manufacturer's guidance and instructions on usage.

FOODS TO AVOID

The following foods always contain flour made from wheat, barley, rye or oats, so must be avoided:
● Wheat berries or grains; wheat bran; wheat flakes; wheat flour, such as plain or strong white flour, brown, granary and wholemeal flours; wheatmeal; wheat protein; wheat starch; bulgur wheat; couscous; cracked wheat, durum wheat (used in pasta); kibbled wheat; pourgouri; rusk; semolina; wheatgerm.
● Pearl barley, pot barley, barley flakes, barley flour, barley meal.
● Rye flakes, rye flour, rye meal.
● Oats, oat flakes, jumbo oats, porridge oats, rolled oats, oatmeal, pinhead oatmeal, oatbran, oatgerm.
● Spelt (flour and American pasta made from a grain related to wheat), kamut (Italian wholegrain pasta).
● Triticale (wheat/rye hybrid grain).

COMMON FOODS THAT MAY CONTAIN GLUTEN

● Dry goods like baking powder, malt, curry powder, mustard powder, MSG (monosodium glutamate flavour enhancer), gravy mixes, spices and spice mixes, pepper compounds and ready-ground white pepper, shredded suet (in packets), stock cubes.
● Pasta (durum wheat pastas are out and some Oriental pastas, though made from other grains, contain wheat).
● Some cornflakes.
● Salad dressings, soy sauce, malt vinegar.
● Some processed cheese spreads, some flavoured yogurts.
● Sausages (and sausage rolls), meat pies, beefburgers, pâtés, foods coated in batter or breadcrumbs.
● Dry roasted nuts.
● Communion wafers (gluten-free wafers are available on mail-order).
● Beers, malted milk drinks.

Above right: Some common foods, such as malt vinegar, pasta made with wheat, dry roasted nuts, mustards and malted milk drinks, contain gluten and must be avoided.

Below: The range of specially manufactured gluten-free foods includes biscuits, cereal, corn pasta and gluten-free flours.

FOOD LABELLING

By law, all manufacturers have to mark or label food with a list of ingredients. Sources of gluten are not always obvious, however. If you read any of the following words on a food label, alarm bells should start to ring and you should ask for more information: binder, binding, cereal, cereal protein, corn, cornstarch, edible starch, flour, food starch, modified starch, rusk, special edible starch, starch, thickener, thickening or vegetable protein.

GLUTEN-FREE COOKING

There is nothing special about gluten-free cooking other than the fact that some ingredients are replaced with alternatives that are equally varied and interesting. Once you familiarize yourself with the list of foods that can safely be served (and note the no-no's), it is simply a matter of making delicious dishes that everyone can enjoy. You will rapidly get into the habit of using a variety of alternative starches for baking, cooking, thickening, binding and coating, and in doing so will discover just how delicious many of the less familiar grains can be.

If you are new to gluten-free cooking, you will probably prefer to start with simple no-risk dishes like grills with fresh vegetables. This will have obvious health advantages, but don't turf out the treats. If you continue to serve pies and puddings, cakes and bakes, but make them gluten-free, everyone in the family will be able to enjoy their favourite foods – and the coeliac won't feel isolated.

USING GLUTEN-FREE FLOURS

Because gluten is the protein that strengthens and binds dough in baking, you may need to find alternative binding agents when using gluten-free flours. Follow recipes for baked goods closely, as they will have been specially formulated to allow for this potential problem. A combination of starches often works better than a single type, and adding egg, pectin powder, grated apple or mashed banana may help to bind gluten-free dough.

BINDING BURGERS AND SAUSAGES

Although burgers and sausages are usually bound with breadcrumbs or rusk, they work equally well without. The best hamburgers are made purely from minced steak, and fresh sausage meat will hold together without additional ingredients. If you must use a binder, add rice flour and egg.

AVOIDING WHEAT CONTAMINATION

If you are baking a batch of breads, cakes and pastries (only some of which are gluten-free), be careful to keep ingredients separate so that there is no risk of wheat flour contaminating the gluten-free foods. Wash all utensils thoroughly after each use. For a highly allergic person, it may be sensible to use separate baking tins and cooking utensils. Alternatively – and this is simpler and safer – use gluten-free ingredients for all your cooking.

QUICK TIPS ON GLUTEN-FREE COOKING

• Do not use breadcrumbs (unless they are gluten-free) for coating foods. Crushed gluten-free cornflakes make a good alternative for coating foods and for gratins.

• Roll gluten-free pastry out on greaseproof paper as this makes it easier to lift and to line the tin.

• Do not dust or coat foods with wheat flour prior to cooking – either avoid dusting food altogether or use naturally gluten-free flours such as maize meal or rice flour.

• If gluten-free pastry is very crumbly, press it over the base and up the sides of the tin (as when making shortbread) rather than trying to roll it out.

• Grease baking tins before use, even if they are non-stick, or line the tins with non-stick baking parchment to prevent sticking.

• It is a good idea to bake a batch of gluten-free breads, cakes and biscuits and pop some into the freezer. Gluten-free baked goods freeze well and will keep fresh for many weeks. Freeze in portions, so that you can thaw exactly what you need for a packed lunch or tea-time treat.

• Potato flour is a useful thickening agent for gravies, stews, casseroles, sauces and soups.

STORE-CUPBOARD ESSENTIALS

Pack your pantry with these items and you'll always have the makings of a gluten-free meal:

- Gluten-free cornflakes, rice crispies, puffed rice cereal.
- Fish, such as anchovies, sardines or tuna, canned in oil, brine or water.
- Canned cooked meat, such as ham or gluten-free corned beef.
- Vegetables canned in water, brine or juice, pickled vegetables.
- Dried vegetables and pulses, plain potato crisps.
- Canned fruit in syrup or juice.
- Plain dried fruit, glacé cherries.
- Fruit juices and squashes (except barley water).
- Rice; also rice noodles and other gluten-free pastas.
- Plain nuts (not dry roasted) and seeds, pure peanut butter.
- Sugars, pure syrups, pure honey, jam, marmalade.
- Dried plain milk, evaporated and condensed milk, tea, pure coffee, good quality plain chocolate.

- Naturally gluten-free flours, which include rice flour, maize flour or maize meal, gluten-free cornflour, potato flour and soya flour; also yeast.
- Ground rice, tapioca, buckwheat flakes, millet flakes, rice flakes.
- Gelatine or agar agar.
- Pure vegetable oils, wine vinegar or cider vinegar.
- Salt, black peppercorns, dried herbs, pure spices.
- Pure food flavourings and colourings.
- Tomato purée, garlic purée, gluten-free soy sauce.

Above: Essential store-cupboard items should include: rice cakes, polenta, pure spices, dried herbs, gluten-free cornflour, rice noodles, rice and gluten-free flour.

Left: Stock up on naturally gluten-free foods, such as jams and marmalades, canned fruits and vegetables, pickled onions, crisps, dried fruit and gluten-free breakfast cereals.

GLUTEN-FREE ACCOMPANIMENTS

Potatoes and rice are particularly good sources of natural, gluten-free carbohydrate. They make ideal accompaniments to many dishes and can be served in a wide variety of ways. Explore the potential of gluten-free pastas, too. Rice noodles and corn pasta are delicious, and polenta is very good with sauced dishes; try it freshly cooked or cooled, cut into wedges and shallow fried.

POTATOES
There are few vegetables as versatile as potatoes. Tiny new potatoes are very good boiled or steamed, baked potatoes make a meal in themselves with a tasty topping, and home-made chips are one treat a gluten-free diet doesn't deny you. Patties, cakes or croquettes, rolled in crushed gluten-free cornflakes or breadcrumbs, make an excellent accompaniment, and mashed potatoes can be served in numerous ways. Always use the right variety of potato for the job. Scrub potatoes and leave the skins on when roasting or making chips for extra texture, flavour and fibre. For a tasty change, try either sweet potatoes or yams.

RICE
There are many different varieties of rice including brown and white, long grain, short grain, pudding rice, basmati and risotto rice (arborio), all of which are gluten-free, as is wild rice. Boiled rice can be served as it is, stir-fried or used as the basis for a salad.

Above: Potatoes, sweet potatoes and yams are all naturally gluten-free.

Below: Don't just opt for plain boiled long grain rice, try cooking wild rice, wholegrain rice or risotto rice, for a change.

RICE NOODLES
These are made from ground rice and water and range in thickness from very thin to wide ribbons and sheets. They are available fresh or dried and are often soaked in warm water before being briefly cooked.

CORN PASTA
Pure corn pasta – made from maize without added binders or starch – is ideal for a gluten-free diet. It comes in a variety of flavours (including parsley, spinach and chilli) and in shapes that range from spaghetti to twists and shells. All versions look pretty on the plate and have a good flavour. Corn pasta makes an excellent alternative to durum wheat pasta.

Above: Corn pasta, rice noodles and polenta make marvellous accompaniments.

POLENTA
Coarsely ground maize, this is a staple food in Italy, where it is often served as an accompaniment instead of rice or pasta. The partly cooked ground grain is whisked into boiling water or stock.

HOW TO COOK POLENTA

Bring 1.2 litres/2 pints/5 cups salted water or stock to the boil in a large saucepan, then sprinkle 175g/6oz/ generous 1 cup polenta into the water, stirring continuously. Cook, uncovered, over a very low heat for about 40 minutes, stirring frequently, until cooked and thick. Season and add flavourings, such as cheese, butter, garlic and herbs. Serve hot.

HOW TO COOK BROWN RICE

Bring 1.4 litres/2¼ pints/5⅔ cups lightly salted water to the boil in a large saucepan. Add 250g/9oz/ 1¼ cups brown rice. Bring back to the boil, then lower the heat and allow to simmer, uncovered, for 25–35 minutes until the rice is tender but retains a bit of bite. Drain in a sieve, rinse with boiling water, then drain thoroughly again.

HOW TO COOK RICE NOODLES

Bring 2 litres/4½ pints/8 cups lightly salted water to the boil in a large saucepan. Turn off the heat and add 250g/9oz/2¼ cups rice noodles. Stir the noodles with a fork to separate them, cover and set aside for 4 minutes. Drain and serve. If serving the noodles cold, rinse in cold water and drain again.

GLUTEN-FREE SNACKS AND FINGER FOODS

We all enjoy snacks at some time, particularly when the munchies strike. When baking, make extra gluten-free cakes and biscuits and freeze the surplus in slices. That way, you can thaw individual portions as needed. Occasional treats, such as a bar of gluten-free chocolate or a packet of plain crisps, won't do any harm, but it is useful to have a good selection of healthy and delicious gluten-free snacks and treats available, ready to keep hunger pangs at bay.

- Fresh fruit, such as apples, pears, mangoes, kiwi fruit, pineapple wedges, peaches, apricots and oranges.
- Ready-to-eat dried fruit, such as apricots, peaches, pears, apples, prunes or dried fruit salad.
- Gluten-free crackers, crispbreads and rice cakes. Serve them with plain cheese, such as Cheddar, Red Leicester, Stilton or Emmental.
- Wedges of gluten-free fruit cake.

- Plain nuts, such as walnuts, almonds or hazelnuts or a mixture of nuts and dried fruit, mixed seeds or a mixture of mixed seeds and plain nuts.
- Plain yogurt to which you can add chopped fresh fruit for a sweet treat, or finely diced cucumber and a trace of

Above: Healthy gluten-free snacks include nuts, mixed nuts and raisins, cheese and rice crackers, and raw vegetable crudités.

crushed garlic for a savoury surprise; also plain or flavoured fromage frais and gluten-free fruit yogurts.

BASIC GLUTEN-FREE RECIPES

There is a wide range of stock products on the market including cubes of various flavours, stock powders or granules and fresh chilled stock, but some of these contain gluten, so it is worth-while making your own gluten-free stocks at home. Home-made stocks add delicious flavour to many different dishes, and they really are simple to make. It is a good idea to prepare one or two batches and freeze them in useful quantities for future use. Cool home-made stocks quickly, pour them into suitable containers (leaving space for expansion) and freeze them for up to 3 months.

CHICKEN STOCK
Makes about 750ml/1¹/₄ pints/3 cups
1 meaty chicken carcass
6 shallots or 1 onion
1 carrot
2 celery sticks
1 bay leaf
salt and ground black pepper

1 Break or chop the chicken carcass into pieces and place in a large saucepan with 1.75 litres/3 pints/7½ cups cold water.

2 Peel and slice the shallots or onion and carrot, then chop the celery. Add the vegetables to the saucepan with the bayleaf. Stir to mix.

3 Bring to the boil, then partially cover and simmer for 2 hours, skimming off any scum and fat that rises to the surface during cooking.

4 Strain the stock through a sieve, then set aside to cool.

5 When cold, remove and discard all the fat and use the stock or freeze. Once cool, cover and store in the fridge for up to 3 days. Season with salt and pepper, as required.

BEEF STOCK
Makes about 750ml/1¹/₄ pints/3 cups
450g/1lb shin of beef on the bone
450g/1lb beef or veal bones
1 onion
1 carrot
1 turnip
2 celery sticks
1 leek
1 bouquet garni
salt and ground black pepper

1 Preheat the oven to 220°C/425°F/Gas 7. Place the meat and bones in a roasting tin and brown in the oven for about 30 minutes, then place in a large pan with 1.75 litres/3 pints/7½ cups cold water.

2 Peel and slice the onion and carrot, then peel and dice the turnip and chop the celery and leek. Add the vegetables to the saucepan with the bouquet garni. Stir to mix.

3 Bring to the boil, then partially cover and simmer for 2 hours, skimming off any scum and fat that rises to the surface during cooking. Strain the stock through a fine sieve, then set aside to cool. Store as for chicken stock.

VEGETABLE STOCK
Makes about 1.5 litres/2¹/₂ pints/6¹/₄ cups
1 large onion, sliced
2 carrots, sliced
1 leek, sliced
3 celery sticks, chopped
1 small turnip, diced
1 small parsnip, sliced
1 bouquet garni
salt and ground black pepper

1 Place all the prepared vegetables in a large saucepan with the bouquet garni. Add 1.75 litres/3 pints/7½ cups cold water and stir to mix.

2 Bring to the boil, then partially cover and simmer for about 1 hour, skimming off any scum.

3 Strain the stock through a sieve, use immediately or set aside to cool. Store in the fridge for up to 3 days. Alternatively, freeze the stock. Season with salt and pepper, as required.

COOK'S TIP
If you have any vegetable trimmings, such as tomato or onion skins, celery tops or cabbage leaves, then add these to the water with the vegetables when making the stock.

GLUTEN-FREE WHITE SAUCE
Makes about 300ml/½ pint/1¼ cups
30ml/2 tbsp gluten-free cornflour
300ml/½ pint/1¼ cups semi-
  skimmed milk
15g/½oz/1 tbsp sunflower
  margarine
salt and ground black pepper

1 Place the cornflour in a bowl and
blend with 60ml/4 tbsp of the milk
to make a smooth paste.

2 Heat the remaining milk in a
saucepan over a medium heat until
boiling, then pour on to the blended
mixture, whisking continuously to
prevent lumps forming.

3 Return the mixture to the
saucepan and bring slowly to the
boil, stirring continuously, until the
sauce thickens. Lower the heat and
simmer gently for 2–3 minutes, then
stir in the margarine, until melted.
Season to taste and serve.

VARIATIONS
● To make a thinner pouring sauce,
reduce the quantity of cornflour to
20–25ml/4–5 tsp.
● Replace half the milk with well-
flavoured vegetable or chicken stock or
use a half-and-half mixture of stock
and white wine in place of the milk.
● Add gluten-free flavourings, such as
grated cheese, chopped mixed fresh
herbs, lightly sautéed onions, tomato
purée, or chopped or sliced, cooked
wild or button mushrooms, to the
sauce for extra flavour.

FRENCH DRESSING
Makes about 150ml/¼ pint/⅔ cup
90ml/6 tbsp sunflower oil
30ml/2 tbsp white wine vinegar or
  lemon juice
5ml/1 tsp Dijon mustard
1.5ml/¼ tsp caster sugar
15ml/1 tbsp chopped fresh
  mixed herbs
salt and ground black pepper

1 Place all the ingredients in a small
bowl and whisk together until
thoroughly mixed. Alternatively, place
all the ingredients in a clean, screw-
top jar, seal and shake well until
thoroughly mixed.

2 Adjust the seasoning and serve
immediately or keep in a screw-top
jar in the fridge for up to 1 week.
Shake thoroughly before serving.

VARIATIONS
● Crush a small garlic clove and add to
the dressing, if you like.
● Use light olive oil in place of some
or all of the sunflower oil.
● Try balsamic vinegar in place of the
white wine vinegar.

MAYONNAISE
Makes about 200ml/7fl oz/scant 1 cup
2 egg yolks
5ml/1 tsp Dijon mustard
15ml/1 tbsp lemon juice
2.5ml/½ tsp salt
ground black pepper
about 150ml/¼ pint/⅔ cup olive or
  sunflower oil

1 Place the egg yolks, mustard, lemon
juice, salt, pepper and 15ml/1 tbsp
oil in a food processor or small blender.
Blend for 30 seconds.

2 With the motor running, gradually
add the remaining oil, pouring it
through the funnel in a slow, steady
stream, until the mayonnaise is thick,
creamy and smooth.

3 Adjust the seasoning, then use
immediately or cover and chill
until required. Store for up to 3 days
in a covered container in the fridge.

VARIATIONS
Add finely chopped garlic, capers,
gherkins or cucumber, crumbled blue
cheese or chopped fresh mixed herbs.

MILK AND DAIRY PRODUCTS

Some people choose a dairy-free diet for either moral or religious reasons, but others have the decision made for them when they develop an intolerance or an allergy to cow's milk. Whatever your reason for omitting cow's milk and its products from your diet, you can still enjoy a wide range of varied and delicious meals. All it takes is a little planning. This book includes plenty of help, advice and information, plus lots of tasty dairy-free recipes for you, your friends and family to enjoy, from soups and starters to main courses, desserts, cakes and bakes.

WHAT EXACTLY ARE DAIRY FOODS?

We all know what dairy foods are, don't we? Maybe not. There is actually quite a lot of confusion about this term. Essentially, it applies to cow's milk, cream, butter, cheese and related items like buttermilk, yogurt, fromage frais and dairy ice cream. Many processed foods contain milk and dairy products. Obvious candidates are milk chocolate and dairy spreads, but there are many other items, too, such as biscuits, cakes, breads, breakfast cereals, pancake and batter mixes, pudding mixes, instant hot chocolate drinks and coffee whiteners.

ARE WE ONLY SPEAKING ABOUT COW'S MILK?

Technically, when we refer to dairy foods, this really only means cow's milk and products derived from cow's milk. Goat's milk and ewe's milk – and foods derived from them, such as cheese and yogurt – are not thought of as dairy foods even though they have a similar composition to cow's milk, and can sometimes cause similar problems for sensitive individuals. Other people who are sensitive to cow's milk, however, are often able to tolerate goat or ewe's milk, and their associated products quite well.

OTHER NAMES FOR MILK AND MILK PRODUCTS

As well as all the foods that we commonly think of as dairy products, such as cheese, yogurt, butter and cream, there are a number of other products that are forms of cow's milk or that have been derived from cow's milk. It is important to look out for these as it is very easy for the uninitiated to miss them and they often crop up in the most unlikely places. It is particularly important to check for them in processed and ready-made foods.

- casein
- caseinates
- ghee
- hydrolyzed casein
- hydrolyzed milk protein
- lactose
- lactalbumin
- milk sugar
- milk solids
- non-fat milk solids
- skimmed milk whey
- skimmed milk powder
- whey
- whey protein
- whey sugar
- whey syrup sweetener

Left: There are a great many cow's milk dairy products, which include (clockwise from top left): milk, evaporated milk, fromage frais, condensed milk, dairy spread, curd cheese, butter, buttermilk and cream, and in the centre, cheese and yogurt.

Left: Regular exercise and a good supply of calcium are needed for strong, healthy bones.

AVERAGE CALCIUM VALUES OF DAIRY AND OTHER MILKS

The daily calcium requirement for the average adult is 700mg. If you are concerned about your calcium intake, use the table below to check that you are getting enough.

Type of milk	Per 100ml
whole cow's milk (including lactose-reduced)	120mg
semi-skimmed and skimmed cow's milk	120–125mg
evaporated milk	290mg
goat's milk	120mg
sheep's milk	170mg
soya milk	13mg
soya milk (with added calcium)	140mg

IS IT OKAY TO GIVE UP MILK?

Before embarking on a dairy-free diet, or even substantially reducing your intake of dairy foods, it is only sensible to seek advice from a doctor or nutritionist. Milk is the most complete food available, providing valuable amounts of protein, fat, carbohydrate (in the form of lactose/milk sugar), vitamin A and – particularly – B_2 (riboflavin). It is rich in readily absorbed calcium and also a good source of phosphorus. In young children, who may be picky about what and how much they eat, milk is often the main source of energy. If you give up milk and other dairy products, whether in the short term or for longer, it is therefore important to look at other ways of providing these nutrients, especially calcium.

THE IMPORTANCE OF CALCIUM IN OUR DIET

Calcium is essential for building strong teeth and bones, normal blood clotting, nerve function and enzyme activity. It is particularly important for young children and teenagers, but even after we stop growing, at around the age of 18 years, the body's need for calcium continues. Requirements for this valuable nutrient are also higher during pregnancy and breastfeeding.

Recent research suggests that having adequate amounts of calcium in early life and building up a strong skeletal structure may help to prevent osteoporosis, or "brittle bone disease" in later life. This condition occurs when calcium is lost faster than it can be replaced, and bones become weak and fragile. Taking regular exercise (especially weight-bearing exercise) also helps to strengthen bones. Vitamin D, which is produced by the action of sunlight on the skin, helps with the absorption of calcium by the body, whereas both smoking and excessive drinking of alcohol deplete calcium reserves.

Non-dairy Calcium Sources

If you are unable to tolerate dairy products, do not despair. Although dairy foods offer a rich and easily absorbable supply of calcium, there are plenty of other foods that can also provide a good supply of the mineral. These include:

- White or brown bread (fortified).
- Leafy dark green vegetables, such as Savoy cabbage, spring greens, curly kale, broccoli and spinach.
- Canned sardines or pilchards in oil or tomato sauce (provided the bones are eaten).
- Canned baked beans in tomato sauce, red kidney beans, chick-peas and lentils.
- Soya beans and tofu (beancurd).
- Nuts, particularly almonds, Brazil nuts and hazelnuts.
- Seeds, such as sesame seeds and sunflower seeds.
- Dried apricots, dried figs and currants.
- muesli

Above: Add extra calcium to your diet by nibbling dried fruit, such as dried figs, or add currants to cakes or dried fruit salads.

Below: Canned sardines are a good source of calcium – as long as you eat the bones.

AVERAGE CALCIUM VALUES OF OTHER FOODS	
Type of food	**Per 100g**
almonds	240mg
apricots, dried	73mg
Brazil nuts	170mg
bread, brown (fortified)	170mg
bread, white (fortified)	110mg
canned baked beans in tomato sauce	48mg
canned sardines (with bones)	500mg
canned pilchards (with bones)	300mg
curly kale, boiled	150mg
figs, dried	230mg
lentils, boiled	22mg
hazelnuts	140mg
muesli, Swiss-style	110mg
red kidney beans, boiled	71mg
Savoy cabbage, boiled	37mg
sesame seeds	670mg
soya beans, boiled	83mg
spinach, boiled	160mg
spring greens, boiled	75mg
sunflower seeds	110mg
tofu (beancurd)	510mg

LACTOSE INTOLERANCE V MILK ALLERGY – WHAT'S THE DIFFERENCE?

LACTOSE INTOLERANCE

This not an allergic reaction but occurs because the body lacks (or does not produce enough of) an enzyme called lactase, which is normally active in the intestinal wall. The function of lactase is to break down lactose (milk sugar) into simpler sugars that can be absorbed by the body. If this doesn't happen, the undigested lactose passes into the large intestine (colon) where it causes irritation and the classic symptoms commonly associated with lactose intolerance. These include bloating, stomach pain, diarrhoea and excessive wind, produced by naturally occurring microflora in the gut, which ferment the undigested lactose and produce gas.

Lactase deficiency is estimated to affect around two-thirds of the world's population. It is more common among non-white/black races, where milk is not a staple food after weaning. However, in Northern Europe, where dairy products are commonly eaten, adults are less likely to have reduced levels of lactase enzyme.

Temporary lactose intolerance can also be triggered by a bout of gastro-enteritis (particularly in young children) or in adults as a consequence of any illness that affects the lining of the small intestine. This sensitivity is generally only short term and usually clears up if the individual avoids cow's milk for a time.

The degree of intolerance varies and may be mild or quite severe. Some people can tolerate small amounts of cow's milk; some find they must avoid drinking milk on its own, but can eat yogurt and some cheeses (which contain little lactose). Some can cope with goat's milk or sheep's milk, although these also contain lactose and can provoke a reaction in susceptible individuals. Other alternative milks, such as soya milk, can also provide suitable substitutes, although for nutritional reasons, establishing an acceptable low level of regular milk is often advised.

MILK ALLERGY

Unlike lactose intolerance, milk allergy is a relatively uncommon condition; and is usually a reaction to the protein (not the lactose) in milk. It is generally restricted to young children, who usually outgrow the problem by the age of two or three. The classic symptoms of an allergy to milk protein are eczema, asthma, allergic rhinitis (a persistent runny nose), vomiting and diarrhoea. In rare instances, the reaction may be severe, and professional guidance should always be sought if an allergy is suspected.

Sometimes, sensitivity to protein and lactose can coexist, particularly after a gastrointestinal upset. The usual treatment is to temporarily exclude milk and dairy products, but again, it is only sensible to seek professional advice from a doctor or nutritionist.

Right: Milk allergy is relatively uncommon and most young children can drink milk.

Below: Although lactase deficiency can affect people from all nationalities, it is more prevalent in black ethnic groups.

DAIRY-FREE FOODS

Recipes and ingredients will vary between different manufacturers, so it is impossible to give a definitive safe list, but there are certain generic food categories that do not contain dairy products. These include:

- Fruit (fresh, canned, frozen).
- Fruit juices (fresh, frozen, canned, bottled and UHT).
- Fish (fresh, frozen without batter, crumb coating or sauce, canned).
- Meat, poultry, game, bacon, offal and Quorn (not processed products).
- Pasta (fresh and dried), rice and other grains.
- Beans and pulses (dried and canned)
- Nuts and seeds.
- Vegetables (fresh, frozen, dried).

In addition, the following items can generally be eaten safely, but always check the labels:

BAKING INGREDIENTS
- Flour, cornflour, arrowroot.
- High quality dark chocolate.

- Mincemeat.
- Marzipan, ready-to-roll icing.
- Desiccated and creamed coconut.
- Dried fruit, glacé cherries, candied peel, canned fruit pie fillings.
- Ready-to-use pastry is safe if made with pure vegetable fat.
- Filo (brush with oil, not butter).

BEVERAGES
- Fresh fruit juices and soft drinks.
- Beef, yeast or vegetable extract drinks.
- Most types of drinking chocolate powder and cocoa powder.

BISCUITS
- Grissini (breadsticks), cream crackers, water biscuits.
- Oatcakes, crispbreads, rice cakes, melba toast and matzos are usually dairy-free.

BREADS AND BAKED GOODS
- Bagels, pitta breads and muffins are usually dairy-free.
- Some ready-made pizza bases are dairy-free.

CAKES AND PASTRIES
- Meringues.
- Some fruit pies are dairy-free.

CEREALS
- Most breakfast cereals, such as Cornflakes, Shreddies and Weetabix are dairy-free.
- Porridge oats and some brands of muesli.
- Couscous, bulgur wheat, semolina.

CONFECTIONERY AND SNACK FOODS
- Sweets such as mints, jellies, pastilles and marshmallows are dairy-free, as well as some brands of plain chocolate and, carob.
- All kinds of nuts, tortilla chips, taco shells, pretzels, poppadums, prawn crackers and some crisps.

DAIRY MILK SUBSTITUTES
- Soya milk drinks.
- Nut milks, rice drinks.
- Goat's or sheep's milk (if tolerated).
- Lactose-reduced milk (if tolerated).

Above: Many baking ingredients are dairy-free. Clockwise from top left, yellow and white marzipan, plain dark cooking chocolate, canned fruit pie filling, desiccated coconut, glacé cherries and cornflour are all safe to include.

Above: Some people with dairy or lactose intolerance can tolerate goat's milk, sheep's milk and lactose-reduced milk.

DELI FOODS

- Cooked, sliced meats.
- Some ready-made salads, such as mixed bean salad, Waldorf salad, carrot and nut salad.
- Florida salad, potato salad, coleslaw in mayonnaise, but check that yogurt has not been used as a substitute for the mayonnaise.

DESSERTS

- Jellies.
- Custard powder (not the instant type).
- Sorbets and pure fruit ice lollies.
- Soya desserts and soya yogurts.
- Goat's and sheep's milk yogurts (these are not lactose-free, however, so eat them with caution).

DIPS

- Taramasalata, hummus and fresh tomato or fruit salsas.

FATS AND OILS

- Pure solid vegetable oil, soya spread/margarine, kosher margarine, lard, beef and vegetable suet.
- Corn, sunflower, safflower, olive, soya, rapeseed and nut oils.
- Mayonnaise, salad cream, Thousand Island dressing (without yogurt) and French dressing.

FISH AND FISH PRODUCTS

- Canned fish or shellfish.
- Smoked fish.

MEAT PRODUCTS

- Most sausages and burgers are dairy-free, but check ingredients.

MISCELLANEOUS

- Bouillon cubes.
- Gravy powders and granules.
- Herbs and spices.
- Olives.
- Onion bhajis.
- Pakoras.
- Samosas.
- Stuffings and breadcrumbs.
- Vegetable spring rolls.
- Vinegar.

Above: Many ready-made deli salsas and salads are dairy-free – and perfect to eat with pitta bread. Try taramasalata, tomato salsa, carrot and nut salad and coleslaw.

Right: Finding the right dairy-free snack shouldn't be too troublesome – you can safely eat tortilla chips, poppadums, some crisps, prawn crackers and taco shells.

SAUCES AND CONDIMENTS

- Relishes, chutneys, pickles.
- Soy sauce.
- Mustard.
- Tomato ketchup, tomato purée, sun-dried tomato paste.
- Most tomato-based pasta sauces.

SOUPS

- French onion, spring vegetable, oxtail, lentil, consommé and minestrone should be safe but many creamed varieties include dairy products.

SOYA PRODUCTS

- Soya mince/chunks.
- Tofu (soya beancurd).
- Soya cheese/spreads.

SWEET AND SAVOURY SPREADS

- Jams and marmalades, honey.
- Peanut butter.
- Sandwich spreads and pastes (check ingredients label).

VEGETARIAN PRODUCTS

- Most burgers, rissoles and sausages are dairy-free, as are all vegan products.

Some "ready meals" (chilled and frozen) are dairy-free. Check the label on individual packages.

FOODS TO AVOID ON A DAIRY-FREE DIET

As well as all the familiar dairy foods, many dairy products and derivatives are used in a wide range of processed foods. Depending on how strict your dairy-free diet needs to be, it may be necessary to avoid all of these foods or just some of them. Check labels if unsure of the ingredients, as there will be variation between products and brands, and take advice from a dietician.

COMMON DAIRY FOODS
- Milk (skimmed, semi-skimmed, whole and powdered).
- Evaporated and condensed milk.
- Cream.
- Crème fraîche.
- Fromage frais.
- Quark.
- Butter.
- Buttermilk.
- Cheese.
- Yogurt.

PROCESSED FOODS THAT MAY CONTAIN DAIRY INGREDIENTS

Beverages and Drinks
- Coffee whitener.
- Malted milk drinks.
- Instant hot chocolate drinks (powdered drinking chocolate and cocoa are usually dairy-free).
- Milkshakes.

BISCUITS
- Most sweet types and some flavoured savoury varieties (for instance, those that are flavoured with cheese).
- Some cereal bars (check label).

Bread and Baked Goods
- Many contain dairy products (check ingredients on individual items).

Breakfast Cereals
- Some muesli-type and some oaty cereals list skimmed milk powder among their ingredients.

Right: There are many processed foods that may contain dairy products, from fairly obvious cream cakes, milk chocolates and cream toffees to less easy-to-spot muesli, savoury biscuits and other baked goods.

Cakes
- Many contain dairy products.

Confectionery
- Milk and some plain chocolate.
- Fudge.
- Toffee.

Desserts
- Custards (ready-made canned, fresh chilled and instant custard mix).

- Ready-made dairy-type desserts and mousses (whether fresh, chilled or frozen).
- Cheesecakes.
- Ice cream (dairy and non-dairy – usually made from skimmed milk and vegetable fat).
- Pancakes and batter mixes.
- Canned rice puddings and other dairy puddings.
- Pudding mixes.

Left: Dairy ice cream and milk chocolate are two dairy foods that unfortunately have to be avoided. Even non-dairy ice cream may have skimmed milk powder or other dairy products added, so always be sure to check the ingredients label.

- Frankfurters and some sausages.
- Some sausage rolls, pies and pastries.
- Pizzas (some pizza bases are dairy-free to use with your own topping).
- Some savoury pie fillings.
- Creamy sauces.
- Many fresh, canned and dried soups.
- Quiches and flans.
- Dips based on yogurt, fromage frais or cheese.

Sweet Preserves and Spreads
- Chocolate spread/chocolate and hazelnut spread.
- Luxury lemon curd.

Vegetables, Canned or Packaged
- Creamed corn.
- Creamed mushrooms.
- Instant mashed potato.
- Spaghetti (canned in tomato sauce).

Fats and Spreads
- Dairy spreads.
- Margarine (most brands contain some buttermilk, skimmed milk or whey powder).
- Low or reduced-fat spreads (may contain buttermilk).

Savoury Foods
- Some breadcrumb- and batter-coated items.
- Yorkshire puddings.
- Some "ready meals" (fresh, chilled and frozen).

WATCHPOINTS

- This list can only serve as a guide as products, particularly processed products, may vary. If one brand is off limits because it contains dairy foods, check all similar products; another brand may be dairy-free. It is also important to check items bought from pharmacies: some sweeteners, medicines and vitamin tablets/capsules may contain dairy ingredients, such as lactose.
- If your doctor has prescribed medication for asthma or eczema, such as inhalers, emollients or steroid creams, you should keep using them at the same time as following your diet.

Below left: Dairy spreads, most margarines, some brands of lemon curd, and chocolate spread all contain dairy products.

Below right: Avoid canned and packaged vegetables, such as creamed sweetcorn and mushrooms, canned spaghetti in tomato sauce and instant mashed potato – they all contain dairy products.

MILK AND DAIRY SUBSTITUTES

There's no need to miss out on choice or taste on a dairy-free diet. A wide range of alternative products is available in supermarkets, health-food shops and wholefood stores as well as from specialist mail-order companies. These substitutes can be used to replace regular cow's milk in hot and cold drinks, on breakfast cereals and for all your favourite recipes. If you can tolerate goat's or sheep's milk, these are also available from large supermarkets and health-food shops, or you may well find a local farm or farm shop with supplies of milk, yogurt and cheese. Milks and creams can be frozen successfully for 2–3 months, which is a real bonus if your supplier lives some distance away.

ALTERNATIVES TO COW'S MILK

Goat's and Sheep's Milk
Both goat's and sheep's milk are just as versatile as cow's milk. Goat's milk has a stronger, tangier taste than cow's milk. Sheep's milk has a higher fat content so is thicker and tastes richer and creamier. It is also slightly sweet, so it is ideal for use in milk puddings. Some individuals who have an intolerance to cow's milk find that they react quite well to these alternatives, but it must be stressed that both goat's milk and sheep's milk can provoke an allergic reaction. Their protein content is similar, although not the same as cow's milk. Neither is lactose-free, so they may well be unsuitable for anyone with more than a mild intolerance. The only way to find out if they are acceptable is to try them and see. (They are not recommended for infants under one year of age.)

Goat's cream is available from some larger supermarkets and health food shops. It has a smooth, sweet taste and can be used as a pouring cream, or whipped and used in desserts and as a topping or filling for cakes.

Soya Milks/Drinks
These drinks are made from soya beans and are widely available, fresh chilled and in UHT cartons, in unsweetened and sweetened versions and as flavoured varieties. They are often fortified with calcium, as soya milk is naturally low in calcium compared with cow's milk, and may also have added vitamins. Soya drinks are lactose-free, low in fat (also some fat-free and full-fat versions are available) and free of cholesterol and may therefore offer positive health benefits. In countries where soya foods are eaten regularly there appears to be less risk of developing certain cancers. The incidence of coronary heart disease and menopausal symptoms also appears to be reduced.

Plain soya milk can be used as a complete milk replacement in both hot and cold beverages, as well as for adding to all kinds of recipes. The flavoured varieties, such as vanilla and chocolate, make an appetizing "milky" drink to replace conventional milkshakes.

However, some allergic individuals may react to the soya protein and – as with goat's and sheep's milk – soya milk is not recommended for infants under the age of 12 months. Where a baby reacts to regular formula milks, dieticians generally advise changing to a special non-allergenic modified formula milk.

Soya cream is a non-dairy alternative to single cream and is widely available in long-life cartons from health-food shops and the larger supermarkets.

Left: Alternative milk drinks include (clockwise from top left) sheep's milk, lactose-reduced milk, soya milk, goat's milk, soya cream, oat drink and rice drink.

Oat Drink

This is a Swedish product made with whole oats, rapeseed oil and pure spring water. It is low in fat and calories, contains no cholesterol and offers another alternative for those on a dairy-free diet. UHT cartons are available from health food shops.

Rice Drink

Another long-life drink, this is made from filtered water, organic rice syrup, sunflower oil, sea salt and vanilla flavouring. It is lactose-free and low in fat and is suitable for vegans or those with a milk allergy or intolerance.

FORMS OF COW'S MILK THAT MAY BE TOLERATED

Lactose-reduced Milk

This is a long-life, full-cream product. Although it is made from cow's milk, its lactose content has been reduced through the addition of a natural lactase enzyme, similar to that normally found in the digestive system.

Heat-treated Milks

Certain milk proteins are affected by heat treatment, which alters their composition and makes them tolerable for older children and adults. You may therefore find that sterilized, UHT and evaporated milk are acceptable if an intolerance is caused by protein rather than lactose.

YOGURTS AND DESSERTS

Yogurt is a fermented milk product, which may contain bacteria with enzymes that can digest the lactose present in the milk to produce lactic acid. It is therefore low in lactose, so even yogurt derived from cow's milk may be acceptable for people with relatively mild lactose intolerance. If cow's milk doesn't suit you but you can tolerate goat's or sheep's milk, you'll find a ready supply of these yogurts. There is also a good range of soya desserts, yogurts and ice cream.

CHEESES

Hard cheeses such as Cheddar, Stilton and Parmesan are relatively low in lactose so small amounts may be safe to eat without causing symptoms.

Alternatively, vegan cheeses, made from soya protein, are available from wholefood or health food shops. There are several types, including variations on Cheddar, Gouda, Stilton, Edam, Parmesan and mozzarella. These cheeses can be used in sandwiches or in cooking, although they may not melt in exactly the same way as similar dairy cheeses.

There's also a good selection of goat's and sheep's cheeses available. Goat's cheeses include Chabichou, Chevrotin, Crottin de Chavignol, Chèvre and Chèvre Roulé, Capricorn and Mendip.

Sheep's (ewe's) milk cheeses include Roquefort and pecorino, and also feta and haloumi. These cheeses are traditionally made from sheep's milk but some brands may be made from or contain some cow's milk, so, as with all food products, it is important to check the label.

Above: The huge range of dairy-free soya products available include (clockwise from top left) soya yogurt, soya dessert, soya milk, marinated tofu (soya beancurd), smoked tofu, hard cheeses, which are similar to Cheddar, Edam and mozzarella, cream cheese and (centre) silken tofu.

FATS AND SPREADS

Choose from dairy-free soya spreads, vegetarian or kosher margarines or pure vegetable fats and oils. These can all be used for spreading, baking, sauces and stir-frying. Check labels on vegetable margarines as they often contain some whey or buttermilk, which is added to bring out the flavour, but is obviously unacceptable to anyone on a dairy-free diet.

TOFU (SOYA BEANCURD)

This is a high-protein, low-fat food made from soya beans. It comes in a block with a firm or soft (silken) texture and is available plain, marinated or smoked. Tofu in all its forms is very versatile and can be used in a wide variety of ways as a basis for both sweet and savoury dishes.

NUTS

Despite nut allergy having been recognized as a real clinical problem, there is still a great deal that is not known about the causes, prevalence and management of this potentially serious disorder. It is not clear why, but the number of people with reported nut allergy seems to be increasing.

A nut, in general terms, is an edible, hard-shelled seed or edible kernel. This definition includes those foods that we traditionally think of as nuts, such as peanuts and hazelnuts, as well as some seeds, such as sesame seeds. Nuts can be broken down into two categories:
Edible tree nuts, which include almonds, Brazil nuts, cashews, hazelnuts, macadamia nuts, pecans, pine nuts, pistachios and walnuts.
Other nuts, which include peanuts, also known as groundnuts or monkey nuts, develop in a seed pod about 10cm/4in below ground level; coconuts (in strict botanical terms the coconut palm is not a tree, but a plant closely related to bamboo and grasses); sesame seeds; and sunflower seeds.

These distinctions are important, because where there is a known allergy to one tree nut, for example, it is advisable to avoid all tree nuts. Similarly, some people with a peanut allergy also report allergy to tree nuts.

NUT ALLERGIES
Individuals who suffer from nut allergy are usually allergic to one of the proteins found in nuts. As with most allergies, the symptoms can vary in type and degree of seriousness, but peanuts are often cited as the culprits because they are the nuts that are usually associated with the life-threatening anaphylactic response.

HOW COMMON ARE NUT ALLERGIES?
It is very difficult to assess the true prevalence, but a limited number of studies have been carried out in the United Kingdom. For example, the incidence of sensitivity to peanuts in four-year-olds in a recent study on the Isle of Wight, was 1.4 per cent. Children as young as one, or even less, have started showing sensitivity, probably because they are being introduced to nut-containing foods early in the weaning diet. In America, it has been suggested that peanuts are second only to milk and eggs in terms of allergy prevalence. Although they are no more allergenic than other tree nuts, peanuts are eaten in larger quantities in the United States than in Europe at present. Peanuts, however, are a cheap source of protein, and are therefore being increasingly incorporated into processed foods in the European market.

SYMPTOMS
These can occur after exposure of the allergen to the mouth or skin, or after ingestion or inhalation. Less serious, although unpleasant, symptoms include: bowel discomfort, a worsening of eczema, nausea, colicky pain and diarrhoea. A rash (urticaria) can develop on the skin within a few minutes of exposure.

Below: There are many different types of nuts and all can be the cause of an allergic reaction.

More serious immediate reactions can be life threatening. These include the swelling of the mouth, tongue and back of the throat, which can make breathing difficult. It is possible to get complete obstruction of the airways. Anaphylactic shock is characterized by a drop in blood pressure, followed by unconsciousness, and, if not treated immediately, death. It can start with a burning sensation in the mouth and throat, and general urticaria. Usually these symptoms can be treated by an immediate adrenaline injection. It is essential, therefore, for people with a known severe sensitivity to nuts to carry emergency adrenaline treatment.

Severe reactions are often associated with people who have a history of asthma, and it is quite common for individuals to have other allergies as well. Unlike other allergies, nut or sesame allergy is generally permanent.

DIAGNOSIS

It is easier to identify the allergen if the reaction is immediate than if there is a delayed reaction. Skin prick tests, in which solutions of the test allergens are applied to the skin, can be used to confirm the diagnosis. These tests are only useful if the reaction involves immunoglobulin E (IgE) antibodies, and are less helpful if there is a delayed response.

Blood levels of IgE can also be measured against a particular antigen using the RAST (Radio Allergo Sorbent Test). This may be more appropriate as it reduces the risk of anaphylactic shock.

MANAGING YOUR DIET

Nuts and nut oils are widely used in the manufacture of cakes, biscuits, confectionery, marzipan, pastries, desserts, breakfast cereals, nut butters and vegetarian dishes. Many ethnic dishes, such as those from China, Thailand and Indonesia, may contain nuts. Sesame seeds are found in many foods, such as hummus, halva, burger buns and sesame oil.

Crude oils may contain traces of protein which can cause a reaction, but refined nut oils (i.e. those which have been neutralized, bleached and deodorized) contain no protein traces, and are considered non-allergenic. Oils to watch are "gourmet" oils which can be blended with crude peanut oil to give them a peanut flavour.

Avoiding the nut(s) that cause problems may be easier said than done because of the widespread use of nuts in manufactured foods. People with a nut allergy have to be very vigilant when reading ingredient labels.

Manufacturers are becoming more diligent in identifying potential allergens in their products. There are specific food safety procedures which manufacturers can put in place to assess the potential risk of contamination of products with nuts, even when they are not an ingredient in the particular food. This assessment forms the basis of the decision whether to include a nut warning on products. It is very unlikely that manufacturers will have a list of their products that are "nut-free", because it is virtually impossible to

Above: Cakes, ice cream and biscuits often contain nuts and nut oils.

prove that this is the case, since cross-contamination from other products can occur. The current guidelines recommended for nut labelling are:
- If a food product contains nuts or a nut ingredient, it must be included in the ingredients list.
- If there is a risk of contamination (for example, from a nut-containing product made on the same production line), a nut warning should be given near to the ingredients list.
- Where there is very low risk of contamination (e.g. a product is made on a site which does not handle nuts), no labelling is needed.

If in any doubt about the nut status of a product, it is best to check first with the manufacturer. People with nut allergy should always inform schools, relatives and friends who may be preparing food for them of their condition. It is also advisable to wear a pendant or MedicAlert identification bracelet stating your food sensitivity in case of an emergency.

FISH AND SHELLFISH

Fish is reported to be one of the most common causes of food allergy in adults. In Scandinavia, where fish is part of the staple diet, fish is the most common cause of food allergies. The most likely culprit is a protein, which is believed to be found in many species of fish.

HOW COMMON IS FISH ALLERGY/INTOLERANCE?

Allergic reactions to shellfish in particular are reportedly common in adults. Shellfish include shrimp, lobster, crawfish and molluscs (clams, oysters, mussels and scallops).

SYMPTOMS

These can vary in severity, depending on how sensitive the individual is. In more severe cases, the reaction may be an immediate one, involving the immunoglobulin E (IgE) antibodies. In such cases, urgent medical attention is required. Other symptoms might include sickness, diarrhoea, abdominal cramps, wheezing rhinitis and urticaria. Simply handling fish can trigger a reaction in a sensitive person.

DIAGNOSIS

Unlike pinpointing an allergy to eggs and milk, identifying a fish intolerance or allergy should not be too difficult, because you are more likely to know when you have eaten fish or shellfish. Eliminate the suspected fish from the diet, and, if symptoms clear up, then the fish can be identified as the culprit.

To confirm diagnosis, a skin test or RAST (Radio Allergo Sorbent Test) is often used.

MANAGING YOUR DIET

As fish and shellfish are not normally "hidden" ingredients in foods, it should be relatively straightforward to avoid fish. Nevertheless, there are still some foods that are derived from fish. Remember that Worcestershire sauce usually contains anchovies, and avoid eating Caesar salad, caviar and roe.

There are different kinds of allergy, however: some people who are sensitive to shellfish may be able to tolerate other types of fish, and vice versa.

Above: A sensitivity to shellfish is not uncommon and crabs, lobsters and prawns are among the most frequent culprits.

Left: Fish allergy is reported to be one of the most common food allergies in adults.

EGGS

It is the white, which makes up about 57 per cent of an egg, that can cause an allergic response in those with a sensitivity to eggs. Albumen, the protein in egg white, is made up of around 40 different proteins. It is some of these that have been identified as allergenic.

HOW COMMON IS EGG INTOLERANCE?

As with all types of food intolerance, it is difficult to give a good estimate of prevalence. It is likely, however, that the incidence is highest in infants under one year, and most have outgrown their sensitivity by the age of two.

SYMPTOMS

The most common reaction is an immediate one (i.e. involving IgE antibodies), occurring within minutes of exposure to egg. Symptoms tend to consist of a rash around the mouth, followed by swelling of the mouth and urticaria (skin rash) on the face. As with severe nut allergy, swelling of the mouth and tongue can occur within minutes, and in severe cases result in anaphylaxis.

In less severe cases, symptoms may not appear until one hour after eating the egg, and might include asthma or a worsening of eczema.

DIAGNOSIS

The diagnosis of egg intolerance relies mainly on medical history. The most reliable way to confirm a suspected egg intolerance is to carry out what is known as a double blind placebo controlled food challenge. In this, neither the person with the suspected allergy nor the observer knows which of the foods being offered contain the test material. Other tests, such as skin prick or RAST, are unreliable for confirming egg intolerance.

MANAGING YOUR DIET

All foods containing egg white, egg yolk, or eggs from hen, turkey, duck, goose or other birds should be avoided by those with an egg allergy. As with nuts, egg is extensively used in a wide range of manufactured foods, such as

cakes, bread, confectionery, custard, mayonnaise, sauces, soufflés, batter mixes and some chocolate products.

Anyone following an egg-free diet should visit a dietician to ensure that their diet is providing them with the right balance of nutrients. The dietician will be able to offer them individually tailored nutritional advice as well as providing some up-to-date information about egg-free products and supplying a "free from" list.

Above and right: Eggs are a common ingredient and are included in many manufactured foods, such as lemon curd, mayonnaise and pasta.

SOYA AND OTHER PROBLEM FOODS

Sensitivity to nuts and milk are well known, but there are a number of other foods that can cause an allergic reaction in sensitive individuals.

These foods include soya beans, cheese, chocolate, coffee, citrus fruits and alcohol, and allergic reactions to them can vary in severity.

SOYA

Hypersensitivity to soya beans is much less common than it is to nuts, for example, but, because soya beans are a major component in processed foods, it is much more difficult to avoid them. It is quite common to have an intolerance to soya beans in addition to a sensitivity to cow's milk.

SYMPTOMS

Some sensitive people will experience an allergic response to soya, although an anaphylactic reaction is rare. As with other food intolerances, the symptoms will vary in severity and type.

DIAGNOSIS

A skin test or RAST (Radio Allergo Sorbent Test) can be useful, but, as with many other allergies, the most reliable way to confirm a soya intolerance is to carry out a double blind placebo controlled food challenge (see Eggs).

MANAGING YOUR DIET

Soya beans and soya bean products are found in many processed foods, such as infant milk formulas, cereals, baked goods, canned tuna, soups and sauces. The allergenic protein in soya bean oils is removed during processing, so refined soya oil is considered safe for those with a sensitivity. Soya lecithin, an emulsifier in many processed foods, is also considered safe, unless symptoms of soya sensitivity continue, in which case it should also be avoided.

Ingredients on food labels which indicate the presence of soya protein:
- soya flour
- soya protein isolate
- tofu (soya beancurd)
- soya protein
- textured vegetable protein
- soy sauce
- miso

Other ingredients to look out for are: vegetable starch, vegetable gum and vegetable broth, as these may contain soya protein.

OTHER PROBLEM FOODS

Cheese, chocolate, coffee and citrus fruits can trigger migraine in sensitive individuals. Alcohol can also cause problems, especially red wine, sherry and port. These foods (and drinks) contain "vasoactive amines", which dilate the blood vessels and can provoke migraines. If you are affected in this way, try to avoid the above foods to see if your symptoms improve.

It's also worth remembering that drinking plenty of water to prevent dehydration and eating regularly (low blood sugar can precipitate a bad headache) can help to prevent recurring headaches.

Above: Cheese, chocolate or red wine can trigger a migraine in sensitive individuals.

Left: Soya beans and products such as tofu (soya beancurd) cause an allergic response in some people.

YEAST

Sensitivity to yeast is sometimes blamed for a number of different complaints, such as thrush, stomach bloating, chronic fatigue and rashes. It is not, however, responsible for causing a true food allergy involving the immune system, and in this sense is not considered a major serious allergen.

A yeast-free and sugar-free diet is often recommended for individuals with a sensitivity to yeast. In some recent studies with patients who had chronic urticaria (skin rash) and a suspected yeast sensitivity, over half found that their skin symptoms cleared up when they followed a low-yeast diet.

Individuals following a yeast-free diet should avoid foods that contain any form of yeast, mould or funghi, such as mushrooms, blue cheese or yeast-leavened breads.

Yeasts in the body do not normally cause any harm. However, there may be some triggers, such as diets rich in sugars and yeasts, oral contraceptives, pregnancy and treatment with certain antibiotics, that can cause yeasts to multiply, resulting in "overgrowth".

Above and left: Foods to avoid on a low-yeast diet include cheese and fermented dairy foods, mushrooms, grapes and mould-ripened cheeses.

Non-dietary treatments include various anti-fungal drugs, such as nyastin, evening primrose oil and garlic capsules. Because yeasts feed on sugar, it is also a good idea to cut down on consumption of sugar and sugary foods and drinks.

Foods to avoid on a low-yeast diet include:
- bread, rolls, pizza, buns
- wine, beer, cider
- grapes, raisins
- mould-ripened cheese
- yeast extract
- vinegar, ketchup, pickles
- fermented dairy products, e.g. yogurt and buttermilk
- malted milk drinks
- tofu (soya beancurd)
- soy sauce

FOOD ADDITIVES

Additives, especially artificial ones, are often blamed for being the cause of all manner of allergic reactions and may produce behavioural problems, especially in young children, though this is a highly contentious subject. Additives are certainly thought to be responsible for upsetting a minority of susceptible people, but the number affected may well be considerably less than is sometimes suggested.

Additives may be natural (extracted directly from natural products), nature identical (made to match something found in nature) or artificial, but those that are man-made are no more likely to cause adverse reactions than natural additives or, indeed, natural foods. It is important, too, to remember why additives are used in food manufacture. Some are purely cosmetic and are used in response to consumer expectations of colour, flavour and texture, but most fulfil important and necessary functions. Without additives, food would not keep as well, so we would have to shop more frequently; there would be a greater risk of food poisoning and we would not be able to enjoy the wide range of convenience foods that we've grown to expect.

WHY ARE ADDITIVES USED?

Additives perform a number of different functions, and they are categorized and grouped according to their function, usually by E number. The E number indicates that the additive has been approved safe by EC regulations. Those listed are the main categories but there are many others, including anti-caking agents, acidity regulators, and so on.

Colours (E100s) These are used to restore colour lost in processing (e.g. canned peas) and to make food look more appetizing. Many are natural colourings, coming from foods such as red peppers, grape skins and beetroot.

Preservatives (E200s) These help keep food safe for longer by preventing the growth of micro-organisms which would cause decay, spoilage and food poisoning. These additives protect our health, reduce wastage and allow us to eat a wider choice of foods all year round.

Antioxidants (E300s) These are used to protect fats and oils in food from turning rancid, changing colour and deteriorating through oxidation. Vitamin E (E306) is used as a natural antioxidant in vegetable oil and ascorbic acid. In fruit drinks vitamin C (E300) prevents the fruit turning brown.

Right: Alcoholic drinks, such as beer, wine and cider, often contain sulphite preservatives and other additives but are not subject to ingredient labelling laws.

Emulsifiers and stabilizers (E400s) Emulsifiers are used to help blend ingredients such as oil and water together and stabilizers are used to prevent them separating again. (These additives are used in soft margarines and salad dressings). Thickeners and gelling agents add smoothness.

Left: The flavour enhancer MSG (monosodium glutamate) is often added to Chinese restaurant food.

them. The azo dyes, which include tartrazine (E102), a yellow colour used in soft drinks and crumb coatings, may be particularly troublesome. Tartrazine has been linked with hyperactivity in children and also affects asthmatics. Annatto (E160b), which is a natural colour, may also trigger asthma attacks and rashes.

Flavour enhancers MSG is a widely used flavour enhancer, particularly in Chinese dishes. Some people develop allergic reactions, including headaches, nausea, dizziness and palpitations, on eating MSG. These reactions have been given the popular name of "Chinese restaurant syndrome". You may want to check with take-aways and restaurants whether MSG is used and ask for it to be omitted.

HYPERACTIVITY IN CHILDREN

Most children are naturally bounding with energy and can sometimes behave badly. This is all a natural part of growing up and learning social boundaries. It shouldn't be confused with hyperactive behaviour, which can be aggressive, unruly and out of control. It is virtually impossible for the child to settle for long and things become intolerable for the rest of the family. In some cases, artificial colours and preservatives may be implicated but take advice from a dietician before jumping to conclusions.

AVOIDING ADDITIVES

Most supermarkets produce lists of "additive-free" foods. Labels on packs that state stating "no artificial preservatives, colours or flavouring" may also be helpful. Check the labels carefully (all additives must be listed by category and E number or name), and avoid any that you believe cause a reaction. Wherever possible, choose fresh foods.

Flavourings A complex range of natural flavourings and artificial chemical flavourings is added to various foods. As yet these additives do not have any serial numbers.

Flavour enhancers These help bring out the flavour of foods, the most common being MSG (monosodium glutamate/E621). Wherever possible, manufacturers usually prefer to use stocks, herbs and spices for boosting or enhancing flavour.

Artificial sweeteners These are used more and more frequently in place of sugar because they are lower in calories and better for dental health. Saccharin, aspartame and acesulfame-k are the principal artificial intense sweeteners used.

WHICH ADDITIVES MAY BE A PROBLEM?

Preservatives Some asthmatics are sensitive to sulphites (E220–E227), such as sulphur dioxide. Sulphite preservatives are used in beer, wine and cider but, as yet, alcoholic drinks are exempt from ingredient labelling laws. Sodium benzoate (E211), another preservative used in soft drinks, sweets, jam and margarine, can cause problems for asthma or urticaria (skin rash) sufferers and has been linked with hyperactivity in children.

Artificial colours These are recognized as upsetting sensitive people, so many manufacturers, acting in response to consumer demand, have reformulated their products to remove

ALLERGY-FREE SHOPPING

The idea of allergy-free shopping may sound like an impossible task, and it is likely to take more effort than usual. However, once you know what foods or food ingredients you are sensitive to, then you can start to think about how best to adapt your diet to ensure it is nutritionally adequate and well balanced. Try not to worry because there are plenty of sources of help.

PROFESSIONAL ADVICE

If your diet is going to be very restricted – cutting out major food groups, such as dairy products, wheat and eggs, for example – you should ask your doctor to refer you to a professional dietician.

Dieticians have expert knowledge in the field of diet and health, and can offer practical help with planning your daily diet. They will also provide "free from" booklets or lists that will help you to avoid manufactured products containing any problem foods. These booklets and lists include branded products, as well as supermarket own-label brands.

READING LABELS

Whatever food, or foods, you are trying to avoid, the most important task you will have to carry out when shopping is to read food labels. Even if you have "free from" lists from a dietician, supermarket or food manufacturer, it is always wise to check the label, as it is possible that the recipe, and therefore ingredients, will change over time (sometimes this will be indicated by a statement such as "New improved recipe").

By law, food labels must include a list of ingredients, which covers all the ingredients present. Although it will be time consuming to start with, you will soon find that you become good at scanning for the particular ingredients you are looking for.

Below: Even when following a restricted diet, there will still be plenty of different foods that you can eat.

WHAT IF THERE ARE NO FOOD LABELS?

There is no legal requirement to include a list of ingredients on foods that are sold loose (e.g. fruit and vegetables) or unpackaged (e.g. on a delicatessen or bakery counter). If there is any doubt about what ingredients are included in a product, ask the sales assistant or department manager, who will be able to help you. He or she may have a product information guide which will include a breakdown of the ingredients.

ADVICE FROM SUPERMARKETS

All major supermarkets now provide detailed lists of their own-label products that are "free-from" various foods and ingredients which may cause allergies, such as gluten, egg, dairy and soya products.

ADVICE FROM MANUFACTURERS

In addition to supermarkets providing "free from" lists, many food manufacturers also have freephone numbers on packs to encourage consumers to telephone for more information about their products.

Bigger companies will have their own nutrition department and customer care team, who will be able to send you the lists you require and supply any further information you are looking for about particular branded products. Once again, product information lists should have a date on them, so do remember that they will go out of date. It would be impossible to keep these updated constantly in line with any product changes, so always remember to read the label before buying the product.

You may also find now that several companies have started highlighting various allergenic ingredients either in the ingredients list or close to the list. This is particularly true in the case of nut labelling, where there may be a nut warning on the pack. This development has made shopping easier for the nut allergy sufferer.

ALLERGY-FREE COOKING

With the wide range of foods of different nationalities that are available in supermarkets and other specialist shops, it is relatively easy to adapt your diet and soon enjoy a new way of eating. It can be fun and inspiring trying out new foods and products that you might not have chosen before. You will have to experiment with different brands to find ones you like. For example, soya milks tend to vary

Above: It can be fun trying out new products that you have not used before, such as soya milk or tofu (soya beancurd).

considerably in taste, depending on the manufacturer. If you are buying substitute foods such as soya milk, try to buy ones that are fortified with the essential nutrients that you might be missing out on, such as calcium. For tasty, easy-to-prepare dishes, turn to the recipes in the second part of this book. You will find plenty of choice to enable you to meet all your dietary requirements (and to satisfy your tastebuds).

Above: Rice pudding made with dairy-free milk and fruit crumble made with pure vegetable margarine make delicious desserts.

Above: Melon with Parma ham makes a delicious – and safe – starter for most allergy sufferers.

Above: Foods that are coated with breadcrumbs, such as chicken Kiev, should be avoided by those with a wheat allergy.

CHILDREN'S ALLERGIES AND FAMILY MEALS

All children need a healthy diet for growth, energy and physical and emotional development. Evidence suggests that if you encourage healthy food choices at a young age, there's a good chance that these will continue into adulthood and beyond. When a child has an allergy or food intolerance, it's important that he or she is not made to feel different from friends and companions, so try to avoid making a fuss over what the child eats, and wherever possible include as much variety of ordinary everyday foods as is practical and appropriate.

COMMON FOOD INTOLERANCES AND ALLERGIES

The most frequently encountered allergy among infants and young children is to milk, and it usually appears when formula milk or cow's milk is introduced during weaning. The usual symptoms are: asthma, eczema, urticaria (skin rash), or vomiting and diarrhoea. In order to protect against the development of allergies in young children, especially if there is a family history of allergies, breastfeeding is recommended, at least until the baby is four months old, and preferably six months. Most grow out of childhood allergies by the age of five, although those with a family history of allergic illness (known as "atopic") are more likely to develop other allergic conditions and possibly food intolerances in later life. Lactose intolerance may also occur on a temporary basis, as a result of a bout of gastroenteritis. This usually clears up when lactose (milk sugar) is avoided for a short while.

Other common food sensitivities in young children include those to wheat and eggs, usually presenting as asthma or eczema. The medical profession recommends that gluten (found in wheat) should not be introduced into

Below: Dairy products are a common cause of allergic reaction in children.

HELPING YOUR CHILD ADAPT

It can be difficult for your child to watch others tuck into jelly and ice cream or chocolate bars if he or she is not able to eat because of a food sensitivity. It is particularly difficult if your child is too young to understand why certain foods aren't allowed. If they are old enough, then explain the reasons why those foods need to be avoided, and focus on all the positive food choices that can be included. Thankfully, there is a much improved selection of alternatives available, such as soya chocolate desserts, which are a delicious choice for children (and adults) on a dairy-free diet.

HEALTHY EATING

The key to a healthy diet containing all the essential nutrients for children's growth and development is balance and variety. It is important to include a range of different foods from the major food groups, in appropriate quantities, every day. Even if you are having to avoid a major food group, such as dairy foods, the diet can still be healthy, as long as suitable alternative foods are included in the diet to make up for lost nutrients. In the case of a diet free from dairy foods, important nutrients that will need to be obtained through other foods include calcium, vitamin A and vitamin B_2 (riboflavin).

If you enjoy your food, and make a feature of cooking and preparing it, it is quite likely that your child will also enjoy helping, so that eating and meal occasions are seen as an important and enjoyable part of the day.

Unless your child has a specific sensitivity to them, you do not necessarily have to avoid convenience foods, such as fish fingers, or even to avoid sweets, cakes and other confectionery. These foods can often still be enjoyed as part of a healthy diet, as long as they are eaten in moderation.

an infant's diet until the age of six months. By this age, it is thought that a baby's intestines are sufficiently developed to cope with gluten, and the risk of coeliac disease is reduced. As far as eggs are concerned, egg yolk can be introduced from around six months, but egg white, which is more allergenic, should not be introduced until babies are nine months old. With babies and young children, it is best to seek advice from your family doctor or health visitor if you are worried about any aspect of your child's health.

Above left: Most children enjoy cooking, so let them help out in the kitchen.

Left: Fruit juice, wholemeal toast and cereal can make a healthy breakfast, but may need adapting if you are avoiding dairy products, wheat or citrus fruits.

Below: Spaghetti with meatballs would make a good dairy-free meal for children.

BREAKFAST IDEAS

Breakfast is one of the most important meals of the day; it helps to boost energy levels for the day ahead. Substitute items such as non-dairy milk and gluten- or wheat-free bread, if necessary:

- Breakfast cereals and milk, or a dairy-free alternative, such as soya milk.
- Yogurt and fresh or dried fruit.
- Cooked breakfasts (e.g. poached egg or boiled egg with toast).
- Baked beans on toast.
- Bagels or muffins with a suitable spread and yeast extract or marmalade.
- Grilled mushrooms on toast.
- For a more substantial breakfast, grilled bacon and tomato on toast makes a good choice.
- Include a glass of fruit juice to boost vitamin C levels and to help the absorption of iron from cereals, toast and baked beans.

ADAPTING THE MAIN FAMILY MEAL

Use the recipe ideas in the second part of this book to plan some weekly menus: this will help with shopping, and ensure variety at mealtimes. For healthy eating, base your meals on a starchy carbohydrate food such as pasta, rice and potatoes, and then decide what else to serve with it. Depending on your child's particular food sensitivity, you may have to adapt the recipe slightly (for example, by substituting soya milk or cheese for cow's milk or cheese). Try some of the following ideas:

- Pasta can be served with a wide range of healthy sauces, from tomato to Bolognese.
- Chicken is delicious simply cooked; try chargrilling it and serving with baked potatoes, a barbecue sauce and a mixed salad.

- Fresh or frozen fish, such as cod or salmon steaks and fillets, can be grilled, poached or steamed and served with or without a sauce.
- Lentils are quick to cook and make a delicious vegetarian dish. Cook them with onions, tomatoes and other vegetables.
- If your children aren't keen on cooked vegetables, you could try puréeing them, or using them to make a delicious and wholesome soup.

SUGGESTED PUDDINGS AND DESSERTS

- Fresh fruit.
- Fruit salad.
- Ice cream (this can be dairy-free if appropriate).
- Fruit crumble or pie.
- Baked apples.
- Poached fruit.
- Fruit or milk (use a dairy-free alternative if needed) jelly, set in a small, covered pot.
- Scones, muffins or meringues (gluten-free if necessary).

SCHOOL LUNCHES

When your child goes to playgroup, nursery or school, it is essential that the staff are fully aware of his or her food sensitivities. The easiest option is for you to prepare a packed lunch with items you know your child will eat and enjoy. Just make sure he or she does not swap food items with friends. If you would prefer your child to have cooked school lunches, then talk to the catering staff, who may be quite willing to provide appropriate dishes.

HEALTHY LUNCH BOX IDEAS

• Bread, which can be gluten-free if needed, filled with tuna, ham, cheese (or soya alternative) and salad.
• Some fresh fruit or vegetables (e.g. apple, banana or carrot).
• A yogurt, or soya alternative.
• A drink e.g. carton of apple juice or low-sugar squash.
• A biscuit, plain cake or packet of raisins or other dried fruit.
• For a savoury snack, opt for breadsticks (or gluten-free alternative) or reduced-fat crisps.

ADDITIVES

If you think that food additives (particularly colours and preservatives) are causing an allergic reaction or affecting your child's behaviour, then aim to cut out all "junk" food for a while, and focus on feeding him or her on fresh, simple, homemade dishes. If you would like some professional advice, go along to your family doctor to talk it through.

Top Right: A healthy packed lunch is often the easiest way to ensure that lunch at school is allergy-free.

Right: Additives, such as colourings and preservatives, that are often contained in "junk" food can be responsible for causing an allergic reaction.

ENTERTAINING AT HOME

Eating is one of life's pleasures, and it is even more enjoyable when you are sharing the experience with friends or family, whether formally or informally. When planning the menu, think about your guests and their particular dietary needs. For example, is anyone vegetarian or do they have diabetes? Plan the choice of food around these needs. Think also about the appearance of the food – the colours – as well as contrasting textures and complementary flavours. Will it be a sit-down meal or a buffet-style menu? How filling do you want the meal to be? Is it to be a light supper or a three-course meal?

Catering for special dietary needs doesn't have to mean more work. If you have a dairy intolerance, for example, there are plenty of dishes to choose from in this book that would be suitable for everyone to enjoy, and this saves you having to make something different for yourself. Similarly, if catering for a nut-sensitive friend or someone with a wheat allergy, there are lots of tasty ideas in this book to help you choose a delicious menu.

CHILDREN'S BIRTHDAY PARTIES

When planning a birthday party at home, keep the food as simple as possible. Usually, children are so excited that they do not eat much, but enjoy nibbling on lots of different bite-size snacks. It can be great fun (but hard work) organizing a party at home, and all that's required for younger children are a few party games and lots of time to play and run around.

The key to a successful birthday party is to keep in mind at the planning stage the food intolerances or allergies you will be coping with. Think ahead about what to offer. A choice of sweet and savoury foods is good, but don't put all the sweet foods out at the start or they are likely to be eaten straightaway.

It is easy to decide which foods are appropriate for someone with an allergy and which are not. If a child is nut sensitive, then avoid obvious foods such as peanut butter sandwiches and cakes or biscuits that have nuts such as almonds or hazelnuts in them. The birthday cake may need adapting if a child is allergic to eggs, for example, or to dairy products, gluten or food colouring.

Right: Children with an allergy need not miss out at birthday parties. There are plenty of recipes for birthday cakes that do not contain eggs, gluten or dairy products.

MENU SUGGESTIONS FOR BIRTHDAY TEAS

There are plenty of party foods that are either free from potential allergens or that can be adapted. Listed below are some ideas to help you plan the perfect party.

MENU 1

Savoury snacks
• Small sandwiches, made with ham, tuna, banana, cheese (or soya alternative) and cucumber.
• Chicken drumsticks.
• Plain potato crisps.
• Cherry tomatoes and cucumber sticks.

Sweet snacks
• Chocolate or carob crispie cakes.
• Jelly and ice cream (or non-dairy alternative).
• Fresh strawberries (in season) or seedless grapes.
• Birthday cake.

Drinks: fruit juice or fruit punch, water or squash.

MENU 2

Savoury snacks
• Cheese or tofu (soya beancurd) and pineapple chunks on sticks.
• Grilled bacon and banana rolls.
• Baked potato skins with a variety of dips (make them yourself if you are unsure of the ingredients), such as herb or garlic yogurt (or soya alternative), tomato salsa or hummus.
• Cherry tomatoes and cucumber sticks.

Sweet snacks
• Seedless grapes.
• Chocolate- or carob-dipped strawberries (simply dip in melted chocolate or carob).
• Chocolate or carob marshmallows (moisten the tops and place a chocolate or carob button on the top).
• Mini muffins or fairy cakes.
• Birthday cake (can be egg-free or gluten-free if required).

Drinks: fruit juice or fruit punch, water or squash.

meal. To make life easier for everyone, it's important that you let your host know if there are any foods you are unable to eat. Then you can discuss what would be suitable options for the meal. You might like to offer to contribute a dish – a dessert, for example – which will help take the pressure off your host.

When eating out in a restaurant, try to choose one where you know the food is freshly prepared. It is easier for the chefs to cater for your needs if they are making up the dishes themselves, since they may not have all the ingredient details of ready-prepared dishes. It's also a good idea to see the menu in advance if you can, and then to talk to the chef personally about any special requirements.

WHAT TO CHOOSE

If you are in any doubt about what's in a dish, play safe and choose something simple with few ingredients, such as plain grilled or roasted meat, fish or poultry, served with vegetables and potatoes, followed by a fruit-based dessert or an egg-free sorbet.

Above: When eating out, it is often easier to choose a dish, such as roast lamb with haricot beans and salad, that does not rely on a large number of different ingredients.

ADULT GUESTS

Entertaining at home is often a time to try something new, and adults are usually happy to taste new dishes. For a gluten sensitivity, try experimenting with different grains such as buckwheat, to make pancakes, savoury rolls or pastries filled with a vegetable or meat filling; you could also consider a rice dish, chargrilled chicken breasts or fish steak (such as cod, tuna or salmon), as these suit most tastes and are simple to prepare.

At the back of this book, you'll find a delicious selection of mouthwatering recipes to try, most of which are suitable for a number of different food sensitivities and allergies. One example of a menu that would suit most special dietary needs would be a simple vegetable soup, such as Summer Tomato Soup, followed by Chicken Baked with Butter Beans and Garlic, and rounded off with Pears with Ginger and Star Anise. There are lots of different options for delicious yet allergy-free starters, main courses and desserts, so approach the situation as an opportunity to expand your repertoire.

EATING OUT

Lunch and Dinner Invitations

Having a food sensitivity does not mean that you can't eat out anymore, nor does it mean you can't enjoy an evening out in a favourite restaurant. It does mean, however, that you need to do a bit of forward planning, particularly if you are going to a friend's or work colleague's house for a

Left: Many foods that people eat every day contain foods that can cause an allergic reaction. Eggs, nuts, dairy products, wheat and nuts are often contained in cakes, quiches and sauces.

enriching or glazing a dish. It is better to be safe than sorry, so always check if you are at all unsure.

• For people with wheat sensitivity, avoid thick stews, casseroles and soups which may have been thickened using wheat flour.

• Pastries, cakes and desserts may contain dairy ingredients, so if you have a cow's milk intolerance, check first, or choose plain desserts such as fruit salad or sorbet. They are also likely to be made with wheat flour, so should be avoided by those with wheat sensitivity.

• Some Indian and Chinese dishes, such as tandoori and tikka dishes, sweet and sour pork and spare ribs, can often contain artificial colours and preservatives.

SAFE SEASONINGS

People with a wheat or gluten sensitivity should avoid seasoning food with ground white pepper – sometimes flour is added to make the pepper last longer. Stick to ground black pepper instead.

FOODS TO AVOID

Depending on the type of food or foods that you are sensitive to, there are a number of foods you might need to avoid in a restaurant. Here are some general guidelines.

• If you are nut sensitive, avoid foods containing nuts and seeds (e.g. cakes, marzipan, some breads, biscuits and cheesecakes). Refined nut oils (e.g. sesame oil) should not cause problems, but if in doubt, choose something that you know does not contain any potential problem foods.

• For people with egg intolerance, watch out for "hidden" eggs, which are often used for binding, thickening,

ALLERGY-FREE MENU SELECTIONS

Below are some safe menu selections which would be suitable for most types of food intolerances as they exclude most of the main food allergens.

STARTERS

• Melon.
• Grapefruit.
• Mixed fruit cocktail.
• Melon with Parma ham.
• Clear soup (e.g. vegetable soup without thickening).

MAIN COURSES

• Plain grilled, roast or fried meat, fish or poultry.
• Simple fish dishes (e.g. poached or steamed fish).
• Rice dishes.
• Vegetable stir-fries.

DESSERTS

• Fresh fruit salad.
• Fruit sorbet (can be egg-free).
• Stewed fruit or dried fruit.
• Pavlova (suitable for wheat-sensitive people but not for people with egg allergy).

WHICH CUISINE IS BEST?

Each cuisine has its own hallmarks, and, depending on your food sensitivity, you will probably find one that suits your tastes and dietary requirements. Here are a few pointers.

- Italian: famous for pasta and pizzas, Italian food is probably least suited for someone with a wheat sensitivity (although you might find some tasty risotto dishes on the menu). You can usually also find fresh fish and plenty of salads on an Italian menu.
- Indian: a variety of different meat and vegetable curries is on offer, so there is usually something to suit most people. Watch out for cream, ghee (clarified butter) and yogurt if you are following a dairy-free diet.

- Chinese: mainly rice and noodle based, with fish, vegetables and some meat. Very little dairy produce is used.
- French: tend to be rich dishes, relying heavily on dairy ingredients, especially cream, butter and cheese.

PICNIC FOOD

There is something very special about eating outdoors. Picnics can be informal snacks or more extravagant affairs which take more thought and time to prepare. Whatever the occasion, it's a good idea to prepare some food in advance. For an informal family picnic, choose a selection of cold meats and fresh crusty bread, with tomatoes, celery and cucumber. Fresh fruit makes an easy dessert.

For a special picnic, try some of the following: chicken drumsticks or wings; slices of pizza; sticks of raw vegetables, such as cucumber, carrot, peppers, celery and mangetouts; cherry tomatoes; a quiche or flan (wheat- or egg-free if appropriate); and a variety of salads, such as pasta or rice salad, a leafy salad or a bean salad. For dessert, take some baked goods, made without problem foods (e.g. an egg- or gluten-free cake with a jam filling or gingerbread), as well as plenty of fresh fruit.

Below: Picnics are great fun for a family day out but, as with meals at home, a little thought as to your choice of food will help to make them a great success.

HEALTHY EATING
FOR DIABETICS

Over the last few years, the recommended diet for people with diabetes

has changed substantially. A diabetic diet need not be all about denial

but should focus, instead, on eating healthy, well-balanced meals —

high in fruit, vegetables and fibre and low in fat, salt and sugar.

This chapter contains all the information you will need,

from diagnosis to management.

INTRODUCTION

By the time you pick up this book you (or someone close to you, such as a friend, child or parent) may already have been diagnosed as diabetic, so you may have a pretty good idea of what being diabetic is and what it involves. However, since understanding a situation is often the key to coping with it, it may be worth reviewing what you actually know.

Don't be intimidated by the wealth of rather technical information in the next few pages. The principles of dealing with diabetes are really very simple and soon become easier to cope with.

Most diabetics, especially those who have been diagnosed recently, lead normal lives, and some go on to excel in sports, which many non-diabetics could only dream of. So, take heart – and read on.

WHAT IS DIABETES?

The name, *diabetes mellitus*, comes from two Greek words (*diabetes* – a siphon; *mellitus* – honey, because the urine of a diabetic tastes sweet) and describes a condition in which the sugar (or glucose) circulating in the blood cannot be absorbed properly. This results in abnormally high blood glucose levels, which can cause both short- and long-term problems.

To explain in a bit more detail: Glucose (a form of sugar) is the body's main fuel – it provides us with our energy. We absorb glucose from starchy and sugary carbohydrate foods, such as potatoes, rice and beans, breads, biscuits, cakes, sugar and sweets. As we chew, enzymes in saliva start breaking down these foods, a process that is continued by the acids in the stomach. As the food progresses on into the gut, digestive juices from the pancreas and gall bladder get to work, and by the time the food reaches the bowel it has been broken down into simple particles (including glucose), which are absorbed through the bowel wall into the blood-stream. The glucose in the bloodstream moves on through the liver where much of it is stored for future use, and into body cells where it is either burned up to provide energy or stored for future use.

However, the glucose in the blood cannot enter the cells in the liver or any other part of the body unless a chemical (insulin) effectively "opens the door" into those cells. Insulin is a hormone that is manufactured in the pancreas (the glandular organ that lies

behind the stomach but in front of the backbone) and stored there until rising glucose levels in the bloodstream set off a chemical reaction, which releases the insulin. Once in the bloodstream, the insulin links into the body's cells through what are called insulin receptors (a procedure which is rather like two space ships docking). This linkage precipitates chemical changes in the cell walls, which allow the glucose through into the cell where it can be converted into energy.

In a non-diabetic this monitoring and replenishment process happens automatically so that the body's cells are continually fed with sufficient glucose for their energy needs, while excess glucose is stored in the cells. In a diabetic the system fails either because the pancreas does not produce any insulin at all (Insulin Dependent Diabetes Mellitus or IDDM) or because the pancreas' supply of insulin is reduced, the supply of insulin receptors is reduced or neither functions very efficiently (Non Insulin Dependent Diabetes or NIDDM).

Despite years of research no one has discovered why it is that the pancreas should (as in the onset of IDDM) suddenly cease to produce insulin, although it would appear that some people have a genetic predisposition to diabetes. In susceptible individuals, a viral disease can act on the immune system to make it turn upon the "beta" cells in the pancreas, which manu-facture the insulin, and destroy them. In NIDDM there seems also to be a radical predisposition: the NIDDM

Above: Children and young adults are more likely to be insulin dependent diabetics than non insulin dependent diabetics.

condition is four times more common in Asian communities than in the rest of the population of Britain, for example. However, with NIDDM, which occurs mainly in older and frequently in overweight people (IDDM usually occurs in thin children and people under 30), there does appear to be a link with obesity. Other possible contributory causes to NIDDM in later years could be pancreatic damage through surgery or alcohol abuse; glucose intolerance during pregnancy, which may disappear after the baby is born but leaves a predisposition to diabetes during later pregnancies or in later life; long-term use of some steroids, which raise the amount of glucose in the blood; and overactivity of the thyroid.

DIAGNOSIS AND SYMPTOMS

Diagnosis of insulin dependent diabetes is normally fairly straightforward as the symptoms, although varied, are pretty obvious and can even be quite dramatic. Non insulin dependent diabetes is another matter, since the fall in insulin production may occur over a number of years and the symptoms may be quite slight. Some people with NIDDM have no symptoms at all.

DIAGNOSIS

If you go to a doctor complaining of any of these symptoms (right), he or she will normally check for diabetes.

The first test might be for excess glucose in the urine although, since the glucose levels in the urine tend to fluctuate (and some people have a low threshold so register as having above the normal level without actually being diabetic), the existence of such an excess is not absolute proof of diabetes. It is more usual to be sent for a blood glucose test. This blood will be taken from a vein, not a finger prick. By the time blood reaches the finger through the small blood vessels or capillaries, it has used up some of the glucose it was originally carrying so does not give an accurate picture. So it is important to measure the glucose in blood taken from a vein (the venous plasma glucose concentration). The normal concentration of glucose that you would expect to find, according to World Health Organization (WHO) criteria, is below 7.8 millimols per litre.

A diabetic, according to the WHO criteria, is one whose "venous plasma glucose concentration" when they have been fasting, remains at 7.8mmol/litre, but rises to above 11.1mmol/litre on a random blood sample. Between "normal" and "diabetic" they list a third category of those with "impaired glucose tolerance" (7.8mmol/litre fasting and between 7.8 and 11.1mmol/litre on a random test). These people may return to normal, may go on to develop full-blown diabetes or

remain at the same level. They should, however, follow a diabetic regime and keep themselves as healthy as possible.

TREATMENT

Although serious, even IDDM has become a treatable condition following the arrival of injectable insulin. Provided you are prepared to stick to your regime, there is no reason why you should not lead a full life.

The key to the management and treatment of both IDDM and NIDDM is to take over the job normally performed by the insulin in the body and keep your blood sugar levels normal. Allowing them to get too high, or too low, can cause a variety of problems and is to be avoided. This does not mean getting paranoid about blood sugar levels or diet – merely keeping a sensible watch on both.

For NIDDMs a change in diet, possibly in conjunction with medication to lower blood glucose levels, will frequently achieve the desired result. Indeed, changes to the diet may improve the health of an individual to such an extent that the onset of their diabetes may be viewed as something of a blessing.

IDDMs have benefited from the development of sophisticated blood testing techniques. These usually involve taking a drop of blood from the finger or ear lobe and have made it much easier to control blood glucose levels, either by changing the diet or the insulin dose.

Whether you have been diagnosed as being an insulin dependent diabetic or a diabetic who is non insulin dependent, your doctor will instruct you in the use of your drugs, insulin and glucose testing equipment. He or she will also give you dietary guidance or send you to a dietitian. The principles of a good diabetic diet are described later in this chapter, and the recipe section contains a wide range of suitable dishes.

SYMPTOMS

Thirst (polydipsia) and passing large quantities of urine (polyuria)
If the levels of glucose in the blood are too high, the kidneys no longer filter all the glucose and some escapes into the urine. The extra glucose thickens the urine, it draws extra water with it to help it to flow through the kidneys, and this causes the bladder to fill. The individual needs to urinate often and in copious amounts. At the same time the body becomes dehydrated, which leads to a terrible thirst.

Constipation
As the body becomes more dehydrated, constipation becomes almost inevitable.

Tiredness and weight loss
Since our bodies acquire their energy from glucose, anyone whose body cannot access the glucose circulating in the blood will be short of energy and therefore tired. In an effort to replace this energy, the body will break down other cells/body tissues thus causing a weight loss that can be dramatic.

Blurred vision
Excess sugar in the blood makes it thick and syrupy. In some diabetics, this can upset the focusing of the eyes – their vision becomes blurred.

Infections
When the blood becomes thick and syrupy due to the presence of excess glucose, this may also affect the functioning of the immune system. The undiagnosed diabetic may be prone to all kinds of infections, including skin eruptions, urinary tract infections, such as thrush or cystitis, and chest infections.

Pins and needles
Changes in the blood glucose levels may also affect nerve functions, resulting in tingling or pins and needles in the hands or feet.

ALTERNATIVE THERAPIES

Once the pancreas has given up on insulin production, it can very rarely be "kicked back into action". However, certain alternative or complementary therapies can stimulate pancreatic function, improve the body's insulin response and moderate glucose levels, so they are worth considering both in cases of non insulin dependent diabetes and in the immediate aftermath of the onset of insulin dependent diabetes, when there may still be some residual function in the pancreas.

Equally important is the diabetic's need to keep as fit and healthy – in both mind and body – as possible. It is recognized that stress does more damage to our health than almost anything else – and that many alternative therapies are very helpful in dealing with stress. Yoga, meditation, reflexology, aromatherapy and massage are some of the best-known stress relievers, but many people find spiritual healers, colour therapists or practising T'ai Chi just as helpful.

CHINESE MEDICINE

The Chinese have recognized diabetes as a disease for many thousands of years. However, Chinese medicine approaches the body, bodily functions and bodily malfunctions from an entirely different angle from Western medicine. To a Chinese doctor, diabetes is a sign of disharmony in the body, whose symptoms appear in the upper body (raging thirst, dry mouth, drinking huge quantities), middle body (large appetite and excessive eating accompanied by weight loss and constipation) and lower body (copious urination, progressive weight loss, etc).

Chinese medical treatment would therefore concentrate on restoring the harmony within the individual with the aim of improving the symptoms and addressing the disease.

Even if this approach does not directly affect insulin production or control, improving the body's natural harmony should improve the diabetic's general health and therefore their ability to cope well with diabetes. However, insulin dependent diabetics must not change their insulin regime if they attend a Chinese physician, except on the express instruction of their diabetes specialist.

RELAXATION AND MASSAGE THERAPIES

It is recognized that stress plays a significant role in the development of diabetes. Any therapy that reduces stress and helps you to relax is therefore likely to have a beneficial effect upon control of your diabetes and your general health.

Yoga and meditation have been found to have a positive impact on blood glucose levels, while moderate exercise helps insulin to work more efficiently in the body.

Reflexology helps to tone and relax the body and, although it cannot address the cause of diabetes, it can alleviate some of the side effects.

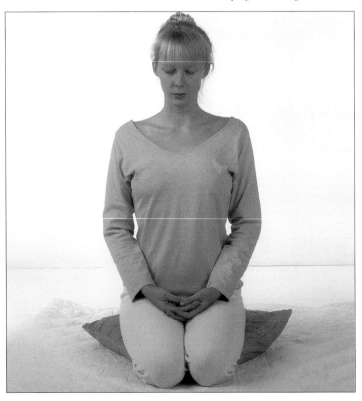

Left: Yoga and meditation are both said to reduce blood glucose levels by helping you to relax and reduce stress.

SELF MASSAGE

Aromatherapy (massage with essential herbal oils) is not only relaxing, but can also improve circulation and therefore help to heal the leg and foot ulcers to which some diabetics are prone.

The therapeutic potential of aromatherapy oils, although recognized in the past, has been largely ignored until recently. However, it is now realized that concentrated oils (made from the plants and herbs that filled our ancestors' medicine chests) can be very helpful for many specific complaints.

Essential oils are easily absorbed through the skin into the bloodstream and so are particularly effective for circulatory problems. Some oils, such as hyssop, are good for the circulation as a whole; others, such as grapefruit, lemon, lime, fennel and white birch, are lymphatic stimulants; while spike lavender, rosemary, eucalyptus, peppermint and thyme stimulate sluggish circulation. Massage is a good way to apply essential oils as it is relaxing, and it also ensures that the oils are effectively absorbed.

LEG AND FOOT MASSAGE

Self-massage is relatively easy and can help considerably in reducing stiffness and sluggishness of blood flow in the legs.

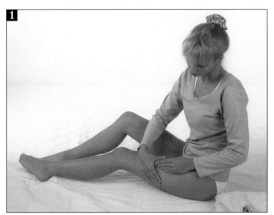

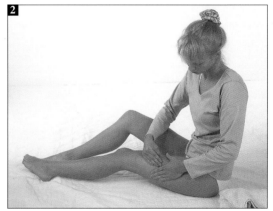

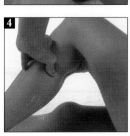

1 Start a leg massage by working on the thighs, so that any fluid in the calves will have somewhere to go as the upper leg relaxes. Using both hands, knead one thigh at a time, by squeezing firmly between the fingers and thumb.

2 Squeeze with each hand alternately for the best effect, working from the knee to the hip and back. Repeat on the other thigh.

3 Around the knees, do a similar kneading action but just using the fingers for a lighter effect and working in smaller circles.

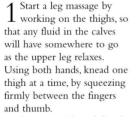

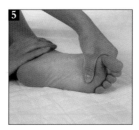

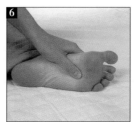

4 Bend your leg, and if possible raise the foot on to a chair or handy ledge. With your thumbs, work on the back of each calf with a circular, kneading action. Repeat this action a few times on each leg, each time working from the ankle up to the knee.

5 Squeeze the foot with your hands, loosening up the muscles and gently stretching the arch.

6 To complete the massage, use firm pressure with your thumb to stretch the foot. Repeat on the other foot.

FOOD AND HERBAL MEDICINES

Certain foods and herbs, although they cannot reinstate pancreatic function, can help the pancreas to function more efficiently. They may also improve the absorption of insulin and lead to better control of glucose levels in the blood by the body and to improved circulation. This may, in part, be due to the nutrients found in these foods and herbs (see Nutritional Medicine below), but there is increasing evidence that certain foods and herbs have important health-giving properties, which cannot be entirely attributed to their vitamin or mineral content.

FOODS WITH HEALTH-GIVING PROPERTIES

- Whole oats, onions, globe artichokes and pulses all have the ability to reduce blood sugar.
- Wheatgerm, underripe bananas, turkey, fish, walnuts, red peppers and cruciferous vegetables, such as broccoli and cauliflower (all good sources of Vitamin B_6), help to control blood sugar levels.
- Shellfish, lean meat, wholegrain cereals, pulses, pumpkin seeds and nuts are all high in chromium and zinc (diabetics are commonly deficient in both minerals).
- Bilberries have been found to help in the control of diabetic retinopathy.
- Wheatgerm, sunflower seeds, rapeseed oils, almonds and sweet potatoes (all containing high levels of Vitamin E) have been shown to help improve diabetic circulation and neuropathy.
- Fresh nettle juice has been used since Roman times to help stimulate the circulation, while dandelions have an equally lengthy pedigree for the stimulation of the liver (which is where glucose is stored).

Above: Dandelions have been used for years as a stimulant for the liver.

NUTRITIONAL MEDICINE

Effects of nutrient deficiencies

Although it has long been recognized that we need a wide range of vitamins and minerals for our bodies to function efficiently, there is a growing belief that many of today's degenerative illnesses, such as diabetes, could be caused by serious deficiencies in essential micronutrients, such as vitamins, minerals and amino acids. These deficiencies, it is argued, have resulted from our eating overprocessed foods, living in a highly polluted environment and subjecting ourselves to hitherto unknown levels of stress. Research is going on all the time and continues to reveal links between certain degenerative conditions and some particular nutrient deficiencies.

Chromium is an essential trace element. Although it is only present in minute quantities in the body, it appears to be necessary for blood sugar control and the proper action of insulin. Unfortunately chromium is lost from refined carbohydrates during processing. Chromium is difficult to take as a supplement but is absorbed from brewer's yeast, black pepper, calf's liver, wheatgerm, wholemeal bread and cheese.

Vitamins B_6 and B_{12} can both help blood sugar control. Vitamin B_{12} levels can be reduced by certain diabetic drugs, so it is useful to include sources of this vitamin (lean meat and dairy produce) in the diet.

Above: Nutritional supplements can help to ensure that you are getting the right amounts of some vitamins, minerals and essential fatty acids.

Vitamin C is known to strengthen fragile blood capillaries, especially in the eye, and to reduce elevated cholesterol levels – both conditions that affect diabetics.

Zinc, magnesium and potassium are all very important for diabetics, but levels can be seriously depleted through excess urination. Zinc is important for combating infections such as eczema, acne and thrush, many of which afflict diabetics. Magnesium is also important for the proper functioning of the kidneys.

Essential fatty acids There is increasing evidence that a diabetic's absorption of essential fatty acids may be impeded by raised blood sugar or insulin deficiency so taking a supplement, such as Evening Primrose oil, may help prevent diabetic complications.

KEEPING BLOOD GLUCOSE LEVELS NORMAL

The ideal state for a diabetic is for blood sugar levels to remain normal. Careful monitoring of these, a good diet and medication where necessary are basic strategies. However, many other aspects of the diabetic's life may impinge on his or her blood sugar levels.

BLOOD GLUCOSE LEVELS

Changing exercise levels, for example, can affect both the efficiency of insulin uptake and the rate at which the sugar in the blood is used up. Stress of any kind may cause adrenalin release that will increase the level of sugar in the blood. Infections, injuries or operations are seen by the body as stress. The body reacts by releasing adrenalin or other hormones into the bloodstream, and these again push up the sugar levels. Pregnancy causes changes in blood sugar levels, as do monthly periods and the menopause. Medical drugs, especially steroids and some diuretics and anti-depressants, can also affect blood sugar levels. If any of these factors apply, it is essential to monitor your blood sugar levels even more carefully than usual, adapting your diet or adjusting your insulin dose or the levels of the drug you take to lower blood glucose, in consultation with your doctor, if necessary.

Serious fluctuations in glucose levels cause hypoglycaemia (too little sugar) and hyperglycaemia (too much sugar). Both have very specific symptoms, which need to be treated immediately. If dramatic rises (and, more especially, falls) in blood sugar are treated immediately, there are unlikely to be long-term effects. However, persistent slightly raised blood sugar levels of about 8–19mmol/litre do have a number of serious consequences in terms of health.

CORONARY HEART DISEASE

Elevated triglycerides (fats in the blood) are a common feature of poorly controlled diabetes and add greatly to the risk of coronary heart disease (when the arteries supplying blood to the heart "fur up", thus depriving the heart muscle of the blood it needs to function properly), so diabetics need to be particularly careful about eating a low-fat diet and ensuring that they are not overweight.

STROKE

High blood pressure is another area which diabetics need to watch. Keeping their weight normal, stopping smoking and eating a low-fat, low-salt diet will usually help a great deal to minimize the risk of strokes.

Below: Pregnancy will affect blood glucose levels, which need to be monitored.

NEUROPATHY

Diabetic neuropathy is very common in long-term and poorly controlled diabetics. Although there are many variations, neuropathy happens when the nerve ends become damaged (as a result of excess glucose flowing through the capillaries or small veins). Neuropathy normally affects the hands and feet (tingling or pins and needles in the hands and feet is one of the symptoms of diabetes) and can, over a period, result in loss of all feeling in the extremities.

Left: Exercise, such as jogging, increases the rate at which sugar in the blood is used up – to prevent a dangerous dip in your blood glucose level, eat a small carbohydrate snack before, or straight after, any exercise.

Neuropathy presents two problems. One is that the circulation to the more remote areas of the body gets worse and this can lead to infected wounds, bad healing and, in the worst cases, gangrene. Feet and legs are especially prone to damage and need to be looked after and monitored with great care. The other problem is that the feet lose all sensation. This not only affects balance and the ability to walk properly but also means that the sufferer is at risk of injury, perhaps by being scalded by getting into too hot a bath, because their feet have become so insensitive to temperature.

Diabetics can also suffer some damage to their "autonomic nerves". These are the nerves that carry the instructions to the various organs, such as heart, kidneys, bladder and bowels, and tell them what to do. Damage to these autonomic nerves can result in poor bowel or bladder control, failure of the stomach to empty properly and similar problems. Normally all these functions will return to normal when the blood glucose levels are also returned to normal.

KIDNEY AND EYE DAMAGE

The kidneys and the eyes are two areas of the body filled with capillaries or tiny blood vessels that are especially prone to diabetic damage. Excess blood sugar can "clog" up both areas, but whereas kidney damage may be reversed or at least controlled by diet and good blood glucose control, damage to the eyes may be irreversible. Maintaining good control of blood glucose levels will minimize the damage. It is particularly important that diabetics have very regular eye checks and that these should include examination of the retina.

SKIN PROBLEMS

Because raised blood sugar makes one more prone to infection, especially skin infection, badly controlled diabetes will often result in boils, pimples, spots and rashes. Most of these will respond well to good diet and improved control.

This disturbing list of symptoms may sound like a life sentence, but diabetics should remember that most of them only occur when they do not look after themselves. These days, a diabetic diet is almost identical to the healthy diet recommended for all of us – so the diabetic should not be singled out as an oddity.

Because of the huge improvement in both monitoring and injection techniques, even insulin dependent diabetics can check their blood sugar levels and administer their insulin both quickly and discreetly.

However, this does not mean that you should keep your diabetes a secret. For a start, there is no reason to as you can live a perfectly full life with diabetes. Secondly, friends, colleagues and even strangers need to know that you are diabetic in case you should suffer a hyper- or hypoglycaemic attack. This is easily dealt with, but very frightening if you or others do not know what is going on. Consider wearing a diabetic bracelet or tag.

All diabetes does require is that you take it seriously and are organized about dealing with it. You must be rigorous about checking your glucose levels, you must always make sure that you have your insulin or drugs available and you must always ensure that you have extra glucose or carbohydrate food should you need it. Finally, you must be aware that your body is more sensitive to change than that of someone without diabetes so you must pay attention to what it tells you in terms of "feeling different" or unwell. Your body is the best possible monitor of its own condition, so it is important to listen to it.

Hyper- and Hypoglycaemia

Hyper- and hypoglycaemia occur when blood sugar levels rise too high (hyper) or fall too low (hypo).

Hyperglycaemia

The symptoms of hyperglycaemia are usually less dramatic than those of hypoglycaemia, but because tissue damage may result if the blood sugar levels remain too high (usually over 11–12mmol/litre), it is important to get the levels down quickly.

Elevated levels of blood sugar can be the result of uncontrolled long-term diabetes, but there can also be more immediate causes. Forgetting to take your insulin or blood glucose drugs will cause your blood sugar levels to rise, as will eating much more than you usually do – or eating a fattier or more sugary meal than normal.

Reducing the amount of exercise you usually take could affect glucose levels. An infection, illness, operation or accident could all cause blood sugar levels to rise, as can pregnancy and menstruation. Careful monitoring will reveal the raised levels quickly – anything over 11mmol/litre is a bad sign – and changes in insulin, drugs or diet should get you back to normal.

Hypoglycaemia

Hypoglycaemia can occur in non-diabetics whose blood sugar levels fall too low; the official definition is below 2.5mmol/litre. However, this reaction is most frequently seen in diabetics who have taken more insulin than they need or eaten too little – or exercised too much – relative to their last dose of insulin or glucose-lowering drugs.

Although hypoglycaemia symptoms can be dramatic, the results of it are seldom serious, and it is extremely easy to treat. All you need is a rapid intake of sugar in the form of glucose tablets (Dextrose, Dextro), sugar lumps, honey, candy, fruit juice or sweet biscuits. Even when the symptoms are quite extreme, the diabetic will be back to normal in a matter of minutes.

Above: Glucose tablets are a simple and speedy remedy to mild hypoglycaemia.

However, they then need to back up the instant injection of glucose with more solid food, as the excess insulin will quickly absorb the initial blast of glucose and will need something further to work on.

The problem with hypoglycaemia is that the brain is utterly dependent on an adequate supply of glucose to function properly. The first sign that a diabetic is suffering from a "hypo" may be a failure in his or her logical reasoning powers. This can manifest itself as a refusal to accept that they may be suffering from a hypo – which is why it is particularly important for friends and colleagues to know that they are diabetic (and for the diabetic to carry a card or consider wearing an identifying bracelet or badge), so that if their hypo symptoms take the form of denial, someone else can get a glucose tablet into their mouth.

Hypo symptoms vary enormously, but they can often include a lack of concentration, difficulty in making even simple decisions or a feeling of being muddled. A common feeling is that you must finish whatever you are doing, even though you are feeling odd. This is particularly dangerous if you are driving a car, so diabetics must make every effort to recognize and combat this compulsion.

Hypos can often cause behavioural changes and quite violent mood swings. Coordination may also be

impaired. They may stagger as if drunk and have difficulty in performing the simplest task – like unwrapping a glucose tablet!

If unrecognized and untreated, a hypo will eventually cause a diabetic to lose consciousness, but even then an injection of glucagon (the antidote to insulin) will bring the diabetic round to the point where they can be fed a proper dose of glucose.

Since symptoms are so varied, it is important that diabetics are aware of changes in their physical or mental states, that they monitor their blood sugar levels regularly, compensate for any changes in their daily routine and always carry glucose tablets (or the equivalent) with them. Long-term diabetics should be aware that over time symptoms of hypo decrease so that their blood sugar may fall without them having any symptoms at all.

A Few Words of Warning

- Ignore rising blood sugar levels at your peril. Your body's reaction will not be as rapid as with low levels, but if ignored rising blood sugar levels can put you into a coma.
- Never give up your insulin or drug regime – even if you are vomiting. The greater the stress on the body, the greater its need for insulin to combat rising blood sugar levels. Vomiting is serious for a diabetic, so maintain your drug regime and consult a doctor.
- Because the body is infinitely adaptable, some people will feel quite ill when their blood sugar is only slightly raised, while others will still feel relatively okay with seriously high levels. Moreover, long-term undiagnosed diabetics may have got used to having high levels of sugar in their blood so they will not even notice feeling ill.
- It is particularly important to monitor your blood sugar levels on a regular basis, even if you feel fine.

A Balanced Diet

Diet is the backbone of both insulin dependent and non insulin dependent diabetic management, and the first line of attack in stabilizing blood sugar control. Today, the diabetic diet varies little from the diet that everyone should be eating: to eat at least five portions of fruit and vegetables each day, to take in less than 30 per cent of calories from fat (with most of it coming from mono- and polyunsaturated fats), to reduce the intake of salt (sodium) and sweet foods and to eat plenty of fibre.

The "Old" Approach

Because sugar is derived from carbohydrates, when the mechanism of carbohydrate absorption was less well understood than it is today, it was thought that diabetics should avoid all carbohydrates. This meant that they had to live on a high-protein, high-fat diet and suffer the side-effects, such as high blood pressure, now associated with such a diet. Moreover, a high-fat diet caused them to gain weight.

Below: Protein is needed for growth and cell repair – wholegrain rice, beans, lentils, tofu (soya beancurd) and walnuts are good sources.

Today's Approach

Research into diabetes over the last 25 years has turned a great deal of this thinking on its head, and, although present-day diabetics still have to monitor their diet and their intake of carbohydrate fairly carefully, they are now encouraged to eat plenty of the right kind of carbohydrate foods, and even sugar is sometimes permitted in small amounts.

The food that we eat is made up of proteins, fats, carbohydrates, fibre, micronutrients (vitamins and minerals) and water. The last four (fibre, vitamins, minerals and water) are all essential for the proper functioning of the body but they do not provide us with energy as such (measured in kilo-calories or kilo-joules). This we need to get from proteins, fats and carbohydrates.

Proteins

Proteins, which can be found in pulses, peas and beans, soya products such as tofu, nuts, cereals, meat, fish and dairy products such as cheese, milk and cream, are essential for growth in children and for cell repair in adults. We need to get up to 20 per cent of our daily energy intake in the form of proteins.

FATS

Fats (found primarily in meat and dairy products, but also in vegetable and fish oils and nuts) are essential to the proper functioning of the body. However, we need the right kind of fat and the right amount. The average Western diet contains far too much of the "wrong" kind of fat – saturated – which leads to obesity, heart problems and strokes. The recommended maximum number of daily calories that should come from fat is between 30 and 35 per cent. However, unfortunately many Westerners obtain well over 40 per cent of their calories from fat.

Fats are broken down into saturated fats (mainly from the fat on meat, but also dairy products, such as cream, full-fat milk, butter and cheese, and nuts), polyunsaturated fats and mono-unsaturated fats (from vegetable oils such as olive oil and sunflower oil and from fish oils).

The subject of fats is a very complex one, but for the purposes of the diabetic diet the main thing to

remember is that saturated fats are to be avoided. These are more likely to cause excess cholesterol to be deposited in the arteries and, because they are higher in calories, obesity is a likely outcome. Diabetics may have high fat concentrations in their blood anyhow (making them more vulnerable to arteriosclerosis), so they should avoid making these levels even higher.

Above: Many different foods, such as (clockwise from top right) milk, pistachio nuts, butter, almonds, cream and cheese, contain fats. Dairy products, such as cheese, butter and milk are all sources of saturated fats, which should be avoided by diabetics, while foods such as nuts are all good sources of polyunsaturated fats, which, along with monounsaturated fats are more beneficial to good health.

Above: Sunflower oil (left) contains mostly polyunsaturated fats, while olive oil is made up of mainly monounsaturated fats.

CARBOHYDRATES

Carbohydrates (known in "diet-speak" as CHOs) also come in different guises – simple and complex carbohydrates.

Simple (refined or sugary) carbohydrates consist of various forms of what we know broadly as sugar or sucrose. In fact, sucrose is made up from glucose and fructose (fruit sugar). Both are essential for providing us with energy, but glucose is particularly important as the brain depends upon it to function efficiently.

Complex (unrefined) carbohydrates are to be found in starchy foods such as pulses (beans), oats, rice, potatoes and bread. Complex carbohydrates are made up of simple carbohydrates, glucose (see above) and fibres. These fibres may be soluble or insoluble. Soluble fibre is found in pulses, beans and legumes; it breaks down into a sort of gluey solution, which contains the carbohydrate. Insoluble fibre, such as that found in bran and such vegetables as celery and cabbage, has no nutritional value but is used by

the body to move food through the system and to push out what is not wanted as waste.

Once they enter the digestive system, complex carbohydrates are broken down by the digestive juices into their components parts – sucrose and fibre. For a diabetic, the virtue of a carbohydrate made up of sucrose and soluble fibre (pulses, peas and beans) is that the gluey solution into which the soluble fibre turns prevents the system from absorbing the glucose too fast, thus giving the diabetic's impaired glucose handling system more time to absorb it. The disadvantage of simple carbohydrates (sugar or sucrose) is that they are absorbed almost immediately into the bloodstream, causing sudden glucose "peaks".

Although studies suggest that if it is eaten along with lots of starchy, high-fibre carbohydrate, a small amount of pure sugar can be successfully absorbed by some diabetics without creating glucose peaks, medical advice would still be to avoid sugar whenever

possible. "Sugar" in this context would include sugar itself (in tea or coffee etc), sweets and candies, jams and jellies, cake and biscuits that have been sweetened with sugar or fructose, and sweetened fizzy drinks.

"DIABETIC" FOODS

Medical advice is also to avoid expensive proprietary diabetic foods. Although their actual sucrose content may be lower than that of the foods they are meant to replace, they may use fructose or sorbitol as sweeteners (in fact, there is little medical evidence that fructose is any better for diabetics than glucose, and sorbitol can cause bowel problems if eaten in large quantities). Finally, these foods may make up for their low sugar content by having a high fat content.

Below: Unrefined or complex carbohydrates, which are found in such foods as (clockwise from top right) wholemeal bread, potatoes, oats, haricot beans, rice and lentils, are absorbed more slowly into the bloodstream.

THE DIABETIC'S DAY-TO-DAY DIET

The first thing that the diabetic must remember is that, because the body's ability to absorb sugar is impaired, the system must never be "overloaded". In practice, this means that he or she should have three regularly spaced, moderately sized meals, usually breakfast, lunch and dinner, with two or three regular snacks in between, such as elevenses, mid-afternoon tea and a snack at bed-time. For an insulin dependent diabetic the meals must be timed to come 15–30 minutes after the insulin injection so that the insulin has had time to be absorbed into the bloodstream and is ready to cope with the food.

If you are a newly diagnosed diabetic and have led a rather disorganized life you may find forcing yourself to stick to specific times for meals difficult, but it will prove worth it. And you can console yourself with the thought that if the rest of us ate on a more regular basis we would all feel a lot better too.

BALANCE

A diabetic should try to ensure that each meal or snack is balanced to include carbohydrates, proteins and fats. This is not difficult to achieve, as many snacks naturally contain all three components in varying amounts. A ham sandwich, for example, includes protein (ham), fat (butter, spread) and carbohydrate (bread).

It is important that the diabetic does not miss out on any one element, especially the carbohydrate. Diabetics used to be given a list of what were known as "carbohydrate exchanges", which allocated a carbohydrate value to each food. They then had to work out how much carbohydrate was in each meal they ate, allocate their meal allowance of carbohydrate and devise a "swap" system if they wanted to change any element of this diet. Today, although diabetic practitioners still allot a total carbohydrate allowance to be spread over the day (based on the diabetic's own lifestyle, eating patterns, medication, etc), this does not need to be as rigid as the old exchange system.

AVOIDING EXCESSIVE CALORIE INTAKE

Whereas insulin dependent diabetics are often very thin, non insulin diabetics, especially long-term ones, tend to obesity – partly of course because the traditional diabetic diet was high in fat and protein. However, it is really important for diabetics to keep their weight down so as to minimize the risk of circulatory and other diseases.

As anyone knows who has tried to diet, the only long-term answer is to reduce the total amount of food that you eat and change the nature of that food.

Reducing the amount of sugar in your diet will set you well on the way; reducing the amount of fat, especially saturated fat, in your diet will help even more. And reduction does not necessarily mean total deprivation.

Right: Fizzy, sweetened drinks, full-sugar jam, sweet biscuits, confectionery, chocolate and cakes aren't completely banned, but consumption of these high-calorie foods should be kept to a minimum.

REDUCING SUGAR

Most diabetic practitioners would prefer their patients to stop sweetening their tea and coffee. However, if the thought is too terrible to contemplate, intense sweeteners, such as Aspartame (NutraSweet, Canderel) or Saccharin (Sweet'n'Low, Hermesetas) are better than sugar, but their consumption should be kept to a minimum.

Sugar in drinks other than coffee and tea – fizzy drinks, colas, etc – should be avoided. Not only do these fizzy drinks give an instant glucose hit (bad for diabetic control), but they are also very calorific (the average cola contains the equivalent of seven teaspoons of sugar). Fizzy water or fresh fruit juice diluted with water are preferred – or, if desperate, the diabetic should try to stick with low-calorie artificially sweetened, fizzy drinks.

Sugar in baking can almost always be replaced with dried or fresh fruits, as is amply illustrated in the recipes that follow. Although fruit contains fructose, this is buried in fibrous flesh, so it is absorbed much more slowly into the system. Fruit also gives a far better flavour to cakes and desserts than granulated sugar, which may be sweet but has no flavour of its own.

Diabetics, indeed all dieters, should also scrutinize labels for added sugar.

Below: Avoid sweetened drinks and opt instead for fizzy water or fresh fruit juice diluted with water.

Sometimes this is easy to avoid – buy fruits canned in fruit juice instead of syrup, for example – but it is not always that clear. Remember, too, that on an ingredients list sucrose, fructose, glucose, malt, maltose, honey, lactose and invert corn syrup are all sugar, even though they appear under different names.

Sweets and chocolate bars are to be avoided except as a snack before or after sport. Like the fizzy drinks, these not only deliver an instant glucose "hit", but they are very high in calories. If total deprivation is not to be borne, try buying chocolate, for example, in thin tablets or drops. It is amazing how satisfying even a morsel of chocolate can be if you nibble it rather than wolfing down a whole bar!

If an apple does not fill that sweet gap, try a few raisins or fresh dates.

They are just as sweet as a mint or a bar of chocolate but the sugar they contain is embedded in fibre.

Below: To avoid sugar, choose fruits canned in fruit juice, and try apples, fresh dates and raisins as an alternative snack.

REDUCING FATS

Reducing the amount of calories from fat – especially saturated fat – will help greatly in overall weight control and will also fit in with the specifically diabetic diet. Again, it need not be that difficult to achieve: Some of the new low-fat spreads are really very palatable and work excellently in pastry and baking. Does one always need butter or a spread? A ham sandwich with mustard needs neither; a cheese sandwich tastes as good, if not better, with a little low-fat mayonnaise and a lettuce leaf as it does with a thick layer of butter.

Use extra virgin olive oil or sunflower oil, not butter or lard, for cooking – and try not to use even that. Meat and vegetables for stews do not need to be fried at the start of cooking. If they are cooked long and slowly enough, they will have plenty of flavour. If the occasional plate of chips is a must, use the oven-ready ones, which have a substantially lower fat content. Ideally the chips should be abandoned in favour of a baked potato – but a baked potato filled with canned tuna and sweetcorn, or canned salmon

or baked beans, rather than with piles of butter or cheese!

Like chips, crisps should really be on the forbidden list. Not only are they calorific and high in fat (even the low-fat ones), but they are very salty – and everyone should be reducing their salt intake! Nuts or (even better) seeds, such as sunflower or pumpkin, maybe lightly salted, are just as good with a drink or as a snack and are very much more nutritious.

Above: Choose a low-fat filling for baked potatoes: here the potatoes are simply spiced with curry-flavoured onions and served topped with a generous dollop of low-fat natural yogurt.

USING WHOLEMEAL BREADS AND FLOURS

Even devoted white bread fans, if they persevere with wholemeal breads, will find that although wholemeal breads are not as soft, they have much more flavour. The same applies to using wholemeal flour in baking. The pastry may not be quite as light, but it will be much more flavoursome. There are several other flours that can be used for "lighter but healthier" baking, the most successful of which is gram or chick-pea flour. This is used a lot in Indian cooking. For a diabetic, it has the advantage of being made from a pulse, so it is filled with soluble fibre. Gram flour can be substituted for white flour in most instances and, although the pastry will be a little crumbly, it will taste delicious.

Left: Wholemeal bread is a healthier option than white bread. However, olive-oil breads, such as ciabatta, flavoured with olives or sun-dried tomatoes, are better than highly processed sliced white breads.

FILLING YOURSELF UP

The best way to prevent yourself nibbling – or having the urge to nibble – is by filling yourself up! Try eating large platefuls of colourful salad leaves and raw vegetables, such as tomatoes, peppers, cucumbers, carrots and radishes, or lightly cooked vegetables (most of which, being low in fat and carbohydrate, are on the "eat as much as your like" list for diabetics). For a main meal, bulk out vegetables and salads with cooked wholemeal rice, pasta or cooked beans and pep them up with plenty of chopped fresh herbs and a simple, tasty dressing made from lemon juice and extra virgin olive oil. It is amazing how satisfying they are. Because the food is full of fibre it will take some time for the body to digest, so that feeling of fullness will not have worn off within half an hour as it so often does after over-indulging on sticky cakes.

MONITORING FAT, SODIUM AND FIBRE INTAKES

Diabetics who do not need to lose weight still need to monitor their fat, sodium (salt) and fibre intakes. It is very important that diabetics keep the cholesterol levels in their blood under control to limit the risk of coronary heart disease. They should also keep their blood pressure down. A healthy, low-fat, low-salt, high-fibre diet will do all of these things.

Above: This pilaff of cooked wholemeal rice combined with plenty of lightly cooked vegetables and prawns is a good example of a simple and satisfying yet low-fat meal.

TIPS FOR CUTTING CALORIES

• Using a slightly smaller plate so that a smaller portion still looks generous is an old, but very successful, trick!

• Chewing rather than gulping one's food is another. Some experts recommend up to 20 "chews" per mouthful, but even eight or nine will extend the eating period so that the food seems to go further.

• If the weight still refuses to come off, keep a food diary, in which all food consumed is written down.

• Don't con yourself into thinking that you are sticking to a diet, if you forget about the broken biscuit you ate because it fell out of the packet, the chunk of cheese you ate while grating a piece for a recipe, the half sausage the children had left on their plates or the lick of the jam spoon as it went into the washing up.

• Cutting out these few unnecessary calories may be all that it takes for the required amount of weight to be lost.

MODERATION

It is very easy, especially for a newly diagnosed diabetic, to become obsessed with his or her diet. This is not only unnecessary but is positively unhelpful: all this does is raise stress levels, and it is well recognized that stress is more debilitating for a diabetic than for anyone else.

FOODS TO EAT AND FOODS TO AVOID

It is very important for diabetics to keep to their diet regime the majority of the time, but the occasional "fall from grace" is not likely to be catastrophic, especially if it can be compensated for by extra vigilance at the next meal.

At first it may be hard to remember what is, and is not, allowed, but this will soon become second nature. Comparing calorie values is an easy way to monitor general food intake, but it is even more useful to memorize the key categories of food.

FREE FOODS
These can be eaten whenever and in whatever quantity you want.
- All green and leafy vegetables.
- Cruciferous vegetables (cauliflower, broccoli, turnip, cabbage, etc).
- Salad vegetables (tomatoes, peppers, cucumbers, etc).
- All members of the onion family.
- Green peas and green beans.
- Mushrooms.
- Fruits, such as redcurrants, cranberries and loganberries.
- Tea, coffee, water, tomato juice (in moderation), clear soups.

Left: Eat as much as you like – there's no restriction on the quantity of fresh green beans and peas that diabetics can eat.

Below: Fruits, such as (clockwise from top) pears, grapes, nectarines, raspberries and plums must be counted as part of a diabetic's daily carbohydrate allocation, but make ideal between-meal snacks as well as instant high-fibre desserts.

Above: Salad vegetables, such as fresh tomatoes, cucumbers and a variety of colourful peppers, can be eaten in whatever quantity you want – they are very low in sugar, fat and calories, yet are a good source of micronutrients.

GOOD CARBOHYDRATE/ PROTEIN FOODS

These are good for diabetics to eat, but must be counted as part of an overall carbohydrate and protein allocation.

- All pulses, beans and peas.
- Brown rice and wholemeal pasta.
- Oats, wholemeal flours, breads, unsweetened biscuits, etc.
- All root vegetables.
- All fresh fruits.
- All canned fruits as long as canned in fruit juice, not syrup.
- Dried fruits.
- Unsweetened breakfast cereals that are also high fibre.
- Lean meats or meat products.
- Fresh and frozen fish.
- Low-fat cheese, skimmed milk and low-fat yogurts.
- All soya products.

Right: Soya beans and tofu (soya beancurd) are good foods for diabetics to eat, although soya margarine, a healthy alternative to butter, is still a fat so use it sparingly.

BORDERLINE FOODS

This list reflects carbohydrate foods and fatty foods that are less good – alright to have sometimes in specific quantities but not to be overindulged in.

- White flour, bread, unsweetened. biscuits, pastry, rice and pasta.
- Cornflour, arrowroot, semolina.
- Unsweetened breakfast cereals.
- Any fried potato products, such as chips and crisps.
- Full-fat cheese, cream, full-fat milk and yogurt.
- Fatty meats, including sausages.
- Salty meats and fish products.
- Fruit juices.
- Reduced-sugar jams, marmalade and other spreads.
- Alcohol.

Left: Borderline foods, such as (clockwise from top) full-fat milk, full-fat, sweetened yogurts, full-fat cheeses and cream, can be eaten occasionally, but don't over-indulge.

Bad Foods

These are to be avoided whenever possible and, when eaten, only to be consumed in very small quantities.

- Sugar: caster, granulated, demerara; also honey and golden syrup.
- Sweets, such as candies, chocolate.
- Full-sugar chewing gum.
- Jams, marmalades and similar spreads that are full-sugar.
- Sweet biscuits, cakes and buns made with white flour and sugar.
- Desserts made with refined flours and refined sugar.

Above: Chocolate biscuits, cakes and buns are best avoided by diabetics.

- Fruit canned in syrup.
- Ice cream and ice lollies.
- Fruit squashes, sweetened drinks (including fizzy drinks and colas).
- Sweetened breakfast cereals.

Below: They are no longer banned entirely, but sweet treats, such as (clockwise from top left) golden syrup, caster sugar, honey, icing sugar and demerara sugar should only be eaten in very small quantities.

Alcohol

Alcohol, such as red wine and lager (*right*), is not entirely off limits for diabetics but must be taken in moderation and calculated into the diet. Beware of low-alcohol drinks. Because less of the sugar has been converted to alcohol, they may contain more sugar. Conversely, low-sugar drinks may contain more alcohol! Remember, too, that alcohol is calorific; if you are trying to lose weight, keep your consumption low. It is also important to remember that excess alcohol consumption puts a strain on the liver and the pancreas – both organs that are already under pressure in a diabetic.

About the Recipes

We hope that many of the recipes in this collection will give you ideas for other dishes that will fulfil the diabetic diet criteria. Any good cookery book should encourage experimentation, so feel free to adapt any of the recipes.

Our aim has been to include many recipes that diabetics can enjoy. We have tried, therefore, to introduce ingredients, such as pulses and beans, that are high in soluble fibre and low in fats and sugars. Many of the main course dishes add lentils or dried beans to meat or vegetables, and use olive or sunflower oil for cooking. Much of the baking makes use of low-fat spreads and fresh or dried fruit (although you will find the occasional chocolate treat).

Sodium Levels Regular stock cubes can be very high in salt, so look out for "natural" or "organic" stock cubes with no added salt. Whenever possible, buy "no added salt or sugar" canned beans and vegetables, avoid fish canned in brine and go for canned fruit in natural juice rather than in a sugar syrup.

ARTHRITIS
PREVENTION

Food has a direct impact on the symptoms of many arthritis sufferers.

Some foods reduce inflammation, and others are rich in the nutrients

essential for the healthy functioning of joints and muscles.

This chapter offers practical advice on managing arthritis, examines

some possible allergy-triggers and explains how to follow

an exclusion diet.

INTRODUCTION

Arthritis is a condition that can affect any of the joints, but is especially prevalent in the load-bearing or particularly hard-working areas, such as the knees, hips, ankles, wrists and hands. In the Western world it is estimated that up to half the population will suffer from an arthritic disorder of the joints at some point in their lives, and that many of these people will be severely troubled by constant pain, stiffness and disability. This is obviously a depressing prospect.

Arthritis cannot be treated as a single disease. There are at least six common forms and up to 100 lesser known types, excluding the rheumatic ailments that are often confused with arthritis. Although it is just as painful as arthritis, rheumatism (including fibrositis/fibromyalgia, bursitis, frozen shoulder and aching neck) is a less serious condition affecting muscles, ligaments and tendons.

Human joints are extremely complex and flexible structures, but they require "good maintenance" for efficient, long-term function. It is when a joint is damaged that arthritis can set in. Damage can be caused by a wide variety of incidents: trauma or accident, abnormal stress, maybe even viral infection or an inflammation. Confusingly, damage may not always lead to arthritis and, as yet, beyond a genetic predisposition, doctors have been unable to identify why some people develop arthritis-related conditions while others do not.

THE STRUCTURE OF A JOINT

A joint is made up of two connecting bones, separated and cushioned by cartilage. Cartilage is water-filled, spongy tissue with no blood vessels and no nerve endings, so cartilage itself never hurts. The joint is held together by a tubular structure attached to the ends of the bones. This is lined with a synovial membrane and lubricated by synovial fluid, which allows the moving parts to rub against each other with minimum friction. The joint is stabilized by muscles, ligaments and tendons on both its inside and outside.

CHANGES IN A DAMAGED AND ARTHRITIC JOINT

The protective cartilage is vital to the proper functioning of the joint. If the cartilage is damaged in any way it is less efficient as the cushion separating the bones.

When the cartilage ceases to perform its cushioning function properly there are several consequences. Initially there appears to be some water loss, after which the cartilage thickens and then softens. Small rips may appear and gradually deepen into tears, which may extend as far as the bone. The bone ends may be damaged or the joint capsule and synovial membrane may become damaged or inflamed. The surrounding tendons and ligaments may also be strained. Eventually, the bone attempts to repair the damage by forming bone spurs, and these stretch the sensitive membrane covering the bone to visibly deform the joints, causing further strain on the surrounding membranes and muscles. The synovial lining, fluid and capsule become inflamed and the joint stiffens.

Although the cartilage has no feeling, the other parts of the joint, including the bone, are very pain sensitive. Increasing pain and stiffness lead to immobility, and experience shows that immobility only makes the condition worse. This explains why most arthritis sufferers find their condition more painful in the morning after lying still all night, than later in the day after moving around.

Left: Osteoarthritis often occurs in the joints that bear the most stress. Keen gardeners may find arthritis particularly painful in their knees, due to long hours of weeding.

Right: Arthritis can affect people of any age, even children. Juvenile arthritis can be particularly distressing, but the good news is that most children outgrow the condition, with no long-term effects.

TYPES OF ARTHRITIS

Although arthritis can take many different forms, the basic joint problem is the same for each type.

OSTEOARTHRITIS

This is the most common form of arthritis, usually associated with increasing age and degeneration. It is also more common in women. Osteoarthritis often occurs in a joint that has been injured or stressed, particularly those joints that do the most work – fingers and thumbs, wrists, knees, hips, ankles and toes. Bony spurs form around the joints and, along with inflammation, make movement difficult and painful.

Progressive joint deterioration can create secondary problems, such as carpal tunnel syndrome, which occurs when arthritis of the wrist causes nerves to be pinched. Not only does this produce pain, but also weakness and loss of control in the hands. Arthritis of the neck can cause severe headaches. Arthritis of the spine can cause radiating pain into the arm or leg (known as sciatica), or injury to the spinal column or to the nerves within the spinal canal.

RHEUMATOID ARTHRITIS

This condition tends to occur in younger people. It is very dramatic and unpredictable and has been known to disappear as suddenly as it appears. It causes inflammation, pain, swelling and joint damage, especially in the hands and wrists, feet, knees and elbows. In severe cases rheumatoid arthritis can affect the internal organs – lungs, heart, liver, kidneys and lymph nodes.

Although no single cause has been found for rheumatoid arthritis, there is evidence to suggest that food allergies,

nutritional deficiencies and viral, parasitic and bacterial infections contribute to the condition.

ANKYLOSING SPONDILITIS

This is an inflammatory condition of the lower back, and it can spread both up and down the spine. It is most common in men.

JUVENILE ARTHRITIS

Symptoms include pain, fever, swelling and skin rash. The condition seems to improve over time, leaving the child with little serious joint damage.

PSORIATIC ARTHRITIS

A condition in which psoriasis (patches of raised, flaky and itching skin) and arthritis are combined.

VIRAL ARTHRITIS

This illness can follow a viral infection, whether or not the person already suffers from arthritis.

LUPUS ERYTHEMATOSUS

This condition causes inflammation of the connective tissue. Symptoms are influenza-like, including aching muscles and joints, fever and fatigue.

GOUT

This is caused by an excess of uric acid in the system. The acid crystals are deposited around joints and tendons, causing inflammation and pain. It can usually be controlled by drugs and by avoiding purines (substances rich in uric acid), which are found in liver, kidneys, shellfish, sardines, anchovies and beer.

TREATING ARTHRITIS

Conventional medicine, on the whole, does not accept a link between food and arthritis. However, there is evidence to suggest that food intolerance and micro-nutrition (essential vitamins, minerals and trace elements) may play a significant role, especially in cases of rheumatoid arthritis.

CONVENTIONAL TREATMENT
Despite the fact that many people are disabled by the various forms of arthritis, medical science can offer no cure. Treatment therefore falls into four areas.
• **Minimizing stress on affected joints** Patients are often advised to lose weight. Although no one is quite sure why, it would appear that being overweight can negatively affect joints, including those that are not weight-bearing (fingers and wrists).
• **Keeping affected joints mobile** Regular, gentle exercise and physiotherapy will keep joints as supple as possible.
• **Reducing the pain of arthritis** Various pain-relieving drugs are used, normally corticosteroids and non-steroidal anti-inflammatory drugs (NSAIDs). Although they may relieve at least some of the inflammation and pain, they do nothing to reverse, or even slow down, the progress of the disease. These drugs can have serious side effects. Even short-term use of steroids can cause weight gain, the one thing that arthritics do not want. Long-term use can cause brittle bone disease or osteoporosis, muscle wasting, skin eruptions and damage, poor wound healing, fluid retention, eye disorders, nutritional deficiencies, even mental disturbance. NSAIDs most frequently cause stomach ulceration.
• **Clearing up infections** Some forms of arthritis (for example, certain cases of rheumatoid arthritis) seem to be set off by bacteria, such as salmonella, campylobacter or yersinai. Joint pains can linger for months or years. In such cases antibiotic treatment may be useful.

ALTERNATIVE TREATMENT
There are occasional cases where dramatic results are achieved by the exclusion or inclusion of one particular food in the diet. However, most people will find that a combined approach, following some of the suggestions below, will result in an improvement in their symptoms, if not a total cure.
• **Dietary manipulation of inflammation** This means eating foods that are most likely to reduce inflammation in the joints.
• **Vitamin and mineral supplementation** Eating a diet rich in the vitamins and minerals needed to minimize the damage caused by arthritis, while taking supplements to counteract possible deficiencies.
• **Exclusion diet** Pinpointing and then removing a particular food, such as wheat or tomatoes, that triggers arthritis or makes the symptoms worse.
• **Weight control** Following a diet to keep body weight down.

OTHER CAUSES
As with most other illnesses, stress seems to make arthritis worse and prevents healing, so minimizing stress is an important part of both complementary and conventional forms of treatment.

There is also some evidence to suggest that, although imbalance in the gut flora (an overgrowth of the yeast *candida albicans*) will not actually cause arthritis, it may well make the symptoms worse.

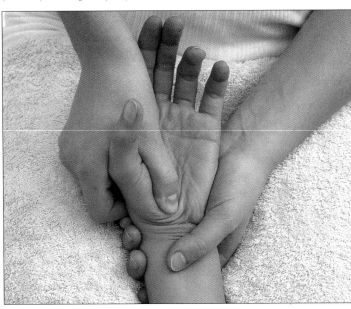

Left: A doctor will often recommend physiotherapy for joints affected by arthritis, as immobility only aggravates the condition. A gentle massage will help to keep your joints as supple as possible.

LOSING WEIGHT

This is a universal recommendation in the treatment of all types of arthritis, and so you need to make it a priority when you are planning your diet. Many of the dietary recommendations for weight loss will also help to increase antioxidant levels and reduce inflammation of the joints.

Most dieticians recommend a gradual weight loss, increasing your intake of vegetables, pulses and some grains, while reducing the fat content of your diet, especially animal fats. In addition, reducing the amount of sugar and refined white flour in a diet will usually put most people well on the way to losing the required amount of weight.

Reducing the intake of sugar and refined flours does not cut out all prospect of desserts, cake or biscuits. Fruits such as dates, prunes, raisins, apples and pears are excellent for sweetening puddings and cakes, and there are many flours, from wholemeal (wheat) flour to rice or chick-pea flour, which are just as versatile as ordinary white flour.

NEW COOKING METHODS
Adjusting the way food is cooked is one easy way to reduce the use of cooking oils.

Deep-fried foods should be banned from the menu. Occasional shallow frying in a little olive oil with a tablespoon of water added (to prevent the oil overheating) is fine, but it is amazing how often grilling, roasting, poaching, steaming, baking or simmering can be used instead of frying. If you are still eating meat, grill sausages, bacon, fish fingers and burgers. Eggs taste delicious poached. Potatoes can be baked or steamed, or, if you are really desperate for chips, treat yourself to the occasional helping of oven chips, which are much lower in fat. Casseroles – for which ingredients are usually first fried in oil – often taste just as good if this step is omitted. Simply combine all the ingredients and cook the whole dish a little longer at a lower temperature, so as to allow the flavours to mature.

Vegetables are much better steamed than boiled as this cooking method does not allow so many nutrients to leach out and the vegetables have less opportunity to overcook.

Sweating is another good cooking method. This needs only a very small amount of oil (about 15ml/1 tbsp) with 15ml/1 tbsp water. Put the vegetables, oil and water into a saucepan with a tight-fitting lid and cook them slowly in their own juices. You will lose very few of the nutrients, apart from some Vitamin C, which will be lost no matter what your cooking method.

EATING LESS MEAT
Vegetarians seem to have less trouble with arthritis than people who eat meat, so there is an argument for trying to reduce the overall consumption of meat. If the idea of a totally vegetarian meal does not appeal, there are a number of meat substitutes that taste fine. Quorn and TVP (textured vegetable protein) have a texture similar

Above: Fatty foods, especially meat and cooking fats derived from animals, can increase the swelling and pain in arthritic joints.

to chicken and, like plain beancurd (tofu), are relatively tasteless but absorb other flavours well. They can all be used with marinades, in curries, casseroles or stews with plenty of herbs and full-flavoured vegetables. Beancurd is also available smoked and ready marinated and can be used in stir-fries, risottos, pilaffs, bean dishes and salads with a good strong dressing (this is a good opportunity to use some inflammation-reducing oil).

Include some totally vegetarian meals in your weekly diet. A good selection of vegetables, roasted with some herbs and a few nuts, makes an excellent and very easy dish. Dishes made with beans, nuts, seeds, herbs, spices and seaweeds (which are now fairly easy to obtain and have a wonderful flavour) are exciting, filling, healthy – and not fattening!

REDUCING INFLAMMATION

Inflammation is the body's way of bringing extra blood, with all its healing nutrients, to an injured area of the body. In the case of arthritis the extra blood, far from healing the injury, creates extra heat and swelling which merely add to the stiffness and soreness of the joint.

The inflammation of the joints that is associated with arthritis can be triggered, often on an ongoing basis, by damage to some part of the joint. Another possible cause is a malfunction in the body's mechanisms for triggering inflammation.

Various foods, especially fats, can influence the inflammatory process in either a negative or a positive way. This is because the chemicals (prostaglandins) that control inflammation are derived from fats in the body. Prostaglandin E2 is the chemical that sparks off the inflammation; it is derived mainly from the fats found in meat and cooking oils. Prostaglandins E1 and E3 act in quite the opposite way, to block swelling and reduce the pain and heat. Prostaglandin E1 is derived from gamma linolenic acid (GLA) found only in a few seed oils – borage, evening primrose, blackcurrant and hemp/linseed. Prostaglandin E3 is derived from alpha linolenic acid (ALA) and is found in green leafy vegetables, rape seed oil, wheat germ oil and oily fish.

Although these fats do not work in exactly the same way for everyone, decreasing the amount of fat in the diet from animal sources and cooking oils and increasing plant foods, seeds and oily fish may help to reduce inflammation without the unwanted side effects caused by drugs. This is one of the reasons why many arthritics find a vegetarian or vegan diet, that is free of animal products, helpful.

GAMMA LINOLENIC ACID (GLA)

Eating more seeds and seed oils is the easiest way to increase GLA intake to make the inflammation-reducing prostaglandins. Evening primrose, borage and blackcurrant oils can all be taken as supplements, but hemp, or linseed, oil has to be taken as an oil and this unfortunately has an unpleasant taste. There is one seed oil

Above: Cod liver oil or cod liver oil capsules are an excellent way of boosting your intake of ALAs, which in turn will help to control the inflammation caused by arthritis.

blended by a Canadian, Professor Udo Erasmus, an acknowledged expert on the role of fats in the diet and in degenerative diseases such as arthritis. Known as Udo's Oil, it tastes pleasant enough to be used as a salad oil and, although expensive, it is an excellent way of boosting GLA intake.

Eating pumpkin, sunflower, sesame and linseeds will also help to boost your intake – they can be eaten as they are or added to almost any dish. Use the seeds whole, when they will have to be chewed well to release the oils, or process them briefly in a pestle and mortar, coffee grinder or a food processor to lightly grind them. Whole seeds can be lightly toasted under the grill to vary their flavour.

Left: Some seeds contain useful amounts of helpful GLAs. Try to use a handful of seeds in every meal. Clockwise from top: sunflower seeds, linseed, sesame seeds and pumpkin seeds.

ALPHA LINOLENIC ACID (ALA)

Reducing your intake of animal fats usually means eating more fresh fruits and vegetables – which boosts consumption of alpha linolenic acid (ALA), used to manufacture prostaglandin E3. Wheatgerm oil supplement will further boost alpha linolenic acid intake – but this is not suitable for those excluding wheat from the diet. Eating oily fish is also a good way to increase ALA in the diet. The term "oily" fish may sound rather unattractive, but, in fact, sardines, anchovies, mackerel, salmon, herrings, kippers and whitebait are one of the tastiest types of seafood. Most can be bought in a form where you do not have to fiddle with fish bones or skin, and some types can be eaten whole. Pre-prepared fish can be bought fresh, frozen or canned. As well as using oily fish as the main dish, add them in small quantities to salads and rice, bean or

GINGER

This spice has been used for centuries in traditional Indian Ayurvedic medicine as an anti-inflammatory food. It blocks the enzymes that make the inflammation-producing prostaglandins. Ginger does not work for everyone, but a dose of 1–2 grams of ground ginger or a 25g/2oz knob of fresh ginger, peeled and grated, taken daily over a period of 3–4 months, appears to produce very positive results in the symptoms of over half the people who try it.

If you like ginger, you can consume it as a drink (there are a number of herbal teas with ginger), in ginger wine or as a confection, coated in chocolate. Ground ginger can be used in puddings, cakes and biscuits, and fresh root ginger is delicious in a wide variety of savoury dishes. You can even eat crystallized or stem ginger in ice cream.

vegetable dishes. Try using anchovies to season some of your dishes instead of salt. As well as boosting your ALA levels, you will be reducing your sodium intake and helping to control high blood pressure.

Below: Oily fish are one of the best foods for reducing inflammation. It is, however, sometimes tricky to know which fish belong to this category. Tuna, for instance, is not an oily fish. Clockwise from bottom left: tuna steak, mackerel, herring, salmon steak.

Increasing Vitamins and Minerals

Even with a balanced and healthy diet, "micro-nutrient malnutrition" may occur, especially as people grow older. This can either be the result of a deficiency of vitamins and minerals in the diet, or of the body's failure to absorb these substances properly from food.

If bones and joints are not receiving enough of the vitamins and minerals needed to maintain them, they are more likely to degenerate. Taking a "broad spectrum" supplement or a multi-vitamin and mineral supplement is helpful, but it may be worth consulting a nutritionist and having a blood test to assess whether the body is deficient in any specific mineral. Iron, zinc, copper, selenium and manganese are all important minerals for joint health, and their absorption can be impeded by consuming too much tea,

coffee and bran. The traditional arthritis remedy of wearing a copper bracelet can be helpful, as small quantities of copper can be absorbed through the skin.

Free Radicals

Most people have heard of free radicals in connection with cancer; they are also relevant in arthritis. As oxygen is processed through the bloodstream and into the tissues, free radical chemicals (including hydrogen peroxide) are released. Although these free radicals

are very unstable and only exist for 1–2 seconds, in this short time they can cause all kinds of damage in the body including taking hydrogen electrons from molecules in body tissues and damaging the tissues in the process. Antioxidants neutralize these free radicals by donating extra hydrogen electrons to them before they can take them from the body tissues. You should eat plenty of foods rich in antioxidants: vitamins A, C, E and betacarotene are the best known of these nutrients, although lycopene (found in tomatoes), zinc and manganese are also important. Many flavonoids (the chemicals that give peppers and fruits such as blueberries, blackberries, cherries and lemons their colour) are also powerful antioxidants.

It is important that anyone with arthritis absorbs plenty of antioxidants, both by eating a diet rich in antioxidants and by taking a vitamin and mineral supplement. Ideally, these supplements should be taken under medical or nutritional supervision, so that they can be adapted to suit your particular needs.

Vitamin A

Found in liver, especially fish liver oils, eggs, orange and yellow fruits, and green leafy vegetables, vitamin A should not be taken in excess, that is, in levels of over 10,000 IUs per day. A spoonful of that old favourite, cod liver oil, is simple, if not the most pleasant, way of increasing Vitamin A intake. Alternatively, include chicken, calf's or lamb's liver in some dishes.

Left: Drinking too much tea and coffee may reduce the absorption of vital minerals, particularly iron. Naturally flavoured fruit teas are a good substitute, and contain almost no calories.

A little chicken liver can be added to a meat stew without changing the flavour too much. However, as arthritis sufferers should be trying to reduce meat consumption, it is better to eat a fairly regular supply of eggs and eat plenty of yellow and orange vegetables (carrots, yellow, orange and red peppers, and yellow squash) and fruits in salads and vegetable dishes.

VITAMIN C

This is found in most fresh fruits and vegetables but is easily destroyed by the cooking process. Eating more fresh, raw fruit and vegetables automatically increases vitamin C consumption. People who are avoiding citrus fruits or members of the solanacae family (potatoes, peppers, chillies, tomatoes, aubergines) as part of an exclusion diet will still find an abundance of other fresh fruits and vegetables that contain substantial quantities of vitamin C.

VITAMIN E

This is found in most vegetable oils (olive, corn and so on), nuts, seeds, avocados (which are also a rich source of vitamin C), peaches, broccoli, spinach and asparagus. The seeds and seed oils that are eaten as part of an anti-inflammatory diet will therefore have the additional benefit of providing a substantial amount of vitamin E.

SELENIUM

Grains and nuts are sources of selenium, but their precise content varies according to the soil in which they were grown. Selenium interacts with vitamin E, making both of these nutrients more powerful. Brazil nuts, grains and pulses (especially lentils), mung beans and red kidney beans are good for boosting the levels in the diet. Fish is also a good source of selenium.

BETACAROTENE

This is the best known of more than 600 carotenoids, which are the plant pigments that give yellow, orange and

Above: Fruit is an excellent natural sweetener and can be used both fresh and dried. It also provides useful amounts of vitamin C and other trace elements.

Right: Supplements can ensure you receive the trace elements that may be missing, and are a useful source of antioxidants.

red fruits their colour. Scientists are greatly interested in carotenoids, which they suspect may be even more powerful antioxidants than the established vitamins A, C and E. Like many of the carotenoids, betacarotene can be converted by the body into vitamin A. Betacarotene is to be found in carrots, apricots, cantaloupe melon, sweet potatoes, pumpkin, spinach, kale and parsley.

FOOD ALLERGIES

Although most conventional specialists dismiss food allergy as being a cause of arthritis, there is a growing body of evidence to suggest that it may be a trigger in a substantial number of cases of rheumatoid arthritis and, to a more limited extent, in other types of arthritis as well.

The amount of the allergic food that is needed to trigger a reaction, the strength of the reaction itself and the improvement that can be achieved by excluding the food from the diet will all vary according to the individual. One sufferer's symptoms may disappear completely when they cut out the relevant food but return if they eat the smallest amount of the allergen. Another person may find that their condition improves to some extent if they cut down on a certain food, but it does not improve further if they cut the food out entirely. It is important that each person experiments with his or her own diet and is not put off by the experiences of other people.

Of course, not everyone will find that changing their diet will cure, or even improve, their arthritis. However, most people will benefit from eating a healthier, balanced diet and most arthritics, unless they are very slim, will probably benefit from losing some weight. There are few statistics, but it would appear that up to 40 per cent of arthritis sufferers (especially those with rheumatoid arthritis) may benefit to some extent by improving their diet. Of that 40 per cent, a small number will find themselves miraculously cured of the condition.

POTENTIALLY ALLERGIC FOODS

There is no food that is guaranteed not to cause an allergic reaction. Every food can provoke an allergy in someone, and it is perfectly possible that the allergy may show itself as arthritis. To complicate the issue, people can have an allergy to more than one food. So, to test properly for an allergic reaction, you need to try all foods, alone and together. Certain families of foods seem to be most frequently involved, however.

• Dairy products such as milk, cheese, cream, butter and yogurt.
• Vegetables from the deadly nightshade or solanacae family such as red, green and yellow peppers, potatoes, tomatoes, tobacco, chillies and aubergines.
• Citrus fruits, especially orange juice.
• Wheat and all wheat derivatives.

Above, clockwise from top: Dairy products include: Cheddar cheese, cow's milk, yogurt made from cow's milk, Brie.

Above: Citrus fruits, and especially oranges and orange juice, can cause a severe allergic reaction in some people.

CANDIDA

If candida (yeast overgrowth in your system) is a problem then a two-pronged strategy is usual: treatment with anti-fungal medication and a diet excluding sugar and all fermented foods, starving the yeast of nourishment.

Above, clockwise from top: The solanacae family includes aubergine, red and green peppers, chillies, potatoes.

Above: Flour and pasta both contain wheat and should therefore be avoided by people following a wheat-free diet.

EXCLUSION DIETS

There is no guarantee that a food allergy has caused or worsened an individual case of arthritis; however, if it has, there are substantial benefits in altering the diet to exclude those foods that trigger the arthritis. They include reduced pain, improved mobility, less joint deterioration, reduced use of drugs and fewer side effects. For a few people, the effects are so positive as to amount to a cure. For most arthritics, excluding foods that their bodies cannot tolerate will not rid them of their arthritis, but it may improve their condition sufficiently to be worth the effort of excluding those foods. Also, if a food upsets the body enough to aggravate arthritis, it may be damaging to your health in other respects, so that excluding it, or at least reducing the amount eaten, will probably be good for your general health.

Before embarking on an exlusion diet, a nutritionist should be consulted by people on a lot of medication; who have health problems in addition to arthritis; who are very young or old; and anyone who is pregnant. A diet that excludes more than one group of foods (dairy products, citrus fruits, wheat and so on) should never be followed in such cases, except under medical supervision.

There are two methods of pinpointing the troublesome food: an allergy test and keeping a food diary.

ALLERGY TESTS

These vary in type and cost, from inexpensive tests offered by healthfood shops (which test for the basic six potential allergens) to a thorough blood analysis covering 100–200 foods and offering back-up information and advice. If you cannot face working through a strict exclusion diet for each of the possible groups of potentially allergic foods, an allergy test may be a worthwhile shortcut. The result still has to be verified by excluding the food from the diet for a period of time.

However, be cautious when reading the test results. If a test records a reaction to a very large number of foods, the advice of a dietician or nutritionist should be taken before excluding them from the diet. More harm than good results from a starvation diet. If there is a genuine bad reaction to a number of foods, professional nutritional guidance must be taken to work through the problem and find a balanced solution.

KEEPING A FOOD DIARY

A food diary will instil the habit of really thinking about all foods that are eaten. It should be kept for a couple of weeks. Note down everything eaten in the day, from licking the marmalade spoon after breakfast to finishing off the children's lunch. The diary must include notes on the arthritis condition – when it is worse or slightly better. There should be least five entries a day for both food and condition.

Above: It is a good idea to talk to your doctor or a nutritionist before embarking on an exclusion diet. He or she will be able to help you plan a diet so that you do not miss out on any essential food group.

DISCOVERING THE CULPRIT

After keeping a detailed food diary for a week or so, some kind of pattern may start to emerge. For example, do you always feel worse 30 minutes after a large glass of fresh orange juice for breakfast? The next step, and the only foolproof way to discover whether a food is having an adverse effect, is to exclude it from your diet for a period of at least one month. You will need to be patient when trying to pinpoint troublesome foods as the process may take several months.

EMBARKING ON AN EXCLUSION DIET

The suspect food family is most likely one of the four usually associated with arthritis – dairy products, citrus fruit, wheat and the solanacae family of vegetables. The food that you suspect you may be allergic to must be rigorously excluded from the diet for at least two weeks, preferably one month. It takes a surprisingly long time for the food to work its way out of the body completely and anyone genuinely sensitive to the food will react to the tiniest trace in the system.

It is relatively easy to exclude some foods from your diet, such as citrus fruits, as it is usually easy to identify them or dishes in which they have been used. It is far more difficult with the other three groups, however, as tomatoes, potatoes, dairy products and wheat products and their derivatives are used in almost every kind of ready-made food.

UNDERSTANDING LABELS

Although it is time-consuming, try to read every food label carefully to ensure that the product does not contain even a trace of the excluded food. To do this efficiently it is necessary to know all the names under which that product may appear on a label. For example, whey and casein are both constituents of milk and modified starch is made from wheat.

FOODS TO AVOID

These lists show some of the products and ingredients that are not necessarily instantly identified as a source of the foods to be excluded. This is extensive enough to highlight the problem – many more individual items could be added.

WHEAT
Foods
Couscous
Curry powder
Farina
Instant hot drinks (such as coffee, tea, chocolate)
Semolina
Soy sauce (except wheat-free tamari)
White pepper in restaurants (can be adulterated with flour)
Ingredients
Cereal filler
Modified starch
Monosodium glutamate
Rusk
Check labels of following:
Chinese sauces
Horseradish creams
Ketchups
Mustards
Prepared meats
Salad dressings
Sauces
Sausages
Seasoning mixes
Soups
Sweets (confectionery)

SOLANACAE
Aubergines
Bell peppers
Chilli peppers
Potatoes
Tomatoes
Spices
Cayenne pepper
Chilli powder
Curry powder
Paprika

DAIRY
Foods
Batter
Butter
Buttermilk
Cheese (including cream, curd and cottage cheeses)
Cream (double, whipping and single)
Créme fraiche
Ghee
Skimmed milk powder
Synthetic cream
Yogurt
Ingredients
Animal fats
Casein
Caseinates
Hydrolysed casein or whey
Lactose
Milk solids
Non-milk fat solids
Whey
Whey protein or sugar
Check labels of following:
Chocolate
Low-fat spreads
Vegetable fats

CITRUS FRUIT
Clementines
Grapefruit
Lemons
Limes
Mandarins
Mineolas
Oranges
Satsumas
Tangelos
Tangerines
Ugli fruits

The number of ready-made dishes that are suitable for people an an exclusion diet is small, although there are a growing number of companies producing foods without dairy products, wheat or other individual ingredients.

ALTERNATIVE INGREDIENTS

It has become fairly easy to find alternatives to some of the basic ingredients that are commonly excluded.

Above: There is now a wide range of non-wheat flours, noodles and pastas.

WHEAT-FREE DIET

Although the number of companies making flour, breads, pastas, pizzas, cake and biscuits without wheat is increasing all the time, they are still relatively few and the products are comparatively expensive. Potato flour or cornflour can be used for thickening soups, sauces and similar dishes, and bread, cakes and biscuits can be made using proprietary wheat-free flours, chick-pea flour or a combination of rice flour and ground oats.

DAIRY-FREE DIET

This means a diet free from cow's milk and all its products, not milk from sheep, goats or other animals.

Goat, sheep, soya or oat milk can be used instead of cow's milk for most savoury dishes, and there are dozens of different soya milks to choose from. For sweet dishes, both rice milk and coconut milk make good alternatives. There are a number of dairy-free spreads (check the ingredients list carefully) that can be substituted for

Above: Soya milk and goat's cheese are useful alternatives to dairy products.

butter, both on bread and for cooking or baking. There is also an increasing range of soya, sheep's milk and goat's milk yogurts and even ice creams. Cheese is a serious problem, as the food industry has still not managed to come up with a cheese substitute that tastes anything remotely like cheese, although there are a couple of soya "cheese" spreads which are perfectly harmless, if not terribly exciting.

Above: Introduce hearty root vegetables such as swede, sweet potato and turnip.

Above: A thick stock can be used instead of tomatoes in many recipes.

SOLANACAE-FREE DIET

This diet excludes potatoes, tomatoes, peppers, chillies and aubergines. There are a number of root vegetables that can be used instead of potatoes in many recipes, such as sweet potatoes, celeriac, Jerusalem artichokes, parsnips, swedes and carrots; firm squashes are also a useful alternative.

Tomatoes are the most difficult item to replace in this family, as there is really no satisfactory substitute for their sweet, acidic flavour and their juice. Use lots of chopped onions and plenty of herbs with a little thick and well-flavoured stock instead of tomatoes in recipes that rely on their juice.

Peppers, chillies and aubergines can be avoided fairly easily. The hot flavour of chilli can be replaced with black or white pepper. Remember, that cayenne pepper is a form of dried chillies and paprika is made from peppers.

Above: Replace chillies with spices such as peppercorns, ground turmeric or ginger.

No Improvement?

A month on an exclusion diet may not yield any improvement in the arthritis. This may be because the wrong food group has been excluded. In that case, try again with another of the food groups. By working through all four of the food families, each will be eliminated in turn; it may be that this diet does not make any difference to the arthritis and that food group is genuinely not implicated in this case. Alternatively, the problem food may not have been located, or there could be more than one food causing the problem. There are a number of therapists who have had great success with specific diets which eliminate more than one type of food. For example, one American therapist, himself an ex-arthritic, recommends a diet regime including only seafood, vegetables and rice.

Food Fasts

If you have not had positive results after excluding the initial four food families, but still feel that food could be implicated, you might like to consider a food fast. On a four to five day fast, nothing but distilled water is consumed. If some food or drink is implicated, it will be excluded automatically during the fast and there should be an improvement. If there is a beneficial result, serious food detective work has to be used to track down the food – or foods – that cause the problem. No one should embark on such a fast lightly. It should ONLY be done when the person has time off, with nothing very much to do, and under the supervision of a doctor, dietician or nutritionist. This applies especially to those who are not in general good health, are on medication or who are very young, old or pregnant. Apart from the fact that not eating for extended periods creates

Right: A food fast should only ever be undertaken when you have time on your hands because you may find yourself reacting badly and feeling quite ill.

a feeling of light-headedness or results in headaches, anyone who reacts badly to certain foods may find that their body takes the opportunity to "detoxify" itself. This process can be quite dramatic and, like an alcoholic or a drug addict who is suddenly deprived of their addictive substance, the person can suddenly feel quite ill.

Using Food to Challenge a Positive Result

If the exclusion diet has produced positive results and the arthritis is improved, if only a little, it has to be confirmed that it was the exclusion of that food that helped, not some other side effect of the diet or a change in lifestyle. Therefore the body has to be "challenged" with the food.

Re-introduce the excluded food in a reasonable quantity for one week. There may be an immediate reaction, or a far more gradual one after a few days. Either way, this confirms that the food is causing a problem. It is then up to the individual to decide whether the improvement in condition was worth the disruption to diet and daily life. It might be worth continuing your investigations into the diet to see whether other foods could be involved and whether further improvement may be possible if those foods are avoided.

A varied diet is always a good thing, and, as you continue to experiment with alternative ways of cooking and eating, you may even find yourself enjoying food more and regarding the experience as an adventure.

EATING TO PREVENT ARTHRITIS

It is one thing knowing the theory, but quite another when it comes to putting it into practice, and this is particularly true of following a special diet. Try to be positive, focusing on different cooking methods and a variety of ingredients rather than on the foods to avoid.

A quick glance at all of these recommendations might give you the impression that you will lose weight very fast, as there may seem to be very little left that you are allowed to eat. However, a diet adjusted to help ease arthritis can include just as much variety as a standard diet. It may take a little extra effort, but there is no reason why the changes should not be included in the family eating pattern. As long as the changes are discreet, even fussy eaters will probably never notice. Adding new foods – especially when many of them are really tasty – is often easier than removing old favourites. In either case, involving the whole family in the diet makes catering easier and can turn into a culinary adventure for everyone.

Browse through a few cookbooks from a range of different cultures for inspiration. Try traditional dishes from India, China, Malaysia and Indonesia, for example, and you will be amazed at the number of fabulous dishes that are low in animal fats and high in the foods and nutrients you should be eating more of.

A FEW SIMPLE POINTS
• Use olive or sunflower oil for cooking rather than butter or lard.
• Try beancurd (tofu) or TVP/soya protein in a well-flavoured curry or stew instead of meat.
• Use soya, oat or rice milk in cooking rather than cow's milk.
• Cut down on chocolate, cakes and biscuits, and increase your intake of fresh fruit.
• Add a few seeds or nuts to savoury and sweet cooked dishes and to salads.
• Increase the number of raw vegetables that you eat.
• Try baking or steaming vegetables rather than frying or roasting them.

Above: A diet suitable for people with arthritis is low in fat and high in vitamins, and should be suitable for all members of the family. You will find it much easier to follow your diet if the rest of the family eat the same foods.

Right: Crushed pumpkin seeds can be used in a wide variety of dishes to increase your intake of GLAs. Try adding them to pastry or wholemeal scones, sprinkling them over salads or stirring them into casseroles or risotto.

KITCHEN IMPROVEMENTS

With arthritis there is a good chance that your hands, and indeed the rest of your body, are not as agile or as mobile as they once were. Although we would hope that changing your diet improves the condition, it is also a good idea to look around the kitchen for anything that could be changed to make cooking easier.

If your hands are stiff or weak, if you use a stick, find it difficult to stand for long, or have trouble bending, there are a number of relatively minor alterations that can be made to kitchen units and fixed appliances to make your life easier. There are also a few special gadgets that are not too expensive and can make quite a difference.

CUPBOARDS

If opening cupboard doors is difficult, take the doors off, leaving open shelves (very fashionable) or add curtains, which can be pulled across easily. Consider taking shelves out of base units to make space for sitting at the counter with your knees underneath or to store a trolley. If the work surfaces are too deep for you to reach the back wall comfortably, try adding a free-standing shallow storage shelf against the back wall. A rail along the front of the units provides extra support when getting around the kitchen and somewhere to hang a stick – as well as a dish towel. Many people prefer to cook sitting down so, if the units are too high, a small table can be ideal for sitting down to carry out some of the tasks involved in food preparation.

ELECTRICS

Rocker switches can be installed (this means changing just the fitment) and you can buy plugs with handles for all appliances, which are much easier to pull out of sockets.

TAPS

Lever taps are easier to operate than the regular type. If you do not want to change the taps, lever tap-turners can be fitted on existing taps.

COOKERS AND MICROWAVES

A split-level cooker with an eye-level grill is very useful for people who cannot bend. Even better, a worktop combination microwave and convection cooker is very accessible. Appliances with a rocker door opener

will be easier to use for anyone with weak hands. A cheaper alternative for a small family is a small microwave and a table-top oven or cooker. All these plug into a standard socket and are easy to use and clean. Table-top cookers get very hot, so care must be taken when using them. Multi-cookers, similar to electric frying pans, are also useful as they sit on a table. They can be used for boiling, stewing, roasting or baking, and some food can be served straight from the pan.

TROLLEYS

A trolley, ideally a fairly tall one, is invaluable in the kitchen for use as a table. It can also be pushed around as a walker-cum-trolley, and its handle provides somewhere for hanging a stick. Retail catalogues listing disabled equipment usually have a selection of reasonably priced, sturdy trolleys suitable for use in the kitchen.

Below: A small table can be ideal for chopping vegetables.

TONGS, KNIVES AND SCISSORS

A pair of long-handled tongs with insulated handles is invaluable for all kinds of tasks. Avoid using knives as far as possible, as it is all too easy to let them slip. Scissors can be used for many types of chopping jobs. Buy scissors with large chunky finger holds or that spring open automatically.

GRATERS, CAN OPENERS AND SCREWTOP OPENERS

Graters, especially the steady four-sided ones, are useful for many jobs. A plastic food mill, which grates by turning, is also handy. An electric can opener may be the answer for those with stiff hands, but a manual opener with chunky handles and an easy-to-grasp turning knob is less expensive. There are a selection of devices for removing tops from jars. Experiment in a gadget shop to find the one that you prefer.

Above: Plastic kitchenware is lighter than metal and therefore easier to lift.

BOWLS AND MEASURING JUGS

Look for kitchen equipment made from lightweight plastic. Replace any ceramic mixing bowls, glass measuring jugs and metal colanders. If you are worried about the plastic bowl slipping when you are mixing, use a wet dish towel or a rubber mat (there are special mats called Dycem which are very good) to stop any movement.

Above: A kettle tipper takes the weight of the water and also makes pouring safer.

KETTLES

A kettle that can be filled through the spout and that is neither too heavy nor too difficult to lift is essential – always test it before buying. Kettle tippers, which save you from having to lift the appliance for pouring, are available.

HANDLES

Choose cutlery and equipment with big, plump handles. If you do not want to buy new items, you can buy large plastic handles that fit over existing ones. Less elegant, but equally effective for cutlery, is a piece of rubber tubing taped firmly in place. Some specialist cutlery has handles that can be bent. The user can move them into the position they find most comfortable.

Above: Cutlery with big, chunky handles is easier to grip.

HELPING HANDS

A pair of magnetic pincers controlled by a lever on the end of a long handle is invaluable for picking up items when your reach is impaired. Helping hands are usually available from larger kitchen or hardware stores.

PROCESSORS, MIXERS AND LIQUIDIZERS

Small, hand-held appliances are easier to use than family-size models, most of which are heavy. Battery-powered cordless mixers are ideal.

Above: A cooking basket will stop you having to lift a heavy pan of boiling water.

SAUCEPANS

Iron casseroles may be wonderful for long, slow cooking, but they are hard for even able-bodied cooks to lift. Look for good-quality, light pans with long handles. The handles must be big and easy to grasp as well as being well insulated. Twin-handled pans are ideal for people with weak hands.

Chose a non-stick pan that will be easy to clean. Cooking in a non-stick pan requires less fat, another important consideration for arthritis sufferers.

A stainless steel cooking basket is a useful investment as it allows you to remove and drain cooked vegetables without lifting a heavy pan of water. The pan can be emptied later when the water is cool.

CANCER PREVENTION

This disease is currently the second highest cause of death in the Western World. Factors such as smoking and sun exposure play a large role in this statistic, but nutrition is also an essential consideration. Studies have shown that a healthy, well-balanced diet can reduce the risk of cancer development. This chapter looks at foods which can help to protect against cancer, which foods to avoid, and how to improve your eating habits and general lifestyle.

INTRODUCTION

Historically, conventional medicine has rejected links between cancer and nutrition. However, recent scientific research shows that better nutrition and healthier eating can definitely help both to prevent and treat cancer, which is now the second highest cause of death in the developed world. Cancer is a conquerable disease.

In choosing better foods for healthier living, it is important to select those that not only sustain life but that also renew and regenerate cells and boost the immune system. Eating healthier foods has been shown to reduce the risk of cancer by between 30 and 60 per cent, which are indeed encouraging statistics!

EVOLVING EATING PATTERNS

Before society became industrialized, food came from the land. People ate a balance of meats, dairy produce, cereals and grains, and natural sugar obtained from fruits and vegetables.

In today's busy world, eating patterns have changed dramatically and modern meals are often unbalanced. They tend to be made up largely of dairy produce and animal foods, while valuable plant foods, such as fruits, vegetables, cereals and wholegrains are left out.

Fast food shops are now popular and provide a supply of cooked foods that are too high in fat, sugar and protein. Processed "convenience" foods and ready-made meals, which are full of additives and preservatives, are also common. As a result, people have developed a taste for unhealthy foods.

Cooking with animal fats and some oils is not only unhealthy, but may actually enourage cancer. Eating too

much protein makes the body acidic, which may cause free-radical damage to cells.

Over-refined foods, such as white sugar and white flour products, do not replenish or nourish the body. Some nutritionists go even further, believing that sugar is actually a poison, feeding cancer cells and draining the body of important nutrients.

So the messages seems clear: if you want to stay healthy, you need to follow a well-balanced diet of fresh and wholesome foods.

DIETS AROUND THE WORLD

There are groups of people around the world, such as the Hunzas of the Himalayas, the Georgians in Russia, and the Vilcamba of Ecuador, who follow nutritious diets of natural,

unrefined foods and often live to be over 100 years of age, and who remain remarkably free of cancer.

The Hunzas' diet, which would appear to lie behind their good health and longevity, consists of rich mineral water; complete proteins of millet, soya beans, barley and buckwheat; natural fibre foods, such as almonds, sesame seeds, leafy green vegetables, berries, peas and freshly sprouted seeds and grains; and enzyme-rich fermented foods, such as yogurt and soured milk.

Similarly, the Seventh Day Adventists in America are vegetarians and have been seen to develop half the number of cases of cancer experienced by the rest of the population.

The Mediterranean diet of tomatoes, olives, onions, garlic, oregano, cold-pressed olive oil and grapes, which is

WHAT CAUSES CANCER?

Cancer develops when abnormal cells divide and multiply, running out of control. These dividing cells form tumours, which can spread relentlessly around the body. Even though thousands of body cells can become malignant every day, a strong immune system can destroy such cells and prevent cancer. Pollution, radiation, smoking and too much sunshine can all cause cancer, but it is believed that many forms develop as a result of an unhealthy and unbalanced diet.

Above: Soup flavoured with miso, which is derived from the nutrient-rich soya bean.

Above: High-fibre dahl is full of protein and helps speed up the digestive process.

high in natural antioxidants and other nutrients, has also been shown to lower the incidence of cancer.

Asian peoples, who also have low cancer rates, eat many plant foods and plenty of pulses, grains, seeds and nuts. The Indian diet uses very little meat or sugar. Dates, raisins, dried apricots and root vegetables are popular, and dahl, which is made from lentils and is one of the most commonly eaten foods in India, possesses anti-cancer nitrilosides. Green tea, a favourite drink in Asian countries, is becoming popular in the West as a highly antioxidant drink that is believed to help in the fight against cancer. Popular foods consumed in Japan, which are considered to have anti-cancer properties, are soya beans, seaweeds, rice and miso.

It should also be noted that many indigenous peoples, including the Aborigines, Polynesians and North American Indians, did not suffer from cancer until they started to follow the over-refined diet of the West. Copying Western eating habits has proved to be a backward step, underlining the need to use fresh, non-processed foods if we wish to improve our chances of maintaining good health.

THE ANTIOXIDANT THEORY

Research suggests that cancer is caused by an antioxidant deficiency. Foods from plants have been proved to possess cancer-preventing qualities and antioxidant nutrients. These anti-cancer properties may prove to be the best solution to conquering the disease. The key nutrients are: vitamins A, C, D and E, co-enzyme Q_{10}, selenium, manganese, zinc, copper, iron, chromium, lycopene and betacarotene.

Vitamin A, in its natural form, is found only in animal products, particularly in fish liver and animal liver. It can also be found in lesser amounts in eggs, milk and butter. The betacarotene in some fruits and vegetables is changed to vitamin A after it has been eaten.

Vitamin E reduces the cells' need for oxygen and is present in dark green vegetables, citrus fruits, seeds, vegetable oils, corn, soya beans, carrots, spinach and apricots. Vitamin E strengthens the immune system. Vitamin C, present in all fresh fruits and vegetables, works with vitamin E to prevent carcinogens forming.

Selenium is a crucial antioxidant nutrient. Although it is present in grains and seeds, depleted soil means that supplementation may be necessary. Other major antioxidant nutrients include iron, manganese, zinc, copper and chromium.

Sulphur-containing compounds, found in cruciferous vegetables such as broccoli, are good cancer inhibitors and block the reaction of certain carcinogens with DNA.

Above: Oranges, lemons and kiwi fruit are rich in vitamin C.

Above: Green tea is high in antioxidants and is a powerful anti-cancer drink.

Above: Eggs, milk and butter contain the antioxidant nutrient, vitamin A.

Above: Dark green vegetables, carrots and apricots contain vitamin E.

EATING FOR HEALTH

Being healthy means taking responsibility for your choices about nutrition. Foods can become used as a remedy, alongside conventional and complementary therapies. A positive change to high nutrient foods that truly feed the body can be an exciting challenge. As tastebuds adapt, so the body cleanses itself and greater energy and well-being are experienced.

WHAT YOU CAN DO

Begin in a relaxed manner, reducing and cutting out over-refined, processed foods and potentially harmful additives, and opting for fresh, high-antioxidant nutrition. Too many rapid changes may result in the fast elimination of toxins leading to skin reactions and head and body aches, so a measured and informed plan is important.

● Build up a stock of natural and organic wholefoods.
● Develop your own personal anti-cancer nutrition lists.
● Study food labels (take a magnifying glass if necessary!) to avoid processed and additive-ridden foods.
● Eat more raw foods. These contain important enzymes, which help to keep the body healthy, but which are destroyed from the heat of cooking.
● Eat more "live" foods, which contain all the nutrients and enzymes that are essential for health.
● Invest in a powerful juicer and drink fresh vegetable and fruit juices.
● Drink green tea, which is high in anti-cancer nitrilosides.

● Drink eight glasses of low-sodium mineral water each day.
● Learn about growing fresh herbs, sprouting seeds and grains and, the powerful anti-cancer plant, wheatgrass.
● Seek out local farms and outlets for organic foods. Buy fresh from the market, where fruits and vegetables are not wrapped in cellophane.
● Give up white sugar and related foods. After a few weeks, your taste-buds will adapt and you won't want sugar any more.
● Cut down on fried foods and avoid hydrogenated products and refined oils and margarines. Processed vegetable fats, including hydrogenated vegetable oils, such as white cooking fats, spreads and margarines, are linked with cancer.
● Use extra virgin olive oil, linseed and sesame oils.
● Eat oily fish, such as sardines, tuna herring, mackerel, salmon and eel, which are rich in omega-3 fatty acids.
● Reduce your consumption of dairy products.
● Boost the good flora in the gut by eating "live" yogurts.

● Cut down on red meats.
● Find an organic meat outlet and favour poultry, which is lower in fat than red meat.
● Focus on complete proteins from plant sources in soya products such as tofu (soya beancurd), sprouted seeds, and pulses such as chick-peas and lentils.
● Increase your natural fibre intake, adding cereals, legumes, nuts, fruits and vegetables.
● Avoid white flour products, such as white breads, pies, cakes and biscuits.
● Choose brown rice, buckwheat and millet. Cooked millet contains all the essential vitamins, minerals and amino acids, does not leach the body of vital calcium, and is high in nitrilosides.
● Use garlic and onions regularly.
● Use herbs such as mint, thyme and rosemary, which have a cleansing effect on the body.
● Check the required balance of salt in your diet. The body needs at least half a gram daily, preferably good sea salt.
● Make sure that you eat at least five portions of fresh vegetables and fruits each day.

Above: Tofu (soya beancurd), lentils and chick-peas are low in fat and high in protein.

Above: Onions and garlic contain valuable cancer-fighting phytochemicals.

Above: Fresh vegetable juices and mineral water both hydrate and cleanse your body.

FOODS TO AVOID

Being aware of all the foods that enter your mouth helps safeguard against eating foods that may be harmful to you.
• Avoid any foods that are burned, charred, rancid or stale.
• Stale foods, such as grains and nuts, can become contaminated with fungi called mycotoxins, thought to cause liver cancer.
• Cut down on fried foods.
• Avoid using hydrogenated and saturated fats and oils found in butters, vegetable fat, margarines and certain oils. Avoid packaged foods that contain these fats.
• Avoid foods that contain artificial colourings, chemicals or additives.
• Try not to eat foods manufactured with added salt.

• Cut out white sugar and related products in cereals, sweets, cakes, pies and biscuits. Refined sugars can create mucus that clogs the system and causes constipation.
• If you choose an alcoholic drink, avoid spirits and pick good wines, or organic wines that have not been through a chemical process.
• Avoid eating refined grains in white bread and white flour. Lack of fibre in these starchy foods can clog the digestive system.
• Cut down on dairy products such as cream, butter, full cream milk, lard and some margarines.
• Check on your protein intake. Too much protein can overload the digestive system.
• Try not to overeat and, instead, end meals still feeling a little hungry.

• Avoid animal protein foods, particularly red meats and cold meats that contain nitrites and other harmful preservatives.
• Check that you have not become a slave to your tastebuds and your appetite. Addictions to foods high in sugars and fats, particularly chocolate, sweets and crisps, are common nowadays. Maintaining the correct weight is important – extra fat tissue is believed to make people more vulnerable to cancers.
• Don't rush meals and be sure to chew foods thoroughly.
• However, as well as being aware of what you eat, avoid becoming over-anxious about which foods to choose. Occasional treats can play an important psychological role in maintaining good health.

Above: Foods to avoid include sugary cakes, biscuits and sweets. Top right: Cooking with butter, lard and vegetable fat may encourage cancer. Right: Organic wine, processed without the use of chemicals, makes a healthier choice than spirits.

THE RIGHT FOODS TO EAT

Eating the right foods will provide you with the nutrients required for good health. Aim to eat balanced meals, using fresh, natural, non-processed foods. Experts favour low-protein, low-calorie, low-fat diets that are high in natural carbohydrates.

Many foods have been highlighted as particularly beneficial in cancer protection. These include fresh fruits and vegetables, oily fish, olive oil, nuts and seeds, soya products, pulses and grains, and drinks that are rich in chlorophyll.

FRUIT AND VEGETABLES

These are seen as the key defence in the fight against cancer. Experts recommend eating between five and seven portions of fruit and vegetables daily. This alone may halve the risk of developing cancer.

Fruit and vegetables are high in fibre and contain many valuable nutrients, including vitamins A, C and E, and folic acid. They also contain powerful phytochemicals, which inhibit the growth of tumours, repair damaged cells and boost the immune system. The most potent anti-cancer fruit and vegetables are watermelon, canteloupe

melon, citrus fruits, berries, tomatoes, broccoli, Brussels sprouts, carrots, garlic, ginger and linseed.

Left: Cantaloupe melon, tomatoes, ginger and Brussels sprouts are anti-cancer foods.

FISH AND FISH OILS

Although fish is an important source of protein, the key element in cancer prevention and intervention is the large amount of omega-3 fatty acids that it contains. Oily fish, such as mackerel, herring, sardine, tuna and salmon, are particularly high in these nutrients and some experts recommend eating them two or three times a week.

Fish oils have been shown to stop established cancers spreading and to strengthen the immune system. Fish that are rich in vitamin D are known to slow down cancer: the best source of vitamin D is eel.

Try to obtain fish from clean salt or fresh water sources that are free of pesticides and chemicals. Select smaller fish because they have had less time to absorb toxins. Never eat fish skins because poisonous chemicals may have been deposited there.

BETACAROTENE

This powerful antioxidant nutrient is changed to vitamin A in the body. It boosts the immune system and provides oxygen to the body's cells, helping to fight cancer.

Above: Orange-fleshed melons, red and yellow peppers, red sweet potatoes and carrots are rich in betacarotene.

Betacarotene is found in orange, red and yellow vegetables and fruits, such as carrots, apricots, cantaloupe melons and sweet potatoes, and in dark green vegetables such as spinach, broccoli, cabbage and Brussels sprouts. Betacarotene is especially effective in treating stomach cancer. It has the power to destroy cancer cells and is an important preventative agent. When combined with vitamin E, betacarotene has an increased anti-cancer effect.

Women who are vulnerable to cervical cancer may be protected by taking a daily supplement of beta-carotene – the suggested intake is between 10,000 and 50,000IU daily – and at least 90mg of vitamin C.

Links have been made between levels of betacarotene in the diet and the incidence of lung cancer. The carcinogenic dangers of breathing polluted air and tobacco smoke may be reduced by betacarotene.

Above: Oily fish, such as mackerel and herring, are rich in omega-3 fatty acids.

Above: Free-range chicken is a good animal protein and has less fat than red meat.

MEAT AND POULTRY

Historically, meat has been linked with strengthening and building the body. But it is high in animal protein and saturated fats, and experts now believe that eating some meats, particularly red ones, can actually increase the chances of developing cancer.

Protein and some of the other vital nutrients provided by meat and poultry can equally well be obtained from complex carbohydrates. It is important to remember that in many societies where there is little or no cancer people eat little or no meat.

Poultry contains less fat than red meat and is easier to digest, but chickens and turkeys that are bred for commercial use are fed with growth hormones and chemicals. Try to buy from farmers who follow free-range and organic processes. Choose lean cuts, or cut off any fat. Avoid prepared cold meats, because these are processed with harmful chemicals.

OILS

A balance of omega-3 and omega-6 essential fatty acids is known to be important for your health. So which oils should you choose?

Restrict omega-6 vegetable oils to sunflower, corn and safflower. Choose cold-pressed olive oil, linseed and rapeseed oils. Linseed and rapeseed oils provide the best balance of essential

fatty acids. Antioxidant olive oils have proven anti-cancer properties. Research has shown that including omega-3 fish oils and olive oil in the diet lowers the rate of breast cancer.

NUTS AND SEEDS

These are a good plant source of protein as well as fibre. They help to provide the body with vital nutrients that can boost the immune system. Sesame seeds also contain generous amounts of calcium.

Nuts have proven anti-cancer properties. Walnuts and almonds, for example, contain the antioxidant oleic acid, while Brazil nuts contain large amounts of selenium, a powerful anti-cancer antioxidant. Walnuts also contain ellagic acid, which is another cancer-fighting antioxidant.

Almost any plant seed can be sprouted. The sprouts, which are loaded with health-giving enzymes and vital nutrients, grow in just a few days.

Above: Choose rapeseed oil, sunflower oil, extra virgin olive oil and linseed oil to obtain essential fatty acids.

Above: Brazil nuts, walnuts and almonds contain powerful antioxidants.

DAIRY PRODUCTS

These foods, which include milk, butter, cream, cheeses, yogurt and ice cream, are sources of protein, vitamin D, sodium and calcium. Anti-cancer diets recommend limiting these foods as they tend to be high in fats, particularly saturated fatty acids, which are thought to increase the risk of many cancers. Cow's milk also contains large amounts of casein, which can clog the digestive system with mucus.

Many of the vital nutrients found in dairy products, such as calcium and protein, can easily be obtained from other sources, such as green vegetables, beans, nuts, sea vegetables, sesame seeds and tahini. Unhydrogenated olive oil margarines are becoming a popular alternative to butter. Goat's milk is a healthy choice for people who have an intolerance to the lactose in cow's milk. Yogurt and fermented milks, such as buttermilk and kefir, are more easily assimilated because fermentation breaks down the lactose. Milk, cheeses and yogurt that come from sheep and goats are available in many shops and are often found to be easier to digest.

SOYA PRODUCTS

Traditional Eastern diets maintain a balance of nutrients through the use of soya beans in conjunction with grains and seaweeds. Soya products are high in protein and low in carbohydrates.

Nutritionists have found that soya products can play an important role in lowering the risk of cancer. Soya beans contain phytochemicals, which help to slow down the rate at which cancer cells divide and allow the body to repair itself.

Many products are produced from soya beans. Tofu and tempeh, which are a mixture of soya beans and rice or barley, are both high in nutrients and low in fat. They are ideal sources of protein and can be eaten instead of meat. Other soya products include soya

Below: Goat's milk, yogurt and cheese are good choices for people who have an intolerance to lactose.

milk, cream and yogurt, flour, soy sauce and miso, which is a tasty, fermented paste. Small amounts of miso can be used to flavour soups, sauces and dressings.

Above: Soya flour, tofu (soya beancurd), tempeh and soya milk and yogurt are rich in protein and can play an important role in lowering the risk of cancer.

PULSES AND CEREALS

In some parts of the world, a mixture of pulses and grains form the basis of the population's diet. These foods provide a rich supply of plant protein, carbohydrates and fibre.

Pulses are high-fibre foods that can speed up the digestive process. There is evidence to suggest that they help to prevent cancer. Popular pulses include soya beans, lentils, chick-peas, black-eyed beans and mung beans.

Cereals, such as wheat bran, have also been shown to reduce levels of cancer by promoting oestrogen in the blood. (However, wheat triggers an allergic reaction in some people.)

Corn and rice are both considered to be anti-cancer grains because they possess protease inhibitors. Rice is thought to be the grain that is the least likely to irritate the immune system. Millet is particularly high in nutrients, and is a key food in populations with a low incidence of cancer.

Above top: A selection of cereals – brown rice, wheat bran and couscous.
Above: Peas and beans are high-fibre foods, which speed up the digestive process.

Drinks

Drinking eight glasses of mineral water a day hydrates and cleanses your body.

Green tea and chlorophyll-rich drinks, such as wheatgrass juice, and shakes made with Klamath Lake blue-green algae and Spirulina, are powerful anti-cancer drinks. They cleanse the blood and increase the oxygen supply, preventing free radicals from forming.

Freshly juiced organic vegetable and fruit juices are also recommended as part of a cancer prevention diet. Carrot juice in particular is believed to have strong anti-cancer properties.

Anti-cancer healing teas are also popular and include horsetail, cat's claw, Pau D'arco and Essiac (which is made from burdock root), Turkish rhubarb, slippery elm and sheep sorrel.

Above: Wheatgrass juice, carrot juice, Spirulina crystals and Klamath Lake blue-green algae increase the supply of oxygen in the blood.

Nutritional Supplements

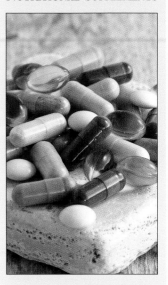

Although food is considered to be the best source of nutrients, the over-refining, processing and cooking of foods can destroy vital nutrients. Conventional cancer treatments can destroy many of the essential vitamins and nutrients found in the body, so people may benefit from taking additional nutritional supplements.

A recent report suggests that taking supplements is generally safe. However, it is recommended that you seek professional advice, particularly if you are taking anticoagulant medication or have high blood pressure.

Many nutritionists believe that antioxidants, including vitamin A, vitamin C, vitamin E, lutein, lycopene, betacarotene and zeaxanthin, can help in the prevention and treatment of cancers. A study of people in 27 countries has shown that the higher the blood selenium level, the lower the incidence of cancer.

JUICING

Freshly juiced vegetables, fruits, grasses and sprouts are an important element of a cancer prevention diet. They supply nutrients that the body may not get from cooked, processed foods and, because they are liquid, juices can be digested in minutes, compared with the hours it takes to digest foods with fibre. Fresh carrot is considered to be the most effective anti-cancer juice.

THE BENEFITS OF LIQUID FOODS

Juices that are taken as part of a health therapy are both nutritious and recuperative. It is important to use a wide variety of fruits and vegetables to obtain all the nutrients needed to combat illness and maintain health. Use organic fruits and vegetables, especially if cancer is already established. If these are not available, choose the freshest produce possible.

Enzymes from juices, which can be killed in cooking, work with the body's own enzymes, enabling better digestion and absorption, and nourishing the body. Drink juices as soon as they are made. Fresh juices made from "live" ingredients contain both oxygen and chlorophyll as well as vitamins, minerals and amino acids, all of which help to rebuild and regenerate body tissues and cells.

Above: Fresh fruit and vegetable juices are full of health-giving nutrients.

The Gerson diet is based on using organic fresh fruit and vegetable juices at regular intervals through the day. This process speeds detoxification and feeds the immune system. Fresh juices cleanse the body. They can also help to prevent constipation and encourage the healing of diverticulitis. Because energy is released so quickly, bringing juices into your diet can bring a joyful feeling that comes from eating live, vital foods.

WHAT TO JUICE

The nutritionist Dr Norman Walker, who lived to be over 100 years old, believed that the best anti-cancer juices were, firstly, fresh raw carrot juice and, secondly, carrot and spinach juice. The carrot juice molecule is exactly parallel to the human blood molecule. One pint or more of fresh carrot juice is recommended as a powerful cleanser and immune booster.

Celery, asparagus, watercress, parsley, kale, turnip and Swiss chard are also effective in cell regeneration and possess restorative healing properties. Some juices, such as beetroot, alfalfa and wheatgrass, can have a strong effect. Begin by sipping small amounts of the juice until you get used to it.

Fruits that are regarded as powerful anti-cancer agents are grapes and citrus fruits. Pear, peach, prune, watermelon, apple and papaya are also cleansing.

HOW TO JUICE

If you want to make therapeutic juices, think about buying a good juicer. You can extract the juice from citrus fruits by squeezing them, but many fruits and vegetables are hard and need a more powerful juicer.

A blender is not suitable for making pure juices. Blended juices take much longer to digest because all the fibre is retained. A high-speed juicer leaves the cellulose and pulp behind. Wheatgrass requires a slow turning juicer because of its tough fibre.

High-speed electric juicers are either "centrifugal" or "masticating" juicers. Many nutritionists consider that one of the best juicers for extracting nutrients is the Champion juicer. It grinds the fruits and vegetables and squeezes them through firm meshing.

Another type of juicer is a hydraulic press, which presses the plant fibres completely to squeeze out the juice. If you want to make fresh juices from wheatgrass or sprouts, you need to buy a fruit press, which is rather like an old-fashioned meat mincer.

If you incorporate regular juicing into your anti-cancer plan, it is worth investing in an efficient juicer, but any form of fresh organic juice is better than no juice at all. You can also chew wheatgrass, sprouts and fruits to extract their juice, and then spit out the fibre.

Above: An old-fashioned juicer can be used to squeeze the juice from citrus fruits.

"Live" and Raw Foods

Cooking kills the enzymes in foods and also many of the vitamins, especially vitamin C, and delicate anti-cancer nutrients such as indoles can be destroyed in the cooking process. Including more raw and live foods in your diet means that you will absorb more enzymes, vitamins, minerals and antioxidants to keep you in good health. It is not a good idea to change suddenly to raw foods, as you may find them hard to digest if you are not used to them. Your tastebuds may need educating, but you will be surprised to find that you soon develop a desire for the freshness of raw foods. Sprouted seeds, grains and legumes are an excellent source of living wholefoods.

"Live" Foods

Sprouts are living anti-cancer foods – they are high in fibre and contain a rich supply of enzymes, vitamins, trace elements, chlorophyll and minerals such as calcium, potassium, phosphorous, iron and magnesium.

Almost any beans, seeds, or grains can be sprouted. It is important to use whole seeds that have not been treated with chemicals. Sesame seeds, aduki beans, mung beans, fenugreek and millet are all good for sprouting. Their flavours differ and the sprouts can sometimes be a little bitter, depending on how long they have been allowed to grow.

Some of the most nutritious and tasty sprouts can be grown from rye, almonds, chick-peas, pumpkin seeds, sesame seeds, sunflower seeds, lentils and mung beans. Mung and aduki bean sprouts are particularly good for transporting oxygen to cells. Sprouted beans and peas are less easy to digest than sprouted grains and seeds.

Above: Live yogurt and sprouted seeds are powerful anti-cancer foods.

Fermented Foods

Praised by many experts as powerful anti-cancer foods, fermented foods, such as "live" bio yoghurt, buttermilk and soured cream, contain a bacteria *Lactobacillus acidophilus,* which is also present in the healthy, large intestine. When it is eaten in fermented foods, the small and large intestines are provided with healthy bacteria, and potentially harmful abnormal bacteria are prevented from forming.

Fermented foods are also rich in living enzymes, which encourage good digestion and absorption of nutrients.

As well as being rich in nutrients, yogurt is a predigested food, which makes it is easier for organs that have been weakened by ill health to digest.

Another fermented food, which is popularly used by centenarians in Russia and Bulgaria, is kefir. It is made by placing kefir grains in milk, then allowing the milk to coagulate.

Salads

It is good to start a meal with a fresh vegetable salad, which acts as an internal cleanser. Grated and chopped carrots, cabbage, beetroot, celeriac, cucumber, watercress, celery, radishes, parsley, avocado, tomatoes and spring onions are all good salad ingredients.

Raw foods, especially fruits, should be chewed thoroughly. Eating them at the beginning of a meal, means they pass through the stomach quickly. Fresh fruits also help to dissolve toxic poisons and draw them through the system. Fresh citrus fruits, such as oranges, lemons, limes and grapefruit, contain over 50 anti-cancer agents.

Above: Raw salad is an internal cleanser.

Herbs

Many herbs are known and used for their medicinal properties, and some are thought to help prevent and treat cancer. Favourite herbs for cleansing and strengthening the system are thyme, parsley, basil, marjoram, tarragon and rosemary. The commonly found stinging nettle is also good for cleansing the blood. Milk thistle is a powerful herb for cleansing the liver, and turmeric, which contains circumin, has been recognized as protecting against cancer.

Astragalus is one of many Chinese herbs that can help to strengthen the immune system, and it is believed to be helpful for people fighting cancer. Fresh ginger is also popular for its anti-cancer properties. Herbalists believe that certain herbs can stop tumours growing and studies have shown that some herbs can be used to shrink tumours. Specialist advice should be sought if you plan to use herbs for medicinal purposes.

WHEATGRASS

Grown from the wholewheat grain, the healing properties of wheatgrass have been recognized for centuries. Wheatgrass juice is one of the best foods for helping to prevent and treat cancer. A powerful detoxifier, wheatgrass is high in enzymes, vitamins C and E, betacarotene, minerals and phytochemicals. It also contains powerful anti-cancer agents including chlorophyll, abscisic acid, and B_{17}. Some nutritionists believe wheatgrass juice to be the best healing food available, especially for bolstering the immune system, cleansing the body, increasing oxygen and rejuvenating cells.

Wheatgrass

JUICING WHEATGRASS

A slow-turning juicer is needed for juicing wheatgrass because of its tough fibre. Keep wheatgrass juice in the fridge and use within a day.

Wheatgrass juice can be very powerful in its effect, and some people may feel dizzy or nauseous the first time they drink it. Begin by sipping small amounts until your body gets used to it.

Wheatgrass is usually grown to make juices rather than to be eaten because it is very fibrous and, in its whole form, is not easy to digest. If you don't have a juicer you can chew wheatgrass and spit out the pulp. However, it takes your body much longer to extract all the plant's vital nutrients in this way.

HOW TO SPROUT WHEATBERRIES

To sprout your own wheatgrass for making juice you will need:
- hard, organic wheatberries
- wide-mouthed glass jar
- nylon mesh or muslin
- 2 plastic trays, about 30 × 35cm/ 12 × 14in
- peat moss, compost or topsoil

1 Fill a cup with wheatberries. Wash and rinse them thoroughly to remove any dirt.

2 Put the wheatberries in a jar, fill with water and leave them to soak overnight.

3 Drain and rinse the berries. Cover the jar with muslin and leave the berries to sprout for 12 hours.

4 Put 2.5cm/1in of soil in one tray and scatter the seeds on top.

5 Water the seeds and cover with the other tray. After about 3 days, remove the top tray and place the tray of sprouting berries on a window ledge. Make sure you do not put them in direct sunlight as this may dry out the berries. Keep the berries moist, but not too wet.

6 Cut the wheatgrass when it is about 18cm/7in high. Try to cut the wheatgrass as close to the soil as possible, as this is where the greatest concentration of nutrients is found.

THE HEALTHY STORE CUPBOARD

When you are tired, ill or worried, you may find it difficult to remember which are the best foods to buy. You may find it helpful to keep a list of healthy foods in your kitchen cupboard, fridge or freezer. All the following foods have been found to have positive effects in preventing or treating cancer. Different foods possess different nutrients, but all help to boost the immune system.

SPICES AND SEASONINGS
Garlic
Miso
Pure soy sauce
Sea salt
Tamari
Turmeric
Umeboshi paste

Above: Onions, garlic and ginger stimulate the body's antioxidant mechanisms.

Basil
Chives
Coriander
Ginger
Mint
Oregano
Rosemary
Sage
Tarragon
Thyme

GRAINS AND PULSES
Barley
Buckwheat
Bulgur wheat
Brown rice
Couscous
Millet
Muesli
Oats
Pasta
Sprouted grain breads
Wheat bran
Wholemeal breads

Above: Organic muesli is high in fibre.

Black-eyed beans
Chick-peas
Lentils
Haricot beans
Kidney beans
Lima beans
Mung beans
Peas

COOKING AND PREPARATION TECHNIQUES
• Use steel cooking utensils; never use aluminium pans.
• Always wash fruit and vegetables to remove any dirt and contaminants. When cleaning vegetables, such as potatoes, turnips and carrots, use a scrubbing brush kept specifically for cleaning vegetables.
• Some fruits and vegetables, such as apples, cucumbers, lemons and aubergines have waxed skins – be sure to remove these before eating.
• Never eat meat that has been burned or charred in cooking.
• Remove all the skin from meat and poultry.

• Do not cook meat and fish in saturated or hydrogenated fats.
• Use extra virgin olive oil for cooking and salad dressings.
• Do not add extra salt to foods when eating your meals.
• Boil, steam, stir-fry and bake foods whenever possible. These are all considered to be effective and healthy ways of preparing foods, and ensure the foods are easy to digest.
• When you prepare a meal, think of it as creating a painting. Foods that are pleasing to the eye can stimulate the digestive juices. Try to balance textures and colours, using herbs as sprigs of colour – they will also exude an enticing aroma.

• Experiment with health-giving herbs to give flavour to foods that may seem bland, especially in the early days of trying a low-fat diet.

Above: Use herbs to add flavour, colour and texture to a dish.

NUTS AND SEEDS

Almonds
Brazil nuts
Nut butters
Pecan nuts
Pine nuts
Poppy seeds
Pumpkin seeds
Sesame seeds
Sunflower seeds
Walnuts

Above: Nut butters are anti-cancer foods.

PACKAGED FOODS

Dried unsulphured fruits, such as dates,
   raisins, sultanas, apricots and prunes
Extra virgin olive oil
Honey
Hummus
Klamath Lake blue-green algae
Linseed oil
Liquorice
Oily fish, such as mackerel, salmon,
   sardines, tuna, herring and eel
Rapeseed oil (canola)
Sauerkraut
Seaweeds, such as nori, laver, arame,
   wakami, kelp and kombu
Spirulina
Tahini
Tofu (soya beancurd)
Tempeh
Whole apple cider vinegar

*Above: Dried fruits are a useful source of
energy and are packed with vitamins and
nutrients, including vitamin C, betacarotene,
potassium and iron.*

FRUITS

Apples
Apricots
Bananas
Blueberries
Blackberries
Blackcurrants
Canteloupe melons
Cherries
Figs
Red grapes
Gooseberries
Grapefruit
Grapes
Kiwi fruits
Lemons
Limes
Peaches
Pineapples
Mangoes
Nectarines
Oranges
Raspberries
Red grapes
Redcurrants
Strawberries
Watermelons
White currants

VEGETABLES

Asparagus
Aubergines
Avocados
Beetroot
Broccoli
Broad beans
Brussels sprouts
Cabbages
Carrots
Cauliflowers
Celery
Kale
Onions
Parsnips
Potatoes
Pumpkins
Shiitake mushrooms
Spinach
Squash
Swedes
Sweet potatoes (yams)
Red, orange, yellow and green peppers
Tomatoes
Turnips

*Above: Dark green vegetables are rich
in folates and contain vitamin E, which
strengthens the immune system.*

DAIRY FOODS

Live yogurt
Low-fat cheeses, such as Quark, ricotta
  and cottage cheese
Organic low-fat milk

*Above: Buttermilk, soured cream and yogurt
are rich in valuable enzymes and healthy
bacteria, which aid the digestion.*

FISH, POULTRY AND EGGS

Fresh oily fish, such as mackerel,
  sardines, trout, salmon, tuna and eel
Organic chicken and turkey
Fresh, organic, free-range eggs

*Above: Eat plenty of oily fish, such as tuna
and salmon, obtained from clean salt or
fresh water sources.*

BEVERAGES

Green, black and ginseng tea
Mineral water (low sodium)
Pure fruit and vegetable juices
Good red wine, preferably organic

*Above: Black tea, green tea and ginseng tea
help cleanse the blood and and increase the
supply of oxygen.*

CHOOSING ORGANIC

Unfortunately, most foods are still grown with the use of agrochemicals, including synthetic fertilizers, growth promoters and pesticides. Studies show that these chemicals in foods can be deposited in fatty body tissue, where they can be harmful to health. All too often, as a result of these farming methods, the soil is depleted of selenium, which is known to be a vital and powerful antioxidant that helps to prevent and treat cancer.

The arguments for choosing to eat organic products are powerful. Fruits and vegetables have a fuller, fresher flavour. It is also reassuring to know that they are unadulterated and completely natural, and haven't been waxed or gassed.

Organic meat is produced from free-range, grass-fed animals, which have not been given antibiotics, hormones, growth-promoters or feed additives. If you choose to eat organic meats and poultry, you will also have the satisfaction of knowing that the animals lived and died humanely.

Organic free-range eggs are produced from hens that are fed on a natural pesticide-free diet, which has not had hormones or artificial colorants added. The hens are able to roam on land that has not been treated with chemical fertilizers and is certified organic.

Organic products often have a better flavour and have no added chemicals, sugar or salt. Always check the labels carefully to ensure that products really are organic.

Many supermarkets are responding to public demand for organic foods. If you would like a greater variety of organic foods, make it known to your local food store – the greater the demand, the more likely your store will be to stock these products, and the lower the price.

*Above: Organic free-range eggs contain
the valuable antioxidant, vitamin A,
and are high in protein.*

A HEALTHIER LIFESTYLE

Even the circumstances under which you eat your meals are important, not only in terms of your enjoyment but also in the way in which it affects your ability to digest food and to assimilate nutrients. You may find it hard to relax and to maintain inner calm in today's hectic world. If you can change any harmful living and eating patterns, you may lessen your chances of getting cancer. You can try to protect your life energy by exercising, practising relaxation and meditation. It is good to think positively, and it is important to recognize strong feelings like anger, fear and sadness and find a safe way to express them. Feeling out of control can depress your immune system.

HARMONIOUS EATING

It is easier to digest food if you eat in a peaceful environment, when you are calm and not stressed. Life is often such a rush that it seems difficult to prepare food with pleasure, gratitude and love. Concentrate fully on your meal rather than watching television or talking too much and gulping in air.

Above: A beautiful table setting will enhance your enjoyment of a meal.

Cultivate your enjoyment of pure, simple foods and do not eat more than you need. Even if you are eating alone, make your table beautiful with a candle or a flower and give yourself the best you can, not only in terms of food but also by creating a harmonious environment.

COMPLEMENTARY THERAPIES

Rather than concentrating on the body alone, complementary medicine offers many therapies that support the person as a whole, and has proved to be effective in treating cancer.

Counselling can provide a safe and non-judgmental environment where you can talk about your often painful thoughts, feelings and experiences and be listened to and supported.

Naturopathy offers guidance on diet, fasting, exercises and hydrotherapy to naturally restore the body to health.

Aromatherapy uses aromatic essences with therapeutic qualities to massage the body. This relaxes the muscles and gives a greater sense of well-being.

Reflexology is a form of massage based on the belief that different areas of the feet relate to parts of the body.

Homeopathy uses minute amounts of natural remedies to stimulate the body's own healing powers.

Traditional Chinese medicine offers herbal treatments, acupuncture and acupressure. Using needles or massage techniques, the energy points in the body are stimulated to create or restore balance, harmony and health.

Herbal medicine uses whole plants as remedies and concentrates on the health of the whole person.

Creative visualization requires you to visualize cancer cells being zapped and dying, and the immune system creating healthy cells and tissue.

In spiritual healing, the healer's hands are gently laid on you or held near you. The body is made well through visualization and prayer.

Yoga offers a simpler approach to living, through proper exercise, breathing, relaxing, eating, positive thinking and meditation.

Oriental forms of exercise have been shown to be good for dealing with cancer. In the East millions of people rise at dawn to practise T'ai Chi, which is seen as essential therapy for health and a long life.

Do-In is a Japanese form of self-massage, which stimulates the body's acupressure points and increases the flow of energy in the body.

RELAXATION AND MEDITATION

Create your own sanctuary of inner peace. Find a comfortable spot in quiet surroundings and choose a regular time to sit there quietly each day for at least ten minutes. Listen to your breathing and still your mind of restless thoughts. It may help to calm your thoughts by playing some soothing music.

Imagine your body being filled with peaceful, white light that washes away your worries and pains. Concentrate on relaxing your muscles in turn, from toes to head. Return to this calm place inside yourself whenever you need to.

Above: Help to eliminate toxins from the body and bring greater vitality and inner peace through relaxation and meditation.

EATING FOR A
HEALTHY HEART

Simple changes to eating habits, such as eating less salt and fat,

eating plenty of fruit, vegetables and meals rich in starchy

foods such as pasta, rice and potatoes, can make a considerable

difference to the health of your heart. This chapter offers a range

of practical tips on choosing the right foods, meal planning

and healthy cooking techniques.

INTRODUCTION

Making simple changes to your diet and your lifestyle can help to reduce the risk of CHD (coronary heart disease). There are three main things you can do to improve your way of life: you can become more active – take 30 minutes moderate exercise five times a week; you can give up smoking – see your general practitioner or call one of the numerous helplines for advice; and you can learn to cope with stress. If you also improve your diet, you will enhance these changes and in addition will help to control the other major risk factors of CHD, which are raised blood cholesterol, raised blood pressure and carrying too much body weight or being obese.

Eating for a healthy heart isn't difficult. As a first step, you should eat at least five portions of vegetables and/or fruit a day, and make sure that at least half your meals consist of starchy carbohydrate foods such as bread, pasta, rice and potatoes, without too much fat. Even simple changes to eating habits can make a considerable difference. Cooking your own food puts you in control and makes it easy to limit the amount of fat (particularly saturated fat), salt and sugar you consume. The recipes in this book prove just how delicious a well-balanced diet can be, and there are numerous techniques and suggestions for eliminating the less desirable elements in your food while retaining – and even enhancing – the flavour. So, change to a healthier lifestyle and follow the food recommendations in this book, then relax and enjoy life – it'll do your heart good.

Above: To maintain a healthy diet you should eat at least five portions of fruit or vegetables daily.

EATING A HEALTHY DIET

Eat a good variety of different foods every day to make sure you get all the nutrients you need.

- Skimmed milk contains the same amount of calcium, protein and B vitamins as whole milk, but a fraction of the fat.
- Natural low-fat yogurt, cottage cheese and fromage frais are all high in calcium and protein, and are good substitutes for cream.
- Starchy foods such as rice, bread, potatoes, cereals, pulses and pasta should be eaten at every meal. These foods provide energy and some vitamins, minerals and dietary fibre.
- Vegetables, salads and fruits should form a major part of the diet; about 450g/1lb should be eaten each day.
- Eat meat in moderation but eat plenty of fish, particularly oily fish such as trout, mackerel, salmon, tuna, herring and sardines.

A few simple changes to a normal diet can reduce fat intake considerably.

The following tips and suggestions are designed to make the change to a healthier diet as easy as possible.

MEAT AND POULTRY

Red meats such as lamb, pork and beef are high in saturated fats, but chicken and turkey contain far less fat. Remove the skin before cooking and trim off any visible fat. Avoid sausages, burgers, pâtés, bacon and minced beef. Buy lean cuts of meat and skim any fat from the surface of stocks and stews.

DAIRY PRODUCTS

Replace whole milk with skimmed or semi-skimmed milk and use low-fat yogurt, low-fat crème fraîche or fromage frais instead of cream. Eat cream, cream cheese and hard cheese in moderation. There are reduced-fat cheeses on the market with 14 per cent fat content which is half the fat content of full-fat cheese. Use these wherever possible.

SPREADS, OILS AND DRESSINGS

Use butter, margarine and low-fat spreads sparingly. Try to avoid using fat and oil for cooking. If you have to use oil, choose olive, corn, sunflower, soya, rapeseed and peanut oils, which are low in saturates. Look out for oil-free dressings and reduced-fat mayonnaise.

HIDDEN FATS

Biscuits, cakes, pastries, snacks, processed meals and curries all contain high proportions of fat. Get into the habit of reading food labels carefully and looking for a low-fat option.

COOKING METHODS

Grill, poach and steam foods whenever possible. If you do fry foods, use as little fat as possible and pat off the excess after browning, with kitchen paper. Make sauces and stews by first cooking the onions and garlic in a small quantity of stock, rather than frying in oil.

Above: Choose a variety of foods from the main food groups to ensure you have all the nutrients your body needs.

EATING LESS SALT

One of the steps you can take to reduce your risk of coronary heart disease is to cut down on the amount of salt you eat. Excessive salt intake can be linked to high blood pressure and is one of the main reasons why blood pressure tends to rise as people get older. (Other risk factors include low potassium intake and being overweight.)

Salt, together with potassium, is essential for a variety of bodily functions, but people tend to have far too much of it, largely through the consumption of processed foods. Canned, pre-packaged or so-called "convenience" foods, takeaways and ready-prepared meals, contribute as much as 80 per cent of the salt in your diet, so preparing and cooking more of your own food is an excellent way of reducing our daily intake to the recommended 6 grammes.

Eating more non-processed foods – such as fresh vegetables, fruit, fish and meat – will have an added bonus in boosting your potassium levels.

Although cutting down on the amount of salt used during cooking and at the table is not enough on its own, it is a valuable step in helping to re-educate your tastebuds. The more salt you have, the more you want.

Gradually reduce the amount added to your food and what used to taste delicious soon seems excessively salty.

It's also a good idea to note which foods are high in salt and keep a check on how many of these you eat.

CUTTING DOWN

People often add salt out of habit; the following are some tips to help you cut down:

- Taste food before you shake on salt – and then use it only sparingly.
- Block up some of the holes in the salt cellar.
- Better still, do not add any kind of salt, including most salt substitutes, to your food, either when cooking or to the finished dish at the table.
- Replace salt in recipes with herbs and spices, garlic and lemon juice, mustard or chilli powder. A small quantity of wine or beer can also be added for extra flavour.
- Use fresh or frozen vegetables instead of canned.
- Chinese food in particular tends to be high in MSG (monosodium glutamate) and salt, so enjoy it as an occasional treat, or make your own.
- Cook with a stock made from celery, onion, carrot and bouquet garni instead of stock cubes.
- Swap to lower-salt breads. Most bread contains 2 per cent salt, but read the labels. "Healthy eating" brands of bread can contain as little as 0.8 per cent salt and some health-food stores sell bread baked with no added salt.

LOW-SALT VEGETABLE STOCK

This is an excellent way of making good use of any leftover vegetables and will produce a healthy, full-flavoured stock.

INGREDIENTS

Makes 1.75 litres/3 pints/7½ cups
1 onion
2 carrots
2 large celery sticks, plus any small amounts from the following: leek, celeriac, parsnip, turnip, courgette, cabbage or cauliflower trimmings, mushroom peelings
30ml/2 tbsp vegetable oil
bouquet garni
6 black peppercorns

2 Heat the oil in a large pan and fry the vegetables until soft and lightly browned. Add the remaining ingredients and cover them with 1.75 litres/3 pints/7½ cups water.

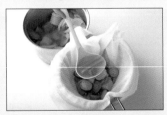

3 Bring to the boil, skim the surface then partially cover and simmer for 1½ hours. Strain the stock and allow to cool. Store in a covered container in the fridge for 2–3 days.

1 Peel the onion and then quarter it. Chop all the vegetables into large pieces.

EATING LESS FAT

Another essential factor in the healthy diet is to reduce the amount of fat you eat, particularly the amount of saturated fat. This lowers your blood cholesterol levels, which, in turn, reduces the risk of CHD (coronary heart disease). At the moment 15–16 per cent of the calories most people eat are from saturated fat. It is recommended that this is reduced to no more than 10 per cent.

WHERE DO SATURATED FATS COME FROM?

As a general rule, saturated fats are solid at room temperature. The list includes lard, butter, hard cheese and the visible fat on meat. Saturated fats can also be "hidden" in products such as pork pies, cakes, biscuits, ice cream, pastry and chocolate. The major sources of saturated fats are full-fat dairy products (milk, cheese, cream), followed by fatty meat products (pies, pasties, sausages).

HOW MUCH FAT?

It is not a good idea to eliminate fat from your diet entirely. Limited amounts of some fats are essential for good health. The ideal is no more than three portions of fat per day. A portion equals:
- 5ml/1 tsp butter, margarine or cooking oil.
- 10ml/2 tsp low-fat spread.
- 5ml/1 tsp salad dressing or mayonnaise.

It is highly preferable to choose polyunsaturated fats, such as those found in vegetable oils, spreads or margarines labelled as being high in polyunsaturates, and oily fish. Meat is a valuable source of protein, iron, B vitamins and minerals, while dairy foods contribute calcium, protein, B vitamins and vitamins A and D. To continue to benefit from these important nutrients, choose lean meat and low-fat dairy products where possible and eat in moderation. Most people will come to no harm if they eat the occasional high-fat food, but as a general rule, it is wise to be wary of cream, cream-based desserts, chocolate, pastries, cakes, biscuits, ice cream, confectionery, crisps, rich sauces and gravies, fatty bacon, sausages and other meat products.

LOW-FAT SWAPS

Make low-fat substitutes wherever possible, such as:
- Skimmed or semi-skimmed milk for full-fat milk.
- Low-fat yogurt for full-fat varieties.
- Small amounts of lean meat for fatty meat products, e.g. sausages, sausage rolls, pâtés, luncheon meats, meat pies and pasties.
- Swap two meat meals a week with fish, especially oily fish (such as sardines, pilchards, herring, mackerel and salmon), which provide "omega 3" fatty acids. These fatty acids help to reduce blood viscosity, making it less likely to clot.

Above: Eat a variety of white and oily fish, such as tuna, plaice, salmon, trout and mackerel.

HIGH-FIBRE FOODS

People who eat a diet rich in fibre tend to have lower blood cholesterol levels and are at a lower risk of CHD (coronary heart diseaase) than those whose diet consists largely of refined foods. High-fibre foods are also filling, which can be an asset when it comes to weight control. There are many types of fibre, but one in particular, soluble fibre, seems to be beneficial in binding cholesterol and preventing it from being deposited in the arteries.

SOURCES OF FIBRE

Foods high in soluble fibre include oats; beans and peas; apples and oranges; and green leafy vegetables, such as cabbage and spinach. To be effective sources of fibre, these vegetables need to be cooked and eaten without additional fats, so do not fry them or smother vegetables with butter or fatty sauces.

The best high-fibre foods are those in which the fibre occurs naturally, such as cereals, vegetables and fruit. These foods are also rich in the protective antioxidant vitamin betacarotene, vitamins C and E and the minerals zinc, selenium, manganese and copper. Antioxidants are substances that delay or prevent oxidation, which is the process by which oxygen combines with other substances. A by-product of oxidation is the production of free radicals. Free radicals in a living organism can be extremely harmful.

One of their effects is to damage artery walls, allowing cholesterol to be deposited and thus increasing the risk of heart disease. We cannot avoid encountering free radicals because we breathe oxygen and pollutants, such as cigarette smoke and chemicals, but we can limit their effect.

EATING MORE FIBRE

The easiest way to boost your fibre intake is to:
- Eat plenty of bread, pasta, rice and potatoes. Choose wholemeal bread and pasta, and brown rice.

- Instead of buying biscuits and cakes, which can be high in sugar, salt and fats, bake wholemeal scones, muffins or buns. Serve them plain or with a mere scraping of low-fat spread.
- Enjoy plenty of breakfast cereal (with low-fat milk and no sugar) but choose wholegrain varieties with little or no added sugar, such as shredded wheat, puffed wheat, porridge oats and muesli. Avoid sugar-coated cereals.
- Use more pulses (beans, peas, lentils, split peas) either alone or to replace some of the meat in dishes such as cottage pie, shepherd's pie, curry,

pasta sauces or chilli con carne. Make frequent use of canned beans, including baked beans.
- Eat at least five portions of vegetables and/or fruit every day.

AVOID BRAN

Bran added to refined food is not as good for you as starchy foods, vegetables and fruits. Too much raw bran can bind minerals, making them unavailable to the body. Bran may conquer constipation, but it does not share the cholesterol-lowering effect of other fibres that are found in starchy foods, fresh vegetables and fruits.

Above: Bread, pasta, rice and muesli are all good sources of fibre.

CHOLESTEROL

Cholesterol is a waxy substance that occurs naturally in the body, when it is referred to as blood cholesterol. It is also present in foods of animal origin (dietary cholesterol). The higher the level of cholesterol in the blood, the greater the risk of heart disease. Some cholesterol is essential for functions such as the making of cell membranes, and the body usually maintains a balance, making more if needed. However, if the blood contains too much cholesterol, this can cause many problems.

GOOD AND BAD CHOLESTEROL

There are two main types of blood cholesterol. The "good" type is HDL (high density lipoprotein), which carries excess cholesterol to the liver for removal from the body. The "bad" type is LDL (low density lipoprotein), which deposits cholesterol on the artery walls. Adequate amounts of HDL lower the risk of coronary heart disease, but excessive amounts of LDL raise the risk.

At one time, it was thought that cholesterol-rich foods were largely responsible for high blood cholesterol levels, but it is now known that the amount of cholesterol we eat is not as significant as our intake of fats. Saturated fats are, once again, the villains of the piece, leading to increased levels of LDL.

WHERE IS CHOLESTEROL FOUND?

Although the link between dietary cholesterol and blood cholesterol is disputed, it can be useful to know which foods are cholesterol-rich. Dietary cholesterol is found only in animal foods: the richest sources are liver, shellfish and eggs. The general advice is to eat no more than four eggs a week. If you like mussels, prawns, shrimps and other shellfish (which, although high in cholesterol, are low in fat), eat them in moderation. Grill, barbecue or cook shellfish in paella and

risotto. Serve them, Asian-style in thin broth, but not in creamy French seafood dishes.

High levels of cholesterol are also found in fatty meat, high-fat cheeses and full-fat milk, but as we have seen, eating for a healthy heart limits these foods anyway. They do not have to be given up completely, just eaten in sensible proportions.

READ THE LABELS

Nutritional labels state how much fat a food contains. Some even state what percentage is saturated but very few labels give information on cholesterol.

Above: Make plenty of salads and cooked vegetable dishes and avoid adding too much fat to your diet.

If there is no statistical data on the label, ingredients are usually listed in descending order by weight. Common names for saturated fat on food labels include hydrogenated vegetable oil or fat; palm oil; coconut oil; cocoa butter; shortening (solid vegetable fat); animal fat; milk solids and non-milk fat. If any of these names appears high up the list of ingredients, the food is likely to be high in saturated fat.

LIFE IS FOR LIVING

People who exercise regularly have lower levels of CHD (coronary heart disease), and those with CHD who exercise are less likely to die as a result of the disease. Most people need to take more exercise but how much is enough? Taking positive action to stop smoking and to lower your stress levels is also an excellent way of leading a healthier lifestyle, while alcohol needs to be treated with caution.

HOW MUCH PHYSICAL ACTIVITY SHOULD YOU DO?

Until recently 20 minutes of vigorous aerobic exercise three times a week was the prescription for preventing CHD. New research, however, shows that even moderate amounts of less intense exercise can be beneficial. Because many people are so sedentary, even getting out of the chair and taking some exercise for half an hour, once or twice a week, can have a positive effect. Regular exercise – say about 30 minutes of moderate intensity for five days out of seven – has substantial benefits. Exercise of moderate intensity makes you breathe slightly harder. Your heart rate will be slightly raised, so you will feel warmer, but you will not be out of breath.

MODERATE INTENSITY ACTIVITY

Aerobic capacity varies between individuals, but examples of moderate intensity activity include brisk walking (6–7 kph/4 mph); heavy do-it-yourself work in the home; gardening (such as raking leaves or using a power mower); washing the car; doing strenuous housework and lifting or carrying heavy loads. Golf, table tennis, social dancing and keep-fit (all at an intensity that makes you breathe hard and sweat a little) are also worthwhile, as are slow stair climbing, cycling at more than 16 kph/10 mph, gentle swimming, playing doubles tennis and doing low-intensity aerobic exercises.

SMOKING

Many doctors consider smoking to be the biggest risk factor when it comes to CHD, with the risk increasing relative to the number of years someone has smoked and how many cigarettes have been smoked. The harmful effects are linked to carbon monoxide in the smoke (which decreases the flow of oxygen to the heart) and nicotine (which makes the heart work harder). In a person with CHD this may cause disturbances in heart rhythm. Both nicotine and carbon monoxide increase the tendency for blood to clot. Free radicals in smoke also increase damage to the artery walls, making it easier for cholesterol to be deposited.

STRESS

Despite the popular view that top grade executives with high levels of responsibility are most likely to suffer stress, current research suggests that it is often the lower grade workers whose jobs make high demands but who have low control over their work (and lives) who suffer more CHD. Research continues into stress and heart disease. Meanwhile it seems that good relaxation techniques, job satisfaction and leisure-time physical activity help us to cope with stress and probably reduce the risk of CHD.

ALCOHOL

Light and moderate drinkers appear to have a lower death rate from CHD than either non-drinkers or heavy drinkers. Light to moderate means 1–3 units a day, or not more than 21 per week for women/28 for men; possibly up to 28 a week for post-menopausal women. Protection may be the result of alcohol raising levels of HDL cholesterol in the blood. Another factor may be the antioxidant properties of some drinks, mainly red wine. If you are a light to moderate drinker, the advice seems to be that it is reasonable to continue, provided you have your doctor's blessing, but the other risks associated with alcohol outweigh any advice to start drinking or to increase the amount of alcohol you drink. Remember, however, that alcohol is very fattening.

Above: Regular exercise, such as golf, swimming, walking or cycling has substantial benefits.

MEAL PLANNING

If all your meals contain generous portions of fresh vegetables, fruit and starchy foods, together with small portions of dairy food or meat, fish and vegetarian alternatives, you cannot go too far wrong. Essentially, eating for a healthy heart means:

- Cutting down on foods that contain a lot of fat, and saturated fat in particular, such as dairy products, meat products, cakes, biscuits, fatty snacks and confectionery, especially chocolate.
- Switching to low-fat dairy produce, cooking with lean meat, avoiding meat pies or pasties, and eating plenty of fish, lean poultry, beans and pulses.
- Using limited amounts of low-fat spreads and oils in cooking, instead of saturated fats.

SAMPLE MENUS

Breakfast

Choose one of the following:
- Wholemeal toast with a thin scraping of low-fat spread and preserve.
- Wholegrain cereal with skimmed milk (add fresh or dried fruit).
- Fruit (fresh or dried fruit compote) and low-fat natural yogurt.
- Poached egg or fish, or boiled egg with wholemeal toast.
- Wholemeal bun or muffin.
- Porridge with skimmed milk.

Lunch

Try one of the following ideas:
- Wholemeal sandwiches or rolls with a small amount of lean meat, fish or cheese and lots of salad.
- Vegetable-based soup with a wholemeal roll.
- Rice or pasta salad.
- A baked potato with a large mixed salad and a small amount of lean meat or cheese.
- Baked beans on toast.

Main Meal

Try one of these suggestions:
- Hearty soup, such as minestrone or a vegetable broth.
- Wholemeal pasta or risotto with vegetable-based sauce.
- Grilled fish or meat plus vegetables and/or salad.
- A baked potato with lean minced beef or pork chilli con carne (or vegetarian equivalent).
- A stir-fry made with a small amount of lean meat or fish with plenty of vegetables and using polyunsaturated oil, served with rice.
- Vegetable and pulse or pasta casserole with wholemeal cobbler or potato topping.
- A vegetable gratin made with a small amount of cheese.

Desserts

Use desserts to add more fruit and low-fat dairy produce to your diet. The following provide essential nutrients without excessive amounts of fat:
- Fresh fruit; fruit salad with yogurt or low-fat frozen yogurt (occasionally with ice cream).
- Canned fruit salad in fruit juice; dried fruit compôte.
- Bread and butter pudding or rice pudding (made with low-fat milk and added fruit).
- Wholemeal pancakes filled with fresh fruit purée.
- Home-made fruit crumble.
- Real fruit jelly, fresh fruit fool made with reduced-fat cream or yogurt or low-fat custard.
- Fruit brûlée made with low-fat yogurt instead of cream.
- Sorbet.

HEALTHY COOKING TECHNIQUES

The aims of cooking for a healthy heart are to avoid adding fat to food, to reduce the saturated fat content of the ingredients where possible, to use techniques that retain the vitamins and minerals and to ensure that the food is delicious by preserving or enhancing its flavour, colour and texture.

STIR-FRYING

This method means that food cooks quickly to retain maximum nutritional value, colour and texture.

Marinate slivers of meat before cooking, to tenderize them and add flavour. Try combining the following: soy sauce, lemon or other fruit juice, tomato purée and vinegar.

Meat and/or vegetables need to be cut into small pieces, so that they cook quickly and evenly.

1 Always heat the wok or frying pan for a minute or so before adding the oil or any other ingredients.

2 Cut the meat and/or vegetables into thin slivers to minimize the cooking time. When adding the first ingredients, quickly reduce the heat a little. This will ensure that they are not overcooked or burnt by the time the other ingredients are added.

3 Once all the ingredients have been added, quickly increase the heat to allow the dish to cook in the least possible time. This will allow the ingredients to retain a crisp texture and prevent them from absorbing too much oil. Be careful not to burn the ingredients. Use a wooden spoon or non-stick slotted spoon to turn the ingredients as you stir-fry.

STEAMING

Food is cooked over boiling liquid (usually water) but it does not touch the liquid. As a result most of the vitamins and minerals are retained. Browning is not part of the process, so fat need never be added.

Steaming preserves the texture of foods and is a good cooking method for those who prefer their vegetables with a bit of bite. It is also very useful for fish, poultry and puddings.

- Prepare ingredients as for stir-frying. Expandable steamers will fit a range of saucepan sizes. Put food straight into the steamer and cover.
- If using a bamboo steamer over either a wok or pan of boiling liquid, place the food in a bowl first, then cover.

MICROWAVING

This is a quick and useful way of cooking vegetables, fruit and fish. Naturally moist foods are cooked without additional liquid, and only a small amount of liquid is added to other foods. As a result, vitamins and minerals do not leach out into cooking water which is then thrown away. Fat is not required for cooking, and microwaved food can be seasoned with fresh chopped herbs instead of salt. The flavour can be sharpened by adding a little lemon juice.

- Place food in a microwave-proof dish, or wrap in a paper parcel. Refer to the manufacturer's handbook for information on power levels and cooking times.

Above: Microwaved jacket potatoes can be cooked in a fraction of the time necessary for a conventional oven.

CASSEROLING

One-pot meals are good for stress-free entertaining and are easy to prepare. They are not necessarily the heavy dishes you may imagine: some are light and fresh, using vegetables according to the season. They also have the advantage that vitamins and minerals are retained in the stock, which is served alongside the other ingredients, and are a delicious way of adding more fibre to your diet if you include pasta, grains and rice. Use only the minimum amount of fat for cooking and make the casserole a day ahead, then cool and chill it. Any fat will solidify on the surface and can easily be lifted off before the casserole is reheated.

PRESSURE COOKING

This method cuts cooking time dramatically, which encourages the frequent consumption of beneficial low-fat foods (brown rice cooks in 7 minutes, and potatoes cook in 6). Like steaming, pressure cooking retains more nutrients because the food is not in contact with the cooking water.

GRILLING

There's no need to add fat when grilling meat, fish or vegetables. Use a rack and any fat that runs from the meat can easily be drained. Brush the rack with oil before cooking to prevent the food from sticking. Cook under a preheated grill and baste with lemon juice, if necessary.

POACHING

This is an excellent way of cooking delicate white fish (plaice) or whole oily fish (mackerel, salmon, trout). Fish steaks, particularly cod, halibut, salmon and tuna also cook well by either method and there is no need to add any fat.
- Poaching can be done either in the oven or on top of the cooker.

1 Trim visible fat from meat or remove skin from poultry.

2 Skim off all excess fat from the surface before reheating the dish.

- To oven-poach fish, pour in boiling liquid to barely cover the fish, add any flavourings and cover with buttered greaseproof paper. Cook in a preheated oven at 180°C/ 350°F/Gas 4.

- To poach on top of the cooker, suspend the fish in the poaching liquid, either in a muslin hammock or on a rack. Cover with liquid, bring to the boil and allow to simmer gently until cooked.

Above: Cook fish or meat on a rack so any excess fat drains away.

EQUIPMENT

There are various pieces of equipment that will help you to prepare food with a minimum amount of fat. Some do not need you to add any fat at all, others allow the fat to drain away.

STEAMERS

These may be oval or round and consist of two pans: a lower one, which holds the boiling water or stock, and a perforated upper pan, which holds the food. Steam enters via the holes, and is trapped by a lid on the top pan. Metal steaming baskets that stand inside a saucepan are suitable for steaming small quantities of food. A metal colander sitting inside a saucepan can also be used as a steamer; find a saucepan lid which will fit on top, or make a lid

from foil to cover. Bamboo steamers come in a range of sizes with multiple layers and will fit either over a saucepan or inside a wok. There are now electrical appliance steamers which are quick and efficient.

ROASTING GADGETS

Placing meat on a trivet or a rack in a roasting tin will allow any excess fat to drain away from the meat. Do not add fat. Cover the meat with aluminium foil if necessary to prevent it from drying out. Chicken roasters hold the chicken so that it stands upright in the roasting tin. This is a very efficient way of draining the fat while retaining all the taste and flavour of the chicken, keeping it moist at the same time.

PASTRY BRUSHES

These inexpensive items are useful for brushing pans and baking tins with a minimal amount of oil.

WOK

This is the perfect utensil for stir-frying. Thanks to its spherical shape, the heat spreads from the base upwards so all the ingredients receive an equal amount of heat. A new wok should be seasoned before it is first used. Wash and dry it thoroughly. Heat the dry wok, remove it from the heat and rub a little oil and salt on to the surface. Return it to a high heat, until the oil burns off. Allow to cool, wipe and use. It should not be necessary to wash the wok again, just wipe it clean after use.

BARBECUE GRILL BASKETS

These allow food to be held securely when placed over the hot coals, at the same time allowing fat to drain away. Non-stick versions are available from most department stores.

NON-STICK PANS

Good quality non-stick frying pans, saucepans and grill pans allow food to be cooked by any method, even frying, without additional fat. Food can also be sweated or sautéed with the minimal amount of added fat. Pans with ribbed bases allow any fat that drains from meat to be poured away. Heavy-based cast-iron pans of good quality also allow cooking on the hob without added fat.

GRAVY SEPARATOR

Available as a glass or plastic jug or ceramic "boat", this item has a low-set spout that takes gravy from the bottom of the jug and avoids the fat floating on the surface of the gravy when pouring.

MOULI OR BLENDER

Use one of these handy appliances to purée vegetables in order to thicken sauces instead of adding a roux, cornflour or eggs. They are also excellent for thickening and lightly blending soups.

BULB BASTER

This works like a syringe when the bulb at the top is squeezed, sucking up fat from the roasting tin.

Although conventionally used as a means of basting a roast with fat, in the hands of a health-conscious cook the utensil proves ideal for skimming fat from soups, sauces and casseroles.

Above: Choose non-stick heavy-based pans, sturdy insulated handles and tight-fitting lids.

Left: Bamboo steamers.

Right: Various styles of woks and pans.

FOLLOWING A
LOW-SALT DIET

Salt is important both for the healthy functioning of the body and as

an excellent way to preserve food. However, in the Western World the

average daily intake of salt is five to ten times more than is necessary

and research has shown that this can be detrimental to good health.

This chapter provides all the essential information, from the effects of

too much salt, to advice on how to follow a low-salt diet.

INTRODUCTION

It may seem difficult to believe that salt, which is now so cheap and so universally available, was once a rare and highly prized mineral. But so it was – just think of expressions such as "worth his salt" or "the salt of the earth". And there was good reason for valuing salt so highly. Salt was, and still is, crucial to the successful functioning of human society for two main reasons. The first is that it is vital to the healthy functioning of the body, although the amount needed to make the body function efficiently is tiny compared to the amount that most of us actually eat, and the second is that, until recent times, salting was one of the very few ways in which food could be successfully preserved. We now know, however, that salt is not such a benign presence in our lives.

WHAT IS SALT?

Salt, or sodium chloride, to give it its chemical name, is a mineral made up of approximately 40 per cent sodium and 60 per cent chloride. Depending on where the salt comes from, it may also include around 1 per cent of other trace minerals.

Salt does occur naturally in foods – mainly in meat and fish – but in much smaller quantities than the amount that we normally consume. A few vegetables, such as celery, beetroot, spinach and watercress, also contain salt, but the majority of vegetables and cereals are virtually salt free. The ones that do contain salt carry it in an organic form, which means that it is contained in a living organism – the vegetable – rather than in an inorganic, or pure mineral, form. The organic form is thought to be more easily and more usefully assimilated by the body.

All the salt that we eat came originally from the sea. On average a litre of sea water contains around 25g/1oz salt, which means that the oceans provide us with a bottomless reservoir of salt. However, the vast majority of the salt in commercial use, rock salt, is mined from the beds of ancient seas, now far inland, which have long since drained away. Sea salt is gathered from coastal deposits – and, in some cases, evaporated from the sea itself.

Above: Sea salt (left) and rock salt. Both are obtainable for culinary use, but sea salt is less widely available.

FOOD PRESERVATION

Salt has the ability to draw water or liquid out of any matter – or foodstuff – to which it is applied. This property inhibits bacterial growth within food, as long as it remains in contact with the salt.

This discovery was the first crucial step in food preservation. In the days before freezers, cans and vacuum packs, this was an enormously important and significant discovery. It meant that food could be preserved from the season of plenty and growth to the season of want. Meat and fish, for example, could be preserved over the winter, thus ensuring communities a regular supply of food throughout the year. It also meant that human beings could travel more freely and widely, as they could now carry preserved food stocks with them, in case no food was found as they moved.

Left: Foods such as meat and fish, and a few vegetables, such as spinach, celery and watercress, naturally contain salt.

This was to be of huge significance right up until the 20th century, especially for sea travel.

Using large quantities of salt to preserve food did however, have the gastronomic disadvantage that most foods tasted very salty. Lengthy cooking was often needed to try to reduce food's saltiness. Salt cod, for example, might need to be boiled for 12 hours just to render it edible. Even so, people's tastebuds became so accustomed to salted foods that low-salt or saltless foods tasted bland – thus encouraging the use of added salt as a seasoning even in foods that had not been salted for preservation.

A Valuable Commodity

The ability of salt to purify and to preserve quickly turned it into a valuable commodity, both financially and spiritually. Throughout the ancient world, salt rapidly became the single most important traded commodity. The wealth of cities such as Venice was built on their salt trade, while salt trading routes criss-crossed Europe and the East.

Salt acquired a "purifying" significance in religions across the world. The ancient Greeks believed salt to be the gift of the gods; the Romans offered it on their altars with incense; and the Hebrews sprinkled every offering to God with salt.

Salt was also a symbol of hospitality and a measure of wealth. Rents were paid in salt, taxes were levied in salt. Indeed, the *gabelle*, or salt tax, was said to be the final straw that sparked off the French Revolution.

From the earliest times, craftsmen laboured to create salt cellars or salt containers from gold, silver and precious stones, which celebrated both the value of the salt itself – and the wealth of its owner.

Right: Equipment for traditional pie- and jam-making laid out on the table, including a remarkably large pillar of salt.

The Pre-history of Salt

Our prehistoric ancestors (the hunter gatherers) lived on a mainly animal diet, so they would easily have absorbed the 2.5g/⅒oz salt (1g/⅕oz sodium) that they needed daily from the meat they ate. Today, the Inuits – who live almost entirely on fish – continue to obtain necessary amounts of salt from the fish and the Bedouins obtain their salt from drinking large quantities of milk.

Around 4000 BC, Neolithic people began to settle in one place and learned how to grow and cook food. Their diet changed to include more vegetables and cereals, both of which carry small to negligible amounts of salt. At more or less the same time, they invented cooking pots that were strong enough to allow them to boil food in water – which is a far more convenient way to cook than roasting, but which leaches the salt out of the food into the water. All of a sudden, their diet became virtually saltless and for reasons of both health and flavour, they needed to replace that salt.

The earliest known salt mines dating from this Neolithic period are in Hallstatt near Salzburg (meaning salt city) in Austria, although there are over a dozen other Neolithic salt mines in Europe, plus a further four sites where salt was extracted from the sea.

THE ROLE OF SALT IN GOOD HEALTH

The human body is over 60 per cent water. This fluid is to be found in the blood, the lymphatic system and the cells of the body. Sodium, together with chloride, potassium and phosphate, control the amount of fluid within and outside the cells of the body, keeping them evenly balanced. Maintaining this balance is absolutely essential to the body's proper functioning.

DIETARY FACTORS: TOO MUCH SODIUM

It is estimated that the average person, in average conditions, requires less than 1g/⅟₂₅oz sodium (which equals around 2.5g/⅟₁₀oz salt) per day for proper bodily function. Yet in the Western World current research estimates that the average person eats 10–15g/⅓–⅗oz salt (4–6g/½–¼oz sodium) a day – which is between five and ten times more than they need.

Unlike in the case of, say, vitamin C, we do not excrete the salt we do not need, so any excess gets absorbed into our body fluids. If excess sodium appears in the blood, in order to reduce its sodium concentration to normal, water will be drawn out of cells into the blood to dilute it. If yet more salt is eaten (and consequently, more sodium is deposited in the blood), the body will crave more fluid to dilute the excess of sodium – in other words, you will get thirsty.

This will cause you to carry excess fluid – up to several litres, which will put a strain on the vascular system and the heart. This is a common cause of high blood pressure.

TOO LITTLE SODIUM

Insufficient sodium, although rare, is just as dangerous as excess sodium and it will also unbalance the body's systems. Symptoms include cramps and aching muscles, lassitude, anorexia, vomiting and mental confusion.

Shortage of sodium will normally only affect those who sweat a great deal, as they excrete sodium along with their sweat. This may be because of continuous exercise, for example, or due to heavy manual labour, or because people are living in a climate to which they are not adapted, as with white-skinned northerners living in the tropics. In either case, they may need to take extra salt to replace the sodium lost in their sweat.

POTASSIUM

Potassium is one of the other vital minerals needed by the body to maintain its fluid balance and there is a good deal of evidence to suggest that high-sodium diets result in an excess loss of potassium. There is also evidence to suggest that the high blood pressure associated with excess sodium intake can sometimes be reduced by an increased consumption of potassium, which is easily available from fruits and vegetables. This may explain, at least in part, why many vegetarians, with their higher intake of potassium-rich fruits and vegetables, such as avocado, bananas and nuts, are less likely to have high blood pressure.

Extra potassium can also be obtained by using a high-potassium salt alternative, now readily available.

Left: Shortage of sodium (found in salt) is usually a problem only for people who exercise strenuously for long periods.

Left: A diet containing fruit, vegetables and unsalted nuts will be rich in potassium.

CORONARY HEART DISEASE

High blood pressure is also closely related to our chances of suffering from coronary heart disease. This happens when the arteries taking blood to and from the heart get clogged with cholesterol deposits, making it difficult for the heart to pump the blood through them.

Although the level of fat in the diet and the blood, and the blood's natural "stickiness" or tendency to clot are also relevant in this process, high blood pressure is recognized to be an important contributory factor. Since nearly 30 per cent of deaths in the Western world are caused by coronary heart disease, all factors are important.

OSTEOPOROSIS

There is now a good deal of evidence to suggest that a high intake of salt/ sodium causes the body to excrete calcium from the bones through the urine. This calcium loss reduces bone density which, if it goes on for long enough, will lead to osteoporosis, loss of height and mobility, and possibly complex fractures. Apart from the suffering and medical expense involved, such fractures in the elderly can often lead to fatal complications.

CANCER

There is some evidence to connect an excessive intake of sodium with cancer of the stomach and of the naso pharynx. Although this evidence is not conclusive, the World Cancer Research Fund – which recently conducted a massive review of cancer research and made wide-ranging dietary recommendations – has suggested that salt consumption should be limited to a maximum of 6g/¼oz salt (2.4g/⅒oz sodium) per day.

Some methods for treating cancer through diet forbid the addition of any salt as part of the therapy.

HIGH BLOOD PRESSURE

There is now a convincing body of scientific evidence to suggest that a higher intake of salt/sodium increases the amount of water in the body. This puts pressure on the veins and the ability of the heart to pump the blood through them, in turn causing the blood pressure to rise and the individual to suffer from high blood pressure, or hypertension.

This evidence also suggests that, in Western societies, the effect of excess salt/sodium is cumulative. In other words, the longer we continue eating too much salt (i.e. the older we get), the higher our blood pressure will get. Research shows that, in non-Western societies where people consume a diet that is lower in salt, blood pressure does not rise with age.

Although it could be argued that there are other lifestyle factors that might influence the health patterns of non-Western societies, the same relation of low-salt diet and low blood pressure can be seen in animals such as chimpanzees.

STROKE

By the late 19th century, salt consumption had reached a peak and it is estimated that the average person may have been eating as much as 20g/ ¾oz per day. Although exact records do not exist, apoplexy (or stroke) was one of the major causes of death at this time.

There is now a vast body of medical and scientific evidence to show that high blood pressure is the strongest predictive factor for a stroke. In other words, high blood pressure is the one physical condition which is more likely to make you have a stroke than any other.

Strokes account for around 10–12 per cent of all the deaths in the Western World. In addition to these fatal strokes, over 20 per cent of the Western population will suffer from non-fatal strokes, which nonetheless cause enormous suffering to those who are partially or totally paralysed, either physically or mentally, and huge financial and emotional costs to those caring for them.

WHY WE EAT SO MUCH SALT

The arrival of freezing and canning techniques means that we now need very little salt to preserve our food, so how is it that we are still consuming well over 10g/⅓oz more salt a day than we need? Have our tastebuds become so accustomed to salt that we are adding it to everything we eat in order to give it "flavour"? Or has the nature of our food changed so much that it provides us with this extra salt whether we wish it to or not? The answer is probably a bit of both.

THE IMPACT OF NEW TECHNOLOGIES ON SALT LEVELS IN FOOD

Thanks to massive advances in food technology since World War II, the vast majority of what the average person eats and drinks today in the Western World has already been processed. Even food that we see as relatively

Below: Salt is often added during the canning process, so always choose fresh products whenever possible.

"natural", such as fruit juices, has been processed in some way to preserve it or make it taste "better".

There is no doubt that many of the techniques used involve a liberal use of salt. This means that whether or not we add extra salt to the food we eat, we still often consume large quantities of it every day. Even when we cook for ourselves, many of the ingredients that we use may already have been manufactured and therefore contain relatively high levels of salt.

WHY DO MANUFACTURERS USE SO MUCH SALT?

The answer probably boils down to one word – money. Because of its abundance, salt is now a cheap commodity on the world food market. It is far cheaper as a seasoning than herbs or any other ingredients that can be used to give flavour to a dish.

Due to its hydroscopic qualities – its ability to draw water to itself – salt can also be used to add water to certain products, such as meat. If the meat is

high in salt, it can be injected with water, which, because of the nature of the salt, it will retain – thus making the meat heavier than it would otherwise be.

Excess salt makes people thirsty, which means that they need to drink more, which often means processed fizzy or packaged drinks. These are not infrequently made by the same company as the one that made the salty foods – so thirst is good for business, too.

Manufacturers claim that, since the food-buying public wants to buy food as economically as possible (most people see price rather than quality as the most important criterion when choosing food), it is their responsibility to make it as cheaply as possible. Using a cheap flavouring ingredient or using salt to increase the water content of some foods to increase bulk and make them cheaper, is therefore justifiable. It should also be said, however, that using cheap ingredients, or those that increase the weight of a product at very little expense to themselves, also allows manufacturers and processors to make larger profits on those foods.

Obviously, processing varies enormously but it is not unusual for the processed variety of a food to have up to 20 times more salt/sodium than the fresh variety – a canned vegetable

or fruit as opposed to a fresh one, for example; bread as opposed to flour, or bacon as opposed to pork.

Manufacturers are becoming aware of increasing concern over the salt/sodium content of their products, and some are already developing low-salt versions of certain dishes. Others are starting gradually to reduce the amount of salt that they use in products such as bread. However, there is still a long way to go, and anyone who is concerned about the amount of salt they eat should try to make themselves familiar with those manufactured foods that are likely to have the highest salt/sodium levels.

Left: Commercially produced sauces, such as soy, ketchup, barbecue and pastes, such as anchovy, can contain relatively large amounts of salt.

Above: Many everyday ingredients have high levels of "hidden" salt: for example, stock cubes, baking powder and hard and pre-sliced cheeses.

SOME KEY INGREDIENTS CONTAINING HIGH LEVELS OF SALT

- Stock cubes or bouillon.
- Baking powders, baking sodas and other chemical raising agents.
- Many commercial sauces, such as Worcestershire, anchovy, brown, soy, ketchup, etc.
- Spreads and salted butters.
- Canned meats and processed meats, such as bacon and ham.
- Canned fish.
- Canned vegetables.
- Breadcrumbs.
- Cheese, particularly pre-sliced cheese and many hard cheeses.

HIGH-SALT MANUFACTURED FOODS

When you are assessing how much salt there is in a dish, remember that the current recommendation is that the average person should eat no more than 6g/¼oz salt (2.4g/⅒oz sodium) per day. If you are on a specifically low-salt diet,

you will have been given an even lower target by your doctor. When considering your salt intake, you may be horrified to discover how many dishes will provide you with as much as 3g/⅛oz salt (half your daily allowance) in just one dish.

ASSESSING SALT LEVELS IN MANUFACTURED FOODS

Because the ingredients of individual dishes vary enormously, the list below is a guide only to manufactured or processed foods and dishes that you might expect to contain excess salt. You should always read the nutrition labels carefully to make quite sure that you know how much salt/sodium there is in that particular version.

Unfortunately, though, the labels won't always help you. A large number of the foods listed here, even when they do give a nutritional breakdown on the pack, do not include salt in that breakdown.

FOODS CONTAINING ADDED SALT

A surprising number of manufactured foods contain salt, the most common ones being listed below:
- Breakfast cereals.
- Breads, especially flavoured ones.
- Biscuits, both sweet and savoury.
- Salted butters and spreads.

- Hard cheeses, such as Cheddar, Cheshire, Parmesan and Pecorino, Gruyère, Gouda, Edam, Samsoe, Havarti and Jarlsberg.
- Soft cheeses, such as ricotta or mozzarella, should not have such a high salt content, though some of the manufactured cheese slices may have more than you expect.
- Savoury snacks, such as crisps, cheesy biscuits, salted crackers, Twiglets and salted nuts.

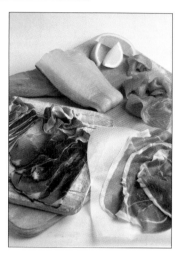

- Bacon and ham, Parma ham.
- All smoked meats.
- Ready meals, including both meat and vegetable dishes.
- Many ready-made pasta dishes, such as meat and vegetable lasagnes, cannelloni and macaroni cheese.
- Pizzas.

- Sandwiches – it may be difficult to tell how much salt is in a sandwich as the label will not usually detail all the ingredients of the bread or spread used, but you can usually assume that it will be high.
- Soups, whether canned, fresh, frozen or dried.
- All smoked fish.
- All ready-made fish dishes, which includes fish pies, fish pastes and pâtés, spreads such as taramasalata, and fish fingers and fish cakes.

- Pies of any kind, including pork, Cumberland, shepherd's pie, Cornish pasty.
- Burgers of any kind, either meat or vegetarian.
- Sausages, sausage rolls, salami.
- Ready-made flans and quiches.
- Takeaway Chinese meals with MSG (monosodium glutamate).
- Ready-made Indian meals.
- Canned vegetables, including baked beans.
- Salad dressings.
- Sauces, including ketchups and soy sauces.

- Commercial desserts and cakes.
- Even drinks can contain processing agents, which may be based on, or contain, sodium.

THE IMPORTANCE OF NUTRITIONAL LABELS

The most obvious way to reduce your intake of ready-made dishes is to cook for yourself – which is what the recipe section of this book is all about. Although cooking all your own food may be the ideal, most people will be only too glad to find a few ready-made dishes that they can still buy. To be able to do so with an easy mind, however, reading the nutritional tables is essential.

As the law stands at the moment, the manufacturers are required only to list the ingredients on the packaging of any product. These ingredients have to be listed in descending order of quantity. In other words, the ingredient of which there is the most has to appear first in the list and so on, down to the ingredient which appears in the smallest quantity. Unfortunately, however, manufacturers do not have to specify exactly how much of each ingredient is in the dish. Also unfortunately, the regulations only apply to the major ingredients in a dish, not to flavourings such as salt.

There is also something called the "25 per cent rule on compound ingredients". This means that if any part of a dish or a food makes up less than 25 per cent of the whole dish (like the dressing in a salad sandwich), the manufacturer does not have to give the ingredients of that part. In other words, you will not be able to tell from the label whether there is any salt in the dressing at all, let alone how much.

No product is currently required to carry a nutritional table, although many do – especially ready-made meals. If there is a nutritional table, you should be better informed. If it is a full table, it will give you the sodium content of both 100g/3¾oz of the food concerned and of a single portion.

This is not entirely ideal, as to learn the salt content of a dish requires some calculations. To find your salt intake, you have to multiply the sodium content by 2.5.

The reason why the table gives the sodium, rather than the salt, content of the food is that it is the sodium that is the active compound that raises blood pressure. This is not helpful, however, for the average shopper who thinks in terms of salt, not sodium. Consumer groups are pressing for the regulations governing salt/sodium declarations to be changed so that labels also include the relevant figure for salt to make the table easier to understand.

The chances are, however, that a large number of foods that you might wish to buy will use a "shorter" form of the nutritional table, which may not include a sodium declaration at all. In that case, if your salt intake is not too critical, you should use the guide on the left to avoid high-sodium foods. And if you are on a strict low-salt diet, you should avoid any ready-made food that does not give you details of its salt/sodium contents.

Finally, bear in mind that any ingredient that includes the word "sodium" – such as sodium bicarbonate – will contain sodium, even in the most unlikely place (a sweet fizzy drink, for example) and even if it is only in a small quantity.

USING THE NUTRITION NOTES IN THIS BOOK

Recipes that are especially suited to people on a low-salt diet include a sodium breakdown in the Nutrition Notes. Remember that the recommended daily amount of sodium for an average person watching their salt intake is 1g/½₀oz, or 2.5g/⅒₀oz salt.

REDUCING THE SALT IN YOUR COOKING

The long-term advantage of any special diet is that it forces you to cook more for yourself at home. Initially this may seem like a terrible punishment, but many people find that once they start they really enjoy more adventurous cooking, and that the health benefits they derive from eating fresh food that also agrees with their dietary requirements are well worth the bit of extra work.

Apart from experimenting with new dishes and flavours, such as those in the recipe section, there are also a few general principles that you can apply to all your cooking.

ADDING LESS SALT

There was a time when no one would ever think of eating a meal without sprinkling salt and pepper on it before they even tasted it. But although this practice has now all but disappeared, many people still cannot imagine cooking potatoes or pasta without salt in the water, making a sauce without a shake of salt "for flavour", roasting a joint without salting the outside, or not adding a pinch of salt to their egg whites when making meringues. In fact, none of these practices is necessary – they are merely habit.

Vegetables have plenty of flavour of their own, which is only masked by putting a lot of salt in the cooking water – although because it is in the nature of salt to leach out of the food into the water rather than from the water into the food, salted cooking water makes for far less salty food than salting the dish itself.

Like any other flavouring – sugar is the prime example – you can always add more to your dish, but you cannot take it out once it is in. As the salt intake decreases, it is amazing how quickly your tastebuds will adapt to a less salty diet and you will suddenly start to discover all kinds of other exciting flavours which have previously been masked by the salt.

Unless you have been told to cut salt out of your diet entirely, reduce the amount of salt that you use gradually: this way, you will scarcely notice.

Above: You can still enjoy vegetables without adding salt during cooking: simply rub them with a little salted butter.

REDUCING YOUR SALT INTAKE GRADUALLY

Taste your food before adding salt, and only add just as much as you really need to make it acceptable. Measure out the amount of salt you would normally use for any dish, then reduce it by 25 per cent. Two weeks later, reduce the new amount that you are using by a further 25 per cent, and so on, until you use none at all. This will allow your tastebuds to adapt gradually to the more varied flavours of less salty foods.

Use salt carriers rather than salt itself. For example, if you cannot bear the thought of a boiled egg without salt, add a tiny bit of salted butter to the egg rather than straight salt – you will end up with less salt but still a good flavour.

Similarly, if you cannot bear not to have salt on your vegetables, lightly rub them with a little salted butter when cooked rather than sprinkling them with salt itself.

HOME-MADE BREAKFAST CEREAL

You will find this nutritious cereal far tastier – and healthier – than any ready-made version.

INGREDIENTS

Makes 1 large bowl
90ml/6 tbsp raw rolled oats
15ml/1 tbsp each unsalted sunflower, pumpkin and sesame seeds
30ml/2 tbsp each unsalted flaked almonds, walnuts and hazelnuts
15ml/1 tbsp wheatgerm
15ml/1 tbsp each dried fruit, such as raisins, sultanas, currants, figs, dates

To serve
fresh fruit, such as bananas, apples, peaches, pears
milk, or yogurt, or fruit juice

1 In a large, clean bowl combine all the dry ingredients and mix thoroughly together.

2 Adjust the quantities of the dry ingredients to suit your taste, then make up enough for a week before storing in a clean, airtight container. When serving, add fresh fruit of your choice and milk.

LOW-SALT COOKING METHODS

Just as water leaches salt out of food, so it leaches out the food's flavour too. Using less water in your cooking will therefore also conserve the natural flavour of food. Cooking any composite dish in its own juices will help retain all the flavour, rather than throwing it out with the cooking water.

STIR-FRYING

- An excellent way to cook finely slivered meats, fishes or vegetables with the minimum fat and salt is to stir-fry them in a wok or large frying pan. Add flavour with herbs and spices, such as garlic, ginger, cumin, lemon juice, mustard seeds, seasoned vinegars and flavoured stir-fry oils.
- Avoid soy sauce and other similar sauces, which are high in salt.

ROASTING/BAKING

- Roasting meats concentrates the flavour by drying them out. They should not need any further seasoning, but you could help them along by sitting them on an appropriate herb – rosemary for lamb, say, sage for pork, horseradish root for beef, tarragon for chicken – or by inserting slivers of garlic into slits in the flesh.

- Larger fish can be successfully roasted or baked either whole or in cutlets. Wrapping fish in foil helps to retain the juices, especially for cutlets or fillets. Add flavouring with lemon slices, dill weed, tarragon or fennel.
- Any combinations of vegetables – both root and leaf – can be roasted together. Lay them in a baking tray with a little olive oil and the herb – dry or fresh – of your choice.

STEAMING

- You can buy an inexpensive steamer from any kitchen shop, and steam all your vegetables rather than boiling them. This is particularly good for root vegetables, such as potatoes, sweet potatoes, carrots, celeriac, beetroot, parsnips and turnips, which will steam in 10–20 minutes, depending on the vegetable and how thick the slices are. Leaf vegetables such as cabbage, sprouts and spinach also steam well, and they are less likely to become soggy cooked in this way. Other vegetables that will benefit from steaming include cauliflower, peas and beans.
- Fish is excellent steamed because this is a far gentler method than poaching or boiling, which tends to break up the flesh. Some meats can be steamed, too, but be sure to use the steaming water in the sauce.

MICROWAVING

- Cook your vegetables in the microwave in a couple of tablespoons of water or stock. Meat works well in the microwave, too, as it retains its juices, though it does not therefore concentrate the flavour quite as well as roasting, which tends to dry out the meat. Fish can be microwaved in a small amount of liquid.
- The microwave is also good for steamed desserts, such as steamed marmalade or treacle pudding.

GRILLING/BARBECUING

- Anything that can be roasted can also be grilled or barbecued. As with roasting, the flavour is concentrated as the food dries out under the influence of the direct heat.
- Herbs placed with the food add flavour, as does marinating it in herbs, spices, chopped fruits, lemon juice, wine or olive oil beforehand.

ALTERNATIVE FLAVOURINGS

There are many alternative ingredients and flavourings that are healthier and tastier than the processed variety. Review the ingredients that you use normally and see where you could substitute a lower-salt version. However, remember that some high-salt ingredients (cheese and smoked fish, for example) contain other important health-giving nutrients, such as calcium and omega-3 fatty acids, so you may want to weigh that up against other high-salt but less nutritious ingredients.

Above: If you don't have time to prepare home-made stock, a quick alternative is a mixture of wine and water.

Above: Choose wholemeal ingredients when possible. The distinctive flavour of brown rice, for example, requires no added salt.

Above: For cooking use virgin oils, which are naturally salt-free and are beneficial to health in other ways too.

STOCK

Most commercial bouillon cubes are notoriously high in salt, so replace them, wherever possible, with home-made stock. This is easy to prepare and can be "stockpiled" by making a large batch and then freezing it in small quantities for future use.

You could also replace the stock altogether by using a mixture of water and wine – replacing 10-25 per cent of the total amount of liquid with wine (red or white depending on the dish) and the rest with water.

Salt-free/no-salt-added stock cubes are available if you really don't have time to make your own stock.

WHOLEMEAL INGREDIENTS

Use wholemeal ingredients (flour, rice, etc.) whenever possible. They have much more natural flavour than the white, highly processed version of the same food. If you think that they will make the resulting dish too heavy (if

using only wholemeal flour in baking, for example) then use half wholemeal and half white.

Bakes such as wholemeal pitta breads, scones, muffins and teacakes make a good, high fibre snack or treat. Choose wholemeal or whole grain varieties whenever possible or make your own bakes at home using wholemeal flour and adding extra dried fruit. Serve bakes such as scones or muffins plain or with a little low-fat spread, honey or reduced-sugar jam for a delicious, filling snack.

OILS

Use oils rather than butter or spreads for all your cooking and baking. Oils are naturally saltless, while spreads and butters can have quite a high salt content. Virgin oils such as olive or sunflower as a cooking medium, for example, will be much better for your overall health. If you do use butter, make sure you buy the saltless variety.

SALAD DRESSINGS

Substitute a little oil and vinegar or oil and lemon juice, two grinds of pepper and a shake of a low-sodium salt for commercial salad dressings, which are nearly always high in salt.

Below: It takes only a few seconds to prepare your own healthy salad dressing using just a little low-sodium salt or with no salt at all.

SAUCES

If you use ready-prepared sauces or ketchups, find the version that has the least salt – and cut down gradually on its use. If you start using other flavourings, you may find that you no longer need bottled sauce.

BAKING

Salt helps to control the activity of yeast, acting as a retardant, so raising agents will be high in salt. If you use a lot of raising agents, try substituting eggs. They will do the job just as well – and with more flavour.

Avoid self-raising flours as they all have built-in raising agents.

Use salt substitutes or low-sodium salts instead of common salt.

HERBS AND SPICES

Herbs and spices give different, subtle and unusual flavours to many dishes. You can use them fresh – you can even grow them on the kitchen windowsill – or dried. Fresh are nicer in raw, salad-type dishes but dried are fine for cooked dishes. Do make sure, however, that dried herbs are not too old, and keep them in an airtight, dark container, as both air and light will make them go stale more quickly. Dried herbs are a good deal stronger than fresh ones, so do not overdo it

Below: When baking, cut down on raising agents, which can contain high levels of salt, by substituting a fine, fresh egg.

when using them for your flavouring. You can use both herbs and spices singly or in combinations. The following list is a guide only; you will need to experiment to find out the combinations that you like best.

- Basil, oregano and marjoram are all excellent both fresh and dried for salads and any casserole dish, especially Italian dishes.
- Mint is lovely fresh and adds greatly to salads.
- Dill weed and caraway seeds are also strong-flavoured and are very popular in northern European cooking – excellent with cabbage and fish dishes.
- Parsley – whether the usual curly variety or the flat-leafed French – has a deliciously robust flavour either cooked or raw. Parsley can be added to almost anything, and it is useful not only for flavour but also for colour and garnishes.

Above: Fresh and dried herbs can be used singly or combined to bring flavour to many savoury dishes.

- Thyme, rosemary, sage and bay leaf, either fresh or dried, are excellent with lamb or pork or in any casserole dish – they are a bit woody to eat uncooked but give very good flavours cooked. You can combine the thyme and bay leaf; the others are probably better on their own.
- Fennel, like coriander, has a distinct flavour of its own, which people either love or hate. It is reminiscent of aniseed and is an excellent herb to use with fish.
- Coriander (both leaf and seed) has become very popular recently and has a wonderful, fresh flavour – although not everyone likes it. Use the fresh leaf in salads, and the seeds or the dried leaf in casseroles or baked dishes.

- Garlic and chives are wonderful flavourings. Garlic can be raw or cooked – boiled, baked in roasts (cut a slit in the roast and insert a peeled clove of garlic), fried or steamed with other vegetables.
- Mustard seeds and horseradish roots are normally found in ready-prepared condiments, but there is no reason why you should not use them raw. Just be careful as both are pretty strong. Peel and grate only the amount needed of fresh horseradish and use in rich, rather fatty foods.
- Salad herbs, such as rocket, sorrel and dandelion, and the more exotic varieties of lettuce, such as radicchio, are now much easier to obtain, and all have a delicious flavour.
- Dried seaweeds are now quite easy to obtain. They are very flavoursome and actually taste "salty", although they contain relatively low amounts of sodium.
- Cumin, turmeric and saffron, all north African spices, are delicious with rice and lamb dishes.

- Ginger, both fresh and dried, is a hugely useful spice. It will give a lift to meats and most vegetables.
- Black and green peppercorns – whole or ground – add excellent flavour to almost any dish.

Above: With skilful use of spices and flavourings in your cooking, you will find that you do not miss salt.

- Cinnamon, nutmeg and cloves, although normally used with sweet dishes, work very well in dark meat casseroles and stews and in some lighter dishes too.
- Chilli peppers – from the mild Hungarian paprika to the sizzling Caribbean hot peppers, choose from a delicious range of flavours.

FRUITS

- Lemons – either the juice or rind or both – are invaluable for adding flavour to sweet and savoury dishes.
- Limes look pretty and have a stronger flavour than lemons.
- Oranges, apples, pears and almost any other fruit can also be used successfully in many savoury and sweet dishes to give fresh and interesting flavours. They also look wonderful as garnishes.

Left: Fruits, particularly the citrus kind, are an excellent way of adding fresh and interesting flavour to both sweet and savoury recipes.

OLIVES, CAPERS, NUTS AND SEEDS

These all add variety to dishes in terms of both taste and texture, but there are some things you must bear in mind if you are not to add to the salt content of your food. Make sure, for example, that olives have not been preserved in brine, i.e. salted water.

Make sure, too, that nuts and seeds are not the salted variety. Add flavour to nuts (peanuts, cashews, almonds, hazelnuts, walnuts, Brazil nuts etc) and seeds (pumpkin, sunflower, sesame, pomegranate etc) by browning them, without fat, in a frying pan or an oven or under a grill.

Above and above left: Nuts, seeds, capers and olives will give a boost to texture and flavour, but be sure to buy them unsalted. Use dried seaweeds for their "salty" flavour and dried chillies for their zing.

REDUCED-SODIUM SALTS

There are now several reduced-sodium salts on the market. Some are available in supermarkets and some are more likely to be found in delicatessens and health-food stores. They include:

- **LoSalt** a reduced-sodium "salt", which contains only 13.22 per cent sodium per gram of salt instead of the normal 40 per cent.
- **Solo** a low-sodium natural sea salt from Iceland which contains 16.28 per cent sodium.
- **Ruthmol** a potassium salt consisting of less than 1 per cent sodium and 23.8 per cent potassium.
- **Seagreens** an organic seaweed from the Arctic, ground into powder, which contains 3.5 per cent sodium, 2.5 per cent potassium and a whole range of other beneficial nutrients.

Although none of these tastes quite the same as a traditional sea salt when you taste them by themselves, they are quite acceptable when they are used in cooking and can even fool some salt enthusiasts.

Above: Reduced-sodium salts and (front) Seagreens, an organic seaweed, which contains a range of nutrients as well as adding flavour.

Menu Planning

Many people think that to eat healthily signifies the end of exciting meals, and entertaining and eating out will be a thing of the past.

A little planning, however, can ensure entertaining at home that is varied, delicious and low in salt. Below are some menu hints to get you started.

Spicy and Aromatic
Chilled Vegetable Soup with Pastis
Aromatic Chicken
Roasted Root Vegetables with
  whole spices

Light Dining
Creamy Aubergine Dip
Tuna with Garlic, Tomatoes and
  Herbs, served with fried potatoes
Couscous Salad

Hearty Winter Fare
Wild Mushroom Soup
Roast Leg of Lamb with Vegetables,
  such as carrots, potatoes and broccoli
Irish Whiskey Cake

Combining Colour and Texture
Calamari with Double Tomato
  Stuffing and Pane Toscana
Beef Tagine with Sweet Potatoes
Provençale Vegetable Stew

A Vegetarian's Delight
Spiced Coconut Mushrooms
Vegetarian Fried Noodles
Sweet-and-sour Artichoke Salad with
  salsa agrodolce

EATING OUT

Although some restaurants are very helpful and will give you detailed ingredients lists for their dishes, there is no legal requirement for them to do so. Even if they can give you ingredients lists, it is unlikely that they will have very much idea of how much salt/sodium those dishes contain, especially if they are not wholly made on the premises, as is the case with many restaurant dishes.

Once again, if your salt intake is not critical, you should use the "high salt" list given earlier and avoid any of the ingredients on it. If you keep your choices to simple dishes such as roasts and plainly cooked vegetables dressed with a little oil or butter and fresh fruits or fruit salads for dessert, you should be OK. If your salt intake is critical, you should speak to the restaurant in advance, explain to them that you are on a no-salt/very low-salt diet and ask them if they can prepare something for you that does not use salt.

The same applies if you are eating out with friends or relatives. Call them in plenty of time, and warn them that you are on a very low-salt diet.

TRYING NEW CUISINES

Many non-Western cuisines rely far less on salt as a flavouring than we do. It is therefore worth experimenting with other cuisines – even if you do not adopt them wholesale. Mediterranean cooking uses rich vegetables and oils to give deep and exciting flavours. Thai and Indonesian foods are full of herbs and spices, while Mexican and South American cuisines use the many flavours of the chilli and the tomato families to add taste to foods.

FOLLOWING A
LOW-CHOLESTEROL DIET

Research has shown that cholesterol plays a significant role in the

incidence of coronary heart disease and high blood pressure.

This chapter explains everything you need to know about cholesterol

and a healthy diet, and tells you which fats can raise blood cholesterol

levels and which foods can help to reduce them. It also contains

a variety of practical tips for low-fat cooking.

INTRODUCTION

Cooking and eating good food are among life's greatest pleasures. Unfortunately, the foods we tend to enjoy most are often fatty, and certain types of fat raise the level of blood cholesterol – a substance strongly implicated in heart disease, stroke and high blood pressure.

Cholesterol is found in the cells of humans and animals, and in the food we eat. Body cholesterol is produced in the liver and is used to carry essential fatty acids around the bloodstream to various organs. The body makes all the cholesterol it needs and any excess accumulates on the walls of the arteries and restricts the passage of blood and oxygen to the heart, which contributes to the risk of heart disease.

Dietary cholesterol is found in saturated fats and in food derived from animals – meat, offal, egg yolk and dairy produce, for instance. Fats derived from vegetables are cholesterol-free. Interestingly, although some low-fat foods such as prawns contain high levels of cholesterol, it seems that blood cholesterol levels are more affected by the amount of saturated fat in the diet than the amount of cholesterol. These foods will not greatly increase blood cholesterol levels even though they contain cholesterol themselves.

When we eat more saturated fat than we need, the body increases cholesterol production and the excess ends up in the bloodstream. So even a diet that is low in cholesterol can raise your blood cholesterol if saturated fats aren't reduced as well.

We need to consume a small amount of fat to maintain a healthy and balanced diet, but almost everyone can afford to, and should, reduce their fat intake, particularly of saturated fats.

By choosing the right types of fat and making small, simple changes to the way you cook and prepare food, you can reduce your overall fat intake quite dramatically and enjoy a low-fat, low cholesterol diet without really noticing any difference.

THE IMPORTANCE OF DIET

A healthy diet is one that provides the body with all the nutrients it needs for growth and repair and to resist disease. It is important to know just how much to eat of each of the main food groups:
- Fruit and vegetables.
- Cereals, rice, potatoes, beans, bread and pasta.
- Meat, poultry, fish and eggs.
- Milk and other dairy foods.
- Fats, oils and sugars.

It is now recommended that we eat at least five portions of fruit and vegetables a day, excluding potatoes. We should also eat a high proportion of energy-producing foods such as cereals, pasta, rice, beans, bread and potatoes; moderate amounts of meat, fish, poultry, eggs and dairy products; and only small amounts of fat and sugar.

You can reduce cholesterol intake by cutting down on fat, particularly the saturated kind. Aim to limit your daily fat intake to no more than 30 per cent of total calories. For an average daily intake of 2000 calories, daily fat intake should come from no more than 600 calories. Each gram of fat provides 9 calories so your total daily fat intake should be no more than 66.6g. Of this amount no more than 10 per cent (6.6g) should consist of saturated fat.

Above: Though not all fats are "bad", only small amounts are needed in the diet.

TYPES OF FAT

All fats contain both saturated and either poly- or mono-unsaturated fatty acids, but if the proportion of saturated is greater than that of unsaturated, the fat is generally said to be "saturated", and vice versa.

Saturated fats are generally solid at room temperature and are mostly found in foods derived from animal sources. However, there are also saturated fats of vegetable origin, notably coconut and palm oils, as well as certain margarines and oils in which some of the unsaturated fatty acids have been processed into saturated ones. These products are labelled "hydrogenated" and are best avoided.

Polyunsaturated fats are usually liquid at room temperature. There are two types: those of vegetable or plant origin (containing fatty acids called omega-6), such as nut, seed and vegetable oils, and soft margarine; and those from oily fish (omega-3), such as herring and sardines. Small quantities are essential for good health, and ideally we should consume equal amounts of omega-6 and omega-3 oils. Most of us need to boost our omega-3 intake.

Monounsaturated fats are found in foods such as olive oil, some nuts such as almonds and walnuts, oily fish and avocado pears. These fats are thought to help reduce blood cholesterol levels, and could explain why there is a low incidence of heart disease in the Mediterranean countries where they are a major part of the diet.

CHOLESTEROL

Although usually associated with fats, cholesterol isn't actually a fat itself; it is a white, waxy material belonging to a group of substances known as lipoproteins. Cholesterol travels round the bloodstream in tiny droplets of lipoprotein, of which there are three densities: very low density lipoproteins (VLDL), low density (LDL) and high density (HDL). When you eat a lot of saturated fats, your liver produces huge quantities of VLDLs and LDLs. Both types are rich in cholesterol and are the culprits when it comes to blocked arteries. HDLs, however, are thought to help prevent clogged arteries. This is why HDLs are sometimes referred to as "good" and LDLs as "bad".

The recommended maximum daily intake of cholesterol is 300mg. This may seem a lot, but it's very easy to exceed the limit if your diet contains high-cholesterol foods (see box).

CUTTING DOWN ON FAT

About one-quarter of the fat we eat comes from meat and meat products, one-fifth from dairy products and margarine, and the rest from cakes, biscuits, pastries and other foods. Many foods, such as nuts, hummus and avocado contain "hidden" fats.

Being aware of high-fat foods, and making simple changes to your eating habits, can help you to reduce the total fat content of your diet, and therefore control cholesterol levels.

BOOSTING FIBRE

Certain types of fibre can help reduce blood cholesterol levels and restrict fat absorption. There are about six types of fibre that divide into two groups.

Soluble fibre contains pectin, which helps prevent cholesterol from being absorbed. As a result, the liver's store of cholesterol becomes depleted and it takes cholesterol from the bloodstream. Foods containing soluble fibre include oats, buckwheat, beans and apples.

Insoluble fibre is made up of cellulose (found in all plant foods) and lignin (a woody substance found in the central core of fibrous vegetables such as old carrots). Lignin helps lower blood cholesterol by binding to bile acids, which emulsify fat, thus increasing their excretion from the body.

CHOLESTEROL CONTENT OF SELECTED FOODS

	mg cholesterol per 100g
Lamb's brains	2200
Egg yolk	1260
Herring roe	575
Whole egg	450
Calfs' liver	370
Lamb's kidneys	315
Caviar (bottled)	285
Mayonnaise	260
Butter	230
Squid	225
Prawns	195
Double cream	140
Pork	110
Salami	79
Lamb, lean	74
Chicken, light meat	70
Cheddar cheese	70
Trout	70
Pork, lean	63
Beef, lean	58
Haddock	36

BOOSTING ANTIOXIDANTS

Our body cells can be damaged by destructive molecules known as free radicals. The process is called oxidation. Some scientists now believe that oxidized fat and cholesterol may be linked to some cancers. Antioxidants provide powerful protection by destroying free radicals, and are also thought to prevent "bad" LDL cholesterol from oxidizing and causing damage to the artery walls.

The main antioxidants are the carotenes, which are found in orange-fleshed fruit and vegetables; vitamin C found in citrus fruit and many other fruits and vegetables; vitamin E found in vegetable oils, seeds and nuts; selenium, zinc and magnesium; and certain proteins found in cabbages as well as other fruits and vegetables.

Left: Cut down on high-cholesterol foods, such as meat, cream and cheese.

KEY CHOLESTEROL-LOWERING FOODS

Try to include the following foods in your daily diet. They all help lower "bad" LDL cholesterol, which can clog the arteries or oxidize, causing damage to the artery walls. These foods also boost "good" HDL cholesterol, which removes LDL cholesterol from the bloodstream.

● **Fish** Oily fish, such as mackerel, sardines, herring, trout and salmon, contain valuable fatty acids known as omega-3. These fatty acids boost HDL cholesterol and are strongly believed to help prevent heart disease. Try to eat oily fish 2–3 times a week. Grill or bake in the oven without any extra oil. Sprinkle with lemon or lime juice and chopped fresh herbs.

● **Nuts** Although nuts are high in fat, it's the monounsaturated kind that lowers "bad" LDL cholesterol and discourages it from oxidizing and damaging the artery walls. Nuts are also a valuable source of vitamin E, which protects against oxidative damage. Almonds and walnuts are said to be particularly effective. Eat just a few nuts each day as a snack, or add them to salads or cakes.

● **Oats** Just 50g/2oz of oats or oat bran a day, as part of a low-fat diet, is known to reduce blood cholesterol dramatically. As well as eating oats in porridge and muesli, add them to homemade bread and biscuits, or sprinkle into crumble mixtures. Sprinkle oat bran over yogurt or fruit and sweeten with a little honey.

● **Olive oil and rapeseed oil** These oils, particularly olive oil, are very high in monounsaturates, which lower "bad" LDL cholesterol and prevent it from causing oxidative damage to the arteries. They slightly raise or keep "good" HDL cholesterol the same. Polyunsaturated oils, such as sunflower and corn oil, lower both types of cholesterol, so you miss out on the protective power of HDL cholesterol. Use "pure" olive oil in moderation for cooking and "extra virgin" for salads.

● **Pulses** Countless studies indicate that pulses – dried beans, lentils and chick-peas – work miracles in fighting high cholesterol when eaten on a daily basis. You can use all types of beans: kidney, pinto, flageolet, butter beans, haricot, soya – even ordinary baked beans. Use canned or precooked pulses to replace some or all of the meat in stews; add cooked pulses to gutsy salads and soups; or whizz them in a blender with garlic, lemon, herbs and a little olive oil to make dips and pâtés.

Below: Certain foods boost "good" cholesterol while reducing the "bad".

FRESH FRUIT AND VEGETABLES

Including plenty of fruit and vegetables in your diet – ideally at least five portions daily (excluding potatoes) – will help control blood cholesterol levels. Almost all are naturally fat-free as well as providing carotene (the plant form of vitamin A), vitamins C and E, minerals and dietary fibre.

Apples A useful source of energy-giving carbohydrate, vitamin C and pectin (a soluble fibre thought to lower blood cholesterol).

Apricots An excellent source of carotene and cholesterol-lowering soluble fibre.

Bananas Packed with carbohydrate, bananas are a fat-free energy booster. Add to yogurt, breakfast cereal and muesli, or mash and spread on wholemeal toast.

Citrus fruit An excellent source of vitamin C and carotene (antioxidants that may help minimize the risk of heart disease). Pectin in the flesh and fibrous membranes is thought to help lower blood cholesterol.

Grapes Red and black grapes are rich in bioflavonoids (antioxidants that may help protect against heart disease and some cancers).

Kiwi fruit Kiwis are an excellent source of vitamin C and also provide pectin, a cholesterol-lowering soluble fibre.

Mangoes Wonderful mixed with yogurt or in a tropical fruit salad, mangoes are packed with betacarotene, vitamin C and soluble fibre.

Prunes Prunes contain masses of pectin, a soluble fibre that accounts for their laxative effect. Pectin also helps lower blood cholesterol levels.

Strawberries Rich in vitamin C and soluble and insoluble fibre that help remove cholesterol from the blood.

Asparagus An excellent source of betacarotene and a useful source of vitamins C and E (all natural antioxidants, which may help lower blood cholesterol).

Avocados Rich in monounsaturates thought to restrict damage caused to arteries by "bad" LDL cholesterol. A good source of vitamin E – a powerful antioxidant – and may be included in a low-fat diet in moderation. Serve with a fat-free dressing.

Broccoli Probably topping the list of disease-fighting vegetables, broccoli is an excellent source of antioxidants carotene, vitamins C and E and cholesterol-lowering soluble fibre.

Carrots A fantastic source of betacarotene, a powerful antioxidant that protects the arteries against damage by "bad" LDL cholesterol. Very rich in cholesterol-lowering soluble fibre.

Garlic An all-round miracle vegetable, strongly believed to thin the blood and reduce blood cholesterol. Use raw in salad dressings, roast whole heads and eat with a selection of roasted vegetables, or sauté gently in stir-fries, sauces and stews.

Kale A rich source of antioxidant vitamins, which help protect against "bad" LDL cholesterol. Tender baby kale can be microwaved or used raw in salads.

Mushrooms Sweat in a little stock rather than butter or slice and use raw

Above: Eating plenty of fruit and vegetables every day can help to control your blood cholesterol levels.

in salads. Eaten daily, Asian shiitake mushrooms are thought to help reduce both blood cholesterol levels and high blood pressure.

Onions Onions are an exceptionally powerful antioxidant and strongly believed to thin the blood and lower cholesterol. An essential flavouring for many savoury dishes; serve them cooked or raw in salads, or baked as a vegetable in their own right.

Parsnips A tasty root vegetable, rich in cholesterol-lowering soluble fibre. Eat them baked, mashed or grated raw in salads.

Potatoes Provide energy-giving carbohydrate, vitamin C and soluble fibre, but are frequently prepared using high-fat cooking methods such as roasting and frying. Boil, steam or bake potatoes instead, and serve with low-fat dressings.

Sweet peppers An excellent source of betacarotene and vitamin C, which help reduce damage caused by "bad" LDL cholesterol. Use raw in salads, add to stir-fries, soups, stews and sauces or roast in the oven.

COOKING WITH LOW-FAT AND FAT-FREE INGREDIENTS

Nowadays many foods are available in reduced-fat or very low-fat versions. In every supermarket you'll find a huge array of low-fat dairy products such as reduced-fat milks and cream, yogurt, hard and soft cheeses and fromage frais. There is also an increasing variety of reduced-fat sweet or chocolate biscuits; reduced-fat or fat-free salad dressings and mayonnaise; reduced-fat crisps and snacks; low-fat, half-fat and very low-fat spreads; and even reduced-fat ready-made meals.

Other foods, such as fresh fruit and vegetables, pasta, rice, potatoes and bread, naturally contain very little fat and they help reduce blood cholesterol levels. Some foods, such as soy sauce, wine, vinegar, cider, sherry and honey, contain no fat at all. By combining these and other low-fat foods with low-fat cooking techniques, you can create delicious dishes that contain very little fat.

Some low-fat or reduced-fat ingredients and products work better than others in cooking, but often a simple substitution of one for another will produce good results.

LOW-FAT SPREADS IN COOKING

There is a huge variety of low-fat, reduced-fat and half-fat spreads available in our supermarkets. Some are suitable for cooking, while others will give disappointing results and are best used only for spreading.

Generally speaking, the very low-fat spreads that have a fat content of around 20 per cent or less have a high water content, which will evaporate on heating. This makes them unsuitable for cooking and, therefore, better for spreading only.

Low-fat or half-fat spreads with a fat content of around 40 per cent are suitable for spreading and can be used for some cooking methods. They are suitable for recipes such as all-in-one cake and biscuit recipes, all-in-one sauce recipes, sautéing vegetables over a low heat, choux pastry and some types of cake icing.

When these low-fat spreads are used for cooking, they may behave slightly differently from full-fat products such as butter or margarine. With some recipes, the cooked result may be slightly different from that produced by the traditional method, but will still be very acceptable. Other recipes will be just as tasty and successful. For example, choux pastry made using half- or low-fat spread is often slightly crisper and lighter in texture than traditional choux pastry and a cheesecake biscuit base made with melted half- or low-fat spread combined with crushed biscuit crumbs may be slightly softer in texture and less crispy than a biscuit base made using melted butter.

Clockwise from left: olive oil, sunflower oil, buttermilk blend, sunflower light, olive oil reduced-fat spread, reduced-fat butter and (centre) very low-fat spread.

LOW-FAT AND VERY LOW-FAT SNACKS

Instead of reaching for a packet of crisps, a high-fat biscuit or a chocolate bar when hunger strikes, choose one of these tasty low-fat snacks to fill that hungry hole.

• A piece of fresh fruit or vegetable, such as an apple, banana or carrot, is delicious, easy to eat and will also increase soluble fibre and help lower blood cholesterol. Keep chunks or sticks wrapped in a polythene bag in the fridge. If you like, skewer fruit pieces on to cocktail sticks or short bamboo skewers to make them into mini kebabs.

• Crackers, such as water biscuits or crispbreads, spread with reduced-sugar jam or marmalade.

• Instead of cream, dollop some very low-fat plain or fruit yogurt or even fromage frais on to puddings.

• Toasted crumpet spread with yeast extract.

• A bowl of wholewheat breakfast cereal or no-added-sugar muesli served with a little skimmed milk. Choose a cereal that is based on oats, if possible.

• A portion of canned fruit in natural fruit juice – serve with a spoonful or two of fat-free yogurt.

•One or two crisp rice cakes or oat cakes – these are delicious on their own, or topped with honey, or reduced-fat cheese. Oats are well known for their cholesterol-lowering properties.

• A handful of dried fruit, such as raisins, apricots or sultanas, will help lower blood cholesterol. These also make a perfect addition to children's packed lunches or can be eaten as school break snacks.

When cooking with half- or low-fat spreads, never heat them over a high heat. Always use a heavy-based pan set over a low heat to avoid burning, spitting or spoiling, and stir the contents all the time. With all-in-one sauces, the mixture should be whisked continuously over a low heat.

Half-fat or low-fat spreads are not suitable for shallow or deep-fat frying, making pastry, rich fruit cakes, some biscuits and shortbread, in place of clarified butter or in preserves such as lemon curd. Remember also, that the keeping qualities of recipes made using half- or low-fat spreads may be reduced slightly, because of the lower fat content of those spreads.

Another way to reduce the fat content of recipes, particularly cake recipes, is to use a dried fruit purée in place of all or some of the fat in a recipe. By using dried fruit, you'll also be increasing your intake of soluble fibre, which, in turn, helps reduce blood cholesterol levels. Many cake recipes work well using dried fruit purée, but other recipes may not be so successful. Pastry does not work well, for instance. Breads work very well – perhaps because the amount of fat is usually small – as do some biscuits and bars, such as brownies and flapjacks.

To make a dried fruit purée to use in recipes, chop 115g/4oz ready-to-eat dried fruit and place in a blender or

food processor with 75ml/5 tbsp water and blend to a fairly smooth purée. Then simply substitute the same weight of this dried fruit purée for all or just some of the amount of fat in the recipe. The purée will keep in the fridge for up to three days.

You can use prunes, dried apricots, dried peaches or dried apples, or substitute mashed fresh fruit, such as ripe bananas or lightly cooked apples, without the added water.

EASY WAYS TO CUT DOWN ON FAT

There are lots of simple, no-fuss ways of reducing fat in your daily diet. Just follow the simple "eat less – try instead" suggestions to discover how easy it is.

Eat less butter, margarine and hard fats

● Try instead – When baking chicken or fish, rather than adding a knob of butter, try wrapping the food in a loosely sealed parcel of foil or greaseproof paper and adding some wine or fruit juice and herbs or spices to the food before sealing the parcel.
● Where possible, use low- and very low-fat spreads, or non-hydrogenated vegetable margarine.

Eat less fatty meats and high-fat products such as meat pâtés, pies and sausages

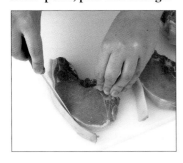

● Try instead – Low-fat meats such as chicken and turkey. Cut off any visible fat and skin before cooking.

● Eat fish much more frequently. White fish is practically fat-free and oily fish contains cholesterol-lowering fatty acids.
● Make gravies and sauces using vegetable water or fat-free stock rather than using meat juices.

Eat less fried foods

● Try instead – Fat-free cooking methods such as grilling, microwaving, steaming or baking whenever possible.
● When grilling foods, the addition of fat is often unnecessary. If the food shows signs of drying, you can lightly brush it with a small amount of monounsaturated oil such as rapeseed or olive oil.
● Steaming or boiling are easy fat-free ways of cooking many foods, especially vegetables, fish and chicken.

● Try cooking in a non-stick wok with only a very small amount of oil.

Eat less hard cooking fats such as lard or hard margarine, and poly-unsaturated oils such as corn, safflower, sunflower and "vegetable" oils

● Try instead – Monounsaturated oils such as olive and rapeseed oils. These protect the arteries by reducing "bad" LDL cholesterol without lowering the level of "good" HDL cholesterol.
● Microwaved and grilled foods rarely need the addition of fat, so add herbs or spices for extra flavour.

Eat less added fat in cooking

● Try instead – To cook with little or no fat. Use heavy-based or good-quality non-stick pans, so that the food doesn't stick.
● Try using a spray oil in cooking to control exactly how much fat you use.

● Always roast or grill meat or poultry on a rack.
● Choose heavy-based or good-quality cookware; you'll find that the amount of fat needed for cooking foods can be kept to an absolute minimum. When making casseroles or meat sauces such as Bolognese, dry-fry the meat to brown it and then drain off all the excess fat before adding the other ingredients. If you do need a little fat, choose an oil that is high in mono-unsaturates such as olive or rapeseed oil and always use as little as possible.

● Use fat-free or low-fat ingredients for cooking, such as fruit juice, low-fat or fat-free stock, wine or even beer.

• When serving vegetables such as boiled potatoes, carrots or peas, resist the temptation to add a knob of butter or margarine. Instead, sprinkle with chopped fresh herbs, freshly ground spices, lemon juice or soy sauce.

• Try poaching foods such as chicken or fish in stock.

• Sauté vegetables in wine, fruit juice or low-fat or fat-free stock.

• Marinate meat or poultry in mixtures of alcohol, herbs or spices, and vinegar or fruit juice. This will help to tenderize the meat as well as adding flavour and colour, and can be used for basting during cooking.

• Cook vegetables in a covered saucepan over a low heat with a little water so they cook in their own juices.

• Try braising vegetables in the oven in wine, low-fat or fat-free stock, or even water with the addition of some herbs.

• Poach fruit in wine for a quick, low-fat dessert. Serve with a dollop of fresh yogurt instead of cream.

Eat less eggs – limit intake to no more than three or four a week

• Try instead – Egg whites in recipes calling for whole eggs. Limit egg yolks to one per serving when making scrambled eggs. For something a little different, make mayonnaise with tofu (soya beancurd) instead of egg yolks.

Eat less rich creamy, salad dressings, such as full-fat mayonnaise, French or Thousand Island

• Try instead – Reduced-fat or fat-free mayonnaise or dressings. Make salad dressings at home with low-fat yogurt or fromage frais, or blender-whipped cottage cheese, ricotta or buttermilk in recipes calling for soured cream or mayonnaise.

• Try lemon juice, soy sauce and fresh herbs on salads – quick and easy but also full of flavour.

Eat less full-fat dairy products such as whole milk, cream, whole-milk yogurts, butter, hard margarine, hard cheese and crème fraîche

• Try instead – Semi-skimmed or skimmed milk, low-fat yogurts, low-fat fromage frais and low- and reduced-fat cheeses and reduced-fat creams.

• Beware of dried skimmed milk and coffee creamers – these may be skimmed of animal fat, but may have vegetable fat added.

Eat less high-fat snacks such as crisps, cakes, muffins, doughnuts, sweet pastries and biscuits – especially chocolate ones

• Try instead – Low-fat and fat-free fresh or dried fruits, breadsticks or vegetable sticks.

• Make your own low-fat cakes, biscuits and breads.

• If you do buy ready-made cakes and biscuits, always choose low-fat and reduced-fat versions.

• Dried fruits are a traditional addition to cakes and quick breads and there is a very wide range available, from banana to apricots and mango. The natural sugars add sweetness to baked goods and keep them moist, making it possible to use less fat.

• Use good-quality bakeware that doesn't need greasing before use.

• If you do have to grease your bakeware, use non-stick baking parchment and grease only lightly.

HOW TO REDUCE OIL IN COOKING

For fat-free or low-fat cooking it's best to avoid roasting and frying as they can increase the overall fat content of food. Instead poach, grill, bake, steam or microwave food – these are all delicious and successful ways of cooking without adding fat. Below are some further clever techniques that may be used for reducing or eliminating the amount of oil used in cooking.

SWEATING VEGETABLES

GOOD FOR: Pan-frying vegetables such as onions, mushrooms, carrots and celery, which would usually be initially fried in oil or butter, as the basis of many savoury recipes.

HOW TO: Put the sliced vegetables into a non-stick frying pan with about 150ml/¼ pint/⅔ cup light stock. Cook for 5 minutes or until the vegetables are tender and the stock has reduced. Add 15ml/1 tbsp dry wine or wine vinegar and continue cooking for a further few minutes until the vegetables are lightly browned.

MARINATING

GOOD FOR: Adding flavour as well as helping to tenderize and keep the food moist during cooking without adding any fat. Useful for meat, fish, poultry and vegetables. The marinade may also be used for basting or it can be added to an accompanying sauce.

HOW TO: Wine, soy sauce, vinegar, citrus juices and yogurt all make excellent fat-free marinade bases with herbs and spices added for extra flavour. Leave fish in the marinade for 1 hour, but marinate meat and poultry overnight if possible.

PARCEL COOKING

GOOD FOR: Fish, chicken, fruit and vegetables. This method allows the food to cook in its own juices and the steam created, holds in all the flavour and nutrient value and eliminates the need for oil or fats.

HOW TO: Enclose food in individual foil or greaseproof parcels and add extra flavourings, such as a little wine, herbs and spices, if liked. Twist or fold the parcel ends to secure and ensure that the juices can't run out, then either bake, steam or, if using foil, cook on a barbecue.

SEARING

GOOD FOR: Sealing the juices into meat and poultry. Even lean cuts trimmed of skin and visible fat contain some hidden fat, so adding extra fat isn't necessary.

HOW TO: Place the meat in a heavy-based pan over a moderate heat and brown evenly on all sides. If the meat sticks slightly, remove from the pan, brush or spray a little olive oil on to the pan's surface, heat, then return the meat to the pan. Drain off any excess fat that comes out of the meat.

LOW-FAT SAUCES

Sauces can introduce an unwelcome amount of fat into a recipe so that naturally low-fat foods such as vegetables, white fish and skinless chicken may end up being served in a rich, high-fat coating.

However, by following the tips and techniques below, it's easy to adapt such sauces without sacrificing flavour and appeal.

BÉARNAISE SAUCE

Some fat savings can be made to this classic piquant sauce by using a small amount of butter and fewer egg yolks.

INGREDIENTS

Makes 350ml/¾ pint/1½ cups
150ml/¼ pint/⅔ cup white wine
60ml/4 tbsp white wine vinegar
15ml/1 tbsp finely chopped shallot
15ml/1 tbsp cornflour
175ml/6fl oz/¾ cup water
2 egg yolks, lightly beaten
40g/1½oz/3 tbsp unsalted
   butter, melted
15ml/1 tbsp chopped fresh tarragon
15ml/1 tbsp chopped fresh parsley
salt and ground black pepper

1 Put the wine, vinegar, shallot and pepper in a saucepan. Bring to the boil and simmer until reduced to 45ml/3 tbsp. Strain, discarding solids.

2 Put the cornflour and water in a bowl over a pan of simmering water. Whisk for 3–4 minutes until thickened. Stir in the vinegar mixture. Remove from the heat, whisk in the egg yolks and half the butter. Return to the heat and stir constantly for 3–4 minutes until thickened.

3 Add the chopped herbs. Whisk in the remaining butter and salt to taste. Use immediately.

EGG-FREE MAYONNAISE

Egg yolks are high in cholesterol and contain saturated fat. Here's a way of making mayonnaise without them.

INGREDIENTS

Makes 250ml/½ pint/1¼ cups
115g/4oz firm tofu (soya beancurd),
   drained and pressed dry
60ml/4 tbsp "light" Greek yogurt or
   low-fat fromage frais
30ml/2 tbsp white wine or vinegar
5ml/1 tsp sea salt
75ml/5 tbsp olive oil
ground black pepper

Put the tofu (soya beancurd), yogurt or fromage frais, wine or vinegar and salt in a blender. Process for 2–3 minutes until very smooth. With the blender running, slowly add the oil until thickened. Season. Use immediately.

OIL-FREE DRESSINGS

Whisk together 90ml/6 tbsp low-fat natural yogurt, 30ml/2 tbsp lemon juice and season to taste with freshly ground black pepper. If you prefer, wine, cider or fruit vinegar or even orange juice could be used in place of the lemon juice. Add chopped fresh herbs, crushed garlic, mustard, honey, or other flavourings, if you like.

VEGETABLE PURÉE

Many recipes for sauces are traditionally thickened by adding cream, beurre manié (a butter and flour paste) or egg yolks, all of which add saturated fat and cholesterol to the sauce. If cooked vegetables are included in the recipe, blend some down in a food processor to make a purée, then stir back into the juices to produce a thickened sauce.

THREE WAYS TO MAKE LOW-FAT SAUCES

The traditional roux method for making a sauce won't work successfully if using a low-fat spread. This is because of the high water content, which will evaporate on heating, leaving insufficient fat to blend with the flour. However, below are three quick and easy low-fat alternatives.

• **The all-in-one method:** Place 30ml/2 tbsp each of low-fat spread and plain flour in a pan with 300ml/½ pint/1¼ cups skimmed milk. Bring to the boil over a moderate heat, whisking constantly, until thickened and smooth.

• **Using stock to replace fat:** Sweat cut-up vegetables, such as onions and mushrooms, in a small amount of stock in a non-stick pan rather than frying in fat.

• **Using cornflour to thicken:** Blend 15ml/1 tbsp cornflour with 15–30ml/1–2 tbsp cold water, then whisk into 300ml/½ pint/1¼ cups simmering stock or milk, bring to the boil and cook for 1 minute, stirring continuously.

LOW-FAT STOCKS

A good stock is invaluable in the kitchen. The most delicious soups, stews, casseroles and sauces rely on a good homemade stock for success. Neither a stock cube nor a canned consommé will do if you want the best flavour. Below are three easy-to-follow recipes for low-fat chicken, meat and vegetable stock, which are all simple and economical to make. Keep in the fridge for 4 days, or freeze for up to 6 months for meat and poultry, 1 month for vegetable.

LOW-FAT CHICKEN STOCK

INGREDIENTS

Makes 1.5 litres/2½ pints/6¼ cups
1kg/2¼lb chicken wings or
  thighs, skinned
1 onion
2 whole cloves
1 bay leaf
1 sprig of thyme
3–4 sprigs of parsley
10 black peppercorns

1 Cut the chicken into pieces and put into a large, heavy-based saucepan. Peel the onion and stud with the cloves. Tie the bay leaf, thyme, parsley and peppercorns in a piece of muslin and add to the saucepan together with the onion.

2 Pour in 1.75 litres/3 pints/7½ cups cold water. Set over a low heat and slowly bring to simmering point, skimming off any scum that rises to the surface with a slotted spoon. Continue to simmer very gently, uncovered, for 1½ hours.

3 Strain the stock through a sieve into a large bowl and leave until cold, then chill. Remove any solidified fat from the surface. Keep chilled in the fridge for up to 3–4 days, or freeze in usable amounts.

LOW-FAT MEAT STOCK

INGREDIENTS

Makes 2 litres/3½ pints/8¾ cups
1.8kg/4lb lean veal bones, trimmed
2 onions, unpeeled, quartered
2 carrots, roughly chopped
2 celery sticks, with leaves if possible,
  roughly chopped
2 tomatoes, coarsely chopped
a handful of parsley stalks
a few fresh thyme sprigs or
  4ml/¾ tsp dried thyme
2 bay leaves
10 black peppercorns, lightly crushed

1 Put the bones and vegetables in a large stockpot. Add 4.5 litres/ 7½ pints/4 quarts of water. Bring just to the boil, skimming to remove the foam from the surface. Add the parsley, thyme, bay leaves and peppercorns.

2 Partly cover the pot and simmer the stock for 4–6 hours. The bones and vegetables should always be covered with liquid, so top up with a little boiling water from time to time.

3 Strain the stock through a colander or sieve. Skim as much fat as possible from the surface. If possible, cool the stock and then refrigerate it; the fat will rise to the top and set in a layer that can be removed easily.

VEGETABLE STOCK

INGREDIENTS

Makes 1.5 litres/2½ pints/6¼ cups
2 carrots
2 celery sticks
2 onions
2 tomatoes
10 mushroom stalks
2 bay leaves
1 sprig of thyme
3–4 sprigs of parsley
10 black peppercorns

1 Roughly chop the vegetables. Place them in a large, heavy-based saucepan. Tie the bay leaves, thyme, parsley and peppercorns in a piece of muslin and add to the pan.

2 Pour in 1.75 litres/3 pints/ 7½ cups cold water. Set over a low heat and slowly bring to simmering point. Continue to simmer very gently, uncovered, for 1½ hours.

3 Strain through a sieve into a large bowl and leave until cold. Keep chilled in the fridge for 3–4 days, or freeze in usable amounts.

LOW-FAT SWEET OPTIONS

Desserts needn't be banned from a low-fat, low-cholesterol diet. Many traditional dairy products, such as cream, are high in fat, but it's a simple matter to adapt recipes and use low-fat alternatives to create delicious results.

Low-fat yogurt (vanilla is particularly delicious for desserts), fromage frais and reduced-fat crème fraîche may be substituted for cream, and skimmed milk can be used in sauces, but here are some further simple ideas to try.

LOW-FAT CREAMY WHIP

A sweetened cream that can be used in place of whipped real dairy cream. It isn't suitable for cooking, but freezes very well.

INGREDIENTS

Makes 150ml/¼ pint/²⁄₃ cup
2.5ml/½ tsp powdered gelatine
50g/2oz/¼ cup skimmed milk powder
15ml/1 tbsp caster sugar
15ml/1 tbsp lemon juice

1 Sprinkle the gelatine over 15ml/ 1 tbsp cold water in a small bowl and leave to "sponge" for 5 minutes. Place the bowl over a saucepan of hot water and stir until dissolved. Remove from the heat and leave to cool.

2 Whisk the skimmed milk powder, caster sugar, lemon juice and 60ml/4 tbsp cold water until frothy. Add the dissolved gelatine and whisk for a few seconds more. Chill in the fridge for 30 minutes.

3 Whisk the chilled mixture again until very thick and frothy. Serve within 30 minutes of making.

YOGURT PIPING CREAM

An excellent alternative to whipped cream for decorating cakes and desserts.

INGREDIENTS

Makes 450ml/¾ pint/scant 2 cups
10ml/2 tsp powdered gelatine
300ml/½ pint/1¼ cups strained yogurt (see right)
15ml/1 tbsp sugar
2.5ml/½ tsp vanilla essence
1 egg white

1 Sprinkle the gelatine over 45ml/ 3 tbsp cold water in a small bowl and leave to "sponge" for 5 minutes. Place the bowl over a saucepan of hot water and stir until dissolved. Remove from the heat and leave to cool.

2 Mix together the strained yogurt, sugar and vanilla essence. Stir in the gelatine. Chill in the fridge for 30 minutes, or until just beginning to set around the edges.

3 Whisk the egg white until stiff and carefully fold it into the yogurt mixture. Spoon into a piping bag fitted with a nozzle and use immediately.

STRAINED YOGURT AND SIMPLE CURD CHEESE

Strained yogurt is simple to make and lower in fat than many commercial varieties. Serve with desserts, instead of cream. Simple curd cheese can be used instead of soured cream, cream cheese or butter for sweet or savoury recipes.

INGREDIENTS

Makes 300ml/½ pint/1¼ cups yogurt or 115g/4oz/½ cup curd cheese
600ml/1 pint/2½ cups natural low-fat yogurt

1 For strained yogurt, line a nylon or stainless-steel sieve with a double layer of muslin. Put over a bowl and pour in the yogurt.

2 Leave to drain in the fridge for 3 hours – the mixture will have separated into thick strained yogurt and watery whey. If liked, sweeten with a little honey.

3 To make simple curd cheese, follow step 1 above, then leave to drain in the fridge for 8 hours or overnight. Spoon the resulting curd cheese into a bowl, cover and chill until required.

THE FAT AND CALORIE CONTENT OF FOODS

The following figures show the weight of fat (g) and the energy content per 100g/3½oz of each food.

VEGETABLES

	FAT (g)	SAT. FAT (g)	CHOL (mg)	ENERGY		FAT (g)	SAT. FAT (g)	CHOL (mg)	ENERGY
Broccoli	0.9	0.2	0	33 Kcals/138 kJ	Onions	0.2	trace	0	36 Kcals/151 kJ
Cabbage	0.4	0.1	0	26 Kcals/109 kJ	Peas	1.5	0.3	0	83 Kcals/344 kJ
Carrots	0.3	0.1	0	35 Kcals/146 kJ	Potatoes	0.2	trace	0	75 Kcals/318 kJ
Cauliflower	0.9	0.2	0	34 Kcals/142 kJ	Chips, home-made in dripping	6.7	3.7	6	189 Kcals/796 kJ
Courgettes	0.4	0.1	0	18 Kcals/74 kJ	Chips, retail (in blended oil)	12.4	1.1	0	239 Kcals/1001 kJ
Cucumber	0.1	trace	0	10 Kcals/40 kJ	Oven-chips, frozen, baked	4.2	1.8	0	162 Kcals/687 kJ
Mushrooms	0.5	0.1	0	13 Kcals/55 kJ	Tomatoes	0.3	0.1	0	17 Kcals/73 kJ

BEANS AND PULSES

	FAT (g)	SAT. FAT (g)	CHOL (mg)	ENERGY		FAT (g)	SAT. FAT (g)	CHOL (mg)	ENERGY
Black-eyed beans, cooked	0.7	0.5	0	116 Kcals/494 kJ	Hummus	12.6	n/a	0	187 Kcals/781 kJ
Butter beans, canned	0.5	0.1	0	77 Kcals/327 kJ	Red kidney beans, canned	0.6	0.1	0	100 Kcals/424 kJ
Chick-peas, canned	2.9	0.3	0	115 Kcals/487 kJ	Red lentils, cooked	0.4	trace	0	100 Kcals/424 kJ

FISH AND SEAFOOD

	FAT (g)	SAT. FAT (g)	CHOL (mg)	ENERGY		FAT (g)	SAT. FAT (g)	CHOL (mg)	ENERGY
Cod fillets, raw	0.7	0.1	46	80 Kcals/337 kJ	Prawns, boiled	0.9	0.2	280	99 Kcals/418 kJ
Crab, canned	0.5	0.1	72	77 Kcals/326 kJ	Roe, cod's, fried	11.9	1.2	500	202 Kcals/861 kJ
Haddock, raw	0.6	0.1	36	81 Kcals/345 kJ	Trout, grilled	5.4	1.1	70	135 Kcals/565 kJ
Lemon sole, raw	1.5	0.2	60	83 Kcals/351 kJ	Tuna, canned in brine	0.6	1.4	50	99 Kcals/422 kJ

MEAT AND MEAT PRODUCTS

	FAT (g)	SAT. FAT (g)	CHOL (mg)	ENERGY		FAT (g)	SAT. FAT (g)	CHOL (mg)	ENERGY
Bacon rasher, streaky, raw	23.6	8.2	65	276 Kcals/1142 kJ	Lamb chops, loin, lean and fat	23.0	10.8	79	277 Kcals/1150 kJ
Beef mince, raw	16.2	4.2	56	225 Kcals/934 kJ	Liver, lamb, raw	6.2	1.7	430	137 Kcals/575 kJ
Beef mince, raw, extra lean	9.6	7.1	60	174 Kcals/728 kJ	Pork, average, lean, raw	4.0	1.4	63	123 Kcals/519 kJ
Chicken fillet, raw	1.1	0.3	70	106 Kcals/449 kJ	Pork chops, loin, lean and fat	21.7	8.0	61	270 Kcals/1119 kJ
Chicken, roasted, meat and skin	12.5	3.4	110	218 Kcals/910 kJ	Pork pie	27.0	10.2	52	376 Kcals/1564 kJ
Duck, meat only, raw	6.5	2.0	110	137 Kcals/575 kJ	Rump steak, lean and fat	10.1	4.3	60	174 Kcals/726 kJ
Duck, roasted, meat, fat and skin	38.1	11.4	99	423 Kcals/1750 kJ	Rump steak, lean only	4.1	1.7	59	125 Kcals/526 kJ
Ham, premium	5.0	1.7	58	132 Kcals/553 kJ	Salami	45.2	n/a	n/a	491 Kcals/2031 kJ
Lamb, average, lean, raw	8.3	3.8	74	156 Kcals/651 kJ	Sausage roll, flaky pastry	36.4	13.4	49	477 Kcals/1985 kJ
					Turkey, meat only, raw	1.6	0.5	70	105 Kcals/443 kJ

Information from *The Composition of Foods* (5th edition 1991) is reproduced with the permission of the Royal Society of Chemistry and the Controller of Her Majesty's Stationery Office.

DAIRY, FATS AND OILS

	FAT (g)	SAT. FAT (g)	CHOL (mg)	ENERGY		FAT (g)	SAT. FAT (g)	CHOL (mg)	ENERGY
Brie	26.9	16.8	100	319 Kcals/1323 kJ	Fromage frais, plain	7.1	4.4	25	113 Kcals/469 kJ
Butter	81.7	54	230	737 Kcals/3031kJ	Fromage frais, very low-fat	0.2	0.1	1	58 Kcals/247 kJ
Cream, double	48.0	30	130	449 Kcals/1849 kJ	Greek yogurt	9.1	5.2	n/a	115 Kcals/477 kJ
Cream, single	19.1	11.9	55	198 Kcals/817 kJ	Greek yogurt, reduced-fat	5.0	3.1	13	80 Kcals/335 kJ
Cream, whipping	39.3	24.6	105	373 Kcals/1539 kJ	Lard	99.0	40.8	93	891 Kcals/3663 kJ
Crème fraîche	40.0	25	105	379 Kcals/1567 kJ	Low-fat spread	40.5	11.2	6	390 Kcals/1605 kJ
Crème fraîche, reduced-fat	15.0	9.4	n/a	165 Kcals/683 kJ	Low-fat spread, extra	25	6.5	n/a	273 Kcals/1128 kJ
Cheddar cheese	34.4	21.7	100	412 Kcals/1708 kJ	Low-fat yogurt, plain	0.8	0.5	4	56 Kcals/236 kJ
Cheddar-type, reduced-fat	15.0	9.4	43	261 Kcals/1091 kJ	Margarine, polyunsaturated	81.6	16.2	7	739 Kcals/3039 kJ
Corn oil	99.9	12.7	0	899 Kcals/3696 kJ	Mayonnaise	75.6	11.1	75	691 Kcals/2843 kJ
Cream cheese	47.4	29.7	95	439 Kcals/1807 kJ	Mayonnaise, reduced calorie	28.1	4.5	n/a	288 Kcals/1188 kJ
Edam cheese	25.4	15.9	80	333 Kcals/1382 kJ	Milk, semi-skimmed	1.6	1.0	7	46 Kcals/195 kJ
Egg, whole	10.8	3.1	385	147 Kcals/612 kJ	Milk, skimmed	0.1	0.1	2	33 Kcals/130 kJ
Egg white	trace	trace	trace	36 Kcals/153 kJ	Milk, whole	3.9	2.4	14	66 Kcals/275 kJ
Egg yolk	30.5	8.7	1120	339 Kcals/1402 kJ	Olive oil	99.9	14	0	899 Kcals/3696 kJ
Fat-free dressing	1.2	0	0	67 Kcals/282 kJ	Parmesan cheese	32.7	20.5	100	452 Kcals/1880 kJ
Feta cheese	20.2	13.7	70	250 Kcals/1037 kJ	Safflower oil	99.9	10.2	0	899 Kcals/3696 kJ
French dressing	49.4	10	0	462 Kcals/1902 kJ	Skimmed milk soft cheese	trace	trace	1	74 Kcals/313 kJ

CEREALS, BAKING AND PRESERVES

	FAT (g)	SAT. FAT (g)	CHOL (mg)	ENERGY		FAT (g)	SAT. FAT (g)	CHOL (mg)	ENERGY
Bread, brown	2.0	0.4	0	218 Kcals/927 kJ	Honey	0	0	0	288 Kcals/1229 kJ
Bread, white	1.9	0.4	0	235 Kcals/1002 kJ	Lemon curd, home-made	0.8	0.3	150	176 Kcals/736 kJ
Bread, wholemeal	2.5	0.5	0	215 Kcals/914 kJ	Madeira cake	16.9	17.3	n/a	393 Kcals/1652 kJ
Chocolate, milk	30.3	17.8	30	520 Kcals/2214 kJ	Pasta, white, uncooked	1.8	0.2	0	342 Kcals/1456 kJ
Chocolate, plain	29.2	16.9	0	510 Kcals/2157 kJ	Pasta, wholemeal, uncooked	2.5	0.4	0	324 Kcals/1379 kJ
Cornflakes	0.7	0.1	0	360 Kcals/1535 kJ	Rice, brown, uncooked	2.8	0.7	0	357 Kcals/1518 kJ
Croissant	20.3	6.5	75	360 Kcals/1505 kJ	Rice, white, uncooked	3.6	0.9	0	383 Kcals/1630 kJ
Digestive biscuit, plain	20.9	8.6	41	471 Kcals/1978 kJ	Shortbread	26.1	17.3	74	498 Kcals/2087 kJ
Doughnut, jam	14.5	4.3	15	336 Kcals/1414 kJ	Sponge cake, fatless	6.1	1.7	223	294 Kcals/1245 kJ
Flapjack	26.6	7.6	43	484 Kcals/2028 kJ	Sugar, white	0	0	0	105 Kcals/394 kJ
Fruit cake, rich	11	3.4	63	341 Kcals/1438 kJ	Sultana bran	1.6	0.4	0	303 Kcals/1289 kJ
Fruit jam	0	0	0	261 Kcals/1116 kJ	Swiss-style muesli	5.9	0.8	trace	363 Kcals/1540 kJ

FRUIT AND NUTS

	FAT (g)	SAT. FAT (g)	CHOL (mg)	ENERGY		FAT (g)	SAT. FAT (g)	CHOL (mg)	ENERGY
Almonds	55.8	4.7	0	612 Kcals/2534 kJ	Hazelnuts	63.5	4.7	0	650 Kcals/2685 kJ
Apples, eating	0.1	trace	0	47 Kcals/199 kJ	Oranges	0.1	trace	0	37 Kcals/158 kJ
Avocados	19.5	4.1	0	190 Kcals/784 kJ	Peaches	0.1	trace	0	33 Kcals/142 kJ
Bananas	0.3	0.1	0	95 Kcals/403 kJ	Peanut butter, smooth	53.7	11.7	0	623 Kcals/2581 kJ
Brazil nuts	68.2	16.4	0	682 Kcals/2813 kJ	Pears	0.1	trace	0	40 Kcals/169 kJ
Dried mixed fruit	0.4	n/a	0	268 Kcals/1114 kJ	Pine nuts	68.6	4.6	0	688 Kcals/2840 kJ
Grapefruit	0.1	trace	0	30 Kcals/126 kJ	Walnuts	68.5	5.6	0	688 Kcals/2837kJ

HEALING RECIPES

The following pages are packed with over 300 exciting and
inspirational recipes to help you put the theories behind your special
diet into practice. Each recipe has been specially chosen for its healing
properties and has been coded with an at-a-glance key, indicating
which potential allergens it is free from. There is also an
easy-to-follow index at the end of the book indicating which recipes
are best suited for each of the health conditions mentioned.

SOUPS

Hot and chunky or chilled and smooth, these soups are low in fat and

packed with nutrients from fresh and wholesome ingredients. As a

light lunch with crusty wholemeal bread, or as a healthy starter, soups

are extremely quick and easy to make. On cold winter days, try a

hearty warming soup, such as Creamed Spinach and Potato Soup or

Chicken Soup with Vermicelli. Alternatively, in summer, try the

cooling flavours of Gazpacho or Chilled Almond Soup.

Summer Tomato Soup

The success of this soup depends on having ripe, full-flavoured tomatoes, so make it when the tomato season is at its peak. It is equally delicious served cold.

INGREDIENTS

Serves 4

15ml/1 tbsp olive oil
1 large onion, chopped
1 carrot, chopped
1kg/2¼lb ripe tomatoes, cored and quartered
2 garlic cloves, chopped
5 thyme sprigs, or 1.5ml/¼ tsp dried thyme
4 or 5 marjoram sprigs, or 1.5ml/¼ tsp dried marjoram
1 bay leaf
45ml/3 tbsp sheep's or goat's milk yogurt, plus a little extra to garnish
salt and ground black pepper
marjoram sprigs, to garnish

1 Heat the olive oil in a large, preferably stainless steel, saucepan or flameproof casserole.

2 Add the onion and carrot and cook for 3–4 minutes, until just softened, stirring occasionally.

VARIATION

To serve the soup cold, omit the yogurt and leave to cool, then chill.

---

3 Add the tomatoes, garlic and herbs. Reduce the heat and simmer, covered, for 30 minutes.

4 Pass the soup through a food mill or press through a sieve into the pan. Stir in the yogurt and season. Reheat gently and serve in warmed soup bowls, garnished with a spoonful of yogurt and a sprig of marjoram.

NUTRITION NOTES	
Per portion:	
Energy	84kcals/335kJ
Protein	2.4g
Fat	4g
saturated fat	0.9g
Carbohydrate	10.2g
Sugar	9.8g
Fibre	3g
Calcium	39mg

Pumpkin Soup

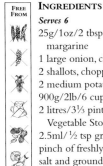

INGREDIENTS

Serves 6

25g/1oz/2 tbsp pure vegetable margarine
1 large onion, chopped
2 shallots, chopped
2 medium potatoes, peeled and cubed
900g/2lb/6 cups cubed pumpkin
2 litres/3⅓ pints/8 cups Chicken or Vegetable Stock
2.5ml/½ tsp ground cumin
pinch of freshly grated nutmeg
salt and ground black pepper
fresh parsley or chives, to garnish

1 Melt the margarine in a large flameproof casserole or saucepan. Add the onion and shallots and cook for 4–5 minutes until just softened.

2 Add the potatoes, pumpkin, stock, cumin and grated nutmeg, and season with a little salt and black pepper. Reduce the heat to low and simmer, covered, for about 1 hour, stirring occasionally, until the vegetables are thoroughly cooked.

NUTRITION NOTES	
Per portion:	
Energy	95kcals/400kJ
Protein	3.2g
Fat	4.6g
saturated fat	1.9g
Carbohydrate	10.9g
Sugar	3.9g
Fibre	2.1g
Calcium	55mg

3 With a slotted spoon, transfer the cooked vegetables to a food processor and process until smooth, adding a little of the cooking liquid if needed. Stir the purée into the cooking liquid remaining in the pan until well mixed. Adjust the seasoning and reheat gently. Garnish the soup with the fresh herbs.

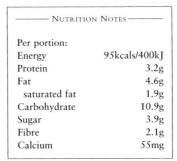

Spicy Carrot Soup with Garlic Croûtons

INGREDIENTS

Serves 6
15ml/1 tbsp olive oil
1 large onion, chopped
675g/1½lb carrots, sliced
5ml/1 tsp each ground coriander,
    ground cumin and hot chilli powder
900ml/1½ pints/3¾ cups vegetable or
    chicken stock
salt and ground black pepper
fresh coriander sprigs, to garnish

For the garlic croûtons
a little olive oil, for frying
2 garlic cloves, crushed
4 slices of gluten-, dairy- and yeast-free
    bread, crusts removed, cut into
    1cm/½in cubes

1 To make the soup, heat the oil in a
large saucepan, add the onion and
carrots and cook gently for 5 minutes,
stirring occasionally. Add the spices.
Cook gently for 1 minute, stirring.

2 Stir in the stock, bring to the boil,
then cover and cook gently for
about 45 minutes until the carrots are
tender, stirring occasionally.

3 Meanwhile, make the garlic
croûtons. Heat a little oil in a frying
pan, add the garlic and cook gently for
30 seconds, stirring. Add the bread
cubes, turn them over in the oil and fry
over a medium heat for a few minutes
until crisp and golden brown all over,
turning frequently. Drain on kitchen
paper and keep warm.

4 Purée the soup in a blender or food
processor until smooth, then season
to taste with salt and pepper. Return
the soup to the rinsed-out saucepan
and reheat gently. Serve hot, sprinkled
with garlic croûtons and garnished with
coriander sprigs.

--- NUTRITION NOTES ---

Per portion:

Energy	127kcals/529kJ
Fat, total	6.1g
saturated fat	0.92g
Protein	2.65g
Carbohydrate	17.2g
sugar, total	7.74g
Fibre	2.94g
Sodium	626mg

Sweet Potato and Parsnip Soup

INGREDIENTS

Serves 6
15ml/1 tbsp sunflower oil
1 large leek, sliced
2 celery sticks, chopped
450g/1lb sweet potatoes, diced
225g/8oz parsnips, diced
900ml/1½ pints/3¾ cups vegetable or
    chicken stock
salt and ground black pepper
15ml/1 tbsp chopped fresh parsley and
    roasted strips of sweet potatoes and
    parsnips, to garnish

1 Heat the oil in a large saucepan,
add the leek, celery, sweet potatoes
and parsnips. Cook gently for about
5 minutes, stirring to prevent them
browning or sticking to the pan.

2 Stir in the vegetable or chicken
stock and bring to the boil, then
cover and simmer gently for about
25 minutes, or until the vegetables are
tender, stirring occasionally. Season to
taste with salt and pepper.

3 Remove the pan from the heat and
allow to cool slightly.

4 Purée the soup in a blender or food
processor until smooth, then return
the soup to the saucepan and reheat
gently. Ladle into warmed soup bowls
to serve and sprinkle over the chopped
fresh parsley and roasted strips of sweet
potatoes and parsnips to garnish.

--- NUTRITION NOTES ---

Per portion:

Energy	115kcals/486kJ
Fat, total	4g
saturated fat	0.46g
Protein	3.1g
Carbohydrate	17.9g
sugar, total	3.72g
Fibre	3.07g
Sodium	780mg

Sweet Potato and Red Pepper Soup

As colourful as it is good to eat, this soup is a sure winner.

INGREDIENTS

Serves 6

500g/1¼lb sweet potato
2 red peppers, about 225g/8oz, seeded and cubed
1 onion, roughly chopped
2 large garlic cloves, roughly chopped
300ml/½ pint/1¼ cups dry white wine
1.2 litres/2 pints/5 cups vegetable or light chicken stock
Tabasco sauce (optional)
salt and ground black pepper
country bread, to serve

1 Peel the sweet potato and cut it into cubes. Put these in a saucepan with the red peppers, onion, garlic, wine and vegetable or chicken stock. Bring to the boil, lower the heat and simmer for 30 minutes or until all the vegetables are quite soft.

2 Transfer the mixture to a blender or food processor and process until smooth. Season to taste with salt, pepper and a generous dash of Tabasco, if liked. Pour into a tureen or serving bowl and cool slightly. Serve warm or at room temperature, with bread.

--- COOK'S TIP ---

Garnish the soup with finely diced red, green or yellow pepper, if you like.

--- NUTRITION NOTES ---

Per portion:

Energy	122kcals/516kJ
Fat, total	0.4g
saturated fat	0.1g
polyunsaturated fat	0.17g
monounsaturated fat	0g
Carbohydrate	21.4g
sugar, total	7.9g
starch	13.2g
Fibre	2.8g
Sodium	37mg

Cream of Celeriac and Spinach Soup

Celeriac has a wonderful flavour that is reminiscent of celery, but also adds a slightly nutty taste. Here it is combined with spinach to make a delicious soup.

INGREDIENTS

Serves 6
1 leek
500g/1¼lb celeriac
1 litre/1¾ pints/4 cups water
250ml/8fl oz/1 cup dry white wine
200g/7oz fresh spinach leaves
semi-skimmed milk (optional)
25g/1oz/⅓ cup pine nuts
salt, ground black pepper and
    grated nutmeg

1 Trim and slit the leek. Rinse it under running water to remove any grit, then slice it thickly. Peel the celeriac and dice the flesh.

2 Mix the water and wine in a jug. Place the leek and celeriac, with the spinach, in a deep saucepan and pour over the liquid. Bring to the boil, lower the heat and let simmer for 10–15 minutes, until soft.

3 Purée the celeriac mixture, in batches if necessary, in a blender or food processor. Return to the clean pan and season to taste with salt, pepper and nutmeg. If the soup is too thick, thin it with a little semi-skimmed milk or water, as your diet demands. Reheat gently.

4 Roast the pine nuts in a dry non-stick frying pan until golden. Sprinkle them over the soup and serve.

NUTRITION NOTES	
Per portion:	
Energy	82kcals/340kJ
Fat, total	3.5g
saturated fat	0.25g
polyunsaturated fat	1.9g
monounsaturated fat	0.85g
Carbohydrate	3.25g
sugar, total	2.7g
starch	0.5g
Fibre	4g
Sodium	124mg

FREE FROM

Mrs Blencowe's Green Pea Soup with Spinach

This lovely green soup was invented by the wife of a 17th-century British Member of Parliament, and it has stood the test of time.

INGREDIENTS

Serves 6

450g/1lb/generous 3 cups podded fresh or frozen peas
1 leek, finely sliced
2 garlic cloves, crushed
2 rindless back bacon slices, finely diced
1.2 litres/2 pints/5 cups gluten-free ham or Chicken Stock
30ml/2 tbsp olive oil
50g/2oz fresh spinach, shredded
40g/1½oz white cabbage, very finely shredded
½ small lettuce, very finely shredded
1 celery stick, finely chopped
large handful of parsley, finely chopped
½ carton mustard and cress
20ml/4 tsp chopped fresh mint
pinch of mace
salt and ground black pepper

1 Put the peas, leek, garlic and bacon in a large saucepan. Add the stock, bring to the boil, then lower the heat and simmer for 20 minutes.

2 About 5 minutes before the pea mixture is ready, heat the oil in a deep frying pan.

3 Add the spinach, cabbage, lettuce, celery and herbs. Cover and sweat the mixture over a low heat until soft.

— COOK'S TIP —

Use 25g/1oz frozen leaf spinach if fresh spinach is not available.

4 Transfer the pea mixture to a blender or food processor; process until smooth. Return to the clean saucepan, add the sweated vegetables and herbs and heat through. Season with mace, salt and pepper and serve.

— NUTRITION NOTES —

Per portion:	
Energy	140kcals/575kJ
Fat, total	7.6g
saturated fat	1.45g
polyunsaturated fat	1.2g
monounsaturated fat	4.4g
Carbohydrate	10g
sugar, total	2.7g
starch	5.8g
Fibre	4.4g
Sodium	165mg

Garlicky Lentil Soup

High in fibre, lentils make a very tasty soup. Unlike many pulses, they do not need to be soaked before being cooked.

INGREDIENTS

Serves 6

225g/8oz/1 cup red lentils, rinsed
  and drained
2 onions, finely chopped
2 large garlic cloves, finely chopped
1 carrot, very finely chopped
30ml/2 tbsp olive oil
2 bay leaves
generous pinch of dried marjoram
  or oregano
1.5 litres/2½ pints/6¼ cups
  vegetable stock
30ml/2 tbsp red wine vinegar
salt and ground black pepper
celery leaves, to garnish
dairy- and egg-free crusty rolls, to serve

COOK'S TIP

If you buy your lentils loose, remember to tip them into a sieve or colander and pick them over, removing any pieces of grit, before rinsing them.

NUTRITION NOTES

Per portion:

Energy	167kcals/748kJ
Fat, total	5.6g
saturated fat	0.8g
polyunsaturated fat	0.65g
monounsaturated fat	3.7g
Carbohydrate	23.6g
sugar, total	2.6g
starch	19.3g
Fibre	2.45g
Sodium	18.5mg

1 Put all the ingredients except the vinegar, garnish and seasoning in a large heavy-based saucepan. Bring to the boil over a medium heat, then lower the heat and simmer for 1½ hours, stirring the soup occasionally to prevent the lentils from sticking to the bottom of the pan.

2 Remove the bay leaves and add the red wine vinegar, with salt and pepper to taste. If the soup is too thick, thin it with a little extra vegetable stock or water. Serve the soup in heated bowls, garnished with celery leaves and accompanied by crusty rolls.

Lentil Soup with Tomatoes

A classic rustic Italian soup flavoured with rosemary.

INGREDIENTS

Serves 4

225g/8oz/1 cup dried green or
   brown lentils
45ml/3 tbsp extra virgin olive oil
3 rindless streaky bacon rashers, cut
   into small dice
1 onion, finely chopped
2 celery sticks, finely chopped
2 carrots, finely diced
2 rosemary sprigs, finely chopped
2 bay leaves
400g/14oz can chopped plum tomatoes
1.75 litres/3 pints/7½ cups
   Vegetable Stock
salt and ground black pepper
bay leaves and rosemary sprigs,
   to garnish

1 Place the lentils in a bowl and cover with cold water. Leave to soak for 2 hours. Rinse and drain well.

2 Heat the oil in a large saucepan. Add the bacon and cook for about 3 minutes, then stir in the onion and cook for 5 minutes until softened. Stir in the celery, carrots, rosemary, bay leaves and lentils. Toss over the heat for 1 minute until thoroughly coated in the oil.

3 Tip in the tomatoes and stock and bring to the boil. Lower the heat, half cover the pan, and simmer for about 1 hour, or until the lentils are perfectly tender.

4 Remove the bay leaves, add salt and pepper to taste and serve with a garnish of fresh bay leaves and rosemary sprigs.

—— NUTRITION NOTES ——

Per portion:
Energy	357kcals/1501kJ
Protein	19.6g
Fat	16.6g
saturated fat	3.9g
Carbohydrate	34.7g
Sugar	6.63g
Fibre	6.8g
Calcium	80mg

Spinach and Rice Soup

Use very fresh, young spinach leaves to prepare this light and clean-tasting soup.

INGREDIENTS

Serves 4

675g/1½ lb fresh spinach, washed
45ml/3 tbsp extra virgin olive oil
1 small onion, finely chopped
2 garlic cloves, finely chopped
1 small fresh red chilli, seeded and
   finely chopped
115g/4oz/generous 1 cup risotto rice
1.2 litres/2 pints/5 cups Vegetable Stock
salt and ground black pepper
60ml/4 tbsp freshly grated Parmesan
   cheese, to serve

1 Place the spinach in a large pan with just the water that clings to its leaves after washing. Add a large pinch of salt. Heat gently until the spinach has wilted, then remove from the heat and drain, reserving any liquid.

2 Either chop the spinach finely using a large knife or place in a food processor and process to a fairly coarse purée.

3 Heat the oil in a large saucepan and cook the onion, garlic and chilli for 4–5 minutes until softened. Stir in the rice, then pour in the stock and the reserved spinach liquid. Bring to the boil, then simmer for 10 minutes. Add the spinach and season to taste. Cook for 5–7 minutes more, until the rice is tender. Serve with Parmesan cheese.

—— NUTRITION NOTES ——

Per portion:
Energy	292kcals/1215kJ
Protein	12.6g
Fat	14.8g
saturated fat	4.4g
Carbohydrate	29.5g
Sugar	3.16g
Fibre	3.8g
Calcium	470mg

Italian Farmhouse Soup

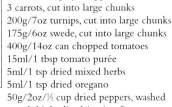

INGREDIENTS

Serves 4

30ml/2 tbsp olive oil
1 onion, roughly chopped
3 carrots, cut into large chunks
200g/7oz turnips, cut into large chunks
175g/6oz swede, cut into large chunks
400g/14oz can chopped tomatoes
15ml/1 tbsp tomato purée
5ml/1 tsp dried mixed herbs
5ml/1 tsp dried oregano
50g/2oz/½ cup dried peppers, washed
    and thinly sliced (optional)
1.5 litres/2½ pints/6¼ cups vegetable
    stock or water
50g/2oz/½ cup dried small egg-free
    macaroni or conchiglie
400g/14oz can red kidney beans, rinsed
    and drained
30ml/2 tbsp chopped fresh flat
    leaf parsley
salt and ground black pepper
freshly grated Parmesan cheese, to serve

1 Heat the oil in a large saucepan, add the onion and cook over a low heat for about 5 minutes until softened. Add the fresh vegetables, canned tomatoes, tomato purée, dried herbs and dried peppers, if using, then stir in salt and pepper to taste.

2 Pour in the stock or water and bring to the boil. Stir well, cover, lower the heat and simmer for 30 minutes, stirring occasionally.

3 Add the pasta and bring to the boil, stirring. Lower the heat and simmer, uncovered, until the pasta is only just *al dente*: about 5 minutes or according to the instructions on the packet. Stir frequently.

4 Stir in the beans. Heat through for 2–3 minutes, then remove from the heat and stir in the parsley. Taste the soup for seasoning. Serve hot with grated Parmesan handed separately.

NUTRITION NOTES

Per portion:

Energy	248kcals/1049kJ
Protein	10.3g
Fat	6.7g
saturated fat	0.9g
Carbohydrate	39g
Fibre	10.5g
Sugars	12.8g
Calcium	143mg

COOK'S TIP

Packets of dried Italian peppers are piquant and firm with a "meaty" bite to them, which makes them ideal for adding substance to vegetarian soups.

VARIATION

Root vegetables form the base of this soup, but you can vary the vegetables according to what you have to hand.

Gazpacho with Avocado Salsa

This classic summer soup, which is loaded with fresh vegetables, chilli and garlic, does not require cooking. Heat can often destroy valuable nutrients, so this soup makes a perfect choice.

INGREDIENTS

Serves 4

2 slices day-old dairy- and egg-free bread
600ml/1 pint/2½ cups chilled water
1kg/2¼lb large vine-ripened tomatoes
1 medium cucumber
1 red pepper, seeded and chopped
1 green chilli, seeded and chopped
2 garlic cloves, chopped
30ml/2 tbsp olive oil
juice of 1 lime and 1 lemon
a few drops of Tabasco
salt and ground black pepper
8 ice cubes, to serve
a handful of basil leaves, to garnish

For the croûtons

2 slices day-old dairy- and egg-free
   bread, crusts removed
1 garlic clove
15ml/1 tbsp olive oil

For the avocado salsa

1 ripe avocado, peeled and diced
5ml/1 tsp lemon juice
2.5cm/1in piece cucumber, diced
½ red chilli, finely chopped

1 Soak the bread in 150ml/¼ pint/ ⅔ cup of the water for 5 minutes.

NUTRITION NOTES	
Per portion:	
Energy	199kcals/836kJ
Protein	5.4g
Fat	10.0g
saturated fat	2.4g
Carbohydrate	23.3g
Fibre	5.8g
Sugars	12.1g
Calcium	59mg

2 Meanwhile, pour boiling water over the tomatoes and leave for 30 seconds–1 minute, then peel, seed and chop the flesh. Peel the cucumber then cut in half lengthways. Scoop out the seeds with a spoon, discard, and chop the flesh into small cubes.

3 Place the bread, tomatoes, chopped cucumber, red pepper, chilli, garlic, olive oil, citrus juices and Tabasco in a food processor or blender with the remaining chilled water and blend until well combined but still chunky. Season to taste and chill for 2–3 hours.

4 To make the croûtons, rub the slices of bread with the garlic clove. Cut into cubes, place in a plastic bag with the olive oil, and shake until coated with the oil. Fry the croûtons until crisp and golden.

5 To make the avocado salsa, toss the avocado in the lemon juice and combine with the cucumber and chilli.

6 Ladle the soup into bowls, add the ice cubes, and top with a spoonful of salsa and croûtons. Garnish with basil just before serving.

FREE FROM

Creamed Spinach and Potato Soup

Spinach fills this low-fat, creamy soup with antioxidant nutrients.

INGREDIENTS

Serves 6
1 large onion, finely chopped
1 garlic clove, crushed
900g/2lb floury potatoes, diced
2 celery sticks, chopped
1.2 litres/2 pints/5 cups
    Vegetable Stock
250g/9oz fresh spinach leaves
200g/7oz/scant 1 cup low-fat
    cream cheese
300ml/½ pint/1¼ cups milk
dash of dry sherry
salt and ground black pepper
croûtons and chopped fresh parsley,
    to garnish

1 Place the onion, garlic, potatoes and celery in a large saucepan. Add the stock and simmer for 20 minutes.

2 Season the soup, add the spinach, then cook for a further 10 minutes. Remove from the heat and leave to cool slightly.

3 Process the soup in batches and return to the saucepan. Stir in the cream cheese and milk, then simmer gently until warmed through. Check the seasoning and add a dash of sherry. Serve garnished with croûtons and chopped parsley.

——— NUTRITION NOTES ———

Per portion:
Energy	170kcals/697kJ
Protein	9.4g
Fat	2g
saturated fat	0.8g
Carbohydrate	30.4g
Fibre	3.4g
Sugars	4.5g
Calcium	116mg

Potato and Garlic Broth

A perfect winter warmer, this wholesome soup is packed with phytochemical-rich garlic, which is believed to help in the fight against cancer.

INGREDIENTS

Serves 6
2 whole heads of garlic
4 potatoes, peeled and diced
1.75 litres/3 pints/7½ cups
    Vegetable Stock
salt and ground black pepper
flat leaf parsley, to garnish

——— HEALTH BENEFITS ———

The American National Cancer Institute rates garlic as one of the top foods for cancer prevention. It is best eaten raw, but cooking does not greatly reduce its beneficial qualities.

1 Preheat the oven to 190°C/375°F/ Gas 5. Place the unpeeled garlic bulbs in a small roasting tin and bake for 30 minutes.

2 Meanwhile, par-cook the potatoes in boiling water for 10 minutes.

3 Simmer the prepared vegetable stock for 5 minutes. Drain the potatoes and add to the stock.

4 Squeeze the garlic pulp into the soup, stir and season to taste.

5 Simmer for a further 15 minutes and then pour into warmed bowls and garnish with flat leaf parsley.

——— COOK'S TIP ———

Too much garlic can be overpowering, but roasting it first mellows its pungent flavour.

——— NUTRITION NOTES ———

Per portion:
Energy	42kcals/172kJ
Protein	1.4g
Fat	0.1g
saturated fat	0.01g
Carbohydrate	9.41g
Fibre	0.8g
Sugars	0.3g
Calcium	3.4mg

Wild Mushroom Soup

Wild mushrooms can sometimes be expensive but dried porcini have an intense flavour, so only a small quantity is needed. The beef stock may seem unusual in a vegetable soup, but it helps to strengthen the earthy flavour of the mushrooms.

INGREDIENTS

Serves 4

25g/1oz/2 cups dried porcini mushrooms
30ml/2 tbsp olive oil
15g/½oz/1 tbsp unsalted butter
2 leeks, finely sliced
2 shallots, roughly chopped
1 garlic clove, roughly chopped
225g/8oz/3 cups fresh wild mushrooms
about 1.2 litres/2 pints/5 cups hot Beef stock
2.5ml/½ tsp dried thyme
150ml/¼ pint/⅔ cup double cream
ground black pepper
fresh thyme sprigs, to garnish

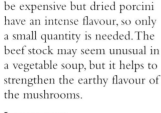

1 Put the porcini in a bowl, add 250ml/8fl oz/1 cup warm water and leave to soak for 20–30 minutes. Lift the porcini out of the liquid and squeeze over the bowl to remove as much of the soaking liquid as possible. Strain all the liquid and reserve to use later. Finely chop the porcini.

2 Heat the oil and butter in a large saucepan until foaming. Add the sliced leeks, chopped shallots and garlic, and cook gently for about 5 minutes, stirring frequently, until softened but not coloured.

3 Chop or slice the fresh mushrooms and add to the pan. Stir over a medium heat for a few minutes until they begin to soften. Pour in the stock and bring to the boil. Add the porcini, soaking liquid, dried thyme and pepper to taste. Lower the heat, half-cover the pan and simmer gently for 30 minutes, stirring occasionally.

4 Pour about three-quarters of the soup into a food processor or blender, and process until smooth. Return to the soup remaining in the pan, stir in the cream and heat through. Taste for seasoning. Serve garnished with thyme sprigs.

NUTRITION NOTES	
Per portion:	
Energy	296Kcals/1223kJ
Protein	4.8g
Fat	27.3g
saturated fat	14.09g
Carbohydrate	8g
Fibre	1.9g
Sodium	50mg

Spicy Lamb Soup

This spicy, filling soup, based on a traditional Moroccan recipe, combines pulses with lamb and fresh tomatoes.

INGREDIENTS

Serves 6

75g/3oz/½ cup chick-peas,
   soaked overnight
15g/½oz/1 tbsp unsalted butter
225g/8oz lamb, cubed
1 onion, chopped
450g/1lb tomatoes, chopped
a few celery leaves, chopped
30ml/2 tbsp chopped fresh parsley
15ml/1 tbsp chopped fresh coriander
2.5ml/½ tsp ground ginger
2.5ml/½ tsp ground turmeric
5ml/1 tsp ground cinnamon
75g/3oz/scant ½ cup green lentils
75g/3oz vermicelli or soup pasta
2 egg yolks
juice of ½–1 lemon
ground black pepper
fresh coriander, to garnish
lemon wedges, to serve

FREE FROM

1 Drain the chick-peas, rinse under cold water and set aside. Melt the butter in a large, flameproof casserole or saucepan and fry the lamb and onion for 2–3 minutes, stirring, until the lamb is just browned.

2 Add the tomatoes, celery leaves, herbs and spices, and season well with black pepper. Cook for about 1 minute and then stir in 1.75 litres/ 3 pints/7½ cups water and add the lentils and chick-peas.

3 Slowly bring to the boil and skim the surface to remove the surplus froth. Boil rapidly for 10 minutes, then reduce the heat and simmer very gently for about 2 hours or until the chick-peas are tender. Season with a little more pepper if necessary.

4 Add the vermicelli or soup pasta and cook for 5–6 minutes until it is just cooked through.

NUTRITION NOTES	
Per portion:	
Energy	256Kcals/1074kJ
Protein	16.3g
Fat	10g
saturated fat	4.51g
Carbohydrate	27g
Fibre	4.1g
Sodium	41mg

5 If the soup is very thick at this stage, add a little more water. Beat the egg yolks with the lemon juice and stir into the simmering soup.

6 Immediately remove the soup from the heat and stir until thickened. Pour into warmed serving bowls and garnish with the fresh coriander. Serve with lemon wedges.

Chilled Vegetable Soup with Pastis

Fennel, star anise and pastis give a delicate aniseed flavour to this sophisticated soup.

INGREDIENTS

Serves 6
175g/6oz leeks, finely sliced
225g/8oz fennel, finely sliced
1 potato, peeled and diced
3 pieces star anise, tied in a square
  of muslin
300ml/½ pint/1¼ cups single cream
10ml/2 tsp pastis
90ml/6 tbsp double cream or
  crème fraîche
ground black pepper
snipped chives, to garnish

COOK'S TIP

To chill the soup quickly, stir in a spoonful
of crushed ice.

1 Pour 900ml/1½ pints/3¾ cups boiling water into a saucepan, add the sliced leek and fennel, the diced potato and star anise and season to taste with pepper. Bring to the boil and simmer for 25 minutes.

2 Remove the star anise with a slotted spoon, then process the vegetables until smooth in a food processor or blender and place in a clean pan.

3 Stir in the single cream, bring to the boil, taste and adjust the seasoning if necessary.

4 Strain through a sieve into a bowl, cover and leave until cold. To serve, stir in the pastis, pour into individual serving bowls, add a swirl of double cream or a spoonful of crème fraîche and garnish with snipped chives.

NUTRITION NOTES

Per portion:

Energy	194Kcals/801kJ
Protein	2.7g
Fat	17g
saturated fat	10.51g
Carbohydrate	7g
Fibre	1.8g
Sodium	36mg

Mediterranean Fish Soup

This traditional soup is a delight for lovers of herbs and is perfect when topped off with a dollop of garlic mayonnaise. Use as many varieties of fish and shellfish as you can find.

INGREDIENTS

Serves 4

450g/1lb mixed fish fillets, such as
   red mullet, monkfish, sea bass
450g/1lb mixed shellfish, such as
   mussels and prawns
a pinch of saffron strands
60ml/4 tbsp olive oil
350g/12oz onions,
   roughly chopped
350g/12oz fennel, halved and thinly
   sliced (about 1 small bulb)
10ml/2 tsp plain flour
400g/14oz can chopped tomatoes
3 garlic cloves, crushed
2 bay leaves
30ml/2 tbsp chopped fresh thyme
pared rind of 1 orange
cayenne pepper, to taste
saltless garlic mayonnaise and crusty
   bread, to serve

1 Wash and skin the fish, if necessary, and cut into large chunks. Clean the shellfish and remove the heads from the prawns. Discard any mussels that are open.

2 Place the saffron strands in a bowl and pour over 150ml/¼ pint/⅔ cup boiling water. Leave the saffron to soak for about 20 minutes. Strain.

3 Heat the oil in a large saucepan and add the onions and fennel. Fry for 5 minutes, stirring occasionally with a wooden spoon, or until they are beginning to soften. Stir in the flour.

4 Strain the tomatoes and gradually blend in with 750ml/1¼ pints/ 3 cups cold water, the garlic, bay leaves, thyme, orange rind, saffron liquid and cayenne pepper. Bring to the boil.

5 Reduce the heat, add the fish (not the shellfish) and simmer gently, uncovered, for about 2 minutes.

6 Add the shellfish and cook for a further 2–3 minutes, or until all the fish is cooked but still holding its shape. Discard any mussels that haven't opened. Adjust the seasoning to taste. Serve with a generous spoonful of garlic mayonnaise and crusty bread.

─── NUTRITION NOTES ───	
Per portion:	
Energy	340Kcals/1412kJ
Protein	29.7g
Fat	18.6g
saturated fat	3.3g
Carbohydrate	14g
Fibre	3.6g
Sodium	205mg

Chilled Almond Soup

Use a food processor to prepare this creamy Spanish soup, which is very simple and refreshing.

INGREDIENTS

Serves 6
115g/4oz fresh dairy- and egg-free
 white bread
115g/4oz/1 cup blanched almonds
2 garlic cloves, sliced
75ml/5 tbsp olive oil
25ml/1½ tbsp sherry vinegar
salt and ground black pepper
toasted flaked almonds and seedless
 green and black grapes, halved and
 skinned, to garnish

1 Break the bread into a bowl and pour over 150ml/¼ pint/⅔ cup cold water. Leave for 5 minutes.

2 Put the almonds and garlic in a blender or food processor and process until very finely ground. Blend in the soaked white bread.

3 Gradually add the oil until the mixture forms a smooth paste. Add the sherry vinegar, then 600ml/ 1 pint/2½ cups cold water and process until smooth.

4 Transfer to a bowl and season with salt and pepper, adding a little more water if the soup is very thick. Chill for at least 2–3 hours.

5 Ladle the soup into bowls and scatter with the toasted almonds and skinned grapes.

——— Nutrition Notes ———	
Per portion:	
Energy	251kcals/1044kJ
Protein	5.8g
Fat	20.4g
saturated fat	2.3g
Carbohydrate	11.7g
Fibre	1.8g
Sugars	2g
Calcium	68mg

Winter Vegetable Soup

Parsnips, pumpkin and carrots give this soup a wonderfully rich texture and a vibrant colour.

INGREDIENTS

Serves 4

15ml/1 tbsp olive or sunflower oil
15g/½oz/1 tbsp soya margarine
1 onion, chopped
225g/8oz carrots, chopped
225g/8oz parsnips, chopped
225g/8oz pumpkin
about 900ml/1½ pints/3¾ cups
  Vegetable or Chicken Stock
lemon juice, to taste
salt and ground black pepper

For the garnish

7.5ml/1½ tsp olive oil
½ garlic clove, finely chopped
45ml/3 tbsp chopped fresh parsley and
  coriander, mixed
good pinch of paprika

FREE
FROM

1 Heat the oil and margarine in a large pan and fry the onion for about 3 minutes until softened, stirring occasionally. Add the carrots and parsnips, stir well, cover and cook over a gentle heat for a further 5 minutes.

2 Cut the pumpkin into chunks, discarding the skin and pith, and stir into the pan. Cover and cook for a further 5 minutes, then add the stock and seasoning and slowly bring to the boil. Cover and simmer very gently for 35–40 minutes until the vegetables are tender.

3 Allow the soup to cool slightly, then purée in a food processor or blender until smooth, adding a little extra water if necessary. Pour back into a clean pan and reheat gently.

4 To make the garnish, heat the oil in a small pan and gently fry the garlic and herbs for 1–2 minutes. Add the paprika and stir well.

5 Adjust the seasoning of the soup and stir in lemon juice to taste. Pour into warmed individual soup bowls and spoon a little garnish on top, which should then be carefully swirled into the soup.

——— NUTRITION NOTES ———

Per portion:

Energy	139kcals/579kJ
Protein	3.8g
Fat	8.4g
saturated fat	2.9g
Carbohydrate	12.7g
Fibre	5.5g
Sugars	7.8g
Calcium	103mg

Chicken Soup with Vermicelli

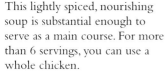

This lightly spiced, nourishing soup is substantial enough to serve as a main course. For more than 6 servings, you can use a whole chicken.

INGREDIENTS

Serves 4

30ml/2 tbsp sunflower oil
15g/½oz/1 tbsp soya margarine
1 onion, chopped
2 chicken legs or breast
    pieces, halved
seasoned flour, for dusting
2 carrots, cut into 4cm/1½in pieces
1 parsnip, cut into 4cm/1½in pieces
1.5 litres/2½ pints/6¼ cups
    chicken stock
1 cinnamon stick
good pinch of paprika
pinch of saffron
2 egg yolks
juice of ½ lemon
30ml/2 tbsp chopped fresh coriander
30ml/2 tbsp chopped fresh parsley
150g/5oz vermicelli
salt and ground black pepper

1 Heat the oil and soya margarine in a saucepan or flameproof casserole and fry the onion for 3–4 minutes until softened. Dust the chicken pieces in flour and fry gently.

2 Transfer the chicken to a plate and add the carrots and parsnip to the pan. Cook over a gentle heat for 3–4 minutes, stirring frequently, then return the chicken to the pan. Add the stock, cinnamon stick, paprika and season well with salt and pepper. Bring the soup to the boil, cover and simmer for 1 hour until the vegetables are very tender.

3 While the soup is cooking, blend the saffron in 30ml/2 tbsp boiling water. Beat the egg yolks with the lemon juice in a separate bowl and add the chopped coriander and parsley. When the saffron water has cooled, stir into the egg and lemon mixture.

4 When the vegetables are tender, transfer the chicken to a plate. Spoon away any excess fat from the soup, then increase the heat a little and stir in the vermicelli. Cook for 5–6 minutes until tender.

5 Meanwhile, remove the skin from the chicken and, if liked, bone and chop into bite-size pieces. If you prefer, simply skin the chicken pieces.

6 When the vermicelli is cooked, reduce the heat and stir in the chicken pieces and the egg, lemon and saffron mixture. Cook over a very low heat for 1–2 minutes, stirring all the time. Adjust the seasoning and serve the soup immediately.

NUTRITION NOTES	
Per portion:	
Energy	352kcals/1482kJ
Protein	24.3g
Fat	14.6g
saturated fat	4.3g
Carbohydrate	33.1g
Fibre	2.5g
Sugars	3.5g
Calcium	53.3mg

Hot-and-sour Soup

This spicy, warming Chinese soup really whets the appetite and is the perfect introduction to a simple meal. Add more vegetables and stock and you can serve it as a main course.

INGREDIENTS

Serves 4

10g/¼oz dried cloud ears
8 fresh shiitake mushrooms
75g/3oz tofu (soya beancurd)
50g/2oz/½ cup sliced, drained, canned
  bamboo shoots
900ml/1½ pints/3¾ cups Vegetable Stock
15ml/1 tbsp caster sugar
45ml/3 tbsp rice vinegar
15ml/1 tbsp light gluten-free soy sauce
1.5ml/¼ tsp chilli oil
2.5ml/½ tsp salt
large pinch of freshly ground
  white pepper
15ml/1 tbsp cornflour
15ml/1 tbsp cold water
1 egg white
5ml/1 tsp sesame oil
2 spring onions, cut into fine rings

1 Soak the cloud ears in hot water for 30 minutes or until soft. Drain, trim off and discard the hard base from each and chop the cloud ears roughly.

2 Discard the stalks from the shiitake mushrooms. Cut the caps into thin strips. Cut the tofu (beancurd) into 1cm/½in cubes. Shred the bamboo shoots.

— NUTRITION NOTES —	
Per portion:	
Energy	66kcals/276kJ
Protein	4.5g
Fat	2.6g
saturated fat	0.4g
Carbohydrate	6g
Fibre	0.5g
Sugars	1.6g
Calcium	109mg

3 Place the stock, mushrooms, bean curd, bamboo shoots and cloud ears in a large saucepan. Bring the stock to the boil, lower the heat and simmer for about 5 minutes.

4 Stir in the sugar, vinegar, soy sauce, chilli oil, salt and pepper. Mix the cornflour to a paste with the water. Add the mixture to the soup, stirring constantly until it thickens slightly.

5 Lightly beat the egg white, then pour it slowly into the soup in a steady stream, stirring constantly. Cook, continuing to stir, until the egg white changes colour.

6 Add the sesame oil just before serving. Ladle the soup into heated bowls and top each portion with spring onion rings.

FREE FROM

STARTERS

This wonderful selection of starters will whet your appetite and help to impress dinner guests. Each recipe uses healthy and nutritious ingredients that will promote good health and fight disease.

In summer, try the Mediterranean-inspired recipes, such as Marinated Baby Aubergines, Genoese Squid Salad, and Globe Artichokes, Green Beans and Garlic Dressing. In winter, enjoy the piping hot flavours of Pepper Gratin and Spicy Potato Wedges with Chilli Dip.

Tuna Carpaccio

Fillet of beef is most often used for carpaccio, but meaty fish such as tuna – and swordfish – make an unusual change. The secret is to slice the raw fish wafer thin, made possible by freezing the fish first, a technique used by the Japanese for making sashimi.

INGREDIENTS

Serves 4

2 fresh tuna steaks, about 450g/1lb
   total weight
60ml/4 tbsp extra virgin olive oil
15ml/1 tbsp balsamic vinegar
5ml/1 tsp caster sugar
30ml/2 tbsp drained bottled green
   peppercorns or capers
salt and ground black pepper
lemon wedges and green salad, to serve

1 Remove the skin from each tuna steak and place each steak between two sheets of clear film or non-stick baking paper. Pound with a rolling pin until flattened slightly.

2 Roll up the tuna as tightly as possible, then wrap tightly in clear film and place in the freezer for 4 hours or until firm.

3 Unwrap the tuna and cut crossways into the thinnest possible slices. Arrange on individual plates.

4 Whisk together the remaining ingredients, season and pour over the tuna. Cover and allow to come to room temperature for 30 minutes before serving with lemon wedges and green salad.

NUTRITION NOTES

Per portion:

Energy	413kcals/1734kJ
Protein	54.2g
Fat	21.8g
saturated fat	4.3g
Carbohydrate	1.6g
Fibre	0
Sugars	1.6g
Calcium	69mg

COOK'S TIP

Raw fish is safe to eat as long as it is very fresh, so check with your fishmonger before purchase, and make and serve carpaccio on the same day. Do not buy fish that has been frozen and thawed.

Pepper Gratin

Serve this simple but delicious dish as a starter with a small watercress, rocket or spinach salad and some good crusty bread to top up the calcium quantity.

INGREDIENTS

Serves 4

2 red peppers
30ml/2 tbsp extra virgin olive oil
60ml/4 tbsp fresh dairy- and egg-free
   white breadcrumbs
1 garlic clove, finely chopped
5ml/1 tsp drained bottled capers
8 stoned black olives, roughly chopped
15ml/1 tbsp chopped fresh oregano
15ml/1 tbsp chopped fresh
   flat leaf parsley
salt and ground black pepper
fresh herbs, to garnish

1 Preheat the oven to 200°C/400°F/ Gas 6. Place the peppers under a hot grill. Turn occasionally until they are blackened and blistered all over. Remove from the heat and place in a plastic bag. Seal and leave to cool.

2 When cool, peel the peppers. (Don't skin them under the tap, as the water would wash away some of the delicious smoky flavour.) Halve and remove the seeds, then cut the flesh into large strips.

3 Use a little of the olive oil to grease a small baking dish. Arrange the pepper strips in the dish.

——— NUTRITION NOTES ———

Per portion:

Energy	63kcals/268kJ
Protein	2.1g
Fat	1.3g
saturated fat	0.2g
Carbohydrate	11.5g
Fibre	1.5g
Sugars	3.9g
Calcium	32mg

4 Scatter the remaining ingredients on top, drizzle with the remaining olive oil and add salt and pepper to taste. Bake for 20 minutes until the breadcrumbs have browned. Garnish with fresh herbs and serve immediately.

Melon and Grapefruit Cocktail

This pretty, colourful starter can be made in minutes, so it is perfect for when you don't have much time to cook, but want something really special to eat.

INGREDIENTS

Serves 4
1 small Galia or
    Ogen melon
1 small Charentais melon
2 pink grapefruit
45ml/3 tbsp freshly squeezed
    orange juice
60ml/4 tbsp red vermouth
seeds from ½ pomegranate
mint sprigs, to decorate

─────── COOK'S TIP ───────

If citrus fruits are a problem, substitute alternative fruits, such as kiwi fruits, and use apple juice in place of the orange.

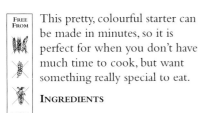

1 Halve the melons and scoop out the seeds. Cut into wedges, peel, then cut into large bite-size pieces.

─────── NUTRITION NOTES ───────

Per portion:
Energy	52kcals/220kJ
Protein	0.8g
Fat	0.2g
saturated fat	0g
Carbohydrate	9.4g
Sugar	9.4g
Fibre (NSP)	1.1g
Calcium	24mg

2 Using a small sharp knife, cut the peel and pith from the grapefruit. Holding the fruit over a bowl to catch the juice, cut between the grapefruit membranes to release the segments. Pour off all the juice into a bowl.

3 Stir the orange juice and vermouth into the reserved grapefruit juice.

4 Arrange the melon pieces and grapefruit segments haphazardly on four individual serving plates. Spoon the dressing over, then scatter with the pomegranate seeds. Decorate with mint sprigs and serve at once.

Parma Ham with Mango

Other fresh, colourful fruits, such as figs, papaya or melon, would go equally well with the ham in this light, elegant starter. Be sure to buy the true prosciutto from Parma for the best flavour. This dish is amazingly simple to prepare and can be made in advance – ideal if you are serving a complicated main course.

INGREDIENTS

Serves 4
16 slices Parma ham
1 ripe mango
ground black pepper
flat leaf parsley sprigs, to garnish

1 Separate the Parma ham slices and arrange four slices on each of four individual plates, crumpling the ham slightly to give a decorative effect.

2 Cut the mango into three thick slices around the stone, then slice the flesh and discard the stone. Neatly cut away the skin from each slice.

3 Arrange the mango slices in among the Parma ham slices. Grind some black pepper over the top and serve garnished with flat leaf parsley sprigs.

─────── NUTRITION NOTES ───────

Per portion:
Energy	73kcals/275kJ
Protein	6.6g
Fat	2.75g
saturated fat	1.4g
Carbohydrate	4.7g
Sugar	4.6g
Fibre (NSP)	0.8g
Calcium	7mg

Layered Vegetable Terrine

FREE FROM

This layered combination of fresh vegetables and herbs is baked in the oven – a healthy and effective way of cooking foods.

INGREDIENTS

Serves 6

3 red peppers, halved
450g/1lb potatoes
115g/4oz spinach leaves, trimmed
25g/1oz/2 tbsp butter
pinch grated nutmeg
115g/4oz vegetarian Cheddar
  cheese, grated
1 courgette, sliced lengthways
  and blanched
salt and ground black pepper

--- COOK'S TIP ---

Get all of the ingredients prepared before you start the layering process, to make sure that you don't forget anything.

1 Preheat the oven to 180°C/350°F/ Gas 4. Place the peppers in a roasting tin and roast them with the cores in place for 30–45 minutes until charred. Remove from the oven. Place in plastic bag to cool. Peel the skins and remove the cores. Peel half the potatoes and boil in plenty of salted water for 10–15 minutes until tender.

2 Blanch the spinach for a few seconds in boiling water. Drain and pat dry on kitchen paper.

3 Line the base and sides of a 900g/ 2lb loaf tin, making sure the leaves overlap slightly.

4 Slice the potatoes thinly and lay one-third of the potatoes over the base, dot with a little of the butter and season with salt, pepper and nutmeg. Sprinkle a little cheese over.

5 Arrange three of the peeled pepper halves on top. Sprinkle a little cheese over and then a layer of courgettes. Lay another one-third of the potatoes on top with the remaining peppers and some more cheese, seasoning as you go. Lay the final layer of potato on top and scatter over any remaining cheese. Fold the spinach leaves over. Cover with foil.

6 Place the loaf tin in a roasting tin and pour boiling water around the outside, making sure the water comes halfway up the sides of the tin. Bake for 45 minutes–1 hour, until soft. Remove from the oven and turn the loaf out. Serve sliced.

--- NUTRITION NOTES ---

Per portion:

Energy	155kcals/684kJ
Protein	7.7g
Fat	7.5g
saturated fat	4.5g
Carbohydrate	17.1g
Fibre	2.4g
Sugars	5.7g
Calcium	179mg

Marinated Baby Aubergines

This recipe has a strong Italian influence and uses traditional Mediterranean ingredients. These are high in antioxidants and have been shown to lower the incidence of cancer.

INGREDIENTS

Serves 4

12 baby aubergines, halved lengthways
250ml/8fl oz/1 cup extra virgin
    olive oil
juice of 1 lemon
30ml/2 tbsp balsamic vinegar
3 cloves
25g/1oz/⅓ cup pine nuts
25g/1oz/2 tbsp raisins
15ml/1 tbsp sugar
1 bay leaf
large pinch of dried chilli flakes
salt and ground black pepper

1 Preheat the grill to high. Place the aubergines, cut side up, in the grill pan and brush with a little of the olive oil. Grill for 10 minutes, until golden brown, turning them over halfway through cooking.

NUTRITION NOTES

Per portion:

Energy	507kcals/2095kJ
Protein	2.7g
Fat	50.6g
saturated fat	6.9g
Carbohydrate	11.6g
Fibre	3.2g
Sugars	11.3g
Calcium	20mg

HEALTH BENEFITS

Aubergines contain bioflavonoids, which are thought to reduce the risk of certain types of cancer. Olive oil and pine nuts are rich sources of the antioxidant vitamin E, which can help fight off free radicals that have the potential to cause cancer.

2 To make the marinade, put the remaining olive oil, the lemon juice, vinegar, cloves, pine nuts, raisins, sugar and bay leaf in a jug. Add the chilli flakes, season with salt and pepper and mix well.

3 Place the hot aubergines in an earthenware or glass bowl, and pour over the marinade. Leave to cool, turning the aubergines once or twice. Serve cold.

Creamy Aubergine Dip

Spread this velvet-textured dip thickly on rounds of toasted bread, then top them with slivers of sun-dried tomato to make wonderful, Italian-style crostini.

INGREDIENTS

Serves 4

1 large aubergine
30ml/2 tbsp olive oil
1 small onion, finely chopped
2 garlic cloves, finely chopped
30ml/2 tbsp chopped fresh parsley
75ml/5 tbsp crème fraîche
Tabasco sauce, to taste
juice of 1 lemon
ground black pepper
toasted rounds of egg- and yeast-free
  bread and sun-dried tomato slivers,
  to serve

1 Preheat the grill. Place the whole aubergine on a baking sheet and grill it for 2–3 minutes, turning occasionally, until the skin is blackened and wrinkled and the aubergine feels soft when squeezed.

2 Cover the aubergine with a clean dish towel and allow to cool for about 5 minutes.

3 Heat the oil in a frying pan and cook the onion and garlic for 5 minutes until softened but not browned.

4 Peel the skin from the aubergine. Mash the flesh with a large fork or potato masher to make a pulpy purée.

5 Stir in the onion, garlic, parsley and crème fraîche. Add the Tabasco sauce, lemon juice and pepper to taste. Transfer the dip to a serving bowl and serve warm, or allow to cool and serve at room temperature, accompanied by slices of toasted bread and slivers of sun-dried tomato.

NUTRITION NOTES	
Per portion:	
Energy	147Kcals/610kJ
Protein	1.9g
Fat	13.5g
saturated fat	5.46g
Carbohydrate	5g
Fibre	2.6g
Sodium	12mg

Mellow Garlic Dip

Two whole heads of garlic may seem like a lot but, once cooked, they develop a sweet and mellow flavour. This is delicious served with crunchy homemade bread sticks and crudités.

INGREDIENTS

Serves 4

2 whole garlic heads
15ml/1 tbsp olive oil
60ml/4 tbsp mayonnaise
75ml/5 tbsp Greek yogurt
5ml/1 tsp wholegrain mustard
ground black pepper
breadsticks, to serve

FREE FROM

1 Preheat the oven to 200°C/400°F/ Gas 6. Separate the garlic cloves and place them, unpeeled, in a small roasting tin.

2 Pour the olive oil over the garlic cloves and turn with a spoon to coat evenly. Roast for 20–30 minutes until the garlic is tender and softened. Leave to cool for 5 minutes.

3 Trim off the root end of each roasted garlic clove. Peel the cloves and discard the skins.

5 Place the garlic in a small bowl and stir in the mayonnaise, yogurt and wholegrain mustard.

NUTRITION NOTES

Per portion:

Energy	175Kcals/720kJ
Protein	1.6g
Fat	18.6g
saturated fat	3.17g
Carbohydrate	0g
Fibre	0.1g
Sodium	40mg

4 Place the roasted garlic cloves on a chopping board and mash with a fork until puréed.

6 Spoon the dip into a serving bowl and season to taste with pepper. Serve accompanied by breadsticks.

Olives with Spicy Marinades

INGREDIENTS

Serves 6
225g/8oz/1⅓ cups green or tan olives
   for each marinade

For the spicy herb marinade
45ml/3 tbsp chopped fresh coriander
45ml/3 tbsp chopped fresh flat
   leaf parsley
1 garlic clove, finely chopped
good pinch of cayenne pepper
good pinch of ground cumin
30–45ml/2–3 tbsp olive oil
30–45ml/2–3 tbsp lemon juice

For the ginger and chilli marinade
60ml/4 tbsp chopped fresh coriander
60ml/4 tbsp chopped fresh flat
   leaf parsley
1 garlic clove, finely chopped
5ml/1 tsp grated fresh root ginger
1 red chilli, seeded and finely sliced
¼ preserved lemon, cut into thin
   strips (optional)

1 Squash the olives, hard enough to break the flesh, but taking care not to crack the stone. Place in a bowl of cold water and leave overnight to remove the excess brine.

2 Drain thoroughly and divide the olives between two jars.

3 Blend the ingredients for the spicy herb marinade and pour into one of the jars of olives, adding more oil and lemon juice to cover, if necessary. Seal the jar.

4 To make the ginger and chilli marinade, mix together the coriander, parsley, garlic, ginger, chilli and preserved lemon, if using. Add to the remaining jar of olives and seal.

5 Store the olives in the fridge for at least one week before use, shaking the jars occasionally.

NUTRITION NOTES

Per portion:
Energy	88kcals/363kJ
Protein	0.4g
Fat	9.6g
saturated fat	1.4g
Carbohydrate	0.12g
Sugar	0.12g
Fibre	0.5g
Calcium	23mg

Broad Bean Dip

This dish is similar to hummus, but uses broad beans instead of chick-peas. It is usually eaten by scooping up the purée with bread, but raw vegetable crudités or potato crisps could be served for dipping.

INGREDIENTS

Serves 6
115g/4oz dried broad beans, soaked
2 garlic cloves, peeled
5ml/1 tsp cumin seeds
about 60ml/4 tbsp olive oil
salt
mint sprigs, to garnish
extra cumin seeds, cayenne pepper and
   vegetable crudités to serve

1 Put the dried broad beans in a pan with the whole garlic cloves and cumin seeds and add enough water just to cover. Bring to the boil, then reduce the heat and simmer until the beans are tender. Drain, cool and then slip off the outer skin of each bean.

2 Purée the beans in a food processor or blender, adding sufficient olive oil and water to give a smooth soft dip. Season to taste with plenty of salt. Garnish with sprigs of mint and serve with extra cumin seeds, cayenne pepper and vegetable crudités.

NUTRITION NOTES

Per portion:
Energy	171kcals/715kJ
Protein	7.5g
Fat	11.8g
saturated fat	1.7g
Carbohydrate	9.3g
Sugar	1.6g
Fibre	7.9g
Calcium	28.7mg

Spicy Potato Wedges with Chilli Dip

Perfect as a starter or light meal, these dry-roasted potato wedges have a crisp, spicy crust, which makes them irresistible, especially when served with a chilli dip.

INGREDIENTS

Serves 2
2 baking potatoes, about 225g/
    8oz each
30ml/2 tbsp olive oil
2 garlic cloves, crushed
5ml/1 tsp ground allspice
5ml/1 tsp ground coriander
15ml/1 tbsp paprika
salt and ground black pepper

For the dip
15ml/1 tbsp olive oil
1 small onion, finely chopped
1 garlic clove, crushed
200g/7oz can chopped tomatoes
1 fresh red chilli, seeded and
    finely chopped
15ml/1 tbsp lemon juice
15ml/1 tbsp chopped fresh coriander,
    plus extra to garnish

1 Preheat the oven to 200°C/400°F/
Gas 6. Cut the potatoes in half, then into eight wedges.

2 Place the wedges in a saucepan of cold water. Bring to the boil, then lower the heat and simmer gently for 10 minutes or until softened slightly. Drain and pat dry on kitchen paper.

---------- COOK'S TIP ----------

To save time, parboil the potatoes and toss them with the spices in advance, but make sure that the potato wedges are perfectly dry and completely covered in the mixture.

3 Mix together the oil, garlic, allspice, coriander and paprika in a roasting tin. Add salt and pepper to taste. Add the potatoes to the pan and shake to coat them thoroughly.

4 Roast the potato wedges for about 20 minutes, turning them occasionally, until they are browned, crisp and fully cooked.

5 Meanwhile, make the chilli dip. Heat the oil in a saucepan, add the onion and garlic and cook for 5–10 minutes until soft. Add the canned tomatoes, with their juice, then stir in the chilli and lemon juice.

6 Cook gently for 10 minutes until the mixture has reduced and thickened. Stir in the fresh coriander and serve hot, with the potato wedges. Garnish the potato wedges with fresh coriander and sprinkle with salt.

--------- NUTRITION NOTES ---------

Per portion:
Energy	344kcals/1439kJ
Protein	6.1g
Fat	17g
saturated fat	2.3g
Carbohydrate	44.1g
Sugar	5.8g
Fibre	40g
Calcium	31mg

Grilled Vegetab...

Chilled Stuffed Courgettes

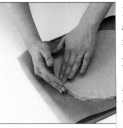

INGREDIENTS

Serves 6

1 courgette, sliced
2 baby aubergines or 1 small
    aubergine, sliced
30ml/2 tbsp olive oil
1 yellow pepper, seeded and
    thickly sliced
115g/4oz/1 cup gluten-free cornmeal
50g/2oz/½ cup potato flour
50g/2oz/½ cup soya flour
5ml/1 tsp gluten-free baking powder
2.5ml/½ tsp salt
50g/2oz/4 tbsp soft margarine
about 105ml/7 tbsp semi-
    skimmed milk
4 plum tomatoes, skinned
    and chopped
30ml/2 tbsp chopped fresh basil
115g/4oz mozzarella cheese, sliced
salt and ground black pepper
fresh basil sprigs, to garnish

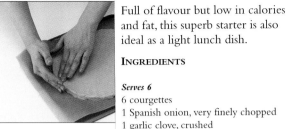

3 Place the dough on a she[...] stick baking paper on a b[...] sheet and roll or press it out [...] 25cm/10in round, making th[...] slightly thicker than the cent[...]

4 Brush the pizza dough w[...] remaining oil, then sprea[...] chopped tomatoes over the d[...]

1 Preheat the grill. Brush the courgette and aubergine slices with a little oil and place on a grill rack with the pepper slices. Cook under the grill until lightly browned, turning once.

2 Meanwhile, preheat the oven to 200°C/400°F/Gas 6. Place the cornmeal, potato flour, soya flour, baking powder and salt in a mixing bowl and stir to mix. Lightly rub in the margarine until the mixture resembles coarse breadcrumbs, then stir in enough of the milk to make a soft but not sticky dough.

Full of flavour but low in calories and fat, this superb starter is also ideal as a light lunch dish.

INGREDIENTS

Serves 6

6 courgettes
1 Spanish onion, very finely chopped
1 garlic clove, crushed
60–90ml/4–6 tbsp well-flavoured
    French dressing
1 green pepper
3 tomatoes, peeled and seeded
15ml/1 tbsp rinsed capers
5ml/1 tsp chopped fresh parsley
5ml/1 tsp chopped fresh basil
salt and ground black pepper
parsley sprigs, to garnish

1 Top and tail the courgettes, but do not peel them. Bring a large shallow pan of lightly salted water to the boil, add the courgettes and simmer for 2–3 minutes until they are lightly cooked. Drain well.

2 Cut the courgettes in half lengthways. Carefully scoop out the flesh, leaving the courgette shells intact, and chop the flesh into small cubes. Place in a bowl and cover with half the chopped onion. Dot with the crushed garlic. Drizzle 30ml/2 tbsp of the dressing over, cover and marinate for 2–3 hours. Wrap the courgette shells tightly in clear film, and chill them until they are required.

3 Cut the pepper in half and remove the core and seeds. Dice the flesh. Chop the tomatoes and capers finely. Stir the pepper, tomatoes and capers into the courgette mixture, with the remaining onion and the chopped herbs. Season with salt and pepper. Pour over enough of the remaining dressing to moisten the mixture and toss well. Spoon the filling into the courgette shells, arrange on a platter and serve garnished with parsley.

FREE FROM

NUTRITION NOTES	
Per portion:	
Energy	326kcals/1362kJ
Fat, total	19.5g
saturated fat	5.8g
Protein	12.2g
Carbohydrate	26.8g
sugar, total	5.1g
Fibre	3.2g
Sodium	365mg

NUTRITION NOTES	
Per portion:	
Energy	95kcals/390kJ
Fat, total	7.3g
saturated fat	1.1g
polyunsaturated fat	0.9g
monounsaturated fat	4.9g
Carbohydrate	5.3g
sugar, total	4.75g
starch	0.2g
Fibre	1.95g
Sodium	60mg

Globe Artichokes, Green

Grilled Vegetable Terrine

Similar to French aïoli, but egg-free and exceptionally garlicky, this creamy, lemon-flavoured dressing makes a perfect partner to freshly cooked vegetables.

INGREDIENTS

Serves 6
225g/8oz green beans
3 small globe artichokes
15ml/1 tbsp olive oil
pared rind of 1 lemon
coarse salt for sprinkling
lemon wedges, to serve

For the garlic dressing
6 large garlic cloves, sliced
10ml/2 tsp lemon juice
250ml/8fl oz/1 cup olive oil
salt and ground black pepper

1 To make the garlic dressing, put the garlic and lemon juice in a blender or mini food processor. With the machine switched on, gradually pour in the olive oil until the mixture is thickened and smooth. Alternatively, crush the garlic to a paste with the lemon juice and gradually beat in the oil using a hand whisk. Season with salt and pepper to taste.

2 To make the salad, cook the beans in boiling water for 1–2 minutes until slightly softened. Drain.

3 Trim the artich the base. Cook a large pan of salted 30 minutes, or unti away a leaf from th

— Coo

Mediterranean b sometimes available kind of salad as, unli can be eaten whole. tender, then cut in artichoke hearts, th sliced, could also be s

This is a colourful layered terrine, using all the vegetables evocative of the Mediterranean, with an added richness from the red wine vinegar.

INGREDIENTS

Serves 6
2 large red peppers, quartered, cored and seeded
2 large yellow peppers, quartered, cored and seeded
1 large aubergine, sliced lengthways
2 large courgettes, sliced lengthways
90ml/6 tbsp olive oil
1 large red onion, finely sliced
75g/3oz/½ cup raisins
15ml/1 tbsp red wine vinegar
400ml/14fl oz/1⅔ cups tomato juice
15g/½oz/2 tbsp powdered gelatine
fresh basil leaves, to garnish

For the dressing
90ml/6 tbsp extra virgin olive oil
30ml/2 tbsp red wine vinegar
ground black pepper

1 Place the prepared peppers skin-side up under a hot grill and cook until the skins are blackened. Transfer to a bowl and cover. Leave to cool.

2 Arrange the aubergine and courgette slices on separate baking sheets. Brush them with a little olive oil and cook under the grill, turning occasionally, until tender and golden.

3 Heat the remaining oil in a frying pan and add the sliced onion, raisins and red wine vinegar. Cook gently until soft and syrupy. Leave to cool in the frying pan.

4 Lightly grease a 1.75 litre/3 pint/7½ cup terrine with oil and then line with clear film, leaving a little hanging over the sides.

5 Pour half the tomato juice into a saucepan and sprinkle with the gelatine. Dissolve gently over a low heat, stirring.

6 Skin and slice the cooled peppers. Place a layer of red peppers in the bottom of the terrine and pour in enough of the tomato juice and gelatine mixture to cover. Next add a layer of aubergine and pour over enough tomato juice to cover.

7 Continue building layers with the courgettes, yellow peppers and onion mixture, finishing with a last layer of red peppers. Pour tomato juice over each layer of vegetables as you go.

8 Add the remaining tomato juice to any left in the pan and pour into the terrine. Give it a sharp tap to disperse the juice. Cover the terrine and chill until set.

9 To make the dressing, whisk together the oil and vinegar and season with pepper. Turn out the terrine and remove the clear film. Serve in thick slices, drizzled with the dressing. Garnish with basil leaves.

Sesame Seed-coated Falafel with Tahini Yogurt Dip

Sesame seeds make a nutritious coating for these spicy patties.

INGREDIENTS

Serves 4

250g/9oz/2⅔ cups dried chick-peas
2 garlic cloves, crushed
1 red chilli, seeded and finely sliced
5ml/1 tsp ground coriander
5ml/1 tsp ground cumin
15ml/1 tbsp chopped fresh mint
15ml/1 tbsp chopped fresh parsley
2 spring onions, finely chopped
1 large egg, beaten
sesame seeds, for coating
sunflower oil, for frying
salt and ground black pepper
pitta bread, to serve

For the tahini yogurt dip

200g/7oz/2⅓ cups live natural yogurt
30ml/2 tbsp light tahini
5ml/1 tsp cayenne pepper, plus extra
  for sprinkling
15ml/1 tbsp chopped fresh mint
1 spring onion, finely sliced

1 Soak the chick-peas overnight in cold water. Drain and rinse the chick-peas, then place in a saucepan and cover with cold water. Bring to the boil and boil for 10 minutes, then reduce the heat and simmer for about 1½ hours until tender. Drain.

2 Meanwhile, make the dip. Place the yogurt, tahini, cayenne and chopped mint in a bowl and mix well. Sprinkle with the sliced spring onion and extra cayenne pepper. Chill in the fridge until required.

3 Combine the chick-peas with the garlic, chilli, ground spices, fresh herbs, spring onions and seasoning, then mix with the egg. Place in a food processor and blend until the mixture forms a coarse paste. If the paste seems too soft, leave it to chill for 30 minutes.

4 Form the chilled chick-pea paste into 12 patties with your hands, then roll each one in the sesame seeds.

5 Heat enough oil in a large frying pan to shallow fry the falafel. Fry for 6 minutes, turning once – you may need to do this in batches.

6 Serve with a spoonful of the yogurt dip and warm pitta bread.

NUTRITION NOTES	
Per portion:	
Energy	348kcals/1458kJ
Protein	19.3g
Fat	15.4g
saturated fat	2.5g
Carbohydrate	35.0g
Fibre	7.4g
Sugars	5.7g
Calcium	258mg

——— HEALTH BENEFITS ———

Chick-peas contain lignins, also known as phytoestrogens, which are thought to protect against certain cancers. Sesame seeds are rich in the antioxidant vitamin E.

Hummus

Blending chick-peas with garlic and olive oil makes a delicious dip or healthy sandwich filler. This creamy purée contains fibre, plant protein and antioxidants – all of which are important in the fight against cancer.

INGREDIENTS

Serves 6

150g/5oz/¾ cup dried chick-peas
juice of 2 lemons
2 garlic cloves, sliced
30ml/2 tbsp olive oil
pinch of cayenne pepper
150ml/¼ pint/⅔ cup tahini paste
extra olive oil and cayenne pepper
  for sprinkling
salt and ground black pepper
black olives, to serve

1 Put the chick-peas in a bowl with plenty of cold water and leave to soak overnight.

2 Drain the chick-peas and cover with fresh water in a saucepan. Bring to the boil and boil rapidly for 10 minutes. Reduce the heat and simmer gently for about 1½–2 hours until soft. Drain.

3 Process the chick-peas in a food processor or blender, to a smooth purée. Add the lemon juice, garlic, olive oil, cayenne pepper and tahini and blend until creamy, from time to time scraping the mixture down from the sides of the bowl.

4 Season the purée with salt and pepper and transfer to a serving dish. Sprinkle with oil and cayenne pepper and serve with olives.

COOK'S TIP

For convenience, canned chick-peas can be used instead. Allow two 400g/14oz cans and drain them thoroughly. Tahini paste can be purchased from most supermarkets and health-food shops.

NUTRITION NOTES

Per portion:

Energy	281kcals/1169kJ
Protein	9.9g
Fat	21.6g
saturated fat	3.0g
Carbohydrate	12.7g
Fibre	4.6g
Sugars	0.8g
Calcium	210mg

FREE FROM

Bacon and Herb Rösti

INGREDIENTS

Serves 4

450g/1lb potatoes, left whole
   and unpeeled
30ml/2 tbsp olive oil
1 red onion, finely chopped
4 lean back bacon rashers, rinded
   and diced
15ml/1 tbsp potato flour
30ml/2 tbsp chopped fresh
   mixed herbs
salt and ground black pepper
fresh parsley sprigs, to garnish

1 Lightly grease a baking sheet. Par-boil the potatoes in a saucepan of lightly salted, boiling water for about 6 minutes. Drain the potatoes and set aside to cool slightly.

2 Once cool enough to handle, peel the potatoes and coarsely grate them into a bowl. Set aside.

3 Heat 15ml/1 tbsp of the oil in a frying pan, add the onion and bacon and cook gently for 5 minutes, stirring occasionally. Preheat the oven to 220°C/425°F/Gas 7.

4 Remove the pan from the heat. Stir the onion mixture, remaining oil, potato flour, herbs and seasoning into the grated potatoes and mix well.

5 Divide the mixture into eight small piles and spoon them on to the prepared baking sheet, leaving a little space between them.

6 Bake for 20–25 minutes until the rösti are crisp and golden brown. Serve immediately, garnished with sprigs of fresh parsley.

— NUTRITION NOTES —	
Per portion:	
Energy	245kcals/1025kJ
Fat, total	12.6g
saturated fat	2.9g
Protein	10.7g
Carbohydrate	23.6g
sugar, total	1.8g
Fibre	2.6g
Sodium	572mg

Persian Omelette

Serve this spiced omelette hot or cold, in wedges as a starter, or cut it into bite-size pieces for serving with drinks. The herbs and nuts add texture and taste.

INGREDIENTS

Serves 8
30ml/2 tbsp olive oil or sunflower oil
2 leeks, finely chopped
350g/12oz fresh spinach, washed and chopped, or 150g/5oz thawed frozen chopped spinach, drained
12 eggs
8 spring onions, finely chopped
2 handfuls fresh parsley, finely chopped
1–2 handfuls fresh coriander, chopped
2 fresh tarragon sprigs, chopped, or 2.5ml/ ½ tsp dried tarragon
handful of fresh chives, chopped
1 small fresh dill sprig, chopped, or 1.5ml/ ¼ tsp dried dill
2–4 fresh mint sprigs, chopped
40g/1½ oz/ ⅓ cup walnuts or pecan nuts, chopped
40g/1½ oz/ ½ cup pine nuts
salt and ground black pepper
salad, to serve

1 Heat the oil in a large shallow pan that can be used under the grill. Add the leeks and fry them gently for about 5 minutes until they are just beginning to soften.

2 If using fresh spinach, add it to the pan containing the leeks and cook for 2–3 minutes over a medium heat until the spinach has just wilted.

3 Beat the eggs in a bowl with a fork. Add the leek and spinach mixture (or the leeks with the thawed frozen spinach), then stir in the spring onions, with all the herbs and nuts. Season with salt and pepper. Pour the mixture into the pan and cover with a lid or foil.

4 Cook over a very gentle heat for 25 minutes or until set. Remove the lid and brown the top under a hot grill. Serve, with salad.

NUTRITION NOTES	
Per portion:	
Energy	258kcals/1073kJ
Fat, total	21g
saturated fat	3.9g
polyunsaturated fat	6.1g
monounsaturated fat	8.7g
Carbohydrate	2.8g
sugar, total	2.3g
starch	0.15g
Fibre	1.9g
Sodium	192mg

FREE FROM

Cheese and Spinach Puffs

INGREDIENTS

Serves 6

150g/5oz cooked, chopped spinach
175g/6oz/¾ cup cottage cheese
5ml/1 tsp grated nutmeg
2 egg whites
30ml/2 tbsp grated Parmesan cheese
salt and ground black pepper

1 Preheat the oven to 220°C/425°F/ Gas 7. Oil six ramekin dishes.

2 Mix the spinach and cottage cheese in a small bowl, then add the nutmeg and seasoning to taste.

3 Whisk the egg whites in a separate bowl until stiff enough to hold soft peaks. Fold them evenly into the spinach mixture, using a spatula or large metal spoon, then spoon the mixture into the oiled ramekins, dividing it evenly, and smooth the tops.

4 Sprinkle with the Parmesan and bake for 15–20 minutes, or until risen and golden. Serve immediately.

— NUTRITION NOTES —

Per portion:

Energy	47Kcals/195kJ
Fat	1.32g
saturated fat	0.52g
Cholesterol	2.79mg
Fibre	0.53g

Lemony Stuffed Courgettes

INGREDIENTS

Serves 4

4 courgettes, about 175g/6oz each
5ml/1 tsp sunflower oil
1 garlic clove, crushed
5ml/1 tsp ground lemon grass
finely grated rind and juice of
    ½ lemon
115g/4oz/1½ cups cooked long
    grain rice
175g/6oz cherry tomatoes, halved
30ml/2 tbsp toasted cashew nuts
salt and ground black pepper
sprigs of thyme, to garnish

— NUTRITION NOTES —

Per portion:

Energy	126Kcals/530kJ
Fat	5.33g
saturated fat	0.65g
Cholesterol	0mg
Fibre	2.31g

1 Preheat the oven to 200°C/400°F/ Gas 6. Halve the courgettes length-ways and use a teaspoon to scoop out the centres. Blanch the shells in boiling water for 1 minute, then drain well.

2 Chop the courgette flesh finely and place in a saucepan with the oil and garlic. Stir over a moderate heat until softened, but not browned.

3 Stir in the lemon grass, lemon rind and juice, rice, tomatoes and cashew nuts. Season well and spoon into the courgette shells. Place the shells in a baking tin in a single layer and cover with foil.

4 Bake for 25–30 minutes, or until the courgettes are tender, then serve hot, garnished with thyme sprigs.

Mushroom Croustades

The rich mushroom flavour of this filling is heightened by the addition of Worcestershire sauce, contrasting deliciously with the crispy French bread toasts.

INGREDIENTS

Serves 2–4

1 short French stick, about 25cm/10in
10ml/2 tsp olive oil
250g/9oz open cup
  mushrooms, quartered
10ml/2 tsp Worcestershire sauce
10ml/2 tsp lemon juice
30ml/2 tbsp skimmed milk
30ml/2 tbsp snipped fresh chives, plus
  extra to garnish
salt and ground black pepper

1 Preheat the oven to 200°C/400°F/ Gas 6. Cut the French bread in half lengthways. Cut a scoop out of the soft middle of each, leaving a thick border all the way round.

2 Brush the bread with oil, place on a baking sheet and bake for about 6–8 minutes, until golden and crisp.

3 Place the mushrooms in a small saucepan with the Worcestershire sauce, lemon juice and milk. Simmer for about 5 minutes, or until most of the liquid is evaporated.

4 Remove from the heat, add the chives and seasoning and spoon into the croustades. Garnish and serve.

NUTRITION NOTES	
Per portion:	
Energy	324Kcals/1361kJ
Fat	6.4g
saturated fat	1.27g
Cholesterol	0.3mg
Fibre	3.07g

Cucumber and Alfalfa Tortillas

Wheat tortillas are extremely simple to prepare at home. Served with a crisp, fresh salsa, they make a marvellous starter, light lunch or supper dish.

INGREDIENTS

Serves 4

225g/8oz/2 cups plain flour, sifted
pinch of salt
45ml/3 tbsp olive oil
100–150ml/4–5fl oz/½–⅔ cup
  warm water
lime wedges, to garnish

For the salsa

1 red onion, finely chopped
1 red chilli, seeded and finely chopped
30ml/2 tbsp chopped fresh dill
  or coriander
½ cucumber, peeled and chopped
175g/6oz/2 cups alfalfa sprouts

For the sauce

1 large ripe avocado, peeled and stoned
juice of 1 lime
15ml/1 tbsp soft goat's cheese
pinch of paprika

1 Mix all the salsa ingredients together in a bowl and set aside.

2 For the sauce, place the avocado, lime juice and goat's cheese in a food processor or blender and process until smooth. Place in a bowl and cover with clear film. Dust with paprika just before serving.

3 For the tortillas, place the flour and salt in a food processor or blender, add the oil and process. Gradually add the water until a stiff dough has formed. Turn out on to a floored board and knead until smooth.

4 Divide the mixture into eight. Knead each piece for 1–2 minutes and form into a ball. Flatten and roll out each ball to a 23cm/9in circle.

5 Heat a non-stick or ungreased heavy-based pan. Cook one tortilla at a time for about 30 seconds on each side. Place the cooked tortillas in a clean dish towel and repeat until you have made eight tortillas.

6 Spread each tortilla with a spoonful of avocado sauce, top with the salsa and roll up. Serve garnished with lime wedges and eat immediately.

— NUTRITION NOTES —

Per portion:

Energy	395Kcals/1659kJ
Fat	20.17g
saturated fat	1.69g
Cholesterol	4.38mg
Fibre	4.15g

— COOK'S TIP —

When peeling the avocado be sure to scrape off the bright green flesh from immediately under the skin as this gives the sauce its vivid green colour.

Aubergine and Smoked Trout Pâté

INGREDIENTS

Serves 6
1 large aubergine
2–3 garlic cloves, unpeeled
4 smoked trout fillets
juice of 1 lemon
sea salt and ground black pepper
toast, to serve

——— NUTRITION NOTES ———

Per portion:

Energy	145kcals/609kJ
Fat, total	4.7g
saturated fat	1.05g
polyunsaturated fat	1.6g
monounsaturated fat	1.6g
Carbohydrate	1.6g
sugar, total	1.1g
starch	0.5g
Fibre	1.1g
Sodium	89mg

1 Slice the aubergine thickly and spread out the slices in a steamer. Tuck the whole garlic cloves among the slices. Steam over boiling water for 10–15 minutes until both the aubergine slices and the garlic cloves are quite soft.

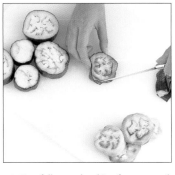

2 Carefully cut the skins from around the aubergine slices using a small sharp knife.

3 Skin the trout fillets and chop them roughly. Put them in a food processor. Pop the garlic flesh out of the skins and add it to the processor with the aubergine slices. Add the lemon juice and process until smooth. Spoon into a bowl and season. Cool, then chill. Serve with toast.

Avocado and Strawberry Salad

The combination of avocado and strawberries works surprisingly well in this refreshing salad.

INGREDIENTS

Serves 6
2 large, ripe avocados
juice of 2–3 lemons
15 strawberries
120ml/4fl oz/½ cup live
   natural yogurt
15–30 ml/1–2 tbsp chopped fresh mint
salt and ground black pepper
sprig of mint, to garnish

——— COOK'S TIP ———

Serve the salad straightaway, before the avocado slices have a chance to discolour.

1 Cut the avocados in half and remove the skin and stones. Cut the avocado flesh into thin slices, then place the slices in a bowl and sprinkle over half the lemon juice.

——— NUTRITION NOTES ———

Per portion:

Energy	93kcals/387kJ
Fat, total	8g
saturated fat	1.75g
polyunsaturated fat	0.9g
monounsaturated fat	4.9g
Carbohydrate	3.5g
sugar, total	2.8g
starch	0g
Fibre	1.5g
Sodium	20mg

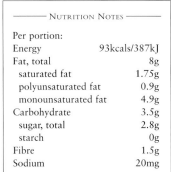

2 Halve or slice the strawberries and toss them lightly with the avocado slices in the bowl. Mix the yogurt with enough cold water to give a pouring consistency. Stir in the mint and season to taste. Spoon the dressing over the salad, garnish with mint and serve.

Chicken Goujons

Herbs and spices ensure these chicken pieces are full of flavour.

INGREDIENTS

Serves 8

4 boned and skinned
  chicken breasts
175g/6oz/3 cups fresh
  saltless breadcrumbs
5ml/1 tsp ground coriander
10ml/2 tsp ground paprika
2.5ml/½ tsp ground cumin
45g/1¾ oz/3 tbsp plain flour
2 eggs, beaten
vegetable oil, for deep frying
ground black pepper
lemon wedges and fresh coriander
  sprigs, to garnish

For the dip

275g/10oz/1¼ cups plain yogurt
30ml/2 tbsp lemon juice
60ml/4 tbsp chopped fresh coriander
60ml/4 tbsp chopped fresh parsley

1 Divide each chicken breast into two fillets. Place them between two sheets of clear film and, using a rolling pin, flatten each one to a thickness of about 5mm/¼in.

2 Cut diagonally across the fillets to form 2.5cm/1in strips.

3 Mix the breadcrumbs with the spices and seasoning. Toss the chicken fillet pieces in the flour, keeping them separate.

4 Dip the fillets into the beaten egg and then coat in the breadcrumbs.

5 Thoroughly mix together all the ingredients for the dip and season with pepper to taste. Cover and chill until required.

6 Heat the oil in a heavy-based pan. It is ready for deep frying when a cube of bread tossed into the oil sizzles on the surface. Fry the goujons in batches until golden and crisp. Drain on kitchen paper and keep warm in the oven until all the goujons have been fried. Garnish with lemon wedges and fresh coriander before serving with the dip.

NUTRITION NOTES	
Per portion:	
Energy	555Kcals/2334kJ
Protein	49.1g
Fat	19.2g
saturated fat	3.2g
Carbohydrate	50g
Fibre	1.8g
Sodium	536mg

Calamari with Double Tomato Stuffing

Calamari, or baby squid, should be cooked only briefly – just until they turn opaque – or they will become tough and rubbery. Turn and baste them often.

INGREDIENTS

Serves 4
500g/1¼lb baby squid, cleaned
1 garlic clove, crushed
3 plum tomatoes, skinned and chopped
8 sun-dried tomatoes in oil, drained and chopped
60ml/4 tbsp chopped fresh basil, plus extra, to serve
60ml/4 tbsp fresh saltless dairy- and egg-free white breadcrumbs
45ml/3 tbsp olive oil
15ml/1 tbsp red wine vinegar
ground black pepper
lemon wedges, to serve

1 Remove the tentacles from the squid and roughly chop them. Leave the body of the squid whole.

2 Mix together the squid tentacles, garlic, plum tomatoes, sun-dried tomatoes, basil and breadcrumbs. Stir in 15ml/1 tbsp of the oil and the vinegar. Season well with pepper.

3 Soak some wooden cocktail sticks in water for 10 minutes before use, to prevent them burning.

4 Fill the squid with the stuffing mixture using a teaspoon: do not overstuff. Secure the open ends with the soaked cocktail sticks.

5 Brush the squid with the remaining oil and cook over a medium-hot barbecue or under a preheated grill for 4–5 minutes, turning often. Sprinkle with basil and serve with lemon wedges.

NUTRITION NOTES	
Per portion:	
Energy	238Kcals/995kJ
Protein	21.8g
Fat	11.4g
saturated fat	1.38g
Carbohydrate	13g
Fibre	1.8g
Sodium	484mg

FREE FROM

Skewered Lamb with Red Onion Salsa

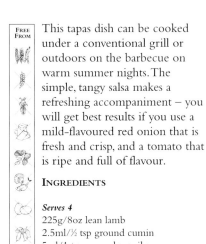

This tapas dish can be cooked under a conventional grill or outdoors on the barbecue on warm summer nights. The simple, tangy salsa makes a refreshing accompaniment – you will get best results if you use a mild-flavoured red onion that is fresh and crisp, and a tomato that is ripe and full of flavour.

INGREDIENTS

Serves 4
225g/8oz lean lamb
2.5ml/½ tsp ground cumin
5ml/1 tsp ground paprika
15ml/1 tbsp olive oil
ground black pepper

For the red onion salsa
1 red onion, finely sliced
1 large tomato, seeded and chopped
15ml/1 tbsp red wine vinegar
3–4 fresh basil or mint leaves, roughly torn
small mint leaves, to garnish

1 Using a sharp knife, chop the lamb into cubes. Place the cubes in a bowl with the cumin, paprika, olive oil and plenty of pepper. Toss well until the lamb is coated with the spices.

2 Cover the bowl with clear film and leave in a cool place for several hours, or in the fridge overnight if possible, so that the lamb absorbs the spicy flavours.

3 When ready to use, spread the lamb cubes on four small skewers – if using wooden skewers, soak them first in cold water for at least 30 minutes to prevent them from burning during cooking.

4 To make the salsa, put the sliced onion, tomato, vinegar and basil or mint leaves in a small bowl and stir together until thoroughly blended. Season to taste with pepper, garnish with mint, then set aside while you cook the skewered lamb.

5 Cook the lamb under a preheated grill or over a hot barbecue for about 5–10 minutes, turning the skewers frequently, until the lamb is well browned but still slightly pink in the centre. Serve hot with the onion salsa, garnished with mint leaves.

NUTRITION NOTES	
Per portion:	
Energy	136Kcals/568kJ
Protein	12.3g
Fat	7.9g
saturated fat	2.77g
Carbohydrate	4g
Fibre	0.8g
Sodium	56mg

Genoese Squid Salad

This is a good salad for summer, when French beans and new potatoes are at their best. Serve it for a first course or light lunch.

INGREDIENTS

Serves 4

450g/1lb prepared squid, cut into rings
4 garlic cloves, roughly chopped
300ml/½ pint/1¼ cups Italian red wine
450g/1lb waxy new potatoes,
   scrubbed clean
225g/8oz French beans, trimmed and
   cut into short lengths
2–3 drained sun-dried tomatoes in oil,
   thinly sliced lengthways
60ml/4 tbsp extra virgin olive oil
15ml/1 tbsp red wine vinegar
salt and ground black pepper

1 Preheat the oven to 180°C/350°F/ Gas 4. Put the squid rings in an earthenware dish with half the garlic, the wine and pepper to taste. Cover and cook for 45 minutes or until the squid is tender.

2 Put the potatoes in a saucepan, cover with cold water and add a good pinch of salt. Bring to the boil, cover and simmer for 15–20 minutes or until tender. Using a slotted spoon, lift out the potatoes and set aside. Add the beans to the boiling water and cook for 3 minutes. Drain.

3 When the potatoes are cool enough to handle, slice them thickly on the diagonal and place them in a bowl with the warm beans and sun-dried tomatoes. Whisk the oil, wine vinegar and the remaining garlic in a jug and add salt and pepper to taste. Pour over the potato mixture.

4 Drain the squid and discard the wine and garlic. Add the squid to the potato mixture and mix together gently. Serve warm with freshly ground black pepper.

——— NUTRITION NOTES ———	
Per portion:	
Energy	369kcals/1545kJ
Protein	19.7g
Fat	18.2g
saturated fat	2.8g
Carbohydrate	20.2g
Fibre	1.3g
Sugars	1.6g
Calcium	29mg

Mussels and Clams with Lemon Grass

Lemon grass has an incomparable flavour and is widely used in Thai cookery, especially with seafood. Coconut cream gives the sauce a creamy consistency. If you have difficulty obtaining the clams for this recipe, use a few extra mussels instead.

INGREDIENTS

Serves 6

1.75kg/4–4½lb mussels
450g/1lb baby clams
120ml/4fl oz/½ cup dry white wine
1 bunch spring onions, chopped
2 lemon grass stalks, chopped
6 kaffir lime leaves, chopped
10ml/2 tsp Thai green curry paste
200ml/7fl oz coconut cream
30ml/2 tbsp chopped fresh coriander
salt and ground black pepper
garlic chives, to garnish

FREE FROM

1 Clean the mussels by pulling off the beards, scrubbing the shells well and removing any barnacles. Discard any mussels that are broken or which do not close when tapped sharply. Wash the clams.

2 Put the wine in a large saucepan with the onions, lemon grass, lime leaves and curry paste. Simmer until the wine has almost evaporated.

3 Add the mussels and clams to the pan, cover tightly and steam over a high heat for 5–6 minutes until they open, shaking the pan occasionally. Transfer the mussels and clams to a heated serving bowl and keep hot. Discard any shellfish that remain closed.

4 Strain the cooking liquid into a clean pan and simmer to reduce to about 250ml/8fl oz/1 cup. Stir in the coconut cream and coriander, with salt and pepper to taste. Heat through. Pour the sauce over the mussels and clams and serve, garnished with garlic chives.

— NUTRITION NOTES —	
Per portion:	
Energy	303kcals/1268kJ
Protein	28.4g
Fat	16.4g
saturated fat	10.6g
Carbohydrate	7.7g
Fibre	0.2g
Sugars	3.4g
Calcium	176mg

MEAT AND POULTRY

The recipes in this chapter have been specially selected to help you make the most of lean cuts of meat in appetizing, low-fat recipes. Whether your preference is for beef, lamb, pork or chicken, you are bound to find a recipe here to please. From exotic Middle Eastern Lamb Tagine to Spiced Grilled Poussins, there are dishes to suit every taste. Combine them with plenty of fresh seasonal vegetables and rice, pasta or potatoes to provide you with a healthy, balanced meal.

Thai Beef Salad

A hearty salad of beef, laced with a chilli and lime dressing.

INGREDIENTS

Serves 6

75g/3oz lean sirloin steaks
1 red onion, finely sliced
½ cucumber, finely sliced
    into matchsticks
1 lemon grass stalk, finely chopped
30ml/2 tbsp chopped spring onions
juice of 2 limes
15–30ml/1–2 tbsp Thai fish sauce
2–4 red chillies, finely sliced,
    fresh coriander, Chinese mustard cress
    and mint leaves, to garnish

NUTRITION NOTES

Per portion:

Energy	101Kcals/424kJ
Fat	3.8g
saturated fat	1.7g
Cholesterol	33.4mg
Fibre	0.28g

COOK'S TIP

Rump or fillet steaks would work just as well in this recipe. Choose good-quality lean steaks and remove and discard any visible fat.

---

1 Grill the sirloin steaks until they are medium-rare, then allow to rest for 10–15 minutes.

2 When cool, thinly slice the beef and put the slices in a large bowl.

3 Add the sliced onion, cucumber matchsticks and lemon grass.

4 Add the spring onions. Toss and season with the lime juice and fish sauce. Serve at room temperature or chilled, garnished with the chillies, coriander, mustard cress and mint.

Beef Rolls with Garlic and Tomato Sauce

Thin slices of beef are wrapped around a richly flavoured stuffing in this classic Italian recipe.

INGREDIENTS

Serves 4

4 thin slices of rump steak, about 115g/4oz each
4 slices smoked ham
150g/5oz/1⅔ cups freshly grated Parmesan cheese
2 garlic cloves, crushed
75ml/5 tbsp chopped fresh parsley
2 eggs, soft-boiled, shelled and chopped (optional)
45ml/3 tbsp olive oil
1 large onion, finely chopped
150ml/¼ pint/⅔ cup passata
2 bay leaves
200ml/7fl oz/scant 1 cup Beef Stock
salt and ground black pepper
flat leaf parsley, to garnish

1 Preheat the oven to 160°C/325°F/ Gas 3. Place the beef slices on a sheet of greaseproof paper. Cover the beef with another sheet of greaseproof paper or clear film and beat with a mallet or rolling pin until very thin. Place a ham slice over each.

2 Mix the cheese in a bowl with the garlic, parsley, eggs if using, and a little salt and pepper. Stir well until all the ingredients are evenly mixed.

3 Spoon the stuffing on to the ham and beef slices. Fold two opposite sides of the meat over the stuffing, then roll up the meat to form neat parcels. Secure with string.

4 Heat the oil in a frying pan. Add the parcels and fry quickly on all sides to brown. Transfer the parcels to an ovenproof dish.

5 Add the onion to the frying pan and fry for 3 minutes. Stir in the passata, bay leaves and stock and season with salt and pepper. Bring to the boil, then pour the sauce over the meat in the dish.

6 Cover the dish and bake for 1 hour. Lift the beef rolls out of the pan using a draining spoon and remove the string. Transfer to warm serving plates.

7 Taste the sauce, season with salt and pepper if necessary, and spoon it over the meat. Serve garnished with flat leaf parsley.

FREE FROM

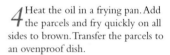

NUTRITION NOTES

Per portion:

Energy	490kcals/2049kJ
Protein	53.5g
Fat	28.1g
saturated fat	12g
Carbohydrate	2.9g
Sugar	2.3g
Fibre	0.6g
Calcium	470mg

Spiced Topside of Beef

A spicy marinade gives the beef a wonderful flavour, while slow cooking keeps it very moist.

INGREDIENTS

Serves 8

10ml/2 tsp coriander seeds
5ml/1 tsp each aniseeds, fennel seeds, dried thyme, ground cloves, salt and ground black pepper
2.5ml/½ tsp ground cinnamon
600ml/1 pint/2½ cups dry white wine
1–1.2kg/2¼–2½lb topside of beef
30ml/2 tbsp olive oil
2 onions, finely chopped
2 carrots, finely chopped
2 celery sticks, finely chopped
1 parsnip, finely chopped
4 French beans, finely chopped
8 mushrooms, finely chopped
300ml/½ pint/1¼ cups homemade jellied beef stock or chicken stock
105ml/7 tbsp red wine
2 fresh parsley sprigs
baked potatoes, to serve

1 Put the seeds in a mortar and pound them with a pestle. Stir in the rest of the spices and seasonings, then tip the mixture into a bowl and stir in the white wine.

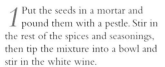

COOK'S TIP

Patience is the secret of this superb casserole. Marinate the meat for the time stated, and cook it very slowly.

2 Put the beef in a deep glass or china bowl. Pour the spicy marinade over the beef, cover the bowl and leave to marinate in the fridge or a cool larder for about 24 hours.

3 Preheat the oven to 150°C/300°F/ Gas 2. Heat the oil in a deep casserole large enough to hold the beef snugly. Add all the vegetables and cook over a gentle heat for 15–20 minutes or until they start to soften.

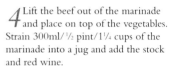

4 Lift the beef out of the marinade and place on top of the vegetables. Strain 300ml/½ pint/1¼ cups of the marinade into a jug and add the stock and red wine.

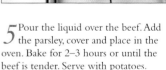

5 Pour the liquid over the beef. Add the parsley, cover and place in the oven. Bake for 2–3 hours or until the beef is tender. Serve with potatoes.

NUTRITION NOTES

Per portion:

Energy	260kcals/1088kJ
Fat, total	7.95g
saturated fat	2g
polyunsaturated fat	0.73g
monounsaturated fat	4.25g
Carbohydrate	4.3g
sugar, total	2.8g
starch	0.8g
Fibre	1.25g
Sodium	203mg

Beef and Lentil Pies

In this variation of cottage pie, lentils are substituted for some of the meat to produce a dish that is lower in fat and higher in fibre. Some red meat is included to boost the iron content.

INGREDIENTS

Serves 4

175g/6oz/1 cup green lentils
225g/8oz extra lean minced beef
1 onion, chopped
2 celery sticks, chopped
1 large carrot, chopped
1 garlic clove, crushed
425g/15oz can chopped tomatoes
10ml/2 tsp yeast extract
1 bay leaf

For the topping

450g/1lb potatoes, peeled and cut into
    large chunks
450g/1lb parsnips, peeled and cut into
    large chunks
60ml/4 tbsp low-fat natural yogurt
45ml/3 tbsp snipped chives
20ml/4 tsp freshly grated
    Parmesan cheese
2 tomatoes, sliced
25g/1oz/¼ cup pine nuts (optional)

1 Place the lentils in a pan and pour in cold water to cover. Bring to the boil, then boil for 10 minutes.

2 Meanwhile, brown the minced beef in a heavy-based saucepan, without adding any extra fat. Stir in the onion, celery, carrot and garlic. Cook over a low heat for 5 minutes, then stir in the tomatoes.

3 Drain the lentils, reserving 300ml/ ½ pint/1¼ cups of the cooking water. Add the lentils to the meat mixture, then dissolve the yeast extract in the cooking water and stir it in. Add the bay leaf and bring to the boil, then lower the heat, cover the pan and cook gently for 20 minutes.

4 Make the topping. Bring a saucepan of lightly salted water to the boil and cook the potatoes and parsnips for about 15 minutes, until tender. Drain, tip into a bowl, and mash with the yogurt and chives.

5 Preheat the grill. Remove the bay leaf from the beef and lentil mixture and discard. Divide the beef and lentil mixture among four small, flameproof dishes. Spoon over the potato and parsnip topping and smooth the surface with a palette knife. Sprinkle evenly with Parmesan and arrange the tomato slices decoratively. Scatter pine nuts over the top, if using, and grill the pies for a few minutes, until the topping is crisp and golden.

NUTRITION NOTES	
Per portion:	
Energy	470Kcals/1985kJ
Fat	10.6g
saturated fat	2.17g
Cholesterol	36.3mg
Fibre	13.3g

Beef Tagine with Sweet Potatoes

This colourful, warming dish is just what is needed on cold winter nights. Only mildly spicy, leave in some of the chilli seeds for a little more zing.

INGREDIENTS

Serves 4

675–900g/1½–2lb stewing beef
30ml/2 tbsp sunflower oil
a good pinch of ground turmeric
1 large onion, chopped
1 red or green chilli, seeded
  and chopped
7.5ml/1½ tsp paprika
a good pinch of cayenne pepper
2.5ml/½ tsp ground cumin
450g/1lb sweet potatoes, sliced
15ml/1 tbsp chopped fresh parsley
15ml/1 tbsp chopped fresh coriander,
  plus extra to garnish
15g/½oz/1 tbsp unsalted butter
ground black pepper

1 Trim the meat and cut into 2cm/¾ in cubes. Heat the oil in a flameproof casserole and fry the meat, together with the turmeric and pepper, over a medium heat for 3–4 minutes until evenly browned. With a wooden spoon, stir frequently to prevent the meat from sticking to the bottom of the pan.

2 Cover the pan tightly and cook for 15 minutes over a fairly gentle heat, without lifting the lid. Preheat the oven to 180°C/350°F/Gas 4.

--- NUTRITION NOTES ---

Per portion:

Energy	450Kcals/1182kJ
Protein	39.8g
Fat	20.3g
saturated fat	7.4g
Carbohydrate	125.1g
Fibre	3.5g
Sodium	116mg

3 Add the onion, chilli, paprika, cayenne pepper and cumin to the pan, together with just enough water to cover the meat. Cover tightly and cook in the oven for 1–1½ hours until the meat is very tender, checking occasionally and, if necessary, adding a little extra water to keep the stew fairly moist.

4 Transfer the sweet potatoes and water to a pan, bring to the boil and simmer for 2–3 minutes until just tender. Drain.

5 Add the herbs to the meat, plus a little extra water if the stew appears dry. Arrange the sweet potato slices over the meat and dot with the butter. Cover and cook in the oven for a further 10 minutes, or until the potatoes feel very tender. Increase the oven temperature to 200°C/400°F/Gas 6 or heat the grill.

6 Remove the lid of the casserole and cook in the oven or under the grill for a further 5–10 minutes until golden. Garnish with coriander.

Beef and Lentil Balls with Tomato Sauce

Mixing lentils with the minced beef not only boosts the fibre content of these meatballs but also adds to the flavour.

INGREDIENTS

Serves 8

15ml/1 tbsp olive oil
2 onions, finely chopped
2 celery sticks, finely chopped
2 large carrots, finely chopped
400g/14oz lean minced beef
200g/7oz/scant 1 cup brown lentils
400g/14oz can plum tomatoes
30ml/2 tbsp tomato purée
2 bay leaves
300ml/½ pint/1¼ cups Vegetable Stock
175ml/6fl oz/¾ cup red wine
30–45ml/2–3 tbsp Worcestershire sauce
2 eggs
2 large handfuls of fresh
   parsley, chopped
salt and ground black pepper
riced potatoes and green salad, to serve

For the tomato sauce
4 onions, finely chopped
2 x 400g/14oz cans chopped tomatoes
60ml/4 tbsp dry red wine
3 fresh dill sprigs, finely chopped

1 Start by making the tomato sauce. Combine the onions, canned plum tomatoes and red wine in a saucepan. Bring to the boil, lower the heat, cover the pan and simmer for 30 minutes. Purée the mixture in a blender or food processor, then return it to the clean saucepan and set it aside.

2 Make the meatballs. Heat the oil in a large heavy-based saucepan and cook the chopped onions, celery and carrots for 5–10 minutes or until the onions and carrots have softened.

3 Add the minced beef and cook over a high heat, stirring frequently, until the meat is lightly browned.

4 Add the lentils, tomatoes, tomato purée, bay leaves, vegetable stock and wine. Mix well and bring to the boil. Lower the heat and simmer for 20–30 minutes until the liquid has been absorbed. Remove the bay leaves, then stir the Worcestershire sauce into the lentil mixture.

5 Remove the pan from the heat and add the eggs and parsley. Season with salt and pepper and mix well, then leave to cool. Meanwhile, preheat the oven to 180°C/350°F/Gas 4.

6 Shape the beef mixture into neat balls, rolling them in your hands. Arrange in an ovenproof dish and bake for 25 minutes. While the meatballs are baking, reheat the tomato sauce. Just before serving, stir in the chopped dill. Pour the tomato sauce over the meatballs and serve. Riced potatoes and salad make excellent accompaniments.

NUTRITION NOTES	
Per portion:	
Energy	272kcals/1154kJ
Fat, total	9.3g
saturated fat	2.9g
polyunsaturated fat	0.8g
monounsaturated fat	4.2g
Carbohydrate	22.65g
sugar, total	9g
starch	11.5g
Fibre	4.5g
Sodium	155mg

Spicy Lamb and Apricots with Pea Rice

INGREDIENTS

Serves 4

675g/1½lb lamb leg fillet
15ml/1 tbsp ghee or butter
1 onion, finely chopped
5ml/1 tsp ground coriander
10ml/2 tsp ground cumin
5ml/1 tsp fenugreek
2.5ml/½ tsp turmeric
pinch of cayenne pepper
1 cinnamon stick
120ml/4fl oz/½ cup Chicken Stock
175g/6oz/¾ cup ready-to-eat apricots
salt and ground black pepper
fresh coriander, to garnish

For the marinade

120ml/4fl oz/½ cup natural yogurt
15ml/1 tbsp sunflower oil
juice of ½ lemon
2.5cm/1in piece root ginger, grated

For the rice

175g/6oz/1 cup chana dhal or yellow
   split peas, soaked for 1–2 hours
225g/8oz/1 cup basmati rice, soaked
15ml/1 tbsp sunflower oil
1 large onion, thinly sliced
1 garlic clove, crushed
10ml/2 tsp finely grated root ginger
5ml/1 tsp turmeric
60ml/4 tbsp natural yogurt
690ml/22fl oz/2¾ cups chicken stock
15ml/1 tbsp chopped fresh coriander
15ml/1 tbsp ghee or butter

1 Cut the meat into bite-size pieces. Mix the marinade ingredients. Add the meat, stir to coat, then cover and leave in a cool place for 2–4 hours.

2 Boil the yellow split peas for 20–30 minutes until tender. Drain and set aside. Cook the drained rice for 5 minutes. Drain well and set aside.

3 Heat the oil and fry the onion rings for 10–15 minutes until golden. Transfer to a plate. Stir-fry the garlic and ginger for a few seconds, then add the turmeric and yogurt and cook for a few minutes. Add the dhal, coriander and salt, stir well and then remove from the heat and set aside. Preheat the oven to 180°C/350°F/Gas 4.

4 Drain the meat, reserving the marinade. Melt the ghee or butter in a flameproof casserole and fry the onion for 3–4 minutes. Add the spices and fry for 1 minute. Add the meat and fry until browned. Spoon in all the remaining marinade, add the stock and apricots and season well. Bring to the boil, cover and cook in the oven for 45–55 minutes until the meat is tender.

5 Meanwhile, finish cooking the rice. Spoon the dhal mixture into a casserole and stir in the rice. Dot with ghee or butter and sprinkle with the onion rings. Cover tightly with a double layer of foil, securing with a lid. Place in the oven about 30 minutes before the lamb is ready. The rice and dhal should be tender, but the grains separate. Serve the rice and spiced lamb garnished with coriander.

———— NUTRITION NOTES ————

Per portion:

Energy	776kcals/3262kJ
Protein	53.3g
Fat	22.6g
saturated fat	9.9g
Carbohydrate	92.1g
Fibre	5.9g
Sugars	21.8g
Calcium	162.5mg

Lamb Casserole with Garlic and Broad Beans

This Spanish-influenced recipe makes a substantial meal, served with creamed potatoes.

INGREDIENTS

Serves 6

45ml/3 tbsp olive oil
1.5kg/3–3½lb fillet lamb, cut into
    5cm/2in cubes
1 large onion, chopped
6 large garlic cloves, unpeeled
1 bay leaf
5ml/1 tsp paprika
120ml/4fl oz/ ½ cup gluten-free
    lamb stock
115g/4oz shelled fresh or frozen
    broad beans
30ml/2 tbsp chopped fresh parsley
salt and ground black pepper

1 Heat 30ml/2 tbsp of the oil in a large frying pan. Add half the meat and brown well on all sides. Transfer to a plate. Brown the rest of the meat in the same way and remove from the pan.

2 Heat the remaining oil in a large saucepan, add the onion and cook for about 5 minutes, until soft. Add the meat and mix well.

3 Add the garlic cloves, bay leaf, paprika and stock. Season with salt and pepper. Bring to the boil, then cover and simmer very gently for 1½–2 hours, until the meat is tender.

4 Add the broad beans about 10 minutes before the end of the cooking time. Stir in the parsley just before serving.

NUTRITION NOTES

Per portion:

Energy	414kcals/1983kJ
Protein	53.1g
Fat	27g
saturated fat	11.3g
Carbohydrate	3.1g
Sugar	1.1g
Fibre (NSP)	1.5g
Calcium	26mg

COOK'S TIP

Use canned beans, such as haricot or flageolet, instead of broad beans.

Roast Leg of Lamb with Mushroom Stuffing

When the thigh bone is removed from a leg of lamb, a stuffing can be put in its place. This not only makes the joint easier to carve but also gives a wonderful flavour to the meat that lessens the need to add salt. Roast potatoes, carrots and broccoli are all excellent accompaniments.

INGREDIENTS

Serves 4

1.75kg/4-4½lb leg of lamb, boned
ground black pepper
watercress, to garnish
lightly cooked carrots and broccoli
 and roast potatoes, to serve

For the stuffing

25g/1oz/2 tbsp unsalted butter
1 shallot or small onion, chopped
225g/8oz assorted wild and cultivated
 mushrooms, such as chanterelles,
 ceps, bay boletus, horn of plenty,
 blewits, oyster, St George's, field
 and Caesar's mushrooms, trimmed
 then chopped
½ garlic clove, crushed
1 fresh thyme sprig, chopped
25g/1oz saltless dairy-free white bread,
 crust removed and diced
2 egg yolks

For the gravy

50ml/3½ tbsp red wine
400ml/14fl oz/1⅔ cups boiling home-
 made chicken stock
5g/⅛oz/2 tbsp dried ceps, bay boletus
 or saffron milk-caps, soaked in
 boiling water for 20 minutes
20ml/4 tsp cornflour
5ml/1 tsp mustard
2.5ml/½ tsp wine vinegar
a knob of unsalted butter

───── COOK'S TIP ─────

If you buy your meat from a butcher, ask
for the thigh bone to be removed.

1 Preheat the oven to 200°C/400°F/ Gas 6. To make the stuffing, melt the butter in a large, non-stick frying pan and gently fry the shallot or onion without colouring.

2 Add the mushrooms, garlic and thyme, and stir the mixture until the mushroom juices begin to run, then increase the heat so that they evaporate completely.

3 Transfer the mushrooms to a large mixing bowl, add the bread, egg yolks and pepper, and mix well. Allow to cool slightly.

───── NUTRITION NOTES ─────

Per portion:	
Energy	967Kcals/4027kJ
Protein	87.1g
Fat	63.4g
saturated fat	32.12g
Carbohydrate	10g
Fibre	0.9g
Sodium	322mg

4 Season the inside cavity of the lamb with pepper and then press the stuffing into the cavity, using a spoon or your fingers. Tie up the end with string and then tie around the joint to help it keep shape.

5 Place the lamb in a roasting tin and roast in the oven for 15 minutes per 450g/1lb for rare meat or 20 minutes per 450g/1lb for medium-rare. For this recipe, cook for 1 hour 20 minutes for medium-rare.

6 Transfer the lamb to a warmed serving plate, cover and keep warm. To make the gravy, spoon off all the excess fat from the roasting tin and brown the sediment over a moderate heat. Add the wine and stir with a flat wooden spoon to loosen the sediment. Add the chicken stock, the dried mushrooms and their soaking liquid.

7 Blend the cornflour and mustard with 15ml/1 tbsp water, stir into the stock and simmer to thicken. Add the vinegar. Season, then stir in the butter. Garnish the lamb with watercress and serve with vegetables.

Green Peppercorn and Cinnamon Crusted Lamb

Racks of lamb are perfect for
dinner parties. This version
has a spiced crumb coating.

INGREDIENTS

Serves 6

50g/2oz ciabatta bread
15ml/1 tbsp drained green peppercorns
   in brine, lightly crushed
15ml/1 tbsp ground cinnamon
1 garlic clove, crushed
2.5ml/½ tsp salt
25g/1oz/2 tbsp pure vegetable
   margarine, melted
10ml/2 tsp Dijon mustard
2 racks of lamb, trimmed
400ml/14fl oz/1⅔ cups lamb stock
30ml/2 tbsp tomato purée
fresh vegetables, to serve

1 Preheat the oven to 220°C/425°F/
Gas 7. Break the ciabatta bread into
pieces, spread out on a baking sheet and
bake for about 10 minutes or until pale
golden. Leave to cool, then process the
bread in a blender or food processor to
make fine crumbs.

2 Tip the crumbs into a bowl and add
the green peppercorns, cinnamon,
garlic and salt. Stir in the melted
margarine. Spread the mustard over the
lamb. Press the crumb mixture on to
the mustard to make a thin, even crust.
Put the racks in a roasting tin and roast
for 30 minutes, covering the ends with
foil if they are starting to brown
too quickly.

3 Remove the lamb to a carving
dish, cover with loosely tented foil
and keep hot.

4 Skim the fat off the juices in the
roasting tin. Stir in the stock and
tomato purée. Bring to the boil, stirring
in any sediment, then lower the heat
and simmer until reduced to a rich
gravy. Carve the lamb and serve with
the gravy and vegetables.

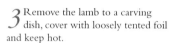

⎯ NUTRITION NOTES ⎯	
Per portion:	
Energy	414kcals/1983kJ
Protein	53.1g
Fat	27.0g
saturated fat	11.3g
Carbohydrate	3.1g
Sugar	1.1g
Fibre	1.5g
Calcium	26mg

Lamb Pie with Mustard Thatch

INGREDIENTS

Serves 4

800g/1¾lb floury potatoes, diced
15ml/1 tbsp gluten-free
   wholegrain mustard
a little pure vegetable margarine
450g/1lb minced lean lamb
1 onion, chopped
2 celery sticks, thinly sliced
2 carrots, diced
30ml/2 tbsp cornflour
150ml/¼ pint/⅔ cup Beef Stock
15ml/1 tbsp vegetarian
   Worcestershire sauce
30ml/2 tbsp chopped fresh rosemary,
   or 10ml/2 tsp dried
salt and ground black pepper
fresh vegetables, to serve

1 Cook the potatoes in boiling lightly salted water until tender. Drain well and mash until smooth, then stir in the mustard, margarine and seasoning to taste. Meanwhile, preheat the oven to 200°C/400°F/Gas 6.

—— NUTRITION NOTES ——	
Per portion:	
Energy	371kcals/1559kJ
Protein	28g
Fat	13.7g
saturated fat	6.8g
Carbohydrate	36g
Sugar	4.5g
Fibre (NSP)	3.5g
Calcium	177mg

2 Fry the lamb in a non-stick pan, breaking it up with a fork, until lightly browned. Add the onion, celery and carrots to the pan and cook for 2–3 minutes, stirring.

—— COOK'S TIP ——

Vegetarian Worcestershire sauce, which doesn't contain anchovies, is available from health-food shops.

3 Blend together the cornflour and stock and stir into the lamb mixture. Bring to the boil, stirring, then remove from the heat. Add the Worcestershire sauce and rosemary and season with salt and pepper.

4 Transfer the lamb mixture to a 1.75 litre/3 pint/7½ cup ovenproof dish and spread the potato topping over evenly, swirling with the edge of a knife. Bake for 30–35 minutes until golden. Serve hot with fresh vegetables.

FREE
FROM

Irish Stew

Although you should be trying to cut down on your consumption of red meat, the carrots and onions in this simple and delicious stew provide vital cancer-fighting nutrients. Always try to buy organic meat.

INGREDIENTS

Serves 6
1.2kg/2½lb boneless lamb chops
15ml/1 tbsp vegetable oil
3 large onions, quartered
4 large carrots, thickly sliced
900ml/1½ pints/3¾ cups water
4 large firm potatoes, cut into chunks
1 large thyme sprig
15ml/1 tbsp butter
15ml/1 tbsp chopped fresh parsley
salt and ground black pepper
Savoy cabbage, to serve (optional)

1 Trim any excess fat from the lamb. Heat the oil in a flameproof casserole, add the lamb and brown on both sides. Remove from the pan.

2 Add the onions and carrots to the casserole and cook for 5 minutes. Return the lamb to the pan with the water. Season with salt and pepper. Bring to a boil then reduce the heat, cover and simmer for 1 hour.

3 Add the potatoes to the pan with the thyme, cover again, and simmer for a further hour.

4 Leave the stew to settle for a few minutes. Remove the fat from the liquid with a ladle, then carefully pour off the liquid into a clean saucepan. Bring to a simmer and stir in the butter, then the parsley. Season well and pour back into the casserole. Serve with Savoy cabbage, if liked.

NUTRITION NOTES	
Per portion:	
Energy	600kcals/2346kJ
Protein	39.2g
Fat	39.8g
saturated fat	15.2g
Carbohydrate	22.7g
Fibre	3.2g
Sugars	7.6g
Calcium	60.3mg

Middle Eastern Roast Lamb and Potatoes

Increase your intake of vitamin E and antioxidants by serving this delicious garlicky lamb with a leafy green vegetable, such as Swiss chard or spinach.

INGREDIENTS

Serves 8
2.75kg/6lb leg of lamb
4 garlic cloves, halved
60ml/4 tbsp olive oil
juice of 1 lemon
2–3 saffron strands, soaked in 15ml/
   1 tbsp boiling water
5ml/1 tsp mixed dried herbs
450g/1lb baking potatoes, peeled and
   thickly sliced
2 large onions, thickly sliced
salt and ground black pepper
fresh parsley, to garnish

1 Make eight incisions in the lamb and press in the garlic. Place the lamb in a glass dish. Mix the oil, lemon juice, saffron mixture and herbs. Rub over the lamb, then marinate for 2 hours.

2 Preheat the oven to 180°C/350°F/ Gas 4. Layer the potatoes and onions in a roasting tin. Lift the lamb out of the marinade and place on top of the potatoes and onions, fat side up.

3 Pour any remaining marinade over the lamb and roast for 2 hours, basting occasionally, until the meat is tender. Remove the lamb from the oven, cover loosely with foil and leave to rest in a warm place for about 15 minutes before carving. Serve garnished with fresh parsley.

NUTRITION NOTES	
Per portion:	
Energy	741kcals/3088kJ
Protein	66.7g
Fat	49.2g
saturated fat	32.8g
Carbohydrate	11.2g
Fibre	1.0g
Sugars	1.4g
Calcium	28.1mg

Turkish Lamb Pilau

INGREDIENTS

Serves 4

45ml/3 tbsp pure vegetable oil
1 large onion, finely chopped
450g/1lb lamb fillet, cut into
  small cubes
2.5ml/½ tsp ground cinnamon
30ml/2 tbsp tomato purée
45ml/3 tbsp chopped fresh parsley
115g/4oz/½ cup ready-to-eat dried
  apricots, halved
450g/1lb long grain rice, rinsed
75g/3oz/¾ cup pistachio nuts,
  chopped (optional)
salt and ground black pepper
flat leaf parsley, to garnish

1 Heat the oil in a large heavy-based pan. Add the onion and cook until golden. Add the lamb and brown on all sides, then stir in the cinnamon, salt and black pepper. Cover and cook gently for 10 minutes.

2 Add the tomato purée and enough water to cover the meat. Stir in the parsley, then bring to the boil. Cover the pan and simmer very gently for 1½ hours, until the meat is tender.

3 Add enough water to the pan to make up to about 600ml/1 pint/ 2½ cups liquid. Add the apricots and rice and stir in the pistachio nuts, if using.

4 Bring to the boil, cover tightly and simmer for about 20 minutes, until the rice is cooked. (You may have to add a little more water, if necessary.) Transfer to a warmed serving dish and garnish with parsley before serving.

NUTRITION NOTES	
Per portion:	
Energy	740kcals/3129kJ
Protein	33.1g
Fat	22.3g
saturated fat	9.3g
Carbohydrate	108g
Sugar	11.8g
Fibre	2.5g
Calcium	92mg

Spiced Lamb with Vegetable Couscous

This delicious stew is packed
with vitamins.

INGREDIENTS

Serves 6

350g/12oz lean lamb fillet, cut into
    2cm/¾in cubes
30ml/2 tbsp wholemeal
    plain flour
10ml/2 tsp sunflower oil
1 onion, chopped
2 garlic cloves, crushed
1 red pepper, seeded and diced
5ml/1 tsp ground coriander
5ml/1 tsp ground cumin
5ml/1 tsp ground allspice
2.5ml/½ tsp hot chilli powder
300ml/½ pint/1¼ cups lamb stock
400g/14oz can chopped tomatoes
225g/8oz carrots, sliced
175g/6oz parsnips, sliced
175g/6oz courgettes, sliced
175g/6oz mushrooms, quartered
225g/8oz frozen broad beans
115g/4oz/⅔ cup sultanas
450g/1 lb quick-cook couscous
salt and ground black pepper
fresh coriander, to garnish

1 Toss the lamb in the flour. Heat the
oil in a large saucepan and add the
lamb, onion, garlic and pepper. Cook
for 5 minutes, stirring frequently.

— NUTRITION NOTES —	
Per portion:	
Energy	439kcals/1844kJ
Fat	8.6g
saturated fat	2.88g
Cholesterol	49.6g
Fibre	7.2g

2 Add any remaining flour and the
spices and cook the mixture for
1 minute, stirring.

3 Gradually add the stock, stirring
continuously, then add the
tomatoes, carrots and parsnips and mix
well. Bring to the boil, stirring then
cover and simmer for 30 minutes,
stirring occasionally.

4 Add the courgettes, mushrooms,
broad beans and sultanas. Cover,
return to the boil and simmer for a
further 20–30 minutes, until the lamb
and vegetables are tender, stirring
occasionally. Season to taste.

5 Meanwhile, soak the couscous and
steam in a lined colander over a pan
of boiling water for about 20 minutes,
until cooked, or according to the
packet instructions. Pile the couscous
on to a warmed serving platter or
individual plates and top with the lamb
and vegetable stew. Garnish with fresh
coriander and serve immediately.

Braised Lamb with Apricots and Herb Dumplings

A rich and fruity lamb casserole, topped with light, herby gluten-free dumplings, which is delicious served with baked jacket potatoes and broccoli.

INGREDIENTS

Serves 6

30ml/2 tbsp sunflower oil
675g/1½lb lean lamb fillet, cut into 2.5cm/1in cubes
350g/12oz button onions, peeled
1 garlic clove, crushed
225g/8oz button mushrooms
175g/6oz/¾ cup small ready-to-eat dried apricots
250ml/8fl oz/1 cup well-flavoured gluten-free lamb or Beef Stock
250ml/8fl oz/1 cup red wine
15ml/1 tbsp tomato purée
salt and ground black pepper
fresh herb sprigs, to garnish

For the dumplings

115g/4oz/1 cup gluten-free self-raising flour
50g/2oz/scant ½ cup gluten-free shredded vegetable suet
15–30ml/1–2 tbsp chopped fresh mixed herbs

—— VARIATIONS ——

Use lean beef or pork in place of the lamb and substitute shallots for the button onions, if you prefer.

—— NUTRITION NOTES ——

Per portion:
Energy	513kcals/3204kJ
Fat, total	28.8g
saturated fat	11.6g
Protein	26.1g
Carbohydrate	31.6g
sugar, total	15.3g
Fibre	3.4g
Sodium	257mg

1 Preheat the oven to 160°C/325°F/Gas 3. Heat the oil in a large, flameproof casserole, add the lamb and cook gently until browned all over, stirring occasionally. Remove the meat from the casserole using a slotted spoon, set aside and keep warm.

2 Add the button onions, garlic and mushrooms to the oil remaining in the casserole and cook gently for about 5 minutes, stirring occasionally.

3 Return the meat to the casserole, add the dried apricots, stock, wine and tomato purée. Season to taste with salt and pepper and stir to mix.

4 Bring to the boil, stirring, then remove the casserole from the heat and cover. Transfer the casserole to the oven and cook for 1½–2 hours until the lamb is cooked and tender, stirring once or twice and adding a little extra stock, if necessary.

5 Meanwhile, make the dumplings. Place the flour, suet, herbs and seasoning in a bowl and stir to mix. Add enough cold water to make a soft, elastic dough. Divide the dough into small, marble-size pieces and, using lightly floured hands, roll each piece into a small ball.

6 Remove the lid from the casserole and place the dumplings on the top of the braised lamb and vegetables.

7 Increase the oven temperature to 190°C/375°F/Gas 5. Return the casserole to the oven and cook for a further 20–25 minutes until the herb dumplings are cooked. Serve, garnished with fresh herb sprigs.

Lamb with Flageolets and Green Peppercorns

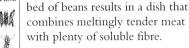

FREE FROM

Roasting the lamb slowly on a bed of beans results in a dish that combines meltingly tender meat with plenty of soluble fibre.

INGREDIENTS

Serves 6

8–10 garlic cloves, peeled
1.75kg/4–4½lb leg of lamb
30ml/2 tbsp olive oil
400g/14oz fresh spinach leaves
400g/14oz can flageolet beans, drained
400g/14oz can butter beans, drained
2 large fresh rosemary sprigs
15–30ml/1–2 tbsp drained green
  peppercorns
potatoes, to serve

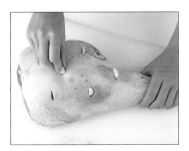

1 Preheat the oven to 150°C/300°F/ Gas 2. Set 4 garlic cloves aside and slice the rest lengthways into three or four pieces. Make shallow slits in the skin of the lamb and insert a piece of garlic in each.

2 Heat the oil in a roasting tin or a heavy flameproof casserole that is large enough to hold the lamb. Add the reserved garlic and the spinach and cook briskly for 4–5 minutes or until the spinach is wilted.

3 Add the flageolets and butter beans and tuck the rosemary sprigs and peppercorns among them. Place the lamb on top. Cover with foil or a lid. Roast the lamb for 3–4 hours until it is cooked to your taste. Serve with the spinach and beans and potatoes.

NUTRITION NOTES	
Per portion:	
Energy	312kcals/1306kJ
Fat, total	14.5g
saturated fat	4.6g
polyunsaturated fat	1.4g
monounsaturated fat	6.9g
Carbohydrate	17.8g
sugar, total	2.3g
starch	14.2g
Fibre	6g
Sodium	172mg

Lamb with Vegetables

INGREDIENTS

Serves 6

juice of 1 lemon
15ml/1 tbsp soy sauce
15ml/1 tbsp dry sherry, optional
1 garlic clove, crushed
10ml/2 tsp chopped fresh rosemary
6 lean chump or loin lamb chops
1 red onion, cut into 8 pieces
1 onion, cut into 8 pieces
1 red, 1 yellow and 1 green pepper,
    seeded and cut into chunks
4 courgettes, thickly sliced
350g/12oz button mushrooms
30ml/2 tbsp olive oil
4 plum tomatoes, peeled
400g/14oz can baby sweetcorn
60ml/4 tbsp chopped fresh basil
15–30ml/1–2 tbsp balsamic vinegar
salt and ground black pepper
fresh herbs and basil, to garnish

1 In a shallow dish, mix together the lemon juice, soy sauce, sherry, if using, garlic and rosemary. Coat the lamb chops in the marinade. Cover and refrigerate for 2 hours.

2 Preheat the oven to 200°C/ 400°F/Gas 6. Put the onions, peppers, courgettes and mushrooms in a roasting tin, drizzle over the olive oil and toss the vegetables to coat. Bake for 25 minutes.

3 Quarter the tomatoes and stir in with the sweetcorn. Bake for a further 10 minutes, until the vegetables are just tender and tinged at the edges. Add the basil, sprinkle over the balsamic vinegar and season to taste, stirring to mix.

4 Preheat the grill. Place the lamb chops under a medium grill for about 6 minutes on each side until cooked, turning over once. Brush the chops with any remaining marinade whilst they are cooking, to prevent them from drying out. Serve the chops with the cooked vegetables and garnish with fresh chopped herbs and a basil sprig.

NUTRITION NOTES	
Per portion:	
Energy	273Kcals/1143kJ
Protein	26.95g
Fat	12.60g
saturated fat	4.22g
Carbohydrate	13.15g
Fibre	4.99g
Sugar	0.10g
Sodium	0.91g

Turkish Kebabs with Tomato and Olive Salsa

FREE FROM

INGREDIENTS

Serves 4

2 garlic cloves, crushed
60ml/4 tbsp lemon juice
30ml/2 tbsp olive oil
1 dried red chilli, crushed
5ml/1 tsp ground cumin
5ml/1 tsp ground coriander
500g/1¼lb lean lamb, cut into cubes
8 bay leaves
salt and ground black pepper

For the tomato and olive salsa
175g/6oz/1½ cups mixed pitted green
    and black olives, roughly chopped
1 small red onion, finely chopped
4 tomatoes, peeled and finely chopped
1 red chilli, seeded and finely chopped
30ml/2 tbsp olive oil

1 Mix the garlic, lemon juice, olive oil, chilli, cumin and coriander in a large shallow dish. Add the lamb cubes, with plenty of salt and pepper to taste. Mix well. Cover and leave to marinate in a cool place for 2 hours.

2 Make the salsa. Put the olives, onion, tomatoes, chilli and olive oil in a bowl. Stir in salt and pepper to taste. Mix well, cover and set aside.

3 Remove the lamb from the marinade and divide the cubes among four skewers, adding the bay leaves at intervals. Grill over a barbecue, on a ridged iron grill pan or under a hot grill, turning occasionally, for 10 minutes, until the lamb is browned and crisp on the outside and pink and juicy inside. Serve with the salsa.

— NUTRITION NOTES —	
Per portion:	
Energy	323kcals/1344kJ
Protein	19.3g
Fat	25.9g
saturated fat	7.1g
Carbohydrate	4.6g
Fibre	2.5g
Sugars	3.7g
Calcium	54mg

Pork in Sweet-and-sour Sauce

This recipe is given extra bite with the addition of crushed mixed peppercorns. Served with shelled broad beans tossed with grilled bacon, it is delectable.

INGREDIENTS

Serves 2
1 whole pork fillet, about 350g/12oz
25ml/1½ tbsp plain flour
30–45ml/2–3 tbsp olive oil
250ml/8fl oz/1 cup dry white wine
30ml/2 tbsp white wine vinegar
10ml/2 tsp sugar
15ml/1 tbsp mixed peppercorns,
   coarsely ground
salt and ground black pepper
broad beans tossed with grilled bacon,
   to serve

1 Cut the pork diagonally into thin slices. Place between two sheets of clear film and pound lightly with a rolling pin to flatten them evenly.

2 Put the flour in a shallow bowl. Season well and coat the meat.

NUTRITION NOTES	
Per portion:	
Energy	601 kcals/2525KJ
Protein	56.7g
Fat	26.2g
saturated fat	18g
Carbohydrate	14.9g
Fibre	0
Sugars	5.5g
Calcium	38mg

3 Heat 15ml/1 tbsp of the oil in a wide heavy-based saucepan or frying pan and add as many slices of pork as the pan will hold. Fry over a medium to high heat for 2–3 minutes on each side until crispy and tender. Remove with a fish slice and set aside. Repeat with the remaining pork, adding more oil as necessary.

4 Mix the wine, wine vinegar and sugar in a jug. Pour into the pan and stir vigorously over a high heat until reduced, scraping the pan to incorporate the sediment. Stir in the peppercorns and return the pork to the pan. Coat the pork with the sauce and heat through. Serve hot with broad beans tossed with grilled bacon.

FREE FROM

Paprika Pork with Fennel and Caraway

Fennel always tastes particularly good with pork, and combined with caraway seeds adds an aromatic flavour to this dish.

INGREDIENTS

Serves 4
15ml/1 tbsp olive oil
4 boneless pork steaks
1 large onion, thinly sliced
400g/14oz can chopped tomatoes
5ml/1 tsp fennel seeds, lightly crushed
2.5ml/½ tsp caraway seeds, crushed
15ml/1 tbsp paprika, plus extra
   to garnish
30ml/2 tbsp soured cream
ground black pepper
noodles tossed with poppy seeds,
   to serve

1 Heat the oil in a large frying pan. Add the pork steaks and brown on both sides. Lift out the steaks and put them on a plate.

2 Add the onion to the oil remaining in the pan. Cook for 10 minutes until soft and golden.

3 Stir in the tomatoes, fennel seeds, caraway seeds and paprika.

4 Return the pork to the pan and simmer gently for 20-30 minutes until tender. Season with pepper.

5 Lightly swirl in the soured cream and sprinkle with a little extra paprika. Serve with noodles that have been tossed in poppy seeds.

NUTRITION NOTES	
Per portion:	
Energy	254Kcals/1064kJ
Protein	30.2g
Fat	10.9g
saturated fat	3.49g
Carbohydrate	9g
Fibre	1.3g
Sodium	142mg

Pork-stuffed Cabbage Parcels

Served with rice, these attractive, tied parcels make a tasty meal.

INGREDIENTS

Serves 4

4 dried Chinese mushrooms, soaked in hot water until soft
50g/2oz cellophane noodles, soaked in hot water until soft
450g/1lb minced pork
4 spring onions, finely chopped, plus 4 spring onions to tie the parcels
2 garlic cloves, finely chopped
30ml/2 tbsp fish sauce
12 large outer green cabbage leaves
30ml/2 tbsp vegetable oil
1 small onion, finely chopped
2 garlic cloves, crushed
400g/14oz can plum tomatoes
pinch of sugar
salt and ground black pepper

1 Drain the mushrooms, remove and discard the stems and coarsely chop the caps. Put them in a bowl.

2 Drain the noodles and cut them into short lengths. Add the noodles to the bowl with the pork, chopped spring onions and garlic. Season with the fish sauce and add pepper to taste.

3 Cut off the stem from each cabbage leaf. Blanch the leaves in batches in a saucepan of boiling salted water for about 1 minute. Remove from the pan and refresh under cold water. Drain and dry on kitchen paper. Add the whole spring onions to the boiling water and blanch in the same fashion. Drain well.

4 Fill one of the cabbage leaves with a generous spoonful of the pork and noodle filling. Roll up the leaf sufficiently to enclose the filling, then tuck in the sides and continue rolling the leaf to make a tight parcel. Make more parcels in the same way.

5 Split each blanched spring onion lengthways into three strands by cutting through the bulb and tearing upwards. Tie each of the cabbage parcels with a length of spring onion.

6 Heat the oil in a large flameproof casserole. Add the onion and garlic and fry for 2 minutes or until soft.

7 In a bowl, mash the tomatoes in their juice with a fork, then stir into the casserole. Season with salt, pepper and a pinch of sugar, then bring to a simmer. Add the cabbage parcels, cover and let them cook gently for 20–25 minutes or until the filling is cooked. Add a little water if necessary.

— NUTRITION NOTES —

Per portion:
Energy	309kcals/1569kJ
Protein	26.5g
Fat	13.9g
saturated fat	3.4g
Carbohydrate	19.4g
Sugar	5.3g
Fibre	2.2g
Calcium	60mg

Honey-roast Pork with Herbs

Herbs and honey add flavour and sweetness to tenderloin – the leanest cut of pork.

INGREDIENTS

Serves 4
450g/1 lb pork tenderloin
30ml/2 tbsp thick honey
30ml/2 tbsp gluten-free Dijon mustard
5ml/1 tsp chopped fresh rosemary
2.5ml/½ tsp chopped fresh thyme
1.5ml/¼ tsp whole tropical peppercorns
fresh rosemary and thyme sprigs,
   to garnish
potato gratin and cauliflower, to serve

For the red onion confit
4 red onions
350ml/12fl oz/1½ cups Vegetable Stock
15ml/1 tbsp red wine vinegar
15ml/1 tbsp caster sugar
1 garlic clove, crushed
30ml/2 tbsp ruby port
pinch of salt

2 Crush the peppercorns using a pestle and mortar. Spread the honey mixture over the pork and sprinkle with the crushed peppercorns. Place in a non-stick roasting tin and cook in the pre-heated oven for 35–45 minutes.

3 For the red onion confit, slice the onions into rings and put them into a heavy-based saucepan.

4 Add the stock, vinegar, sugar and garlic clove to the saucepan. Bring to the boil, then reduce the heat. Cover and simmer for 15 minutes.

5 Uncover and pour in the port and continue to simmer, stirring occasionally, until the onions are soft and the juices thick and syrupy. Season to taste with salt.

6 Cut the pork into slices and arrange on four warmed plates. Serve garnished with rosemary and thyme and accompanied with the red onion confit, potato gratin and cauliflower.

1 Pre-heat the oven to 180°C/350°F/ Gas 4. Trim off any visible fat from the pork. Put the honey, mustard, rosemary and thyme in a small bowl and mix them together well.

--- NUTRITION NOTES ---

Per portion:
Energy	258Kcals/1080kJ
Fat	8.9g
saturated fat	2.92g
Cholesterol	77.6mg
Fibre	12g

Pork Fillet with Sage and Orange

Sage is often partnered with pork – there seems to be a natural affinity. The addition of orange brings complexity and balances the sometimes overpowering flavour of sage.

INGREDIENTS

Serves 4

2 pork fillets, about 350g/12oz each
15g/½oz/1 tbsp pure vegetable
   margarine
300ml/ ½ pint/ 1¼ cups well-flavoured
   chicken stock
2 garlic cloves, very finely chopped
grated rind and juice of
   1 unwaxed orange
3 or 4 sage leaves, finely chopped
10ml/2 tsp cornflour or arrowroot
salt and ground black pepper
orange wedges and sage leaves,
   to garnish

1 Season the pork fillets lightly with salt and pepper. Melt the margarine in a heavy flameproof casserole over a medium-high heat, then add the meat and cook for 5–6 minutes, turning to brown all sides evenly.

2 Add the stock, boil for about 1 minute, then add the garlic, orange rind and sage. Bring to the boil; reduce the heat to low, then cover and simmer for 20 minutes, turning once, until the meat can be pierced with a knife. Transfer the pork to a warmed platter; cover.

3 Bring the sauce to the boil. Blend the cornflour or arrowroot and orange juice and stir into the sauce, then boil gently over a medium heat for a few minutes, stirring frequently, until the sauce is slightly thickened. Strain into a gravy boat or serving jug.

4 Slice the pork diagonally and pour the meat juices into the sauce.

5 Arrange the pork slices on warmed plates and spoon a little sauce over the top. Garnish with orange wedges and sage leaves and serve the remaining sauce separately.

NUTRITION NOTES	
Per portion:	
Energy	330kcals/1378kJ
Protein	36.2g
Fat	15.5g
saturated fat	5.7g
Carbohydrate	2.65g
Sugar	0.3g
Fibre	0g
Calcium	16.7mg

Fruity Cider Pork with Parsley Dumplings

Pork, cider and fruit are a time-honoured combination. If you don't want to make dumplings, serve creamy mashed potatoes with the stew.

INGREDIENTS

Serves 6

115g/4oz/½ cup pitted prunes, roughly chopped
115g/4oz/½ cup dried apricots, roughly chopped
300ml/½ pint/1¼ cups dry cider
30ml/2 tbsp plain flour
675g/1½lb lean boneless pork, cut into cubes
30ml/2 tbsp oil
350g/12oz onions, roughly chopped
2 garlic cloves, crushed
6 celery sticks, roughly chopped
475ml/16fl oz/2 cups hot homemade chicken stock
12 juniper berries, lightly crushed
30ml/2 tbsp chopped fresh thyme
115g/4oz/1 cup self-raising flour
50g/2oz/generous ⅓ cup vegetable suet
45ml/3 tbsp chopped fresh parsley
425g/15oz can black-eyed beans, drained
ground black pepper

1 Preheat the oven to 180°C/350°F/ Gas 4. Place the chopped prunes and apricots in a small bowl. Pour over the cider and leave to soak for at least 20 minutes.

2 Season 30ml/2 tbsp flour with pepper. Toss the pork in the plain flour to coat, and reserve any flour that remains. Heat the oil in a flameproof casserole. Brown the meat in batches, then remove.

3 Add the onions, garlic and celery to the casserole and cook for about 5 minutes. Add any remaining flour and cook for 1 minute. Blend in the stock, cider and fruit, juniper berries, thyme and plenty of seasoning. Bring to the boil, add the pork, cover and cook in the oven for 50 minutes.

4 Just before the end of the cooking time prepare the dumplings. Sift the self-raising flour into a bowl, then stir in the suet and parsley. Add about 90ml/6 tbsp water and mix together to form a smooth dough.

5 Remove the casserole from the oven, stir in the beans and adjust the seasoning. Divide the dumpling mixture into six, form into rounds and place on top. Return to the oven, covered, and cook for a further 20–25 minutes, or until the dumplings are cooked and the pork is tender.

NUTRITION NOTES	
Per portion:	
Energy	487Kcals/2041kJ
Protein	33.3g
Fat	16.7g
saturated fat	5.58g
Carbohydrate	51g
Fibre	6.3g
Sodium	254mg

Pancetta and Broad Bean Risotto

This delicious risotto makes a healthy and filling meal, served with cooked fresh seasonal vegetables or a mixed green salad.

INGREDIENTS

Serves 4
15ml/1 tbsp olive oil
1 onion, chopped
2 garlic cloves, finely chopped
175g/6oz smoked pancetta, diced
350g/12oz/1¾ cups risotto rice
1.2 litres/2 pints/5 cups Chicken Stock
225g/8oz frozen baby broad beans
30ml/2 tbsp chopped fresh mixed
    herbs, such as parsley, thyme
    and oregano
salt and ground black pepper
chopped fresh flat leaf parsley,
    to garnish
shavings of Parmesan cheese, to serve

1 Heat the oil in a large saucepan or frying pan. Add the onion, garlic and pancetta and cook gently for about 5 minutes, stirring occasionally.

2 Add the rice to the pan and cook for 1 minute, stirring. Add 300ml/½ pint/1¼ cups of the stock and simmer, stirring frequently until it has been absorbed.

3 Continue adding the stock, a ladleful at a time, stirring frequently until the rice is *al dente* and creamy, and almost all the liquid has been absorbed. This will take 30–35 minutes. It may not be necessary to add all the stock.

4 Meanwhile, cook the broad beans in a saucepan of lightly salted, boiling water for about 3 minutes until tender. Drain and keep warm.

5 Stir the beans, mixed herbs and seasoning into the risotto. Serve sprinkled with shavings of Parmesan cheese and garnished with parsley.

NUTRITION NOTES	
Per portion:	
Energy	485kcals/2031kJ
Fat, total	9.9g
saturated fat	1.7g
Protein	22.35g
Carbohydrate	74.7g
sugar, total	1.93g
Fibre	4.36g
Sodium	1969mg

Smoked Bacon, Sausage and Bean Casserole

This casserole is the perfect choice for a winter's evening.

INGREDIENTS

Serves 6

150g/5oz/²⁄₃ cup each dried black-
   eyed, pinto and cannellini beans
15ml/1 tbsp olive oil
6 rindless smoked streaky bacon rashers
6 large country pork sausages
3 large carrots, halved
3 large onions, halved
1 small garlic bulb, separated
   into cloves
4 bay leaves
2 fresh thyme sprigs
15–30ml/1–2 tbsp dried
   green peppercorns
300ml/½ pint/1¼ cups unsalted
   Vegetable Stock or water
300ml/½ pint/1¼ cups red wine
salt and ground black pepper
thyme sprigs, to garnish
green salad, to serve

1 Bring a large saucepan of unsalted water to the boil. Add the beans and boil vigorously for 30 minutes. Drain and set aside.

— NUTRITION NOTES —

Per portion:

Energy	410kcals/1714kJ
Fat, total	20.5g
saturated fat	6.7g
polyunsaturated fat	2.3g
monounsaturated fat	10.25g
Carbohydrate	33.8g
sugar, total	5.4g
starch	25.6g
Fibre	7g
Sodium	467mg

2 Pour the olive oil into a large heavy-based flameproof casserole, then lay the bacon rashers on top. Add the whole sausages and the halved carrots and onions. Peel but do not slice the garlic cloves, then press into the mixture with the bay leaves, thyme sprigs and dried peppercorns. Spoon the cooked, drained beans over the top of the mixture.

3 Pour in the stock or water and wine. Cover the casserole and bring the liquid to the boil over a medium heat. Reduce the heat to the lowest setting and cook for 4–6 hours, stirring periodically and topping up the liquid if necessary. Stir the mixture and season before serving, garnished with thyme. Serve from the casserole, accompanied by a green salad.

Pan-grilled Veal Chops

Veal chops from the loin are an expensive cut but are well worth it and are shown to their best advantage when cooked quickly and simply. The flavour of fresh basil goes well with veal, but other herbs can be used instead if you prefer.

INGREDIENTS

Serves 2

30ml/2 tbsp unsalted butter, softened
15ml/1 tbsp gluten-free mustard
15ml/1 tbsp chopped fresh basil
olive oil, for brushing
2 veal loin chops, 2.5cm/1in thick (about 225g/8oz each)
ground black pepper

1 Cream the butter with the mustard and chopped basil in a small bowl, then season to taste with pepper.

2 Lightly oil a heavy, cast iron skillet. Set over high heat until very hot but not smoking. Brush both sides of each chop with a little oil and season with a little pepper.

3 Place the chops on the skillet and reduce the heat to medium. Cook for about 5 minutes, then turn and cook for a further 3–4 minutes until done as preferred (medium-rare meat will still be slightly soft when pressed, medium meat will be springy and well-done firm). Top each chop with half the basil butter and serve at once.

NUTRITION NOTES	
Per portion:	
Energy	324Kcals/1359kJ
Protein	38.7g
Fat	18.3g
saturated fat	8.6g
Carbohydrate	1g
Fibre	0g
Sodium	421mg

Veal Escalopes with Tarragon

Aromatic tarragon has long been popular for flavouring sauces.

INGREDIENTS

Serves 4

4 veal escalopes (115–150g/4–5oz each)
15ml/1 tbsp unsalted butter
30ml/2 tbsp brandy
250ml/8fl oz/1 cup homemade stock
15ml/1 tbsp chopped fresh tarragon
ground black pepper
fresh tarragon sprigs, to garnish

NUTRITION NOTES	
Per portion:	
Energy	200Kcals/839kJ
Protein	25.3g
Fat	8.5g
saturated fat	4.37g
Carbohydrate	1g
Fibre	0g
Sodium	135mg

1 Place the veal escalopes between two sheets of wax or greaseproof paper and pound with the flat side of a meat mallet or roll them with a rolling pin to flatten to about 5mm/¼in thickness. Season with pepper.

2 Melt the butter in a large frying pan over medium-high heat. Add enough meat to fit easily in one layer (cook in batches if necessary) and fry for 1½–2 minutes, turning once. Be careful not to overcook. Transfer to a plate and keep warm.

3 Add the brandy to the pan, then pour in the stock and bring to the boil. Add the chopped tarragon and continue to boil until the liquid is reduced by half. Return the veal to the pan with any accumulated juices and heat through. Serve immediately, garnished with tarragon sprigs.

COOK'S TIP
Take care not to overcook the veal as the thin slices cook very quickly.

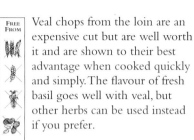

Chicken with Tomatoes and Prawns

This Piedmontese dish was created especially for Napoleon. Versions of it appear in both Italian and French recipe books.

INGREDIENTS

Serves 4

120ml/4fl oz/½ cup olive oil
8 chicken thighs on the bone, skinned
1 onion, finely chopped
1 celery stick, finely chopped
1 garlic clove, crushed
350g/12oz ripe Italian plum tomatoes, peeled and roughly chopped
250ml/8fl oz/1 cup dry white wine
2.5ml/½ tsp chopped fresh rosemary
15ml/1 tbsp unsalted butter
8 small triangles thinly sliced egg-free white bread, without crusts
175g/6oz large raw prawns, shelled
ground black pepper
finely chopped flat leaf parsley, to garnish

1 Heat about 30ml/2 tbsp of the oil in a frying pan. Add the chicken thighs and sauté over a medium heat for about 5 minutes until they have changed colour on all sides. Transfer to a flameproof casserole.

2 Add the onion and celery to the frying pan and cook gently, stirring frequently, for about 3 minutes until softened. Add the garlic, tomatoes, wine, rosemary and pepper to taste. Bring to the boil, stirring.

3 Pour the tomato sauce over the chicken. Cover and cook gently for 40 minutes, or until the chicken is tender when pierced.

4 About 10 minutes before serving, add the remaining oil and the butter to the frying pan and heat until hot but not smoking. Add the triangles of bread and shallow fry until crisp and golden on each side. Drain.

5 Add the prawns to the casserole and heat until the prawns are cooked. Taste the sauce for seasoning. Dip one of the tips of each fried bread triangle in parsley. Serve the dish hot, garnished with the bread triangles.

——— NUTRITION NOTES ———	
Per portion:	
Energy	659Kcals/2747kJ
Protein	57.2g
Fat	37.7g
saturated fat	8.24g
Carbohydrate	14g
Fibre	1.7g
Sodium	380mg

Chicken with Lemons and Olives

This tangy chicken dish makes a healthy choice, but be sure to buy a free-range or organic chicken if you can, which has not been fed with hormones.

INGREDIENTS

Serves 4

2.5ml/½ tsp ground cinnamon
2.5ml/½ tsp ground turmeric
1.5kg/3–3½lb chicken
30ml/2 tbsp olive oil
1 large onion, thinly sliced
5cm/2in piece fresh root ginger, grated
600ml/1 pint/2½ cups chicken stock
2 preserved lemons or limes, or fresh
   ones, cut into wedges
75g/3oz/¾ cup pitted brown olives
15ml/1 tbsp clear honey
60ml/4 tbsp chopped fresh coriander
salt and ground black pepper
coriander sprigs, to garnish

1 Preheat the oven to 190°C/375°F/ Gas 5. Mix the ground cinnamon and turmeric in a bowl with a little salt and pepper and rub all over the chicken skin to give an even coating.

2 Heat the oil in a large sauté or shallow frying pan and fry the chicken on all sides until it turns golden. Transfer the chicken to an ovenproof dish.

3 Add the sliced onion to the pan and fry for 3 minutes. Stir in the grated ginger and the chicken stock and bring just to the boil. Pour over the chicken, cover with a lid and bake in the oven for 30 minutes.

4 Remove the chicken from the oven, add the lemons or limes and brown olives and drizzle with the honey. Bake, uncovered, for a further 45 minutes until the chicken is tender.

5 Stir in the chopped coriander and season to taste. Garnish with coriander sprigs and serve at once.

NUTRITION NOTES	
Per portion:	
Energy	375kcals/1580kJ
Protein	57.7g
Fat	14.8g
saturated fat	4.1g
Carbohydrate	2.8g
Fibre	0.5g
Sugars	2.8g
Calcium	34mg

HEALTH BENEFITS

Olives contain the natural antioxidant vitamin E, which can help fight off the free radicals that damage cells in the body and have the potential to cause cancer.
Vitamin C, found in lemons and limes, has also been found to help combat cancer, and research has shown that ginger may halt certain cancers, too.

Chicken with Chianti

Together the full-flavoured, robust red wine and red pesto give this sauce a rich colour and almost spicy flavour, while the grapes add a delicious sweetness. Serve the stew with grilled polenta if you like and accompany with a calcium-rich salad, such as rocket, spinach or watercress, tossed with a fruity flavoured dressing.

INGREDIENTS

Serves 4

45ml/3 tbsp olive oil
4 part-boned chicken breasts, skinned
1 red onion
30ml/2 tbsp red pesto
300ml/½ pint/1¼ cups Chianti
300ml/½ pint/1¼ cups water
115g/4oz red grapes, halved lengthways
    and seeded if necessary
salt and ground black pepper
fresh basil leaves, to garnish
rocket salad, to serve

1 Heat 30ml/2 tbsp of the oil in a large frying pan, add the chicken breasts and sauté over a medium heat for about 5 minutes until they have changed colour on all sides. Remove with a slotted spoon and drain on kitchen paper.

2 Cut the onion in half, through the root. Trim off the root, then slice the onion halves lengthways to create thin wedges.

3 Heat the remaining oil in the pan, add the onion wedges and red pesto and cook gently, stirring constantly, for about 3 minutes until the onion is softened, but not browned.

4 Add the Chianti and water to the pan and bring to the boil, stirring, then return the chicken to the pan and add salt and pepper to taste.

5 Reduce the heat, then cover the pan and simmer gently for about 20 minutes or until the chicken is tender, stirring occasionally.

------ NUTRITION NOTES ------

Per portion:

Energy	283kcals/1394kJ
Protein	27.8g
Fat	16.8g
saturated fat	3.7g
Carbohydrate	5.5g
Fibre	0.4g
Sugars	5.1g
Calcium	65mg

6 Add the grapes to the pan and cook over a low to medium heat until heated through, then taste the sauce for seasoning. Serve the chicken hot, garnished with basil leaves and accompanied by the rocket salad.

------ WATCHPOINT ------

Commercial pesto contains Parmesan, which is relatively low in lactose, so most people who are avoiding dairy products will find that they can eat this small amount of pesto without causing adverse symptoms. However, if you'd prefer, and can tolerate soya, make home-made pesto and add grated soya Parmesan instead.

------ VARIATION ------

Substitute a dry white wine such as Pinot Grigio for the Chianti, then finish with seedless green grapes.

Stoved Chicken

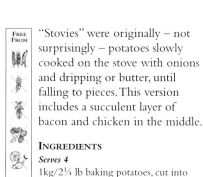

"Stovies" were originally – not surprisingly – potatoes slowly cooked on the stove with onions and dripping or butter, until falling to pieces. This version includes a succulent layer of bacon and chicken in the middle.

INGREDIENTS

Serves 4

1kg/2¼ lb baking potatoes, cut into
    5mm/¼in slices
2 large onions, thinly sliced
15ml/1 tbsp chopped fresh thyme
25g/1oz/2 tbsp butter
15ml/1 tbsp pure vegetable oil
2 large bacon slices, chopped
4 large chicken joints, halved
600ml/1 pint/2½ cups Chicken Stock
1 bay leaf
salt and ground black pepper

1 Preheat the oven to 150°C/300°F/ Gas 2. Arrange a thick layer of half the potato slices in the bottom of a large baking dish, then cover with half the onions. Sprinkle with half of the thyme, and season.

2 Heat the butter and oil in a large heavy-based frying pan, add the bacon and chicken and brown on all sides. Using a slotted spoon, transfer the chicken and bacon to the baking dish. Reserve the fat in the pan.

3 Sprinkle the remaining thyme over the chicken, season with salt and pepper, then cover with the remaining onions, followed by a neat layer of overlapping potato slices. Season well.

4 Pour the stock over the potatoes. Tuck in the bay leaf and brush the potatoes with the reserved fat. Cover and bake for 1–1½ hours until the chicken is tender.

5 Preheat the grill. Uncover the baking dish and grill until the potato is brown and crisp. Remove the bay leaf and serve hot.

NUTRITION NOTES	
Per portion:	
Energy	565kcals/2377kJ
Protein	47g
Fat	22.5g
saturated fat	8.7g
Carbohydrate	45g
Sugar	3.1g
Fibre	3.7g
Calcium	37mg

Moroccan Harissa-spiced Roast Chicken

The spices and dried fruit in this stuffing give the roast chicken an unusual flavour and help to keep it moist.

INGREDIENTS

Serves 4–5

1.5kg/3–3½lb chicken
30–60ml/2–4 tbsp garlic and spice oil
   (see Cook's Tip)
a few bay leaves
10ml/2 tsp clear honey
10ml/2 tsp tomato purée
60ml/4 tbsp lemon juice
150ml/¼ pint/⅔ cup hot
   Chicken Stock
2.5–5ml/½–1 tsp harissa

For the stuffing

25g/1oz/2 tbsp unsalted butter
1 onion, chopped
1 garlic clove, crushed
7.5ml/1½ tsp ground cinnamon
2.5ml/½ tsp ground cumin
225g/8oz/1⅓ cups dried fruit, soaked
   for several hours or overnight in
   water to cover
25g/1oz/¼ cup blanched almonds,
   finely chopped
ground black pepper

1 Make the stuffing. Melt the butter in a saucepan. Add the chopped onion and garlic and cook gently for 5 minutes until soft. Add the ground cinnamon and cumin and cook, stirring, for 2 minutes.

2 Drain the dried fruit, chop it roughly and add to the stuffing with the almonds. Season with pepper and cook for 2 minutes more. Tip into a bowl and leave to cool.

3 Preheat the oven to 200°C/400°F/ Gas 6. Using a spoon, stuff the neck of the chicken with the fruit mixture, reserving any excess. Generously brush the garlic and spice oil all over the chicken. Place the chicken in a roasting tin, tuck in the bay leaves and roast for 1–1¼ hours, basting occasionally with the juices, until golden brown and well cooked.

4 Transfer the chicken to a carving board. Pour off any excess fat from the roasting tin. Stir the honey, tomato purée, lemon juice, stock and harissa into the juices in the tin. Bring to the boil and simmer for 2 minutes, stirring. Meanwhile, reheat any excess stuffing. Carve the chicken and serve with the stuffing and sauce.

COOK'S TIP

To make garlic and spice oil, steep garlic, bay leaves, mustard seeds, peppercorns and chillies in olive oil for 2 weeks.

NUTRITION NOTES

Per portion:

Energy	659Kcals/2747kJ
Protein	44.7g
Fat	34.1g
saturated fat	10.81g
Carbohydrate	46g
Fibre	2.3g
Sodium	165mg

FREE FROM

Mediterranean Roasted Chicken

FREE
FROM

This is a delicious alternative to a traditional roast chicken. Use a corn-fed or free-range bird, if available, and choose organic vegetables. This recipe also works well with guinea fowl.

INGREDIENTS
Serves 4

1.75kg/4–4½lb roasting chicken
150ml/¼ pint/⅔ cup extra virgin
   olive oil
½ lemon
few sprigs of fresh thyme
450g/1lb small new potatoes
1 aubergine, cut into 2.5cm/1in cubes
1 red pepper, seeded and quartered
1 fennel bulb, trimmed and quartered
8 large garlic cloves, unpeeled
coarse salt and ground black pepper

3 Remove the chicken from the oven and season with salt. Turn the chicken right side up, and baste with the juices from the tin.

4 Surround the bird with the new potatoes, roll the potatoes in the tin juices until coated, and return the tin to the oven and continue roasting for 30 minutes.

1 Preheat the oven to 200°C/400°F/ Gas 6. Rub the chicken all over with some of the extra virgin olive oil and season with pepper.

2 Place the lemon half inside the bird, with a sprig or two of thyme. Put the chicken breast-side down in a large roasting tin. Transfer to the oven and roast for about 30 minutes.

5 Remove the tin from the oven and add the aubergine, red pepper, fennel and garlic cloves. Drizzle with the remaining olive oil, and season with salt and pepper.

6 Add any remaining thyme to the vegetables. Return the tin to the oven, and cook for 30–50 minutes more, basting and turning the vegetables occasionally.

7 To find out if the chicken is cooked, push the tip of a sharp knife between the thigh and breast. If the juices run clear, it is done. If not, return the chicken to the oven for about 10 minutes and test again. The vegetables should be tender and just beginning to brown.

8 Serve the chicken and vegetables from the tin, or transfer the vegetables to a serving dish, joint the chicken and place it on top. Serve the skimmed juices in a gravy boat.

--- COOK'S TIP ---

Extra virgin olive oil is the highest quality, obtained by a single cold pressing of the finest olives. It has a pure fruity flavour which makes it ideal for cooking.

--- NUTRITION NOTES ---

Per portion:

Energy	724kcals/3040kJ
Protein	70g
Fat	40g
saturated fat	8.1g
Carbohydrate	22.2g
Sugar	5.4g
Fibre	3.72g
Calcium	52mg

Chicken with Lemon Sauce

Succulent chicken breast fillets with a refreshing lemony sauce and just a hint of lime make a dish that is a sure winner. Serve with stir-fried pak choi or dark green Chinese cabbage.

INGREDIENTS

Serves 4
4 small skinless chicken breast fillets
5ml/1 tsp sesame oil
15ml/1 tbsp dry sherry
1 egg white, lightly beaten
30ml/2 tbsp cornflour
15ml/1 tbsp vegetable oil
salt and ground black pepper
chopped coriander leaves and spring onions and lemon wedges, to garnish

For the sauce
45ml/3 tbsp fresh lemon juice
30ml/2 tbsp lime cordial
45ml/3 tbsp caster sugar
10ml/2 tsp cornflour
90ml/6 tbsp cold water

1 Place the chicken breasts in a bowl and add the sesame oil and sherry.

NUTRITION NOTES

Per portion:

Energy	349kcals/1460kJ
Protein	42.2g
Fat	9.7g
Saturated Fat	2.7g
Carbohydrate	23.4g
Fibre	0
Sugars	14g
Calcium	17.2mg

2 Stir in 2.5ml/½ tsp salt and 1.5ml/¼ tsp pepper, then cover and leave to marinate for 15 minutes.

3 Mix together the egg white and cornflour. Add the mixture to the chicken and turn the chicken with tongs until thoroughly coated. Heat the vegetable oil in a non-stick frying pan or wok and fry the chicken fillets for about 15 minutes until the fillets are golden brown on both sides.

4 Meanwhile, make the sauce. Combine all the ingredients in a small pan. Add 1.5ml/¼ tsp salt. Bring to the boil over a low heat, stirring constantly until the sauce is smooth and has thickened slightly.

5 Cut the chicken into pieces and arrange on a warm serving plate. Pour over the sauce, garnish with the coriander leaves, spring onions and lemon wedges and serve.

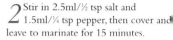

Chicken and Leek Pie

Crisp and light gluten-free pastry, flavoured with fresh herbs, tops a tarragon-flavoured chicken and leek sauce to make this tempting savoury pie a popular choice.

INGREDIENTS

Serves 4

175g/6oz/1½ cups gluten-free
  plain flour
pinch of salt
90g/3½oz/7 tbsp sunflower margarine
15ml/1 tbsp chopped fresh mixed herbs
3 leeks, sliced
45ml/3 tbsp cornflour
400ml/14fl oz/1⅔ cups semi-
  skimmed milk
15−30ml/1−2 tbsp chopped
  fresh tarragon
350g/12oz cooked, skinless, boneless
  chicken breast, diced
200g/7oz can sweetcorn
  kernels, drained
salt and ground black pepper
fresh herbs and salt flakes,
  to garnish

1 Make the pastry. Place the flour and salt in a bowl and lightly rub in 75g/3oz/6 tbsp of the margarine until the mixture resembles breadcrumbs. Stir in the mixed herbs and add a little cold water to make smooth, firm dough. Wrap the pastry in a plastic bag and chill for 30 minutes.

2 Preheat the oven to 190°C/375°F/ Gas 5. Steam the leeks for about 10 minutes until just tender. Drain thoroughly and keep warm.

3 Meanwhile, blend the cornflour with 75ml/5 tbsp of the milk. Heat the remaining milk in a saucepan until it is just beginning to boil, then pour it on to the cornflour mixture, stirring continuously. Return the mixture to the pan and heat gently until the sauce comes to the boil and thickens, stirring continuously. Simmer gently for about 2 minutes, stirring.

4 Add the remaining margarine to the pan with the chopped tarragon, leeks, chicken and sweetcorn. Season to taste with salt and pepper and mix together well.

5 Spoon the chicken mixture into a 1.2 litre/2 pint/5 cup pie dish and place the dish on a baking sheet. Roll out the pastry to a shape slightly larger than the pie dish. Lay it over the dish, and press to seal. Trim, decorate the top with the trimmings, if liked, and make a slit in the centre.

6 Bake for 35−40 minutes until the pastry is golden brown. Serve at once, sprinkled with herbs and salt.

NUTRITION NOTES

Per portion:

Energy	598kcals/2504kJ
Fat, total	24g
saturated fat	5.6g
Protein	37.2g
Carbohydrate	59.9g
sugar, total	9.2g
Fibre	2.27g
Sodium	265mg

VARIATION

Use half milk and half chicken or vegetable stock, if preferred.

Aromatic Chicken

FREE FROM

This is best cooked ahead so that the flavours permeate the chicken flesh, making it even more delicious. Serve cucumber alongside if you wish, which is the traditional accompaniment.

INGREDIENTS

Serves 4

1.5kg/3–3½lb chicken, quartered, or 4 chicken quarters
5ml/1 tsp sugar
30ml/2 tbsp coriander seeds
10ml/2 tsp cumin seeds
6 cloves
2.5ml/½ tsp ground nutmeg
2.5ml/½ tsp ground turmeric
1 small onion
2.5cm/1in fresh root ginger, peeled and sliced
300ml/½ pint/1¼ cups hot Chicken Stock or water
ground black pepper
boiled rice, to serve

1 Cut each chicken quarter in half to obtain eight pieces. Place in a flameproof casserole, sprinkle with sugar and toss together. This helps release the juices in the chicken. If using a whole chicken, use the backbone and any remaining carcass to make the stock for this recipe, if liked.

2 Dry-fry the coriander, cumin and cloves until the spices give off a good aroma. Add the nutmeg and turmeric and heat briefly. Grind in a food processor or a pestle and mortar.

3 If using a processor, process the onion and ginger until finely chopped. Otherwise, finely chop the onion and ginger and pound to a paste with a pestle and mortar. Add the ground spices and chicken stock or water and mix well.

4 Pour the onion mixture over the chicken in the flameproof casserole. Cover with a lid and cook over a gentle heat for 45–50 minutes, or until the chicken pieces are really tender.

5 Season with pepper to taste, then serve portions of the chicken, with the sauce, on boiled rice.

NUTRITION NOTES

Per portion:

Energy	337Kcals/1317kJ
Protein	31.6g
Fat	23.1g
saturated fat	6.2g
Carbohydrate	1g
Fibre	0.2g
Sodium	158mg

Chicken Baked with Butter Beans and Garlic

A one-pot meal which combines chicken with leeks, fennel and garlic-flavoured butter beans.

INGREDIENTS

Serves 6
2 leeks
1 small fennel bulb, roughly chopped
4 garlic cloves, peeled
2 x 400g/14oz cans butter beans, drained
2 large handfuls fresh parsley, chopped
300ml/½ pint/1¼ cups dry white wine
300ml/½ pint/1¼ cups Vegetable Stock
1.5kg/3lb chicken
parsley sprigs, to garnish
cooked green vegetables, to serve

FREE FROM

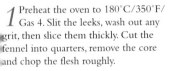

1 Preheat the oven to 180°C/350°F/ Gas 4. Slit the leeks, wash out any grit, then slice them thickly. Cut the fennel into quarters, remove the core and chop the flesh roughly.

NUTRITION NOTES

Per portion:

Energy	304kcals/1288kJ
Fat, total	3.4g
saturated fat	0.8g
polyunsaturated fat	0.9g
monounsaturated fat	1.2g
Carbohydrate	26.2g
sugar, total	3.2g
starch	21.2g
Fibre	8g
Sodium	105mg

2 Mix the leeks, fennel, whole garlic cloves, butter beans and parsley in a bowl. Spread out the mixture on the bottom of a heavy-based flameproof casserole that is large enough to hold the chicken. Pour in the white wine and vegetable stock.

3 Place the chicken on top. Bring to the boil, cover the casserole and transfer it to the oven. Bake it for 1–1½ hours, until the chicken is cooked and falls off the bone. Garnish with parsley and serve with lightly cooked green vegetables.

Spiced Grilled Poussins

These tasty poussins are a healthy choice because they contain less fat than red meat.

INGREDIENTS

Serves 4
2 garlic cloves, roughly chopped
5ml/1 tsp ground cumin
5ml/1 tsp ground coriander
pinch of cayenne pepper
1 small onion, chopped
60ml/4 tbsp olive oil
salt
2 poussins
lemon wedges, to garnish

——— VARIATION ———

Chicken portions and quail can also be cooked in this way.

1 Combine the garlic, cumin, coriander, cayenne pepper, onion, olive oil and salt in a blender or food processor. Process to make a paste that will spread smoothly.

2 Cut the poussins in half lengthways. Place them skin-side up in a shallow dish and spread with the spice paste. Cover and leave to marinate in a cool place for 2 hours.

3 Grill the poussins for about 20 minutes, turning them frequently, until they are cooked and have become crispy on the outside.

4 Serve the poussins immediately, garnished with lemon wedges.

——— NUTRITION NOTES ———

Per portion:

Energy	214kcals/891kJ
Protein	19.2g
Fat	15.2g
saturated fat	2.8g
Carbohydrate	0g
Fibre	0g
Sugars	0g
Calcium	8mg

Chicken with 40 Cloves of Garlic

Garlic is renowned for its healing properties, so this recipe is a "must try" for anyone pursuing an anti-cancer diet.

INGREDIENTS

Serves 6
½ lemon
fresh rosemary sprigs
1.5–1.75kg/3–4½lb chicken
4 or 5 heads of garlic
60ml/4 tbsp olive oil
salt and ground black pepper
steamed broad beans and spring onions, to serve

——— COOK'S TIP ———

Make sure that each guest receives an equal portion of garlic. They can then mash it into the pan juices for an aromatic sauce.

1 Preheat the oven to 190°C/375°F/ Gas 5. Place the lemon half and the rosemary sprigs in the chicken. Separate three or four of the garlic heads into cloves and remove the papery husks, but do not peel. Slice the top off the other garlic head.

2 Heat the oil in a large flameproof casserole. Add the chicken, turning it in the hot oil to coat completely. Season and add all the garlic.

3 Cover the casserole with a sheet of foil, then the lid, to seal in the steam and the flavour. Cook for about 1¼ hours until the chicken is cooked.

4 Serve the chicken with the garlic, accompanied by steamed broad beans and spring onions.

——— NUTRITION NOTES ———

Per portion:

Energy	316kcals/1326kJ
Protein	40.1g
Fat	15.9g
saturated fat	3.6g
Carbohydrate	3.4g
Fibre	0.9g
Sugars	0.3g
Calcium	19mg

Two-way Chicken with Vegetables

This tender slow-cooked chicken makes a tasty lunch or supper. The remaining stock and vegetables can be eaten as soup.

INGREDIENTS

Serves 6

1.5kg/3lb chicken
2 onions, quartered
3 carrots, thickly sliced
2 celery sticks, chopped
1 parsnip or turnip, thickly sliced
50g/2oz/½ cup button mushrooms, with stalks, roughly chopped
1–2 fresh thyme sprigs or 5ml/1 tsp dried thyme
4 bay leaves
large bunch of fresh parsley
115g/4oz/1 cup wholemeal pasta shapes
salt and ground black pepper
new potatoes or pasta, mangetouts or French beans and dairy- or egg-free bread, to serve

1 Trim the chicken of any extra fat. Put it in a flameproof casserole and add the vegetables and herbs. Pour in water to cover. Bring to the boil, skimming off any scum. Lower the heat and simmer for 2–3 hours.

2 Carve the meat neatly, discarding the skin and bones, but returning any small pieces to the pan. Serve the chicken with some of the vegetables from the pan, plus new potatoes or pasta and mangetouts or French beans.

3 Remove any large pieces of parsley and thyme from the pan, let the remaining mixture cool, then chill it overnight. Next day, lift off the fat that has solidified on the surface. Reheat the soup gently.

4 When the soup comes to the boil, add the pasta shapes, with salt, if required, and cook for 10–12 minutes or until the pasta is tender. Season with salt and pepper, garnish with parsley and serve immediately.

— NUTRITION NOTES —	
Per portion:	
Energy	212kcals/896kJ
Fat, total	3.3g
saturated fat	0.8g
polyunsaturated fat	0.8g
monounsaturated fat	1.3g
Carbohydrate	17.5g
sugar, total	3.7g
starch	12.7g
Fibre	3.15g
Sodium	130mg

Thai Chicken and Vegetable Stir-fry

INGREDIENTS

Serves 6

1 piece lemon grass (or the rind of
  ½ lemon)
1cm/½in piece fresh root ginger
1 large garlic clove
30ml/2 tbsp sunflower oil
275g/10oz lean chicken, thinly sliced
½ red pepper, seeded and sliced
½ green pepper, seeded and sliced
4 spring onions, chopped
2 carrots, cut into matchsticks
115g/4oz fine green beans
25g/1oz peanuts, lightly crushed
30ml/2 tbsp oyster sauce
pinch of sugar
salt and ground black pepper
coriander leaves, to garnish

--- NUTRITION NOTES ---

Per portion:

Energy	203Kcals/849kJ
Fat	11.0g
saturated fat	2.0g
Cholesterol	29.6mg
Fibre	2.6g

1 Thinly slice the lemon grass or lemon rind. Peel and chop the ginger and garlic. Heat the sunflower oil in a frying pan over a high heat. Add the lemon grass or lemon rind, ginger and garlic and stir-fry for 30 seconds, until brown.

2 Add the chicken strips and stir-fry for 2 minutes. Then add the red and green peppers, spring onions, carrots and green beans and stir-fry for 4–5 minutes, until the chicken is lightly coloured and cooked through and the vegetables are almost cooked.

3 Finally, stir in the peanuts, oyster sauce and sugar and season to taste with salt and pepper. Stir-fry for another minute to blend the flavours. Serve at once, sprinkled with the coriander leaves and accompanied by boiled rice.

--- COOK'S TIP ---

Make this quick supper dish a little hotter by adding more fresh root ginger, if liked.

Barbecued Chicken

FREE FROM

INGREDIENTS

Serves 4 or 8
8 small chicken pieces
2 limes, cut into wedges, 2 red chillies,
    finely sliced, and 2 lemon grass stalks,
    to garnish
steamed rice, to serve

For the marinade
2 lemon grass stalks, chopped
2.5cm/1in piece fresh root ginger
6 garlic cloves
4 shallots
½ bunch coriander roots
15ml/1 tbsp palm sugar
120ml/4fl oz/½ cup coconut milk
30ml/ tbsp Thai fish sauce
30ml/2 tbsp soy sauce

--- COOK'S TIP ---

Don't eat the skin of the chicken – it's only
left on to keep the flesh moist during
cooking and to give the dish an attractive
appearance. Coconut milk makes a good
base for a marinade or sauce, as it is low in
calories and fat.

--- NUTRITION NOTES ---

Per portion:

Energy	100Kcals/420kJ
Fat	2.8g
saturated fat	0.89g
Cholesterol	35.6mg
Fibre	0.3g

1 To make the marinade, put all the ingredients into a food processor and process until smooth.

2 Put the chicken pieces in a dish and pour over the marinade. Leave in a cool place to marinate for at least 4 hours or overnight.

3 Preheat the oven to 200°C/400°F/ Gas 6. Arrange the chicken pieces on a rack on a baking tray. Brush generously with the marinade and bake in the oven for about 20–30 minutes, or until the chicken is cooked through and golden brown. Turn the pieces over halfway through and brush with more marinade.

4 Garnish the chicken with lime wedges, finely sliced red chillies and lemon grass stalks. Serve at once with steamed rice.

Hot Chicken Curry

This curry has a flavourful thick sauce, and includes red and green peppers for extra colour. Serve with plain boiled rice.

INGREDIENTS

Serves 4
30ml/2 tbsp corn oil
1.5ml/¼ tsp fenugreek seeds
1.5ml/¼ tsp onion seeds
2 onions, chopped
1 garlic clove, crushed
2.5ml/½ tsp grated fresh root ginger
5ml/1 tsp ground coriander
5ml/1 tsp chilli powder
5ml/1 tsp salt
400g/14oz can tomatoes
30ml/2 tbsp lemon juice
350g/12oz chicken without skin and
    bone, cubed
30ml/2 tbsp chopped fresh coriander
3 green chillies, chopped
½ red pepper, cut into chunks
½ green pepper, cut into chunks
fresh coriander leaves, to garnish

FREE FROM

1 Heat the oil in a medium saucepan, and fry the fenugreek and onion seeds, stirring, until they turn a shade darker. Add the onions, garlic and ginger and fry for about 5 minutes, until the onions are golden. Reduce the heat to very low.

— COOK'S TIP —

For a milder version of this dish, remove the seeds of the fresh green chillies before chopping the flesh and adding to the curry.

2 Meanwhile mix together the ground coriander, chilli powder, salt, tomatoes and lemon juice.

3 Add to the pan, increase the heat to medium and stir-fry for 3 minutes.

— NUTRITION NOTES —

Per portion:
Energy	216Kcals/900kJ
Fat	10.0g
saturated fat	2.06g
Cholesterol	49.9mg
Fibre	2.2g

4 Add the chicken and stir-fry for about 5–7 minutes. Take care not to overcook the chicken.

5 Add the fresh coriander, green chillies and the red and green pepper chunks. Lower the heat, cover, and simmer for about 10 minutes, until cooked. Serve hot, garnished with fresh coriander leaves.

Chicken with Cashew Nuts

FREE FROM

An all-time favourite, this classic Chinese dish is delicious served with noodles or rice.

INGREDIENTS

Serves 4

350g/12oz skinless chicken breast fillets
1.5ml/¼ tsp salt
pinch of ground white pepper
15ml/1 tbsp dry sherry
300ml/½ pint/1¼ cups chicken stock
15ml/1 tbsp vegetable oil
1 garlic clove, finely chopped
1 small carrot, cut into cubes
½ cucumber, about 75g/3oz, cut into
    1cm/½in cubes
50g/2oz/½ cup drained canned
    bamboo shoots, cut into cubes
5ml/1 tsp cornflour
15ml/1 tbsp light soy sauce
5ml/1 tsp caster sugar
25g/1oz/¼ cup dry roasted cashew nuts
2.5ml/½ tsp sesame oil
noodles or rice, to serve

1 Cut the chicken into 2cm/¾in cubes. Place the cubes in a bowl, stir in the salt, pepper and sherry, cover and marinate for 15 minutes.

2 Bring the stock to the boil in a large saucepan. Add the chicken and cook, stirring, for 3 minutes. Drain, reserving 90ml/6 tbsp of the stock, and set aside.

3 Heat the vegetable oil in a non-stick frying pan until very hot, add the garlic and stir-fry for a few seconds. Add the carrot, cucumber and bamboo shoots and continue to stir-fry over a medium heat for 2 minutes.

4 Stir in the chicken and reserved stock. Mix the cornflour with the soy sauce and sugar and add to the pan. Cook, stirring, until the sauce thickens slightly, then add the cashew nuts and sesame oil. Toss thoroughly and serve with noodles or rice.

NUTRITION NOTES	
Per portion:	
Energy	243kcals/1016kJ
Protein	29.4g
Fat	10.9g
saturated fat	2.5g
Carbohydrate	5.9g
Fibre	0.9g
Sugars	2.9g
Calcium	28mg

Spicy Indonesian Chicken Satay

INGREDIENTS

Serves 4

4 skinless, boneless chicken breasts,
  about 175g/6oz each
30ml/2 tbsp deep fried onions

For the marinade

1 fresh red chilli, seeded and
  finely chopped
2 garlic cloves, crushed
60ml/4 tbsp gluten-free soy sauce
20ml/4 tsp lemon juice

1 Make the marinade by mixing
together the chilli, garlic, soy sauce
and lemon juice. Cut the chicken into
2.5cm/1in cubes, add to the marinade
and mix thoroughly. Cover and leave
in a cool place to marinate for at least
1 hour. Soak eight bamboo skewers in
cold water for 30 minutes.

2 Tip the marinated chicken into a
sieve placed over a saucepan. Leave
to drain for a few minutes. Set the
chicken aside. Add 30ml/2 tbsp hot
water to the marinade and bring to the
boil. Lower the heat and simmer for
2 minutes, then pour into a bowl and
leave to cool. When cool, add the deep
fried onions.

FREE
FROM

——— NUTRITION NOTES ———	
Per portion:	
Energy	310kcals/1305kJ
Protein	53.7g
Fat	9.4g
saturated fat	2.9g
Carbohydrate	2.9g
Fibre	0.4g
Sugars	0.9g
Calcium	23mg

3 Drain the skewers, thread them
with the chicken and grill or
barbecue for about 10 minutes, turning
regularly until the chicken is golden
brown and cooked through. Serve with
the marinade as a dip.

Thai Chicken and Vegetable Curry

For this curry, chicken and vegetables are cooked in a Thai-spiced coconut sauce.

INGREDIENTS

Serves 4
15ml/1 tbsp sunflower oil
6 shallots, finely chopped
2 garlic cloves, crushed
450g/1lb skinless, boneless chicken
    breasts, cut into 1cm/½in cubes
5ml/1 tsp ground coriander
5ml/1 tsp ground cumin
20ml/4 tsp Thai green curry paste
1 green pepper, seeded and diced
175g/6oz baby sweetcorn, halved
115g/4oz French beans, halved
150ml/¼ pint/⅔ cup Chicken Stock
150ml/¼ pint/⅔ cup coconut milk
30ml/2 tbsp cornflour
fresh herb sprigs and toasted cashew
    nuts, to garnish
boiled rice, to serve

1 Heat the oil in a saucepan, add the shallots, garlic and chicken and cook for 5 minutes until the chicken is coloured all over, stirring occasionally.

2 Add the coriander, cumin and curry paste and cook for 1 minute.

— COOK'S TIP —

Add more Thai green curry paste for a hotter curry, if you like.

3 Add the green pepper, baby sweetcorn, beans, stock and coconut milk and stir to mix.

4 Bring to the boil, stirring all the time, then cover and simmer for 20–30 minutes until the chicken is tender, stirring occasionally.

5 Blend the cornflour with about 45ml/3 tbsp water in a small bowl. Stir into the curry, then simmer gently for about 2 minutes, stirring all the time, until the sauce thickens slightly. Serve hot, garnished with fresh herb sprigs and toasted cashew nuts and accompanied by boiled rice.

— NUTRITION NOTES —	
Per portion:	
Energy	207kcals/809kJ
Fat, total	5.7g
saturated fat	0.8g
Protein	29.4g
Carbohydrate	9.8g
sugar, total	7.9g
Fibre	2.6g
Sodium	801mg

Fragrant Thai-spiced Chicken Curry

This is perfect for a party as the chicken and sauce can be prepared in advance and combined at the last minute.

INGREDIENTS

Serves 4

45ml/3 tbsp sunflower oil
1 onion, roughly chopped
2 garlic cloves, crushed
15ml/1 tbsp Thai red curry paste
115g/4oz creamed coconut dissolved
    in 900ml/1½ pints/3¾ cups
    boiling water
2 lemon grass stalks, roughly chopped
6 kaffir lime leaves, chopped
150ml/¼ pint/⅔ cup soya yogurt
30ml/2 tbsp apricot jam
1 cooked chicken, about 1.5kg/3–3½lb
30ml/2 tbsp chopped fresh coriander
salt and ground black pepper
kaffir lime leaves, shredded coconut and
    fresh coriander, to garnish
boiled rice, to serve

1 Heat the oil in a saucepan. Add the onion and garlic and fry over a low heat for 5–10 minutes until soft. Stir in the curry paste. Cook, stirring, for 2–3 minutes. Stir in the creamed coconut, then add the lemon grass, lime leaves, soya yogurt and apricot jam. Stir well. Cover and simmer for 30 minutes.

> COOK'S TIP
>
> If you prefer the sauce a little thicker, stir in a little more creamed coconut after adding the chicken.

2 Process the sauce in a blender or food processor, then strain it back into a clean pan, pressing as much of the puréed mixture through the sieve as possible.

3 Remove the skin from the chicken, slice the meat off the bones and cut into bite-size pieces. Add to the sauce.

4 Bring the sauce back to simmering point. Stir in the fresh coriander and season with salt and pepper. Serve with rice, garnished with extra lime leaves, shredded coconut and coriander.

NUTRITION NOTES

Per portion:	
Energy	667kcals/2786kJ
Protein	61g
Fat	43.2g
saturated fat	22.3g
Carbohydrate	9.2g
Fibre	0.3g
Sugars	8.4g
Calcium	39mg

Turkey Tonnato

This low-fat version of the Italian dish "vitello tonnato" is garnished with strips of red pepper instead of the traditional anchovy fillets.

INGREDIENTS

Serves 4
450g/1lb turkey fillets
1 small onion, sliced
1 bay leaf
4 black peppercorns
350ml/12fl oz/1½ cups Chicken Stock
200g/7oz can tuna in brine, drained
75ml/5 tbsp low-fat mayonnaise
30ml/2 tbsp lemon juice
2 red peppers, seeded and thinly sliced
about 25 capers, drained
pinch of salt
salad, lemon wedges and tomatoes,
    to serve

1 Put the turkey fillets in a single layer in large, heavy-based saucepan. Add the onion, bay leaf, peppercorns and stock. Bring to the boil and reduce the heat. Cover and simmer for 12 minutes, or until tender.

2 Turn off the heat and leave the turkey to cool in the stock, then remove with a slotted spoon. Slice thickly and arrange on a serving plate.

3 Boil the stock until reduced to about 75ml/5 tbsp. Strain and leave to cool.

4 Put the tuna, mayonnaise, lemon juice, 45ml/3 tbsp of the reduced stock and salt into a blender or food processor and purée until smooth.

5 Stir in enough of the remaining stock to reduce the sauce to the thickness of double cream. Spoon over the turkey.

6 Arrange the strips of red pepper in a lattice pattern over the turkey. Put a caper in the centre of each square. Chill in the fridge for 1 hour and serve with a fresh mixed salad and tomatoes and lemon wedges.

NUTRITION NOTES	
Per portion:	
Energy	239Kcals/1004kJ
Protein	38.45g
Fat	7.55g
saturated fat	0.69g
Carbohydrate	4.45g
Fibre	0.58g
Sugar	3.2g
Sodium	0.41g

Turkey and Macaroni Cheese

A tasty low-fat alternative to macaroni cheese, the addition of turkey rashers ensures this dish is a family favourite. Serve with a mixed leaf salad.

INGREDIENTS

Serves 4
1 medium onion, chopped
150ml/¼ pint/⅔ cup Vegetable or
    Chicken Stock
25g/1oz/2 tbsp low-fat margarine
45ml/3 tbsp plain flour
300ml/½ pint/1¼ cups skimmed milk
50g/2oz reduced-fat Cheddar
    cheese, grated
5ml/1 tsp dry mustard
225g/8oz egg-free macaroni
4 smoked turkey rashers, cut in half
2–3 firm tomatoes, sliced
a few fresh basil leaves
15ml/1 tbsp freshly grated
    Parmesan cheese
salt and ground black pepper

─── NUTRITION NOTES ───	
Per portion:	
Energy	152Kcals/637kJ
Fat	2.8g
saturated fat	0.7g
Cholesterol	12mg
Fibre	1.1g

1 Put the chopped onion and stock into a non-stick frying pan. Bring to the boil, stirring occasionally, and cook for 5–6 minutes, or until the stock has reduced entirely and the onion is translucent.

2 Put the margarine, flour, milk and seasoning into a saucepan and whisk together over the heat until thickened and smooth. Draw aside and add the cheese, mustard and onion.

3 Cook the macaroni in a large pan of boiling, salted water according to the instructions on the packet. Preheat the grill. Drain the macaroni thoroughly and stir into the sauce. Transfer to a shallow flameproof dish.

4 Arrange the turkey rashers and tomatoes overlapping on top of the macaroni cheese. Tuck in the basil leaves, then sprinkle with Parmesan and grill to brown the top lightly.

Duck with Pineapple

The great thing about Chinese food is that it very rarely contains dairy products, so the dishes make a good choice for a dairy-free diet. The combination of duck, vinegar and pineapple gives this dish a wonderfully subtle sweet-and-sour flavour.

INGREDIENTS

Serves 4

15ml/1 tbsp dry sherry
15ml/1 tbsp dark soy sauce
2 small skinless duck breasts
15ml/1 tbsp vegetable oil
2 garlic cloves, finely chopped
1 small onion, sliced
1 red pepper, seeded and cut into 2.5cm/1in squares
75g/3oz/½ cup drained canned pineapple chunks
90ml/6 tbsp pineapple juice
15ml/1 tbsp rice vinegar
5ml/1 tsp cornflour
15ml/1 tbsp cold water
5ml/1 tsp sesame oil
salt and ground white pepper
1 spring onion, shredded, to garnish

1 Combine the sherry and soy sauce with plenty of salt and pepper. Lay the duck breasts in a dish, add the marinade, cover and leave for 1 hour.

2 Drain the duck and grill under a medium to high heat for 10 minutes on each side. Cool, then cut into bite-size pieces.

3 Heat the oil in a non-stick frying pan or wok and stir-fry the garlic and onion for 1 minute. Add the red pepper, pineapple chunks, duck pieces, pineapple juice and rice vinegar and stir-fry for 2 minutes.

4 Mix the cornflour to a paste with the water. Add the mixture to the pan with 1.5ml/¼ tsp salt. Cook, stirring, until the sauce thickens. Stir in the sesame oil and serve at once, garnished with spring onion shreds.

— NUTRITION NOTES —	
Per portion:	
Energy	246kcals/1029kJ
Protein	24.6g
Fat	12.9g
saturated fat	3.07g
Carbohydrate	7.1g
Fibre	1.1g
Sugars	4.7g
Calcium	24mg

FISH AND SHELLFISH

Most types of fish and seafood are low in fat, high in protein and full

of nutrients that can help to sustain good health. Oily fish, such as

mackerel, herring and tuna, are believed to be particularly beneficial to

health because of their rich supplies of omega-3 fatty acids. Try some

recipes from around the world, such as Baked Fish with Tahini Sauce

from North Africa, traditional Coconut Fish with Rice Noodles

from Burma, or Sardine Gratin from the Mediterranean.

Fennel and Smoked Haddock Chowder

This soup is substantial enough to serve as a main meal.

INGREDIENTS

Serves 8

1 large fennel bulb
2 large leeks, very finely sliced
225g/8oz new potatoes, scrubbed, halved or quartered if large
5ml/1 tsp dill seed
2 large garlic cloves, thinly sliced
½ lemon
1.5 litres/2½ pints/6¼ cups water
300ml/½ pint/1¼ cups dry white wine
225g/8oz smoked haddock fillet, skinned
salt and ground black pepper
chopped fresh parsley, to garnish

1 Quarter the fennel, cut away the core and slice each piece very finely. Place in a saucepan with the leeks, potatoes, dill seed and garlic. Cut the half lemon into thick slices and add these to the pan. Pour the water and wine into the pan.

2 Season with plenty of pepper, then bring to the boil, lower the heat and simmer for about 30 minutes or until the potatoes and fennel are both cooked through.

3 Cut the haddock into chunks, add to the pan and simmer the mixture for 10 minutes more. Remove the lemon slices. Stir the soup gently. Add salt and pepper to taste. Sprinkle with parsley and serve.

NUTRITION NOTES	
Per portion:	
Energy	75kcals/316kJ
Fat, total	0.5g
saturated fat	0.1g
polyunsaturated fat	0.15g
monounsaturated fat	0.1g
Carbohydrate	6g
sugar, total	1.5g
starch	4.35g
Fibre	1.2g
Sodium	221mg

Tuna and Flageolet Bean Salad

Two cans of tuna form the basis of this delicious and easy-to-make store-cupboard salad.

INGREDIENTS

Serves 6
90ml/6 tbsp reduced calorie
  mayonnaise
5ml/1 tsp mustard
30ml/2 tbsp capers
45ml/3 tbsp chopped fresh parsley
pinch of celery salt
2 × 200g/7oz cans tuna in
  brine, drained
3 little gem lettuces
400g/14oz can flageolet beans, drained
12 cherry tomatoes, halved
400g/14oz can baby artichoke
  hearts, halved

——— NUTRITION NOTES ———	
Per portion:	
Energy	299Kcals/1255kJ
Fat	13.91g
saturated fat	2.12g
Cholesterol	33mg
Fibre	3.36g

1 Combine the mayonnaise, mustard, capers and parsley in a bowl.

2 Season to taste with celery salt. Flake the tuna into the dressing and toss gently.

3 Arrange the lettuce leaves on four plates, then spoon the tuna mixture on to the leaves.

——— COOK'S TIP ———

If flageolet beans are not available, use cannellini beans.

4 Spoon the flageolet beans to one side of the tuna mixture, followed by the cherry tomato halves and artichoke hearts, and serve.

FREE
FROM

Marinated Monkfish with Tomato Coulis

A light but well-flavoured dish, perfect for summertime eating and enjoying *al fresco*.

INGREDIENTS

Serves 4

30ml/2 tbsp olive oil
finely grated rind and juice of
 1 lime
30ml/2 tbsp chopped fresh
 mixed herbs
5ml/1 tsp gluten-free Dijon mustard
4 skinless, boneless monkfish fillets
salt and ground black pepper
fresh herb sprigs, to garnish

For the coulis

4 plum tomatoes, peeled and chopped
1 garlic clove, chopped
15ml/1 tbsp olive oil
15ml/1 tbsp tomato purée
30ml/2 tbsp chopped fresh oregano
5ml/1 tsp light soft brown sugar

1 Place the oil, lime rind and juice, herbs, mustard and salt and pepper in a small bowl or jug and whisk together until thoroughly mixed.

COOK'S TIP

The coulis can be served hot, if you prefer. Simply make as directed in the recipe and heat gently in a saucepan until almost boiling, before serving.

2 Place the monkfish fillets in a shallow, non-metallic container and pour over the lime mixture. Turn the fish several times in the marinade to coat it. Cover and chill for 1–2 hours.

3 Meanwhile, make the coulis. Place all the coulis ingredients in a blender or food processor and process until smooth. Season to taste, then cover and chill until required.

4 Preheat the oven to 180°C/350°F/ Gas 4. Using a fish slice, place each fish fillet on a sheet of greaseproof paper big enough to hold it in a parcel.

5 Spoon a little marinade over each piece of fish. Gather the paper loosely over the fish and fold over the edges to secure the parcel tightly. Place on a baking sheet.

6 Bake for 20–30 minutes until the fish fillets are cooked, tender and just beginning to flake.

7 Carefully unwrap the parcels and serve the fish fillets immediately, with a little of the chilled coulis served alongside, garnished with a few fresh herb sprigs.

NUTRITION NOTES

Per portion:

Energy	210kcals/821kJ
Fat, total	12.26g
saturated fat	1.82g
Protein	20.75g
Carbohydrate	4.72g
sugar, total	3.8g
Fibre	1g
Sodium	77mg

Italian Fish Kebabs

INGREDIENTS

FREE FROM

Serves 4

120ml/4fl oz/½ cup olive oil
finely grated rind and juice of
   1 large lemon
5ml/1 tsp crushed chilli flakes
350g/12oz monkfish fillet, cubed
350g/12oz swordfish fillet, cubed
350g/12oz thick salmon fillet, cubed
2 red, yellow or orange peppers, cored,
   seeded and cut into squares
30ml/2 tbsp finely chopped fresh flat
   leaf parsley
salt and ground black pepper

For the sweet tomato and chilli salsa
225g/8oz ripe tomatoes,
   finely chopped
1 garlic clove, crushed
1 fresh red chilli, seeded and chopped
45ml/3 tbsp extra virgin olive oil
15ml/1 tbsp lemon juice
15ml/1 tbsp finely chopped fresh flat
   leaf parsley
pinch of sugar

1 Put the oil in a shallow glass or china bowl and add the lemon rind and juice, the chilli flakes and pepper to taste. Whisk to combine, then add the fish chunks. Turn to coat evenly.

2 Add the pepper squares, stir, then cover and marinate in a cool place for 1 hour, turning occasionally.

3 Thread the fish and peppers on to eight oiled metal skewers, reserving the marinade. Barbecue or grill the fish for 5–8 minutes, turning once.

4 Meanwhile, make the salsa by mixing the ingredients and seasoning to taste with salt and pepper.

5 Heat the reserved marinade, then remove from the heat and stir in the parsley, with salt and pepper to taste. Serve the kebabs hot with the marinade, accompanied by the salsa.

— NUTRITION NOTES —

Per portion:	
Energy	621kcals/2586kJ
Protein	48.9g
Fat	44.0g
Saturated Fat	6.9g
Carbohydrate	7.8g
Fibre	2.2g
Sugars	0.2g
Calcium	56mg

Fish Boulettes in Hot Tomato Sauce

This is an unusual and flavoursome dish that needs scarcely any preparation and produces very little washing up, as it is all cooked in one pan. It serves four people as a main course, or eight as a starter.

INGREDIENTS

Serves 4

675g/1½lb cod, haddock or sea
  bass fillets
pinch of saffron
½ bunch flat leaf parsley
1 egg
25g/1oz/½ cup dairy-free
  white breadcrumbs
25ml/1½ tbsp olive oil
15ml/1 tbsp lemon juice
salt and ground black pepper
fresh flat leaf parsley and lemon wedges,
  to garnish

For the sauce

1 onion, very finely chopped
2 garlic cloves, crushed
6 tomatoes, peeled, seeded
  and chopped
1 green or red chilli, seeded and
  finely sliced
90ml/6 tbsp olive oil
150ml/¼ pint/⅔ cup water
15ml/1 tbsp lemon juice

--- NUTRITION NOTES ---

Per portion:

Energy	240kcals/997kJ
Protein	4.8g
Fat	21g
Saturated Fat	3.3g
Carbohydrate	8.7g
Fibre	1.9g
Sugars	5.2g
Calcium	41mg

1 Skin the fish and, if necessary, remove any bones. Cut the fish into large chunks and place in a blender or a food processor.

2 Dissolve the saffron in 30ml/2 tbsp boiling water and pour into the blender or food processor with the parsley, egg, breadcrumbs, olive oil and lemon juice. Season well with salt and pepper and process for 10–20 seconds until the fish is finely chopped and all the ingredients are combined.

3 Mould the mixture into small balls about the size of walnuts and place them in a single layer on a plate.

4 To make the sauce, place the onion, garlic, tomatoes, chilli, olive oil and water in a saucepan. Bring to the boil and then simmer, partially covered, for 10–15 minutes until the sauce is slightly reduced.

5 Add the lemon juice, then place the fish balls in the simmering sauce. Cover and simmer very gently for 12–15 minutes until the fish balls are cooked through. Serve immediately, garnished with flat leaf parsley and lemon wedges.

Cajun Blackened Fish with Papaya Salsa

This is an excellent way of cooking fish, leaving it moist in the middle and crisp and spicy on the outside. The hot, fresh salsa makes a delicious alternative to creamy sauces.

INGREDIENTS

Serves 4
1 quantity Cajun spice (see Cook's Tip)
4 × 225–275g/8–10oz skinned fish
  fillets such as snapper or bream
50g/2oz/¼ cup soya margarine, melted
wedges of lime and coriander leaves,
  to garnish

For the papaya salsa
1 papaya
½ small red onion, diced
1 fresh red chilli, seeded and finely
  chopped
45ml/3 tbsp chopped fresh coriander
grated rind and juice of 1 lime
salt

1 Make the salsa: halve the papaya, scoop out the seeds, then remove the skin and dice the flesh. Add the onion, chilli, coriander, lime rind and juice, with salt to taste. Mix well.

--- COOK'S TIP ---

To make Cajun spice, combine 5ml/1 tsp each of black pepper, ground cumin, gluten-free mustard powder, chilli powder, dried oregano and salt with 10ml/2 tsp each of paprika and thyme.

2 Preheat a heavy-based frying pan over a medium heat for about 10 minutes. Spread the Cajun spice on a plate. Brush the fish fillets with melted soya margarine, then dip them into the spices until well coated.

3 Place the fish in the hot pan and cook for 1–2 minutes on each side until blackened. Serve with the papaya salsa. Garnish with wedges of lime and coriander leaves.

--- NUTRITION NOTES ---

Per portion:

Energy	352kcals/1482kJ
Protein	54g
Fat	13.9g
saturated fat	2.9g
Carbohydrate	2.9g
Fibre	0.7g
Sugars	2.9g
Calcium	118mg

Caribbean Fish Steaks

In this quick and easy recipe, a mixture of fresh and ground spices adds an exotic accent to a tomato sauce for fish.

INGREDIENTS

Serves 4
45ml/3 tbsp oil
6 shallots, finely chopped
1 garlic clove, crushed
1 fresh green chilli, seeded and
  finely chopped
400g/14oz can chopped tomatoes
2 bay leaves
1.5ml/¼ tsp cayenne pepper
5ml/1 tsp crushed allspice
juice of 2 limes
4 cod steaks
5 ml/1 tsp brown muscovado sugar
10ml/2 tsp angostura bitters
salt

1 Heat the oil in a frying pan. Add the shallots and cook for 5 minutes until soft.

2 Add the garlic and chilli and cook for 2 minutes, then stir in the tomatoes, bay leaves, cayenne pepper, allspice and lime juice, with a little salt to taste.

--- NUTRITION NOTES ---

Per portion:

Energy	261kcals/1103kJ
Protein	38.6g
Fat	9.72g
saturated fat	1.6g
Carbohydrate	5.5g
Fibre	0.9g
Sugars	4.9g
Calcium	36mg

3 Cook gently for 15 minutes, then add the cod steaks and baste with the tomato sauce. Cover and cook for about 10 minutes or until the steaks are cooked. Transfer the steaks to a warmed dish and keep hot.

4 Stir the sugar and angostura bitters into the sauce, simmer for about 2 minutes, then pour over the fish. Serve with okra or green beans.

Halibut with Tomato Vinaigrette

The tomato vinaigrette, an uncooked mixture of tomatoes, aromatic fresh herbs and olive oil, can either be served at room temperature or slightly warm.

INGREDIENTS

Serves 2

3 large ripe beefsteak tomatoes, peeled, seeded and chopped
2 shallots or 1 small red onion, finely chopped
1 garlic clove, crushed
90ml/6 tbsp chopped mixed fresh herbs, such as parsley, coriander, basil, tarragon, chervil or chives
120ml/4fl oz/ ½ cup extra virgin olive oil, plus extra for brushing
4 halibut fillets or steaks, about 175–200g/6–7oz each
salt and ground black pepper
green salad, to serve

1 In a medium bowl, mix together the tomatoes, shallots or onion, garlic and herbs. Stir in the oil and season with salt and ground pepper. Cover the bowl and leave the sauce at room temperature for about 1 hour to allow the flavours to blend.

2 Preheat the grill. Line a grill pan with foil and brush the foil lightly with oil.

3 Season the fish with salt and pepper. Place the fish on the foil and brush with a little extra oil. Grill the fish for 5–6 minutes until the flesh is opaque and the top is lightly browned.

4 Pour the tomato vinaigrette into a saucepan and heat gently for a few minutes. Serve the fish with the sauce and a green salad.

NUTRITION NOTES	
Per portion:	
Energy	652kcals/1360kJ
Protein	44.5g
Fat	49.5g
saturated fat	7.3g
Carbohydrate	7.2g
Sugar	6.6g
Fibre	1.9g
Calcium	90.5mg

Cod, Tomato and Pepper Bake

The wonderful sun-drenched flavours of the Mediterranean are brought together in this appetizing, potato-topped bake. Lightly cooked courgettes make a tasty accompaniment.

INGREDIENTS

Serves 4

450g/1lb potatoes, cut into
    thin slices
30ml/2 tbsp olive oil
1 red onion, chopped
1 garlic clove, crushed
1 red pepper, seeded and diced
1 yellow pepper, seeded and diced
225g/8oz mushrooms, sliced
400g/14oz and 225g/8oz cans
    chopped tomatoes
150ml/¼ pint/⅔ cup dry white wine
450g/1lb skinless, boneless cod fillet,
    cut into 2 cm/¾in cubes
50g/2oz/½ cup pitted black
    olives, chopped
15ml/1 tbsp chopped fresh basil
15ml/1 tbsp chopped fresh oregano
salt and ground black pepper
fresh oregano sprigs, to garnish
cooked courgettes, to serve

1 Preheat the oven to 200°C/400°F/ Gas 6. Par-boil the potatoes in a saucepan of lightly salted, boiling water for 4 minutes. Drain thoroughly, then add 15ml/1 tbsp of the oil and toss together to mix. Set aside.

2 Heat the remaining oil in a saucepan, add the onion, garlic and red and yellow peppers and cook for 5 minutes, stirring occasionally.

3 Stir in the mushrooms, tomatoes and wine, bring to the boil and boil rapidly for a few minutes until the sauce has reduced slightly.

—— NUTRITION NOTES ——	
Per portion:	
Energy	336kcals/1412kJ
Fat, total	10.6g
saturated fat	1.5g
Protein	26.5g
Carbohydrate	29.2g
sugar, total	9g
Fibre	4.6g
Sodium	424mg

4 Add the fish, olives, herbs and seasoning to the tomato mixture.

5 Spoon the mixture into a lightly greased casserole and arrange the potato slices over the top, covering the fish mixture completely.

6 Bake, uncovered, for about 45 minutes until the fish is cooked and tender and the potato topping is browned. Garnish with fresh oregano sprigs and serve with courgettes.

FREE FROM

Cod Creole

INGREDIENTS

Serves 6

450g/1lb cod fillets, skinned
15ml/1 tbsp lime or lemon juice
10ml/2 tsp olive oil
1 medium onion, finely chopped
1 green pepper, seeded and sliced
2.5ml/½ tsp cayenne pepper
2.5ml/½ tsp garlic salt
400g/14oz can chopped tomatoes

——— NUTRITION NOTES ———

Per portion:

Energy	130Kcals/546kJ
Fat	2.61g
saturated fat	0.38g
Cholesterol	51.75mg
Fibre	1.61g

1 Cut the cod fillets into bite-size chunks and sprinkle with the lime or lemon juice.

2 In a large, non-stick pan, heat the olive oil and fry the onion and green pepper gently until softened. Add the cayenne pepper and garlic salt.

3 Stir in the cod with the chopped tomatoes. Bring to the boil, then cover and simmer for about 5 minutes, or until the fish flakes easily. Serve with boiled rice or potatoes.

Five-Spice Fish

Chinese mixtures of spicy, sweet and sour flavours are particularly successful with fish, and dinner is ready in minutes.

INGREDIENTS

Serves 4

4 white fish fillets, such as cod, haddock or hoki (about 175g/6oz each)
5ml/1 tsp Chinese five-spice powder
20ml/4 tsp cornflour
15ml/1 tbsp sesame or sunflower oil
3 spring onions, shredded
5ml/1 tsp chopped fresh root ginger
150g/5oz button mushrooms, sliced
115g/4oz baby corn cobs, sliced
30ml/2 tbsp soy sauce
45ml/3 tbsp dry sherry or apple juice
5ml/1 tsp sugar
salt and ground black pepper

1 Toss the fish in the five-spice powder and cornflour to coat.

2 Heat the oil in a frying pan or wok and stir-fry the spring onions, ginger, mushrooms and corn cobs for about 1 minute. Add the fish and cook for 2–3 minutes, turning once.

3 Mix together the soy sauce, sherry or apple juice and sugar, then pour over the fish. Simmer for 2 minutes, adjust the seasoning, then serve with noodles and stir-fried vegetables.

——— NUTRITION NOTES ———

Per portion:

Energy	213Kcals/893kJ
Fat	4.41g
saturated fat	0.67g
Cholesterol	80.5mg
Fibre	1.08g

Monkfish with Tomatoes and Olives

This makes a really delicious lunch or light supper dish. Alternatively, serve as a starter for six to eight people.

INGREDIENTS

Serves 4

8 tomatoes
675g/1½lb monkfish
30ml/2 tbsp plain flour
5ml/1 tsp ground coriander
2.5ml/½ tsp ground turmeric
25g/1oz/2 tbsp soya margarine
2 garlic cloves, finely chopped
15–30ml/1–2 tbsp olive oil
40g/1½oz/4 tbsp pine nuts, toasted
small pieces of preserved lemon
12 black olives, pitted
salt and ground black pepper
whole slices of preserved lemon and
   chopped fresh parsley, to garnish

1 Peel the tomatoes by placing them briefly in boiling water, then cold water. Quarter them, remove the cores and seeds and chop roughly.

2 Cut the fish into bite-size chunks. Blend together the flour, coriander, turmeric and seasoning. Dust the fish with the seasoned flour, shake off any excess, and set aside.

3 Melt the soya margarine in a medium non-stick frying pan and gently fry the tomatoes and garlic for 6–8 minutes until the tomatoes have broken down, are very thick and most of the liquid has evaporated.

4 Push the tomatoes to the edge of the frying pan, moisten the pan with a little olive oil and fry the monkfish pieces in a single layer over a moderate heat for 3–5 minutes, turning frequently. You may have to do this in batches, so as the first batch of fish pieces cooks, place them on top of the tomatoes and fry the remaining fish, adding a little more olive oil to the pan, if necessary.

5 When all the fish is cooked, add the pine nuts and stir, scraping the bottom of the pan to remove the glazed tomatoes. The sauce should be thick and slightly charred in places.

6 Rinse the preserved lemon in cold water, discard the pulp and cut the peel into strips. Stir into the sauce with the olives, adjust the seasoning and serve garnished with whole slices of preserved lemon and chopped parsley.

— NUTRITION NOTES —	
Per portion:	
Energy	337kcals/1414kJ
Protein	29.9g
Fat	19.4g
saturated fat	5.1g
Carbohydrate	11.6g
Fibre	2.2g
Sugars	5.8g
Calcium	39mg

Pan-fried Red Mullet with Basil and Citrus

Red mullet is popular all over the Mediterranean. This Italian recipe combines it with oranges and lemons, which grow in abundance in the area.

INGREDIENTS

Serves 4

4 red mullet, about 225g/8oz each, filleted
90ml/6 tbsp olive oil
10 peppercorns, crushed
2 oranges, one peeled and sliced and one squeezed
1 lemon
30ml/2 tbsp plain flour
15g/½oz/1 tbsp soya margarine
2 drained canned anchovies, chopped
60ml/4 tbsp shredded fresh basil
salt and ground black pepper

FREE FROM

1 Place the fish fillets in a shallow dish in a single layer. Pour over the olive oil and sprinkle with the crushed peppercorns. Lay the orange slices on top of the fish. Cover the dish, and leave to marinate for at least 4 hours.

2 Halve the lemon. Remove the skin and pith from one half using a small sharp knife, and slice thinly. Squeeze the juice from the other half.

3 Lift the fish out of the marinade, and pat dry on kitchen paper. Reserve the marinade and orange slices. Season the fish with salt and pepper and dust lightly with flour.

4 Heat 45ml/3 tbsp of the marinade in a frying pan. Add the fish and fry for 2 minutes on each side. Remove from the pan and keep warm.

5 Discard the marinade left in the pan. Melt the soya margarine with any of the remaining original marinade. Cook the anchovies until softened. Stir in the orange and lemon juice, then check the seasoning and simmer until slightly reduced. Stir in the basil. Pour the sauce over the fish and garnish with the reserved orange and lemon slices.

— NUTRITION NOTES —	
Per portion:	
Energy	507kcals/2121kJ
Protein	44.9g
Fat	31.5g
saturated fat	4.7g
Carbohydrate	11.9g
Fibre	5g
Sugars	6.3g
Calcium	204mg

Mediterranean Baked Fish

INGREDIENTS

Serves 4

3 potatoes
30ml/2 tbsp olive oil, plus extra
for drizzling
2 onions, halved and sliced
2 garlic cloves, very finely chopped
675g/1½lb thick skinless fish fillets,
such as turbot or sea bass
1 bay leaf
1 thyme sprig
3 tomatoes, peeled and thinly sliced
30ml/2 tbsp orange juice
60ml/4 tbsp gluten-free fish stock
2.5ml/½ tsp saffron threads, steeped in
60ml/4 tbsp boiling water
salt and ground black pepper

1 Cook the potatoes in boiling salted water for 15 minutes, then drain and allow to cool. When the potatoes are cool enough to handle, peel off the skins and slice them thinly.

— NUTRITION NOTES —

Per portion:

Energy	300kcals/1262kJ
Protein	32.2g
Fat	10.4g
saturated fat	2.03g
Carbohydrate	17.9g
Sugar	4.7g
Fibre	2.1g
Calcium	100mg

2 Meanwhile, heat the olive oil in a heavy-based frying pan and fry the onions over a medium-low heat for about 10 minutes, stirring frequently. Add the garlic and continue cooking for a few minutes until the onions are soft and golden.

3 Preheat the oven to 190°C/375°F/ Gas 5. Layer half the potato slices in a 2 litre/3⅓ pint/8 cup baking dish. Cover with half the onions. Season with salt and pepper.

4 Place the fish fillets on top of the vegetables and tuck the herbs in between them. Top with the tomato slices and then the remaining onions and potatoes.

5 Pour the orange juice, stock and saffron liquid over, season with salt and pepper and drizzle a little extra olive oil on top. Bake, uncovered, for about 30 minutes until the potatoes are tender and the fish is cooked.

Fish with Spinach and Lime

The fish is marinated in a fragrant herb marinade called a *charmoula* in Middle Eastern cooking.

INGREDIENTS

Serves 4

675g/1½lb white fish, such as haddock, cod, sea bass or monkfish
sunflower oil, for frying
500g/1¼lb potatoes, sliced
1 onion, chopped
1–2 garlic cloves, crushed
5 tomatoes, peeled and chopped
375g/12oz fresh spinach, chopped
lime wedges, to garnish

For the *charmoula*

5 spring onions, chopped
10ml/2 tsp fresh thyme
60ml/4 tbsp chopped flat leaf parsley
30ml/2 tbsp chopped fresh coriander
10ml/2 tsp paprika
generous pinch of cayenne pepper
60ml/4 tbsp olive oil
grated rind of 1 lime and 60ml/4 tbsp lime juice
salt

1 Cut the fish into large pieces, discarding any skin and bones, and place in a large shallow dish.

2 Blend together the ingredients for the *charmoula* and season well with salt. Pour over the fish, stir to mix and leave in a cool place, covered with clear film, for 2–4 hours.

--- NUTRITION NOTES ---

Per portion:

Energy	369kcals/1549kJ
Protein	36.5g
Fat	13.6g
saturated fat	2.06g
Carbohydrate	26.3g
Sugar	7.4g
Fibre	4.5g
Calcium	174mg

3 Heat about 5mm/¼in oil in a large heavy-based pan and fry the potatoes until cooked through and golden. Drain on kitchen paper.

4 Pour off all but about 15ml/1 tbsp of the oil and add the chopped onion, garlic and tomatoes. Cook over a gentle heat for 5–6 minutes, stirring occasionally, until the onion is soft.

5 Place the potatoes on top of the onion and tomato mixture, then add the chopped spinach to the pan.

6 Place the fish pieces on top of the spinach and pour in all of the marinade. Cover tightly and cook for 15–18 minutes. After about 8 minutes, carefully stir the contents of the pan so that the fish is distributed evenly throughout the dish. Cover the pan again and continue cooking, but check occasionally – the dish is cooked once the fish is tender and opaque and the spinach has wilted.

7 Serve immediately on individual serving plates, garnished with wedges of lime.

FREE FROM

Spiced Fish with Pumpkin Rice

This North African dish is a contrast of mild spicy fish and slightly sweet pumpkin. This orange-fleshed vegetable is a good source of the powerful antioxidant, betacarotene, which boosts the immune system, provides oxygen to the cells and helps the body to fight cancer.

INGREDIENTS

Serves 4

450g/1lb sea bass or other
   firm fish
30ml/2 tbsp plain flour
5ml/1 tsp ground coriander
1.5–2.5ml/¼–½ tsp ground turmeric
about 500g/1¼lb piece of pumpkin
30–45ml/2–3 tbsp olive oil
about 6 spring onions,
   sliced diagonally
1 garlic clove, finely chopped
275g/10oz/1½ cups basmati
   rice, soaked
salt and ground black pepper
lime or lemon wedges and fresh
   coriander sprigs, to garnish

**For the coriander and ginger
   flavouring mixture**
45ml/3 tbsp finely chopped
   fresh coriander
10ml/2 tsp finely chopped fresh
   root ginger
½–1 fresh chilli, seeded and very
   finely chopped
45ml/3 tbsp lime or lemon juice

——— NUTRITION NOTES ———	
Per portion:	
Energy	479kcals/2004kJ
Protein	28.7g
Fat	11.8g
saturated fat	1.8g
Carbohydrate	63.9g
Fibre	1.7g
Sugars	2.7g
Calcium	212mg

1 Carefully remove and discard any skin or bones from the fish and cut into 2cm/¾in chunks. Mix together the flour, coriander, turmeric and a little salt and pepper in a plastic bag. Then add the chunks of fish and shake for a few seconds so that each piece is evenly coated in the spice mixture. Set aside.

2 Make the coriander and ginger flavouring mixture by stirring the ingredients together in a small bowl.

3 Cut the skin from the pumpkin with a sharp knife and scoop out the seeds. Then cut the flesh into 2cm/¾in chunks.

4 Heat 15ml/1 tbsp of the oil in a wok or flameproof casserole and stir-fry the spring onions and garlic for a few minutes until slightly softened and golden. Add the pumpkin and cook over a fairly low heat, stirring frequently, for 4–5 minutes or until the flesh softens.

5 Drain the rice, add to the wok or casserole and stir-fry over a brisk heat for 2–3 minutes. Then stir in the stock together with a little salt. Bring to simmering point, then cover and cook over a low heat for about 15 minutes until the rice and pumpkin are tender.

6 About 4 minutes before the rice is ready, heat the remaining oil in a frying pan and fry the fish over a moderately high heat for 3 minutes until the outside is lightly browned and crisp and the flesh is cooked through but still moist.

7 Just before serving, carefully stir the coriander and ginger flavouring mixture into the rice and transfer to a warmed serving dish. Lay the fish pieces on top of the rice or, alternatively, stir into the rice. Serve garnished with lime or lemon wedges and sprigs of fresh coriander.

Fish Fillets with a Chilli Sauce

Fish fillets, marinated with fresh coriander and lemon juice, then grilled and served with a chilli sauce, are simply delicious served with saffron rice.

INGREDIENTS

Serves 4
4 flatfish fillets, such as plaice, sole or flounder, about 115g/4oz each
30ml/2 tbsp lemon juice
15ml/1 tbsp finely chopped fresh coriander
15ml/1 tbsp vegetable oil
lime wedges and coriander leaves, to garnish

For the sauce
5ml/1 tsp fresh root ginger
30ml/2 tbsp tomato purée
5ml/1 tsp sugar
5ml/1 tsp salt
15ml/1 tbsp chilli sauce
15ml/1 tbsp wine vinegar
300ml/½ pint/1¼ cups water

1 Rinse, pat dry and place the fish fillets in a medium bowl. Add the lemon juice, fresh coriander and oil and rub into the fish. Leave to marinate for at least 1 hour. The flavour will improve if you can leave it for longer.

2 To make the sauce, mix together all the sauce ingredients, pour into a small saucepan and simmer gently over a low heat for about 6 minutes, stirring occasionally.

3 Preheat the grill to medium. Cook the fillets under the grill for about 5–7 minutes.

4 When the fillets are cooked, remove and arrange them on a warmed serving dish.

5 The chilli sauce should now be fairly thick – about the consistency of a thick chicken soup.

6 Spoon the hot chilli sauce over the fish fillets, garnish with the lime wedges and coriander leaves and serve with saffron rice.

NUTRITION NOTES	
Per portion:	
Energy	142Kcals/599kJ
Fat	5.3g
saturated fat	0.75g
Cholesterol	48.3mg
Fibre	0.2g

Fresh Tuna and Tomato Stew

This tuna stew has a delicious Italian flavour.

INGREDIENTS

Serves 4

12 baby onions, peeled
900g/2lb ripe tomatoes
675g/1½lb fresh tuna
45ml/3 tbsp olive oil
2 garlic cloves, crushed
45ml/3 tbsp chopped fresh herbs
2 bay leaves
2.5ml/½ tsp caster sugar
30ml/2 tbsp sun-dried tomato paste
150ml/¼ pint/⅔ cup gluten-free
    fish stock
salt and ground black pepper
baby courgettes and fresh herbs, to garnish

1 Leave the onions whole and cook in a pan of boiling water for 4–5 minutes until softened. Drain.

2 Plunge the tomatoes into boiling water for 30 seconds, then rinse in cold water. Peel away the skins and chop the tomatoes roughly.

3 Cut the tuna into 2.5cm/1in chunks. Heat the oil in a large pan and quickly fry the tuna until browned. Drain on kitchen paper.

4 Add the onions, garlic, tomatoes, chopped herbs, bay leaves, sugar, tomato paste and stock and bring to the boil, breaking up the tomatoes with a wooden spoon.

5 Reduce the heat and simmer gently for 5 minutes. Return the fish to the sauce in the pan and cook for a further 5 minutes. Season, and serve hot, garnished with baby courgettes and fresh herbs.

--- COOK'S TIP ---

The best fresh herbs to use as a garnish for tuna are basil, parsley or chives.

--- NUTRITION NOTES ---

Per portion:

Energy	412kcals/1728kJ
Protein	42.5g
Fat	18.7g
saturated fat	3.7g
Carbohydrate	13.1g
Sugar	11.3g
Fibre	3.3g
Calcium	66mg

FREE FROM

Red Mullet with Cumin

INGREDIENTS

Serves 4
8–12 red mullet, depending on the size
of the fish
fresh parsley and finely pared strips of
lemon rind, to garnish

For the marinade
10ml/2 tsp ground cumin
5ml/1 tsp paprika
60ml/4 tbsp lemon juice
45ml/3 tbsp olive oil
30ml/2 tbsp chopped fresh parsley
salt and ground black pepper

For the fresh tomato sauce
5 large tomatoes
2 garlic cloves, chopped
60ml/4 tbsp chopped fresh parsley
and coriander
30ml/2 tbsp olive oil
30ml/2 tbsp lemon juice

1 Make 2–3 slashes along the sides of
the fish and place them in a shallow
non-metallic dish. Blend together the
ingredients for the marinade and rub
into the fish on both sides. Set aside for
2 hours in a cool place.

2 Make the fresh tomato sauce. Peel
the tomatoes and cut into small
pieces, discarding the core and seeds.
Place in a bowl and stir in the
remaining ingredients. Set aside in the
fridge or a cool place.

3 Heat the grill or prepare the
barbecue. Grill or barbecue the fish
for 3–4 minutes on each side, until the
flesh is tender. Garnish with parsley and
lemon rind and serve immediately with
the fresh tomato sauce.

NUTRITION NOTES

Per portion:
Energy	334kcals/1399kJ
Protein	33.1g
Fat	21.1g
saturated fat	2.1g
Carbohydrate	3.65g
Sugar	3.65g
Fibre	1.1g
Calcium	130mg

Spicy Fish Brochettes

INGREDIENTS
Serves 4 as a starter
450g/1lb white fish fillets, such as cod,
haddock, monkfish or sea bass
olive oil, for brushing
lime wedges and fresh tomato sauce,
to serve

For the spicy marinade
½ onion, grated or very finely chopped
2 garlic cloves, crushed
30ml/2 tbsp chopped fresh coriander
15ml/1 tbsp chopped fresh parsley
5ml/1 tsp ground cumin
10ml/2 tsp paprika
good pinch of ground ginger
25ml/1½ tbsp white wine vinegar
30ml/2 tbsp lime juice
salt and cayenne pepper

1 First make the marinade. Blend all
the ingredients and season to taste
with salt and cayenne pepper.

2 Cut the fish into 1cm/½in cubes,
discarding the skin and bones. Place
in a shallow non-metallic dish. Add the
marinade and stir to coat the fish
thoroughly. Cover with clear film and
set aside for about 2 hours.

3 Preheat the grill. Thread the fish on
to 12 small or 8 larger metal skewers.
Place on a grill pan and brush with a
little olive oil. Cook the brochettes for
7–10 minutes until the fish is cooked
through, turning and brushing with
more oil occasionally. Serve with
wedges of lime and fresh tomato sauce.

NUTRITION NOTES

Per portion:
Energy	77kcals/330kJ
Protein	17.7g
Fat	0.4g
saturated fat	0.1g
Carbohydrate	0.7g
Sugar	0.5g
Fibre	0.1g
Calcium	11mg

Fish Pie with Sweet Potato Topping

INGREDIENTS

Serves 6

175g/6oz/1 cup basmati rice, soaked
450ml/¾ pint/scant 2 cups
   well-flavoured stock
175g/6oz broad beans
675g/1½lb skinned haddock or
   cod fillets
about 450ml/¾ pint/scant 2 cups milk
40g/1½oz/3 tbsp butter
30–45ml/2–3 tbsp plain flour
15ml/1 tbsp chopped fresh parsley
salt and ground black pepper
sugar-snap peas, to serve

For the topping

450g/1lb sweet potatoes
450g/1lb floury white potatoes, such as
   King Edwards
butter and milk, for mashing
15ml/1 tbsp single cream (optional)
10ml/2 tsp chopped fresh parsley
5ml/1 tsp chopped fresh dill

1 Preheat the oven to 190°C/375°F/
  Gas 5. Drain the rice and then
cook in the lightly salted stock in a
covered pan for about 10 minutes
or according to the instructions on
the packet.

2 Cook the broad beans in lightly
  salted water until tender and drain.
When cool enough to handle, skin the
beans, discarding the outer skin.

3 To make the topping, cook the
  sweet and white potatoes separately
in boiling salted water. Mash them both
with a little milk and butter, adding the
cream, if using. Add the parsley and dill
to the sweet potatoes.

4 Place the fish fillets in a shallow pan
  and add about 350ml/12fl oz/
1½ cups of the milk or enough to just
cover the fish. Dot with 15ml/1 tbsp
of the butter and season with salt and
pepper. Heat gently and then simmer
for about 6 minutes until the fish is
just tender.

5 Break the fish into large pieces.
  Then pour the cooking liquid into
a measuring jug and make up to
450ml/¾ pint/scant 2 cups with the
remaining milk.

6 Make a white sauce. Melt the
  remaining butter in a saucepan and
stir in the flour. Add the milk from the
fish and cook, stirring, to make a fairly
thin white sauce. Stir in the parsley
and season.

7 Place the cooked rice at the
  bottom of a casserole. Add the broad
beans and fish on top and pour over
the white sauce. Spoon the mashed
potatoes over the top to make an
attractive pattern. Dot with a little extra
butter and bake for 15 minutes until
lightly browned. Serve with the
sugar-snap peas.

NUTRITION NOTES	
Per portion:	
Energy	663kcals/2695kJ
Protein	39g
Fat	15.9g
saturated fat	9.4g
Carbohydrate	88.1g
Fibre	7.1g
Sugars	8.7g
Calcium	100mg

Coconut Fish with Rice Noodles

This spicy dish from Burma is the ideal way to introduce more oily fish, and all its valuable nutrients, into your diet. Some experts recommend eating oily fish, such as mackerel, two or three times a week.

INGREDIENTS

Serves 8

675g/1½lb huss, cod or mackerel, cleaned but left on the bone
3 lemon grass stalks
2.5cm/1in piece fresh root ginger, peeled
30ml/2 tbsp fish sauce
3 onions, roughly chopped
4 garlic cloves, roughly chopped
2–3 fresh red chillies, seeded and chopped
5ml/1 tsp ground turmeric
75ml/5 tbsp groundnut oil, for frying
400ml/14fl oz/1⅔ cups canned coconut milk
45ml/3 tbsp rice flour
45ml/3 tbsp chick-pea flour (besan)
500g/1¼lb drained canned bamboo shoot, cut into chunks
salt and ground black pepper

To serve

450g/1lb dried or fresh rice noodles, cooked according to the instructions on the packet
wedges of hard-boiled egg; thinly sliced onions; chopped spring onions and fried prawns and chillies

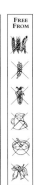

NUTRITION NOTES	
Per portion:	
Energy	497kcals/2073kJ
Protein	20.8g
Fat	21.0g
saturated fat	4.3g
Carbohydrate	109.2g
Fibre	3.7g
Sugars	8.5g
Calcium	102.5mg

1 Place the fish in a large pan and pour in cold water to cover. Bruise two lemon grass stalks and half the ginger and add to the pan. Bring to the boil, add the fish sauce and cook for 10 minutes.

2 Lift out the fish and allow to cool while straining the stock into a large bowl. Discard the skin and bones from the fish and reserve the flesh, which will be in small pieces.

3 Cut off the lower 5cm/2in of the remaining lemon grass stalk and chop it roughly. Put it in a food processor or blender along with the remaining ginger, the onions, garlic, chillies and turmeric.

4 Process to a smooth paste. Heat the oil in a frying pan and fry the paste until it gives off a rich aroma. Remove from the heat and add the fish.

5 Stir the coconut milk into the reserved fish stock. Add enough water to make up to 2.4 litres/4 pints/10 cups and pour into a large pan. In a jug, mix the rice and chick-pea (besan) flours to a thin cream with some of the stock. Stir this into the coconut and stock mixture and bring to the boil, stirring all the time.

6 Add the bamboo shoots and cook for about 10 minutes until just tender. Stir in the fish. Check the seasoning, cover and heat through. Guests pour soup over the noodles and choose their own accompaniments.

Baked Trout with Wild Mushrooms

INGREDIENTS

Serves 4

4 whole rainbow trout, cleaned
juice of 1 lemon
15ml/1 tbsp chopped fresh parsley
30ml/2 tbsp olive oil
2 shallots, finely chopped
1 garlic clove, crushed
350g/12oz mixed fresh wild
    mushrooms, chopped
15ml/1 tbsp ruby port or Madeira
30ml/2 tbsp crème fraîche
salt and ground black pepper
chopped fresh parsley, to garnish

1 Preheat the oven to 180°C/350°F/
Gas 4. Place the trout, side by side,
in a lightly greased, shallow, ovenproof
dish. Pour over the lemon juice and
sprinkle over the parsley.

2 Cover with foil and bake for
30–40 minutes until the fish is
cooked, tender and beginning to flake.

3 Meanwhile, heat the oil in a frying
pan, add the shallots and garlic and
cook gently for 3–5 minutes until the
shallots have softened, stirring them
occasionally. Add the mushrooms and
cook gently for about 5 minutes until
they are just cooked, stirring frequently.

4 Add the port or Madeira, increase
the heat and cook, stirring, for a
few minutes until most of the liquid has
evaporated. Add the crème fraîche,
season to taste with salt and pepper and
mix well.

5 Place the cooked trout on four
warmed serving plates and spoon a
little of the mushroom sauce over each
fish or on either side of it. Sprinkle a
little chopped parsley over each fish and
serve immediately.

——— NUTRITION NOTES ———

Per portion:
Energy	330kcals/924kJ
Fat, total	18.4g
saturated fat	3.9g
Protein	38.3g
Carbohydrate	1.92g
sugar, total	1.62g
Fibre	1.3g
Sodium	102mg

Chargrilled Salmon Steaks with Mango Salsa

INGREDIENTS

Serves 4

1 medium, ripe mango
115g/4oz cucumber
2 spring onions
30ml/2 tbsp chopped fresh coriander
4 salmon steaks, each about 175g/6oz
juice of 1 lemon or lime
salt and ground black pepper
fresh coriander sprigs and lemon
    wedges, to garnish

1 Make the mango salsa. Peel and
stone the mango, finely chop the
flesh and place in a bowl. Peel, seed and
finely chop the cucumber; chop the
spring onions. Add to the mango with
the coriander and salt and pepper. Mix,
cover and leave for 30 minutes.

2 While the salsa is standing to allow
the flavours to mingle, preheat a
barbecue or grill. Place the salmon
steaks on a ridged grill pan, drizzle over
the lemon or lime juice and cook for
about 6 minutes on each side until the
steaks are tender and just beginning to
flake. Alternatively, cook over a hot
barbecue or under a moderate grill.

3 Transfer the salmon to serving
plates, spoon some mango salsa
alongside each steak and serve
immediately, garnished with coriander
sprigs and lemon wedges.

——— NUTRITION NOTES ———

Per portion:
Energy	350kcals/1460kJ
Fat, total	19.5g
saturated fat	3.4g
Protein	36.2g
Carbohydrate	7.84g
sugar, total	4.3g
Fibre	2g
Sodium	98mg

Baked Trout with Rice and Sun-dried Tomatoes

Trout, with its rich supply of omega-3 fatty acids and other cancer-fighting nutrients, is always a healthy choice.

INGREDIENTS

Serves 4

2 fresh, filleted trout, each about 500g/1¼lb unfilleted weight
75g/3oz/½ cup mixed unsalted cashews, pine nuts, almonds or hazelnuts
25ml/1½ tbsp olive oil, plus extra for cooking
1 small onion, finely chopped
10ml/2 tsp grated fresh root ginger
175g/6oz/1 cup cooked long grain rice
4 tomatoes, peeled and finely chopped
4 sun-dried tomatoes, chopped
30ml/2 tbsp chopped fresh tarragon
salt and ground black pepper
salad leaves, to garnish

1 Ask your fishmonger to fillet the trout, or use a sharp knife and cut away the bones, leaving as little flesh on the bones as possible. Check for any tiny bones and remove using tweezers.

2 Preheat the oven to 190°C/375°F/ Gas 5. Put the nuts in a shallow baking tin and bake in the oven for 3–4 minutes until golden, shaking the tin occasionally. Chop roughly.

3 Heat the oil in a small frying pan and fry the onion for 3–4 minutes until soft and golden. Stir in the ginger and cook for another minute and spoon into a mixing bowl. Stir in the rice, tomatoes, sun-dried tomatoes, toasted nuts and tarragon, and season with salt and pepper.

4 Place the two trout on pieces of oiled foil and spoon the stuffing into the filleted cavities. Bring the foil round to encircle each fish and add a sprig of tarragon and a drizzle of olive oil to each.

5 Fold the foil over to secure and place the fish parcels in a large roasting tin. Cook in the oven for 20–25 minutes until the fish is just tender – test with a knife.

6 Cut the fish into thick slices and serve, garnished with salad leaves.

NUTRITION NOTES

Per portion:

Energy	726kcals/3045kJ
Protein	55.7g
Fat	38.7g
saturated fat	7.8g
Carbohydrate	41.4g
Fibre	1.6g
Sugars	3.1g
Calcium	111mg

Salmon Marinated with Thai Spices

This Scandinavian recipe has been transformed using Thai spices and provides a good source of vitamin D.

INGREDIENTS

Serves 4

tail piece of 1 salmon, about
    675g/1½lb, cleaned and prepared
    (see Cook's Tip)
20ml/4 tsp coarse sea salt
20ml/4 tsp sugar
2.5cm/1in piece fresh root
    ginger, grated
2 lemon grass stalks, coarse outer leaves
    removed, thinly sliced
6 kaffir lime leaves, finely chopped
    or shredded
grated rind of 1 lime
1 fresh red chilli, seeded and
    finely chopped
5ml/1 tsp black peppercorns,
    coarsely crushed
30ml/2 tbsp chopped fresh coriander
coriander and kaffir limes, to garnish

**For the coriander and
    lime dressing**
150ml/¼ pint/⅔ cup mayonnaise
juice of ½ lime
10ml/2 tsp chopped fresh coriander

1 Carefully remove all the bones from the salmon (a pair of tweezers is the best tool). Mix together the salt, sugar, ginger, lemon grass, lime leaves, lime rind, chilli, peppercorns and coriander in a bowl.

NUTRITION NOTES

Per portion:

Energy	593kcals/2465kJ
Protein	34.8g
Fat	48.3g
saturated fat	7.5g
Carbohydrate	5.2g
Fibre	0g
Sugars	5.1g
Calcium	44.8mg

---

2 Place one quarter of the spice mixture in a shallow dish. Place one fillet, skin down, on top. Spread two-thirds of the remaining mixture over the flesh then place the other fillet on top, flesh down. Sprinkle the rest of the spice mixture over the fish.

COOK'S TIP

Ask your fishmonger to scale the fish, split it lengthways and remove it from the backbone in two matching fillets.

---

3 Cover the fish with foil, then place a chopping board on top. Add some weights, such as clean cans of fruit. Chill for 2–5 days, turning the fish daily in the spicy brine.

4 Make the dressing by mixing the mayonnaise, lime juice and chopped coriander in a bowl.

5 Scrape the spices off the fish. Slice it as thinly as possible. Serve with the lime dressing, garnished with coriander and wedges of kaffir limes.

Buckwheat Noodles with Smoked Trout

These earthy flavours mix perfectly with the crisp pak choi.

INGREDIENTS

Serves 4

350g/12oz buckwheat noodles
30ml/2 tbsp vegetable oil
115g/4oz fresh shiitake
    mushrooms, quartered
2 garlic cloves, finely chopped
15ml/1 tbsp grated fresh root ginger
225g/8oz pak choi
1 spring onion, finely sliced diagonally
15ml/1 tbsp dark sesame oil
30ml/2 tbsp mirin
30ml/2 tbsp tamari
2 smoked trout, skinned and boned
salt and ground black pepper
30ml/2 tbsp coriander leaves and
    10ml/2 tsp sesame seeds, toasted,
    to garnish (optional)

1 Cook the buckwheat noodles in boiling water for 7–10 minutes until just tender or according to the packet instructions.

2 Meanwhile, heat the oil in a large frying pan. Add the mushrooms and cook, stirring, over a medium heat for 3 minutes. Add the garlic, ginger and pak choi, and continue to cook for 2 minutes.

3 Drain the noodles and add them to the mushroom mixture with the spring onion, sesame oil, mirin and tamari. Toss and season with salt and pepper to taste.

4 Break the smoked trout into bite-size pieces. Arrange the noodle mixture on individual serving plates. Place the smoked trout on top of the noodles.

5 Garnish the noodles with coriander leaves and sesame seeds, if you wish, and serve them immediately.

——— NUTRITION NOTES ———	
Per portion:	
Energy	513kcals/2437kJ
Protein	27.2g
Fat	16.7g
saturated fat	1.5g
Carbohydrate	67.2g
Sugar	2.9g
Fibre	3.5g
Calcium	65mg

Linguine with Smoked Salmon

INGREDIENTS

Serves 6

30ml/2 tbsp olive oil

115g/4oz/1 cup button mushrooms, finely sliced

250ml/8fl oz/1 cup dry white wine

7.5ml/1½ tsp fresh dill or 5ml/1 tsp dried dill weed

handful of fresh chives, snipped

300ml/½ pint/1¼ cups very low-fat unsweetened soya cream or very low-fat fromage frais

225g/8oz smoked salmon, cut into thin strips

lemon juice

350g/12oz fresh egg-free spaghetti

salt and ground black pepper

whole chives, to garnish

FREE FROM

1 Heat the oil in a wide, shallow saucepan. Add the mushrooms and fry over a gentle heat for 4–5 minutes until softened but not coloured.

2 Pour the white wine into the pan. Increase the heat and boil rapidly for about 5 minutes, until the wine has reduced considerably.

3 Stir in the herbs and the soya cream or fromage frais. Fold in the salmon and reheat gently, but do not let the sauce boil or it will curdle. Stir in pepper and lemon juice to taste. Cover the pan and keep the sauce warm.

4 Cook the pasta in a large saucepan of lightly salted boiling water until just tender. Drain, rinse thoroughly in boiling water and drain again. Turn into a warmed serving dish and toss gently with the salmon sauce before serving, garnished with chives.

NUTRITION NOTES

Per portion:

Energy	346kcals/1464kJ
Fat, total	8.3g
saturated fat	1.35g
polyunsaturated fat	1.6g
monounsaturated fat	4.5g
Carbohydrate	42.4g
sugar, total	5.8g
starch	36.5g
Fibre	5.16g
Sodium	800mg

COOK'S TIP

Soya cream may be an acquired taste, but it is a very successful low-fat substitute for dairy cream in dishes such as this one, with a strong flavour of their own.

Trout with Almonds

This simple and quick recipe can also be made with hazelnuts.

INGREDIENTS

Serves 2

2 trout (about 350g/12oz each), cleaned
40g/1½oz/⅓ cup plain flour
50g/2oz/4 tbsp unsalted butter
25g/1oz/¼ cup sliced almonds
30ml/2 tbsp dry white wine
ground black pepper

——— NUTRITION NOTES ———	
Per portion:	
Energy	636Kcals/2667kJ
Protein	46.3g
Fat	42.1g
saturated fat	17.63g
Carbohydrate	17g
Fibre	1.7g
Sodium	100mg

1 Rinse the trout and pat dry. Put the flour in a large polythene bag and season with pepper. Place the trout, one at a time, in the bag and shake to coat with flour. Shake off the excess flour from the fish and discard the remaining flour.

2 Fry the trout in half the butter in a frying pan for 6–7 minutes on each side, until golden brown and cooked through. Transfer the fish to warmed plates and keep warm.

3 Add the remaining butter to the pan and cook the almonds until just lightly browned. Add the wine to the pan and boil for 1 minute, stirring constantly, until slightly syrupy. Pour or spoon over the fish and serve at once.

Tuna with Garlic, Tomatoes and Herbs

This Provençal dish owes its full flavour to the generous use of local herbs, such as thyme, rosemary and oregano, which grow wild on the hillsides and feature in many recipes from the region.

INGREDIENTS

Serves 4

4 tuna steaks, about 2.5cm/1in thick (175–200g/6–7oz each)
30–45ml/2–3 tbsp olive oil
3 or 4 garlic cloves, finely chopped
60ml/4 tbsp dry white wine
3 ripe plum tomatoes, peeled, seeded and chopped
5ml/1 tsp dried herbes de Provence
ground black pepper
fresh basil leaves, to garnish
fried potatoes, to serve

1 Season the tuna steaks with pepper. Set a heavy frying pan over high heat until very hot, add the oil and swirl to coat.

2 Add the tuna steaks and press down gently, then reduce the heat to medium and cook for 6–8 minutes, turning once, until just slightly pink in the centre.

——— NUTRITION NOTES ———	
Per portion:	
Energy	313Kcals/1314kJ
Protein	42.4g
Fat	13.8g
saturated fat	2.98g
Carbohydrate	3g
Fibre	1g
Sodium	90mg

3 Transfer the steaks to a serving plate, cover and keep warm. Add the garlic and fry for 15–20 seconds, stirring all the time, then pour in the wine and boil until it is reduced by half. Add the tomatoes and dried herbs and cook for 2–3 minutes until the sauce is bubbling. Season with pepper and pour over the fish steaks. Serve garnished with fresh basil leaves and accompanied by fried potatoes.

Lemon Sole en Papillote

Make sure that these paper parcels are well sealed, so that none of the delicious juices can escape.

INGREDIENTS

Serves 4

4 lemon sole fillets, each weighing
    about 150g/5oz
½ small cucumber, sliced
4 lemon slices
60ml/4 tbsp dry white wine (optional)
sprigs of fresh dill, to garnish
new potatoes and braised celery,
    to serve

For the yogurt hollandaise
150ml/¼ pint/⅔ cup low-fat yogurt
5ml/1 tsp lemon juice
2 egg yolks
5ml/1 tsp gluten-free Dijon mustard
salt and ground black pepper

1 Preheat the oven to 180°C/ 350°F/Gas 4. Cut out four heart shapes from non-stick baking paper, each about 20 x 15cm/8 x 6in.

2 Place a sole fillet on one side of each heart. Arrange the cucumber and lemon slices on top of each fillet. Sprinkle with the wine, if using, and close the parcels by turning the edges of the paper and twisting to secure. Put on a baking tray and cook in the preheated oven for 15 minutes.

3 For the hollandaise, beat together the yogurt, lemon juice and egg yolks in a double boiler or bowl placed over a saucepan. Cook over simmering water, stirring for 15 minutes, or until thickened. (The sauce will become thinner after 10 minutes, but will thicken again.)

4 Remove from the heat and stir in the mustard. Season to taste. Open the fish parcels, garnish with a sprig of dill and serve accompanied with the sauce, new potatoes and braised celery.

NUTRITION NOTES	
Per portion:	
Energy	186Kcals/793kJ
Protein	29.5g
Fat	5.4g
Saturated Fat	1.25g
Carbohydrate	3.16g
Fibre	0.05g
Sugar	3.12g
Sodium	0.21g

Oatmeal-crusted Mackerel

An appetizing way of serving fresh mackerel. Serve with baked potatoes and cooked mangetouts for a tasty and filling meal.

INGREDIENTS

Serves 4

4 mackerel, each weighing about
    175–225g/6–8oz
juice of 1 lemon
50g/2oz/½ cup fine oatmeal
50g/2oz/½ cup medium oatmeal
30ml/2 tbsp chopped fresh mixed herbs
salt and ground black pepper
tomato quarters and fresh herb sprigs,
    to garnish

1 Remove and discard the heads from the mackerel, gut and then clean the fish.

2 Sprinkle the inside of each mackerel with lemon juice and a little seasoning.

— NUTRITION NOTES —

Per portion:

Energy	480Kcals/2001kJ
Protein	36.30g
Fat	30.15g
Saturated Fat	6.18g
Carbohydrate	16.63g
Fibre	1.88g
Sugar	0.00g
Sodium	0.0g

3 Mix together the oatmeals and herbs and press the oatmeal mixture firmly on to the outside of each fish.

— COOK'S TIP —

Sardines or trout can be used in place of the mackerel in this recipe and are equally healthy and tasty.

4 Preheat the grill. Grill the fish under a fairly high heat for 6–8 minutes, turning once, until the fish is cooked and is just beginning to flake. Garnish with tomato quarters and fresh herb sprigs.

Tuna, Courgette and Pepper Frittata

This nutritious Italian omelette is quick and easy to make. Serve it simply, with a lightly dressed mixed or green leaf salad.

INGREDIENTS

Serves 4

15ml/1 tbsp sunflower oil
1 onion, chopped
1 courgette, thinly sliced
1 red pepper, seeded and sliced
4 eggs
30ml/2 tbsp semi-skimmed milk
200g/7oz can tuna in brine or water, drained and flaked
10ml/2 tsp dried herbes de Provence
50g/2oz/ ½ cup grated Red Leicester cheese
salt and ground black pepper
mixed or green leaf salad, to serve

1 Heat half the oil in a shallow saucepan, add the onion, courgette and red pepper and cook for 5 minutes, stirring frequently.

2 Beat the eggs with the milk in a small bowl. Heat the remaining oil in a heavy-based omelette pan. Add the cooked courgette and red pepper, flaked tuna and herbs, and season well.

3 Pour the egg mixture into the frying pan on top of the vegetable mixture and cook over a medium heat until the eggs are beginning to set. Pull the sides into the middle to allow the uncooked egg to run on to the pan, then continue cooking undisturbed until the frittata is golden underneath. Meanwhile, preheat the grill.

4 Sprinkle the cheese over the top of the frittata and grill until the cheese has melted and the top is golden.

5 Cut the frittata into wedges and serve immediately with a mixed or green leaf salad.

— NUTRITION NOTES —	
Per portion:	
Energy	250kcals/1046kJ
Fat, total	15.3g
saturated fat	5.2g
Protein	24g
Carbohydrate	4.7g
sugar, total	3.1g
Fibre	0.8g
Sodium	330mg

Tuna with Pan-fried Tomatoes

INGREDIENTS

Serves 2

2 tuna steaks, about 175g/6oz each
90ml/6 tbsp olive oil
30ml/2 tbsp lemon juice
2 garlic cloves, chopped
5ml/1 tsp chopped fresh thyme
4 canned anchovy fillets, drained and
 finely chopped
225g/8oz plum tomatoes, halved
30ml/2 tbsp chopped fresh parsley
4–6 black olives, pitted and chopped
ground black pepper
crusty bread, to serve (optional)

3 Meanwhile, heat the remaining oil in a frying pan. Add the tomatoes and fry for 2 minutes only on each side.

4 Divide the tomatoes equally between two serving plates and scatter the chopped parsley and olives over. Top each with a tuna steak.

5 Add the remaining marinade to the pan juices and warm through. Pour over the tomatoes and tuna steaks and serve at once with crusty bread (if your diet allows) for mopping up the juices.

NUTRITION NOTES	
Per portion:	
Energy	578kcals/2405kJ
Protein	21.8g
Fat	21.6g
saturated fat	7.2g
Carbohydrate	3.6g
Sugar	3.6g
Fibre	1.4g
Calcium	57mg

1 Place the tuna steaks in a shallow non-metallic dish. Mix 60ml/ 4 tbsp of the oil with the lemon juice, garlic, thyme, anchovies and pepper. Pour this mixture over the tuna and leave to marinate in a cool place for at least 1 hour.

2 Lift the tuna from the marinade and place on a grill rack. Grill for 4 minutes on each side, or until firm to the touch, basting with the marinade. Take care not to overcook.

Baked Fish with Tahini Sauce

INGREDIENTS

FREE FROM

Serves 4

1 whole fish, about 1.2kg/2½lb, scaled
    and cleaned
10ml/2 tsp coriander seeds
4 garlic cloves, sliced
10ml/2 tsp harissa sauce
90ml/6 tbsp olive oil
6 plum tomatoes, sliced
1 mild onion, sliced
3 preserved lemons or 1 fresh lemon
salt and freshly ground black pepper
plenty of fresh herbs, such as bay leaves,
    thyme and rosemary

For the sauce

75ml/3fl oz/⅓ cup light tahini
juice of 1 lemon
1 garlic clove, crushed
45ml/3 tbsp finely chopped fresh
    parsley or coriander
extra herbs, to garnish

1 Preheat the oven to 200°C/400°F/
Gas 6. Grease the base and sides of
a large, shallow ovenproof dish or
roasting tin.

2 Slash the fish diagonally on both
sides with a sharp knife. Finely
crush the coriander seeds and garlic
with a pestle and mortar. Mix with the
harissa sauce and about 60ml/4 tbsp of
the olive oil.

3 Spread a little of the coriander,
garlic and harissa paste inside the
cavity of the fish. Spread the remainder
over each side of the fish and set aside.

4 Scatter the tomatoes, onion and
preserved or fresh lemon into the
dish. (Thinly slice the lemon if using
fresh.) Sprinkle with the remaining oil
and season with salt and pepper. Lay the
fish on top and tuck plenty of herbs
around it.

5 Bake, uncovered, for about
25 minutes, or until the fish has
turned opaque – test by piercing the
thickest part with a knife.

6 Meanwhile, make the sauce. Mix
the tahini, lemon juice, garlic and
parsley or coriander in a small saucepan
with 120ml/4fl oz/½ cup water and
add a little salt and pepper. Cook gently
until smooth and heated through. Serve
with the fish.

NUTRITION NOTES	
Per portion:	
Energy	481kcals/2002kJ
Protein	46g
Fat	31.1g
saturated fat	4.6g
Carbohydrate	4.2g
Fibre	2.6g
Sugars	3.8g
Calcium	187mg

Sardine Gratin

Sardines are an excellent choice of fish because they contain high levels of omega-3 fatty acids, which play a key role in cancer prevention and intervention.

INGREDIENTS

Serves 4

15ml/1 tbsp light olive oil
½ small onion, finely chopped
2 garlic cloves, crushed
40g/1½oz/6 tbsp blanched
 almonds, chopped
25g/1oz/2 tbsp sultanas,
 roughly chopped
10 pitted black olives, chopped
30ml/2 tbsp capers, roughly chopped
30ml/2 tbsp roughly chopped
 fresh parsley
50g/2oz/1 cup egg-free breadcrumbs
16 large sardines, scaled and gutted
25g/1oz/⅓ cup freshly grated
 Parmesan cheese
salt and ground black pepper
flat leaf parsley, to garnish

1 Preheat the oven to 200°C/400°F/
Gas 6. Lightly oil a large, shallow ovenproof dish.

2 Heat the oil in a frying pan and fry the onion and garlic gently for 3 minutes. Stir in the almonds, sultanas, olives, capers, parsley and 25g/1oz/½ cup of the breadcrumbs. Season lightly with salt and pepper.

3 Make 2–3 diagonal cuts on each side of the sardines. Fill the cavities with stuffing and lay the sardines in the prepared dish.

4 Mix the remaining breadcrumbs with the cheese and scatter over the fish. Bake for about 20 minutes until the fish is cooked through. Test by piercing one sardine through the thickest part with a knife.

5 Garnish with parsley and serve immediately with a leafy salad.

NUTRITION NOTES

Per portion:

Energy	450kcals/1886kJ
Protein	39.3g
Fat	26.3g
saturated fat	6.6g
Carbohydrate	15.3g
Fibre	1.5g
Sugars	5.5g
Calcium	260mg

HEALTH BENEFITS

Almonds contain the antioxidant vitamin E, which, like omega-3 fatty acids, is associated with a lower risk of cancer.

Sardine and Spinach Parcels

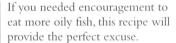

If you needed encouragement to eat more oily fish, this recipe will provide the perfect excuse.

INGREDIENTS

Serves 6

2 x 120g/4¼oz cans large sardines in oil
3 leeks, finely chopped
300g/11oz fresh spinach leaves, finely shredded
2 tomatoes, peeled, seeded and finely chopped
lemon juice
24 sheets of filo pastry, about 20cm/8in square, thawed if frozen
30ml/2 tbsp olive oil, for brushing filo
salt and ground black pepper
salad leaves, to garnish

1 Preheat the oven to 180°C/350°F/ Gas 4. Drain the oil from one of the cans of sardines into a frying pan. Set six sardines aside. Heat the oil and fry the leeks for 5 minutes. Add the spinach and tomatoes and cook over a low heat for 5 minutes until soft. Add salt, pepper and lemon juice to taste.

2 Stack four sheets of filo, brushing each sheet with olive oil and laying each sheet at an angle of 45° to the one below. Spoon a sixth of the vegetable mixture into the centre of the top sheet. Press a sardine into the middle of the vegetable mixture.

3 Fold over the filo to make a parcel, brushing each fold with olive oil. Brush the top of the parcel with oil and place it on a baking sheet. Make five more parcels. Bake the filo parcels for 20 minutes, or until the filo is crisp and brown. Garnish with salad leaves.

NUTRITION NOTES	
Per portion:	
Energy	251kcals/1048kJ
Fat, total	12g
saturated fat	1.9g
polyunsaturated fat	2.8g
monounsaturated fat	5.65g
Carbohydrate	22.5g
sugar, total	2.5g
starch	20g
Fibre	2.2g
Sodium	253mg

Turkish Prawn Pilaff

INGREDIENTS

Serves 6

60ml/4 tbsp olive oil
1 onion, finely chopped
2 large red peppers, seeded and
    finely chopped
2 garlic cloves, finely chopped
350g/12oz/1½ cups brown rice
5ml/1 tsp ground allspice
5ml/1 tsp ground cumin
10ml/2 tsp dried mint or basil
225g/8oz cooked peeled prawns,
    thawed if frozen
45ml/3 tbsp currants
juice of 2 large lemons
2 handfuls fresh parsley, finely chopped
salt and ground black pepper
fresh green salad, to serve

1 Heat the oil in a shallow saucepan. Fry the onion, peppers and garlic over a low heat for 10 minutes until the onion has softened but not browned.

— NUTRITION NOTES —	
Per portion:	
Energy	383kcals/1612kJ
Fat, total	12.6g
saturated fat	2g
polyunsaturated fat	1.7g
monounsaturated fat	7.9g
Carbohydrate	58g
sugar, total	10g
starch	47g
Fibre	2.4g
Sodium	606mg

2 Add the rice, spices and mint or basil. Stir over the heat for 2–3 minutes, then add enough water to cover the rice. Bring to the boil, lower the heat and simmer, uncovered, for 10–15 minutes or until the rice is just tender, but still has a bite to it.

3 Add the prawns, currants and a little salt, to taste. Cook for about 4 minutes more, until the prawns have heated through, then add the lemon juice and chopped parsley. Add pepper to taste. Serve the pilaff warm or cold, with a fresh green salad.

Seafood Risotto

Risotto is one of Italy's most popular rice dishes and it is made with everything from fresh diced pumpkin to squid ink. On the Mediterranean shores, seafood is the most obvious addition.

INGREDIENTS

Serves 4
60ml/4 tbsp sunflower oil
1 onion, chopped
2 garlic cloves, crushed
225g/8oz/generous 1 cup arborio rice
105ml/7 tbsp white wine
1.5 litres/2½ pints/6¼ cups hot
   fish stock
350g/12oz mixed seafood, such as raw
   prawns, mussels, squid rings or clams
grated rind of ½ lemon
30ml/2 tbsp tomato purée
15ml/1 tbsp chopped fresh parsley
salt and ground black pepper

1 Heat the oil in a heavy-based pan, add the onion and garlic and cook until soft. Add the rice and stir to coat the grains with oil. Add the wine and cook over a moderate heat, stirring, for a few minutes until absorbed.

2 Add 150ml/¼ pint/⅔ cup of the hot stock and cook, stirring constantly, until the liquid is absorbed by the rice. Continue stirring and adding stock in 150ml/¼ pint/⅔ cup quantities, until half is left. This should take about 10 minutes.

3 Stir in the seafood and cook for 2–3 minutes. Add the remaining stock as before, and continue cooking until the rice is creamy and the grains *al dente*.

4 Stir in the lemon rind, tomato purée and parsley. Season with salt and pepper and serve warm.

NUTRITION NOTES		
Per portion:		
Energy	438kcals/	1843kJ
Protein		22.4g
Fat		15.4g
saturated fat		2.1g
Carbohydrate		51.3g
Fibre		0.8g
Sugars		3.5g
Calcium		70mg

Italian Prawn Skewers

Crunchy crumb-coated prawns make a delicious starter, or serve as a light lunch with a crisp green salad and warm ciabatta bread.

INGREDIENTS

Serves 4
900g/2lb raw tiger prawns, peeled
60ml/4 tbsp olive oil
45ml/3 tbsp vegetable oil
75g/3oz/1¼ cups very fine dry
   ciabatta breadcrumbs
1 garlic clove, crushed
15ml/1 tbsp chopped fresh parsley
salt and freshly ground black pepper
lemon wedges, to serve

1 Slit the prawns down their backs and remove the dark vein. Rinse the prawns in cold water and pat dry using kitchen paper.

2 Put the olive oil and vegetable oil in a large bowl and add the prawns, mixing them to coat evenly. Add the breadcrumbs, garlic and parsley and season with salt and pepper. Toss the prawns thoroughly, to give them an even coating of breadcrumbs. Cover and leave to marinate for 1 hour.

NUTRITION NOTES	
Per portion:	
Energy	387kcals/1619kJ
Protein	41.4g
Fat	20.4g
saturated fat	2.9g
Carbohydrate	9.8g
Fibre	0.5g
Sugars	0.6g
Calcium	204mg

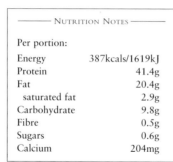

3 Thread the prawns on to four metal or wooden skewers, curling them up as you do so, so that the tail is skewered in the middle.

4 Preheat the grill. Place the skewers in the grill pan and cook for about 2 minutes on each side, until the breadcrumbs are golden. Serve with lemon wedges.

Prawns with Vegetables

This is a light and nutritious dish. It is excellent served on a bed of lettuce leaves with boiled rice.

INGREDIENTS

Serves 4

30ml/2 tbsp chopped fresh coriander
5ml/1 tsp salt
2 green chillies, seeded if required
45ml/3 tbsp lemon juice
30ml/2 tbsp vegetable oil
20 cooked king prawns, peeled
1 courgette, thickly sliced
1 onion, cut into 8 chunks
8 cherry tomatoes
8 baby corn
mixed salad leaves, to serve

—— NUTRITION NOTES ——	
Per portion:	
Energy	142Kcals/592kJ
Fat	6.6g
saturated fat	0.68g
Cholesterol	125.4mg
Fibre	1.2g

1 Place the chopped coriander, salt, green chillies, lemon juice and oil in a food processor or blender and process for a few seconds.

2 Remove the spice paste from the processor and transfer to a medium-size mixing bowl.

3 Add the peeled prawns to the paste and stir to make sure that all the prawns are well coated. Set aside to marinate for about 30 minutes.

4 Preheat the grill to very hot, then turn the heat down to medium.

5 Arrange the courgette slices, onion chunks, cherry tomatoes, baby corn and prawns alternately on four skewers. When all the skewers are ready, place them under the preheated grill for about 5–7 minutes, until they are cooked and browned.

6 Serve the skewers immediately on a bed of mixed salad leaves.

—— COOK'S TIP ——
King prawns are quite an expensive luxury, but worth choosing for a very special dinner party or a treat. For a more economical variation, replace the king prawns with 450g/1lb/2½ cups peeled Atlantic prawns.

Glazed Garlic Prawns

Peel the prawns as this helps them to absorb maximum flavour. Serve as a main course with a variety of accompaniments, or with a salad as a starter.

INGREDIENTS

Serves 4

15ml/1 tbsp sunflower oil
3 garlic cloves, roughly chopped
3 tomatoes, chopped
2.5ml/½ tsp salt
5ml/1 tsp crushed dried red chillies
5ml/1 tsp lemon juice
15ml/1 tbsp mango chutney
1 green chilli, chopped
15–20 cooked king prawns, peeled
fresh coriander leaves and 2 chopped
    spring onions, to garnish

NUTRITION NOTES	
Per portion:	
Energy	101Kcals/421kJ
Fat	3.6g
saturated fat	0.41g
Cholesterol	95.0mg
Fibre	0.9g

1 Heat the oil in a medium saucepan and add the chopped garlic.

2 Lower the heat. Add the chopped tomatoes together with with the salt, crushed chillies, lemon juice, mango chutney and fresh chilli.

COOK'S TIP
Be careful not to overcook the prawns or they will lose both texture and flavour.

3 Finally, add the king prawns, increase the heat to medium-high and stir-fry quickly until they are just heated through and thoroughly coated in the sauce.

4 Transfer to a warmed serving dish. Serve immediately, garnished with fresh coriander leaves and chopped spring onions.

Asparagus with Crabmeat Sauce

The subtle flavour of fresh asparagus is enhanced by the equally delicate taste of crabmeat in this classic dish.

INGREDIENTS

Serves 4

450g/1lb asparagus, trimmed
15ml/1 tbsp vegetable oil
4 thin slices of fresh root ginger
2 garlic cloves, chopped
115g/4oz/⅔ cup fresh or thawed
   frozen white crabmeat
5ml/1 tsp dry sherry
150ml/¼ pint/⅔ cup semi-
   skimmed milk
15ml/1 tbsp cornflour
45ml/3 tbsp cold water
salt and freshly ground white pepper
1 spring onion, thinly shredded,
   to garnish

1 Bring a large pan of lightly salted water to the boil. Poach the asparagus for about 5 minutes until just crisp-tender. Drain well and keep hot in a shallow serving dish.

2 Heat the oil in a non-stick frying pan or wok. Cook the ginger and garlic for 1 minute to release their flavour, then lift them out with a slotted spoon and discard them.

3 Add the crabmeat, sherry and milk to the flavoured oil and cook, stirring often, for 2 minutes.

4 In a small bowl, mix the cornflour to a paste with the water and add to the pan slowly. Cook, stirring constantly, until the sauce is thick and creamy. Season to taste with salt and pepper, spoon over the asparagus, garnish with shreds of spring onion and serve.

NUTRITION NOTES	
Per portion:	
Energy	128 Kcals/533 KJ
Protein	10.6g
Fat	5.6g
saturated fat	0.9g
Carbohydrate	8.9g
Fibre	2.0g
Sugar	4.2g
Sodium	0.25g

Prawn Curry

This is a rich, flavoursome curry made from succulent prawns and a delicious blend of aromatic spices.

INGREDIENTS

Serves 4

675g/1½lb raw tiger prawns
4 dried red chillies
50g/2oz/1 cup desiccated coconut
5ml/1 tsp black mustard seeds
1 large onion, chopped
45ml/3 tbsp oil
4 bay leaves
2.5cm/1in piece root ginger,
    finely chopped
2 garlic cloves, crushed
15ml/1 tbsp ground coriander
5ml/1 tsp chilli powder
4 tomatoes, finely chopped
unpeeled cooked prawns,
    to garnish
boiled rice, to serve

1 Peel the prawns. Run a sharp knife along the back of each prawn to make a shallow cut and carefully remove the thin, black intestinal vein.

——— NUTRITION NOTES ———	
Per portion:	
Energy	344Kcals/1429kJ
Protein	33.1g
Fat	18.7g
saturated fat	7.78g
Carbohydrate	12g
Fibre	3.3g
Sodium	351mg

2 Put the dried red chillies, coconut, mustard seeds and onion in a large frying pan. Dry fry for 8–10 minutes or until the mixture begins to brown. Put into a food processor or blender and process to a coarse paste.

3 Heat the oil in the frying pan and fry the bay leaves for 1 minute. Add the chopped ginger and the garlic and fry for 2–3 minutes.

4 Add the coriander and chilli and fry for about 5 minutes. Stir in the tomatoes and about 175ml/6fl oz/ ¾ cup water and allow to simmer for 5–6 minutes, or until thickened.

5 Add the prawns and cook for about 4–5 minutes, or until they turn pink and the edges are curling slightly. Serve with boiled rice, garnished with unpeeled cooked prawns.

FREE FROM

Fish Balls with Chinese Greens

Tasty fish balls are partnered with a selection of green vegetables to make a fresh and appetizing stir-fry with a Chinese flavour.

INGREDIENTS

Serves 4

450g/1lb white fish fillets, skinned, boned and cubed
3 spring onions, chopped
1 back bacon rasher, chopped
15ml/1 tbsp Chinese rice wine
30ml/2 tbsp tamari
1 egg white

For the vegetables

5ml/1 tsp cornflour or arrowroot
15ml/1 tbsp tamari
150ml/¼ pint/⅔ cup fish stock
30ml/2 tbsp vegetable oil
2 garlic cloves, sliced
2.5cm/1in piece fresh root ginger, cut into thin shreds
75g/3oz green beans
175g/6oz mangetouts
3 spring onions, sliced diagonally into 5–7.5cm/2–3in lengths
1 small head pak choi, stems trimmed and leaves torn
salt and ground black pepper

COOK'S TIP

Tamari is a wheat-free type of soy sauce and can be found in Asian shops. If you are not allergic to wheat or gluten, you can subsitute soy sauce, if you prefer.

NUTRITION NOTES

Per portion:

Energy	201kcals/1115kJ
Protein	26.5g
Fat	8.75g
saturated fat	1.5g
Carbohydrate	3.9g
Sugar	3.2g
Fibre	2.2g
Calcium	67mg

1 Put the fish, spring onions, bacon, rice wine, tamari and egg white in a food processor. Process until smooth. With wetted hands, form the mixture into about 24 small balls.

2 Steam the fish balls in batches in a lightly greased bamboo steamer in a wok for 5–10 minutes until firm. Transfer to a plate and keep warm.

3 In a small bowl, blend together the cornflour or arrowroot, tamari and stock until smooth. Set aside.

4 Heat a wok until hot, add the oil and swirl it around. Add the garlic and ginger and stir-fry for 1 minute. Then add the beans and stir-fry for 2–3 minutes, then add the mangetouts, spring onions and pak choi. Stir-fry for 2–3 minutes.

5 Add the stock mixture to the wok and cook, stirring, until it has thickened and the vegetables are tender but still crisp. Taste, and adjust the seasoning, if necessary. Serve at once with the steamed fish balls.

Spiced Prawns with Coconut

This delicious, fragrant and spicy dish is based on a traditional Indonesian recipe. Serve with a bowl of plain boiled rice.

INGREDIENTS

Serves 4

2–3 fresh red chillies, seeded and chopped
3 shallots, chopped
1 lemon grass stalk, chopped
2 garlic cloves, chopped
thin sliver of dried shrimp paste
2.5ml/ ½ tsp ground ginger
5ml/1 tsp ground turmeric
5ml/1 tsp ground coriander
15ml/1 tbsp pure vegetable oil
250ml/8fl oz/1 cup water
2 fresh kaffir lime leaves
5ml/1 tsp light brown soft sugar
2 tomatoes, peeled, seeded and chopped
250ml/8fl oz/1 cup coconut milk
675g/1½lb large raw prawns, peeled and deveined
squeeze of lemon juice
salt, to taste
shredded spring onions and toasted flaked coconut, to garnish

1 In a mortar, pound the chillies, shallots, lemon grass, garlic, shrimp paste, ginger, turmeric and coriander with a pestle until it forms a paste. Alternatively, process the ingredients in a food processor or blender.

NUTRITION NOTES

Per portion:

Energy	188kcals/770kJ
Protein	30.3g
Fat	4.1g
saturated fat	0.6g
Carbohydrate	8.1g
Sugar	7.7g
Fibre	0.6g
Calcium	159mg

2 Heat a wok until hot, add the oil and swirl it around. Add the spiced paste and stir-fry for about 2 minutes. Pour in the water and add the kaffir lime leaves, sugar and tomatoes. Simmer for 8–10 minutes until most of the liquid has evaporated.

3 Add the coconut milk and prawns and cook gently, stirring, for about 4 minutes until the prawns are pink. Taste and adjust the seasoning with salt and a squeeze of lemon juice. Serve at once, garnished with shredded spring onions and toasted flaked coconut.

VEGETARIAN DISHES

Fresh vegetables and wholefoods such as grains and pulses are

an essential part of a nutritious diet. This chapter makes the best use

of these wholesome ingredients, offering a delicious array of exciting,

health-giving dishes that are high in nutrients and taste. Take your

pick from hearty, warming dishes such as Rice Noodles with

Vegetable Chilli Sauce, or mouth-watering temptations such as

Red Pepper Risotto, and Mushroom and Sunflower Seed Flan.

Vegetable Moussaka

This is a really flavoursome vegetarian alternative to classic meat moussaka. Serve it with warm, gluten- and yeast-free bread and a glass of red wine.

Ingredients

Serves 6

450g/1lb aubergines, sliced
115g/4oz whole green lentils
600ml/1 pint/2½ cups Vegetable Stock
1 bay leaf
45ml/3 tbsp olive oil
1 onion, sliced
1 garlic clove, crushed
225g/8oz mushrooms, sliced
400g/14oz can chick-peas, rinsed
   and drained
400g/14oz can chopped tomatoes
30ml/2 tbsp tomato purée
10ml/2 tsp dried herbes de Provence
45ml/3 tbsp water
300ml/½ pint/1¼ cups natural yogurt
3 eggs
50g/2oz/½ cup grated mature
   Cheddar cheese
salt and ground black pepper
flat leaf parsley, to garnish

1 Sprinkle the aubergine slices with salt and place in a colander. Cover and leave for 30 minutes to allow the bitter juices to be extracted.

2 Meanwhile, place the lentils, stock and bay leaf in a saucepan. Cover, bring to the boil and simmer for about 20 minutes until the lentils are just tender. Drain well and keep warm.

3 Heat 15ml/1 tbsp of the oil in a large saucepan, add the onion and garlic and cook for 5 minutes, stirring. Stir in the lentils, mushrooms, chick-peas, tomatoes, tomato purée, herbs and water. Bring to the boil, cover and simmer gently for 10 minutes.

4 Preheat the oven to 180°C/350°F/Gas 4. Rinse the aubergine slices, drain and pat dry. Heat the remaining oil in a frying pan and fry the slices in batches for 3–4 minutes, turning once.

5 Season the lentil mixture with salt and pepper. Arrange a layer of aubergine slices in the bottom of a large, shallow, ovenproof dish or roasting tin, then spoon over a layer of the lentil mixture. Continue the layers until all the aubergines slices and lentil mixture are used up.

6 Beat together the yogurt, eggs and plenty of salt and pepper and pour the mixture into the dish. Sprinkle the grated cheese on top and bake for about 45 minutes until the topping is golden brown and bubbling. Serve immediately, garnished with flat leaf parsley.

Nutrition Notes	
Per portion:	
Energy	348kcals/1463kJ
Fat, total	17.3g
saturated fat	4.4g
Protein	20.6g
Carbohydrate	29.5g
sugar, total	9g
Fibre	7.1g
Sodium	722mg

Rice Noodles with Vegetable Chilli Sauce

INGREDIENTS

Serves 4

15ml/1 tbsp sunflower oil
1 onion, chopped
2 garlic cloves, crushed
1 fresh red chilli, seeded and
  finely chopped
1 red pepper, seeded and diced
2 carrots, finely chopped
175g/6oz baby sweetcorn, halved
225g/8oz can sliced bamboo shoots,
  rinsed and drained
400g/14oz can red kidney beans, rinsed
  and drained
300ml/½ pint/1¼ cups passata or
  sieved tomatoes
15ml/1 tbsp tamari
5ml/1 tsp ground coriander
250g/9oz rice noodles
30ml/2 tbsp chopped fresh coriander
  or parsley
salt and ground black pepper
fresh parsley sprigs, to garnish

1 Heat the oil, add the onion, garlic, chilli and red pepper and cook for 5 minutes, stirring. Stir in the carrots, sweetcorn, bamboo shoots, kidney beans, passata or sieved tomatoes, soy sauce and ground coriander.

COOK'S TIP

After handling chillies, wash your hands. Chillies contain volatile oils that can irritate and burn sensitive areas, such as the eyes, if they are touched.

2 Bring to the boil, then cover, reduce the heat, and simmer gently for 30 minutes until the vegetables are tender, stirring occasionally. Season with salt and pepper to taste.

3 Meanwhile, place the noodles in a bowl and cover with boiling water. Stir with a fork and leave to stand for 3–4 minutes, or according to the packet instructions. Rinse with boiling water and drain thoroughly.

4 Stir the coriander or parsley into the sauce. Spoon the noodles on to warmed serving plates and top with the sauce. Garnish with parsley and serve.

NUTRITION NOTES

Per portion:

Energy	409kcals/1717kJ
Fat, total	5.2g
saturated fat	0.6g
Protein	13.5g
Carbohydrate	77.3g
sugar, total	10.6g
Fibre	8.7g
Sodium	1156mg

Harvest Vegetable and Lentil Casserole

INGREDIENTS

Serves 6

15ml/1 tbsp sunflower oil
2 leeks, sliced
1 garlic clove, crushed
4 celery sticks, chopped
2 carrots, sliced
2 parsnips, diced
1 sweet potato, diced
225g/8oz swede, diced
175g/6oz whole brown
  or green lentils
450g/1lb tomatoes, skinned, seeded
  and chopped
15ml/1 tbsp chopped fresh thyme
15ml/1 tbsp chopped fresh marjoram
900ml/1½ pints/3¾ cups well-
  flavoured Vegetable Stock
15ml/1 tbsp cornflour
salt and ground black pepper
fresh thyme sprigs, to garnish

1 Preheat the oven to 180°C/350°F/
Gas 4. Heat the oil in a large
flameproof casserole. Add the leeks,
garlic and celery and cook over a low
heat for 3 minutes, stirring occasionally.

NUTRITION NOTES

Per portion:

Energy	254kcals/1075kJ
Fat, total	11g
saturated fat	0.15g
Protein	11.5g
Carbohydrate	37.8g
sugar, total	10.8g
Fibre	7.1g
Sodium	722mg

2 Add the carrots, parsnips, sweet
potato, swede, lentils, tomatoes,
herbs, stock and seasoning. Stir well.
Bring to the boil, stirring occasionally.

3 Cover and bake for about
50 minutes until the vegetables and
lentils are cooked and tender, removing
the casserole from the oven in order to
stir the vegetable mixture once or twice
during the cooking time.

4 Remove the casserole from the
oven. Blend the cornflour with
45ml/3 tbsp water in a small bowl. Stir
it into the casserole and heat gently,
stirring continuously, until the mixture
comes to the boil and thickens, then
simmer gently for 2 minutes, stirring.

5 Spoon the casserole on to warmed
serving plates or into bowls and
serve garnished with thyme sprigs.

Herby Rice Pilaff

A quick and easy recipe to make, this simple pilaff is delicious to eat. Serve with a selection of cooked fresh seasonal vegetables such as broccoli florets, baby sweetcorn and carrots.

INGREDIENTS

Serves 4

225g/8oz mixed brown basmati and
    wild rice
15ml/1 tbsp olive oil
1 onion, chopped
1 garlic clove, crushed
5ml/1 tsp each ground cumin and
    ground turmeric
50g/2oz/ ½ cup sultanas
750ml/1¼ pints/3 cups Vegetable Stock
30−45ml/2−3 tbsp chopped fresh
    mixed herbs
salt and ground black pepper
fresh herb sprigs and 25g/1oz/ ¼ cup
    pistachio nuts, chopped, to garnish

1 Wash the rice in a sieve under cold running water, then drain well. Heat the oil in a saucepan, add the onion and garlic and cook gently for 5 minutes, stirring occasionally.

2 Add the spices and rice and cook gently for 1 minute, stirring. Stir in the sultanas and stock, then bring to the boil, cover and simmer gently for 20−25 minutes until the rice is cooked and just tender and almost all the liquid has been absorbed, stirring occasionally.

3 Stir in the chopped mixed herbs and season to taste with salt and pepper. Spoon the pilaf into a warmed serving dish and garnish with fresh herb sprigs and a scattering of chopped pistachio nuts. Serve immediately.

— NUTRITION NOTES —	
Per portion:	
Energy	326kcals/1363kJ
Fat, total	8.6g
saturated fat	0.15g
Protein	1.0g
Carbohydrate	56g
sugar, total	10.2g
Fibre	1.4g
Sodium	630mg

Cheese-topped Roast Baby Vegetables

A simple way of serving baby vegetables that really brings out their flavour.

INGREDIENTS

Serves 6

1kg/2¼lb mixed baby vegetables, such
    as aubergines, onions or shallots,
    courgettes, sweetcorn and button
    mushrooms
1 red pepper, seeded and cut into
    large pieces
1−2 garlic cloves, finely chopped
15−30ml/1−2 tbsp olive oil
30ml/2 tbsp chopped fresh mixed herbs
225g/8oz cherry tomatoes
115g/4oz/1 cup coarsely grated
    mozzarella cheese
salt and ground black pepper
black olives, to serve (optional)

1 Preheat the oven to 220°C/425°F/ Gas 7. Cut all the mixed baby vegetables in half lengthways.

2 Place the baby vegetables and peppers in an ovenproof dish with the garlic and seasoning. Drizzle the oil over and toss the vegetables to coat them. Bake for 20 minutes until tinged brown at the edges, stirring once.

3 Remove the dish from the oven and stir in the herbs. Scatter the tomatoes over the surface and top with the mozzarella cheese. Return to the oven and bake for 5−10 minutes more until the cheese has melted and is bubbling. Serve at once, with black olives, if liked.

— NUTRITION NOTES —	
Per portion:	
Energy	162kcals/679kJ
Fat, total	10g
saturated fat	3.4g
Protein	8.2g
Carbohydrate	10.6g
sugar, total	7g
Fibre	3.1g
Sodium	172mg

Wild Mushroom and Broccoli Flan

FREE FROM

Gluten-free potato and cheese pastry combines well with a mushroom and broccoli filling to ensure this savoury flan is a family favourite. Lightly cooked, sliced leeks can be used instead of broccoli florets, if preferred.

INGREDIENTS

Serves 8
115g/4oz small broccoli florets
15ml/1 tbsp olive oil
3 shallots, finely chopped
175g/6oz mixed wild mushrooms, such as ceps, shiitake mushrooms and oyster mushrooms, sliced or chopped
2 eggs
200ml/7fl oz/scant 1 cup semi-skimmed milk
15ml/1 tbsp chopped fresh tarragon
50g/2oz/½ cup grated Cheddar cheese
salt and ground black pepper
fresh herb sprigs, to garnish

For the pastry
75g/3oz/¾ cup brown rice flour
75g/3oz/¾ cup gluten-free cornmeal
pinch of salt
75g/3oz/6 tbsp soft margarine
115g/4oz cold mashed potatoes
50g/2oz/½ cup grated Cheddar cheese

2 Stir in the mashed potatoes and cheese and mix to form a smooth, soft dough. Wrap in a plastic bag and chill for 30 minutes.

3 Roll out the pastry between two sheets of greaseproof paper and use to line a 24cm/9½in loose-bottomed flan tin, gently pressing the pastry into the sides of the flan tin. Carefully trim around the top edge of the pastry case with a sharp knife. Cover the pastry, and chill while making the filling.

5 Heat the oil in a frying pan, add the shallots and cook gently for 3 minutes, stirring. Add the mushrooms and cook gently for 2 minutes.

6 Spoon into the pastry case and top with broccoli. Beat the eggs, milk, tarragon and seasoning together and pour over the vegetables. Top with cheese. Bake for 10 minutes, reduce the oven temperature to 180°C/350°F/Gas 4 and bake for about 30 minutes until lightly set. Serve warm or cold, garnished with fresh herbs.

1 First make the pastry. Place the rice flour, cornmeal and salt in a mixing bowl and stir to mix. Lightly rub in the margarine with your fingertips until the mixture resembles breadcrumbs.

4 Preheat the oven to 200°C/400°F/Gas 6. Cook the broccoli florets in a saucepan of lightly salted, boiling water for 3 minutes. Drain thoroughly and set aside.

— NUTRITION NOTES —	
Per portion:	
Energy	265kcals/1102kJ
Fat, total	17.2g
saturated fat	5.54g
Protein	8.8g
Carbohydrate	18.5g
sugar, total	1.95g
Fibre	1g
Sodium	209mg

Savoury Nut Loaf

FREE FROM

This delicious nut loaf makes perfect picnic food.

INGREDIENTS

Serves 8

15ml/1 tbsp olive oil
1 onion, chopped
1 leek, chopped
2 celery sticks, finely chopped
225g/8oz mushrooms, chopped
2 garlic cloves, crushed
425g/15oz can lentils, rinsed
  and drained
115g/4oz/1 cup mixed nuts, such as
  hazelnuts, cashew nuts and almonds,
  finely chopped
50g/2oz potato flour
50g/2oz/½ cup grated mature
  Cheddar cheese
1 egg, beaten
45–60ml/3–4 tbsp chopped fresh
  mixed herbs
salt and ground black pepper
chives and flat leaf parsley, to garnish

1 Preheat the oven to 190°C/375°F/ Gas 5. Lightly grease and line the base and sides of a 900g/2lb loaf tin.

2 Heat the oil in a large saucepan, add the chopped onion, leek, celery and mushrooms and the crushed garlic, then cook gently for 10 minutes until the vegetables have softened, stirring occasionally.

3 Add the lentils, mixed nuts, potato flour, grated cheese, egg and herbs to the pan. Season with salt and pepper and mix thoroughly.

4 Spoon the nut, vegetable and lentil mixture into the prepared loaf tin and level the surface. Bake, uncovered, for 50–60 minutes or until the nut loaf is lightly browned on top and firm to the touch.

5 Cool the loaf slightly in the tin, then turn it out on to a large serving plate. Serve hot or cold, cut into slices, and garnished with snipped chives and chopped flat leaf parsley.

NUTRITION NOTES	
Per portion:	
Energy	230kcals/953kJ
Fat, total	13.1g
saturated fat	2.9g
Protein	12.5g
Carbohydrate	16.8g
sugar, total	1.9g
Fibre	4.3g
Sodium	67mg

Provençal Stuffed Peppers

INGREDIENTS

Serves 4

15ml/1 tbsp olive oil
1 red onion, sliced
1 courgette, diced
115g/4oz mushrooms, sliced
1 garlic clove, crushed
400g/14oz can chopped tomatoes
15ml/1 tbsp tomato purée
40g/1½oz/scant ⅓ cup pine nuts
30ml/2 tbsp chopped fresh basil
4 large peppers
50g/2oz/½ cup finely grated Red
    Leicester cheese
salt and ground black pepper
fresh basil leaves, to garnish

1 Preheat the oven to 180°C/350°F/ Gas 4. Heat the oil in a pan, add the onion, courgette, mushrooms and garlic and cook gently for 3 minutes, stirring occasionally.

2 Stir in the tomatoes and tomato purée, then bring to the boil and simmer, uncovered, for 10–15 minutes, stirring occasionally, until thickened slightly. Remove from the heat and stir in the pine nuts, basil and seasoning.

3 Cut the peppers in half lengthways and seed them. Blanch in a pan of boiling water for 3 minutes. Drain.

4 Place in a shallow, ovenproof dish and fill with the vegetable mixture.

5 Cover the dish with foil and bake for 20 minutes. Remove the foil, sprinkle each pepper with a little grated cheese and bake, uncovered, for a further 5–10 minutes until the cheese is melted and bubbling. Garnish with basil leaves and serve at once.

VARIATIONS

Use the vegetable sauce to stuff other vegetables, such as large courgettes or baby aubergines, in place of the peppers. Try grated Parmesan in place of Red Leicester.

NUTRITION NOTES

Per portion:	
Energy	211kcals/881kJ
Fat, total	15.7g
saturated fat	3.8g
Protein	8.2g
Carbohydrate	10g
sugar, total	8.6g
Fibre	4.1g
Sodium	136mg

Mixed Mushroom and Parmesan Risotto

A classic risotto of mixed mushrooms, herbs and fresh Parmesan cheese, best simply served with a mixed leaf salad.

INGREDIENTS

Serves 4
15ml/1 tbsp olive oil
4 shallots, finely chopped
2 garlic cloves, crushed
10g/¼oz dried porcini mushrooms, soaked in 150ml/¼ pint/⅔ cup hot water for 20 minutes
450g/1lb mixed mushrooms, such as closed cup, chestnut and field mushrooms, sliced or chopped
250g/9oz long grain brown rice
900ml/1½ pints/3¾ cups well-flavoured Vegetable Stock
30–45ml/2–3 tbsp chopped fresh flat leaf parsley
50g/2oz/⅔ cup freshly grated Parmesan cheese
salt and ground black pepper

1 Heat the oil in a large saucepan, add the shallots and garlic and cook gently for 5 minutes, stirring. Drain the porcini, reserving their liquid, and chop roughly. Add all the mushrooms to the pan along with the porcini soaking liquid, the brown rice and 300ml/½ pint/1¼ cups of the stock.

2 Bring to the boil, reduce the heat and simmer, uncovered, until all the liquid has been absorbed, stirring frequently. Add a ladleful of hot stock and stir until it has been absorbed.

3 Continue cooking and adding the hot stock, a ladleful at a time, until the rice is cooked and creamy but *al dente*, stirring frequently. This should take about 35 minutes and it may not be necessary to add all the stock.

4 Season with salt and pepper to taste, stir in the chopped parsley and grated Parmesan and serve at once. Alternatively, sprinkle the Parmesan over the risotto just before serving.

—— NUTRITION NOTES ——

Per portion:
Energy	358kcals/1511kJ
Fat, total	10.9g
saturated fat	3.65g
Protein	12.8g
Carbohydrate	55.4g
sugar, total	2.2g
Fibre	3.4g
Sodium	738mg

Spring Vegetable Omelette

INGREDIENTS
Serves 4
50g/2oz asparagus tips
50g/2oz spring greens, shredded
15ml/1 tbsp sunflower oil
1 onion, sliced
175g/6oz cooked baby new potatoes, halved or diced
2 tomatoes, chopped
6 eggs
15–30ml/1–2 tbsp chopped fresh mixed herbs
salt and ground black pepper
salad, to serve

1 Steam the asparagus tips and spring greens over a saucepan of boiling water for 5–10 minutes until tender. Drain the vegetables and keep warm.

2 Heat the oil in a large frying pan, add the onion and cook gently for 5–10 minutes until softened, stirring.

3 Add the baby potatoes and cook for 3 minutes, stirring. Stir in the tomatoes, asparagus and spring greens. Lightly beat the eggs with the herbs and season with salt and pepper.

4 Pour the eggs over the vegetables, then cook over a gentle heat until the bottom of the omelette is golden brown. Preheat the grill to hot and cook the omelette under the grill for 2–3 minutes until the top is golden brown. Serve with salad.

—— NUTRITION NOTES ——

Per portion:
Energy	221kcals/923kJ
Fat, total	14.2g
saturated fat	3.4g
Protein	13.6g
Carbohydrate	10.4g
sugar, total	3.4g
Fibre	2.1g
Sodium	142mg

Ratatouille

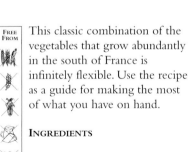

This classic combination of the vegetables that grow abundantly in the south of France is infinitely flexible. Use the recipe as a guide for making the most of what you have on hand.

INGREDIENTS

Serves 6

2 aubergines, about 450g/1lb total, cut into 2cm/³⁄₄in slices
60–75ml/4–5 tbsp olive oil
1 large onion, halved and sliced
2 or 3 garlic cloves, very finely chopped
1 large red or yellow pepper, seeded and cut into thin strips
2 large courgettes, cut into 1cm/ ½in slices
675g/1½lb ripe tomatoes, peeled, seeded and chopped, or 400g/14oz can chopped tomatoes
5ml/1 tsp dried mixed herbs
salt and ground black pepper

--- COOK'S TIP ---

Roasting the pepper not only allows you to remove the skin, it adds a delicious, smoky flavour to the ratatouille. Quarter the pepper and grill, skin-side up, until blackened. Enclose the pepper in a sturdy polythene bag and set aside until cool. Peel off the skin, then remove the core and seeds and cut the pepper into strips. Add to the mixture with the cooked aubergine.

--- NUTRITION NOTES ---

Per portion:
Energy	95kcals/396kJ
Protein	1.9g
Fat	7.7g
saturated fat	1.2g
Carbohydrate	7.4g
Sugar	4.3g
Fibre	1.9g
Calcium	28mg

1 Preheat the grill. Brush the aubergine slices with oil on both sides. Grill until lightly browned, turning once, then cut into chunks.

2 Heat 15ml/1 tbsp of the olive oil in a large flameproof casserole and cook the onion for about 10 minutes until lightly golden, stirring frequently. Add the garlic, pepper and courgettes and cook for a further 10 minutes.

3 Add the tomatoes, aubergine, dried herbs and salt and pepper. Simmer gently, covered, over a low heat for about 20 minutes, stirring occasionally. Uncover and continue cooking for a further 20–25 minutes, stirring occasionally, until all the vegetables are tender and the cooking liquid has thickened slightly. Serve hot or at room temperature, if you prefer.

Risotto with Spring Vegetables

This is one of the prettiest risottos, especially if you can get yellow courgettes.

INGREDIENTS

Serves 4

150g/5oz/1 cup shelled fresh peas
115g/4oz/1 cup French beans, cut into
   short lengths
30ml/2 tbsp olive oil
75g/3oz/6 tbsp butter
2 small yellow courgettes, cut
   into matchsticks
1 onion, finely chopped
275g/10oz/1½ cups risotto rice
120ml/4fl oz/½ cup Italian dry
   white vermouth (optional)
about 1 litre/1¾ pints/4 cups boiling
   Chicken Stock
75g/3oz/1 cup freshly grated
   Parmesan cheese
a small handful of fresh basil leaves,
   finely shredded, plus a few whole
   leaves, to garnish
salt and ground black pepper

1 Blanch the peas and beans in a large saucepan of lightly salted boiling water for 2–3 minutes until just tender. Drain, refresh under cold running water, drain and set aside.

2 Heat the oil and 25g/1oz/2 tbsp of the butter in a medium saucepan until foaming. Add the courgettes and cook gently for 2–3 minutes or until just softened. Remove the courgettes with a slotted spoon and set aside. Add the onion to the pan and cook gently for about 3 minutes, stirring frequently, until softened.

3 Stir in the rice until the grains start to swell and burst, then add the vermouth, if using. Stir until the vermouth stops sizzling and most of it has been absorbed by the rice, then add a few ladlefuls of the stock, with salt and pepper to taste. Stir over low heat until the stock has been absorbed.

4 Continue cooking and stirring for 20–25 minutes, adding the remaining stock a few ladlefuls at a time. The rice should be *al dente* and the risotto should have a moist and creamy appearance. Gently stir in the vegetables and the remaining butter.

5 Stir in half the Parmesan. Heat through, then stir in the shredded basil and taste for seasoning. Garnish with basil leaves and serve with the remaining Parmesan handed separately.

——— NUTRITION NOTES ———	
Per portion:	
Energy	602kcals/2500kJ
Protein	17.2g
Fat	28.9g
saturated fat	15g
Carbohydrate	59.3g
Sugar	3.9g
Fibre	2.9g
Calcium	272mg

Stuffed Vine Leaves

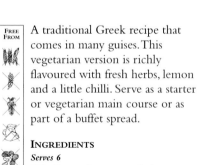

A traditional Greek recipe that comes in many guises. This vegetarian version is richly flavoured with fresh herbs, lemon and a little chilli. Serve as a starter or vegetarian main course or as part of a buffet spread.

INGREDIENTS

Serves 6

225g/8oz packet preserved vine
  leaves, drained
1 onion, finely chopped
½ bunch of spring onions,
  finely chopped
60ml/4 tbsp chopped fresh flat
  leaf parsley
10 large mint sprigs, chopped
finely grated rind of 1 lemon
2.5ml/½ tsp crushed dried chillies
7.5ml/1½ tsp fennel seeds, crushed
175g/6oz/scant 1 cup long grain rice
120ml/4fl oz/½ cup extra virgin
  olive oil
salt
lemon wedges and mint leaves, to
  garnish (optional)

COOK'S TIP

To check that the rice is cooked, lift out one stuffed leaf and cut in half. The rice should have expanded and softened to make a firm parcel. If necessary, cook the stuffed leaves a little longer, adding boiling water if the pan is becoming dry.

1 Rinse the vine leaves in plenty of cold water. Put in a bowl, cover with boiling water and leave for 10 minutes. Drain thoroughly.

2 In a bowl, mix together the onion, spring onions, parsley, mint, lemon rind, chilli, fennel seeds, rice and 25ml/1½ tbsp of the olive oil. Mix thoroughly and season with salt.

3 Place a vine leaf, veined side facing upwards, on a work surface and cut off any stalk. Place a heaped teaspoonful of the rice mixture near the stalk end of the leaf.

4 Fold the stalk end of the leaf over the rice filling, then fold over the sides and carefully roll up into a neat cigar shape.

5 Repeat with the remaining filling to make about 28 stuffed leaves. If some of the vine leaves are quite small, use two and patch them together to make parcels of the same size.

6 Place any remaining leaves in the base of a large heavy-based saucepan. Pack the stuffed leaves in a single layer in the pan. Spoon the remaining oil over then add about 300ml/½ pint/1¼ cups boiling water.

7 Place a small plate over the leaves to keep them submerged in the water. Cover the pan and cook on a very low heat for 45 minutes.

8 Transfer the stuffed leaves to a serving plate and garnish with lemon wedges and mint, if you like.

--- NUTRITION NOTES ---

Per portion:

Energy	256kcals/1072kJ
Protein	3.9g
Fat	15.8g
saturated fat	2.3g
Carbohydrate	26.3g
Sugar	1.6g
Fibre	0.5g
Calcium	170mg

Red-cooked Tofu with Chinese Mushrooms

FREE FROM

Red-cooked is a term applied to Chinese dishes cooked with dark soy sauce. Tamari is a type of soy sauce available in Asian shops that is wheat-free.

INGREDIENTS

Serves 4 as a side dish

225g/8oz firm tofu (soya beancurd)
45ml/3 tbsp tamari
30ml/2 tbsp Chinese rice wine or
    medium-dry sherry
10ml/2 tsp soft dark brown sugar
1 garlic clove, crushed
15ml/1 tbsp grated fresh root ginger
2.5ml/½ tsp Chinese five-spice powder
pinch of ground, roasted
    Szechuan peppercorns
6 dried Chinese black mushrooms
5ml/1 tsp cornflour
30ml/2 tbsp pure vegetable oil
5–6 spring onions, white and green
    parts separated, sliced into 2.5cm/
    1in lengths
small basil leaves, to garnish
rice noodles, to serve

1 Drain the tofu (soya beancurd), pat dry and cut into 2.5cm/1in cubes. Place in a shallow dish.

2 In a small bowl, mix together the tamari, rice wine or sherry, sugar, garlic, ginger, five-spice powder and Szechuan peppercorns. Pour the marinade over the tofu, toss well and leave to marinate for about 30 minutes. Drain, reserving the marinade.

3 Meanwhile, soak the dried black mushrooms in warm water for 20–30 minutes until soft. Drain, reserving 90ml/6 tbsp of the soaking liquid. Squeeze out any excess liquid from the mushrooms, remove the tough stalks and slice the caps. In a small bowl, blend the cornflour with the reserved marinade and mushroom soaking liquid.

4 Heat a wok until hot, add the oil and swirl it around to coat the pan. Add the tofu and fry for 2–3 minutes until evenly golden. Remove from the wok and set aside.

5 Add the mushrooms and white parts of the spring onions to the wok and stir-fry for 2 minutes. Pour in the marinade mixture and stir for 1 minute until thickened.

6 Return the tofu to the wok with the green spring onions. Simmer gently for 1–2 minutes. Serve at once, garnished with basil leaves, on a bed of rice noodles.

NUTRITION NOTES	
Per portion:	
Energy	90kcals/374kJ
Protein	4.5g
Fat	7.9g
saturated fat	1.1g
Carbohydrate	0.4g
Sugar	0.2g
Fibre	0g
Calcium	287mg

Polenta with Mushroom Sauce

Polenta, made from corn, forms the starchy base for many Italian dishes. Its subtle taste works well with the rich mushroom sauce.

INGREDIENTS

Serves 4

1.2 litres/2 pints/5 cups Vegetable Stock
350g/12oz/3 cups polenta
50g/2oz/⅔ cup freshly grated
  Parmesan cheese
salt and ground black pepper

For the sauce

15g/½oz/1 cup dried
  porcini mushrooms
15ml/1 tbsp olive oil
50g/2oz/¼ cup pure
  vegetable margarine
1 onion, finely chopped
1 carrot, finely chopped
1 celery stick, finely chopped
2 garlic cloves, crushed
450g/1lb/6 cups mixed chestnut
  and large flat mushrooms,
  roughly chopped
120ml/4fl oz/½ cup Vegetable Stock
400g/14oz can chopped tomatoes
15ml/1 tbsp tomato purée
15ml/1 tbsp chopped fresh
  thyme leaves

1 Make the sauce. Put the dried mushrooms in a bowl, add 150ml/¼ pint/⅔ cup hot water and soak for 20 minutes. Drain the mushrooms, reserving the liquid, and chop them roughly.

NUTRITION NOTES	
Per portion:	
Energy	550kcals/2293kJ
Protein	17.2g
Fat	21.3g
saturated fat	7.6g
Carbohydrate	68.4g
Sugar	5g
Fibre	3.1g
Calcium	201mg

2 Heat the oil and margarine in a saucepan and add the onion, carrot, celery and garlic. Cook over a low heat for about 5 minutes until the vegetables are beginning to soften, then raise the heat and add the fresh and soaked dried mushrooms to the pan of vegetables. Cook for 8–10 minutes until the mushrooms are softened and golden.

3 Add the stock and let boil for 2–3 minutes until reduced, then add the tomatoes and mushroom liquid. Stir in the tomato purée, thyme and salt and pepper. Lower the heat and simmer for 20 minutes until thickened.

4 Meanwhile, heat the stock for the polenta in a large heavy saucepan. Add a generous pinch of salt. As soon as it simmers, tip in the polenta in a fine stream, whisking until the mixture is smooth. Cook for 30 minutes, stirring constantly, until the polenta comes away from the pan. Remove from the heat and stir in half the Parmesan and some black pepper.

5 Divide the cooked polenta among four heated bowls and top each serving with the mushroom sauce. Sprinkle with the remaining Parmesan and serve at once.

Spinach with Beans, Raisins and Pine Nuts

This Mediterranean dish is traditionally made with chickpeas, but can be made with haricot beans as here.

INGREDIENTS

Serves 4

115g/4oz/scant ¾ cup haricot beans soaked overnight, or 400g/14oz can, drained
60ml/4 tbsp olive oil
1 thick slice dairy-free white bread
1 onion, chopped
3–4 tomatoes, peeled, seeded and chopped
2.5ml/½ tsp ground cumin
450g/1lb spinach
5ml/1 tsp paprika
1 garlic clove, halved
25g/1oz/3 tbsp raisins
25g/1oz/¼ cup pine nuts, toasted
salt and ground black pepper
dairy- and egg-free bread, to serve

1 Simmer the dried haricot beans in clean water for about 1 hour until tender. Drain.

2 Heat 30ml/2 tbsp of the oil in a frying pan and fry the bread until golden. Transfer to a plate.

3 Fry the onion in a further 15ml/ 1 tbsp of the oil over a gentle heat until soft but not brown, then add the tomatoes and cumin and continue cooking over a gentle heat.

4 Wash the spinach thoroughly, removing any tough stalks. Heat the remaining oil in a large pan, stir in the paprika and then add the spinach and 45ml/3 tbsp water. Cover and cook for a few minutes until the spinach has wilted.

5 Add the onion and tomato mixture to the spinach and stir in the beans, then season with salt and pepper.

6 Place the garlic and fried bread in a food processor and blend until smooth. Stir into the spinach and bean mixture, together with the raisins. Add 175ml/6fl oz/¾ cup water and then cover and simmer very gently for 20–30 minutes, adding more water if necessary.

7 Place the spinach on a warmed serving plate and scatter with toasted pine nuts. Serve hot with bread.

— NUTRITION NOTES —	
Per portion:	
Energy	372kcals/1352kJ
Protein	12.5g
Fat	17.6g
saturated fat	2.4g
Carbohydrate	30.5g
Fibre	9.2g
Sugars	9.5g
Calcium	279mg

Crispy Noodles with Mixed Vegetables

In this dish, rice vermicelli noodles are deep fried until crisp, then tossed into a colourful mixture of stir-fried vegetables.

INGREDIENTS

Serves 4
pure vegetable oil, for deep frying
115g/4oz dried vermicelli rice noodles
  or cellophane noodles, broken into
  7.5cm/3in lengths
115g/4oz yard-long beans or green
  beans, cut into short lengths
2.5cm/1in piece fresh root ginger, cut
  into shreds
1 fresh red chilli, sliced
115g/4oz/1½ cups fresh shiitake or
  button mushrooms, thickly sliced
2 large carrots, cut into fine sticks
2 courgettes, cut into fine sticks
a few Chinese cabbage leaves,
  coarsely shredded
75g/3oz/1 cup beansprouts
4 spring onions, cut into fine shreds
30ml/2 tbsp tamari
30ml/2 tbsp Chinese rice wine
5ml/1 tsp sugar
30ml/2 tbsp roughly torn
  coriander leaves

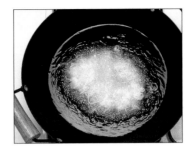

1 Half-fill a wok with oil and heat it to 180°C/350°F. Deep fry the raw noodles, a handful at a time, for 1–2 minutes until puffed and crispy. Drain on kitchen paper. Carefully pour off all but 30ml/2 tbsp of the oil.

2 Reheat the oil in the wok. When hot, add the beans and stir-fry for 2–3 minutes. Add the ginger, red chilli, mushrooms, carrots and courgettes and stir-fry for 1–2 minutes.

3 Add the Chinese cabbage, beansprouts and spring onions to the wok. Stir-fry for 1 minute, then add the tamari, rice wine and sugar. Cook, stirring, for about 30 seconds.

4 Add the noodles and coriander and toss to mix, taking care not to crush the noodles too much. Serve at once, piled up on a plate.

----- COOK'S TIPS -----

If a milder flavour is preferred, remove the seeds from the chilli.

  Tamari is a type of soy sauce that is wheat-free. It is available from Asian shops and some health-food shops.

----- NUTRITION NOTES -----

Per portion:

Energy	184kcals/766kJ
Protein	3.7g
Fat	6.1g
saturated fat	0.9g
Carbohydrate	27.5g
Sugar	3.9g
Fibre	2.2g
Calcium	41mg

Potato Rösti and Tofu with Tomato Sauce

Soya products can play an important role in lowering the risk of cancer. This deliciously flavoursome tofu dish is a natural choice if you want to improve your chances of good health.

INGREDIENTS

Serves 4

425g/15oz/3¾ cups tofu (soya beancurd), cut into 1cm/½in cubes
900g/2lb large potatoes
40g/1½oz/3 tbsp butter, melted
50ml/2fl oz/¼ cup vegetable oil
30ml/2 tbsp sunflower seeds, toasted, to serve
salt and ground black pepper

For the marinade
30ml/2 tbsp tamari
15ml/1 tbsp clear honey
2 garlic cloves, crushed
4 cm/1½in piece fresh root ginger, grated

For the sauce
15ml/1 tbsp olive oil
8 vine-ripened tomatoes, halved, seeded and chopped

1 Mix together all the marinade ingredients in a shallow dish and add the tofu (soya beancurd). Spoon the marinade over the tofu and leave to marinate in the fridge for at least 1 hour. Turn occasionally to allow the marinade to soak into the tofu.

2 To make the rösti, par-boil the potatoes for 10–15 minutes until almost tender. Leave to cool, then grate coarsely. Season, stir in the melted butter and mix well. Heat half the oil in a large, heavy-based frying pan and divide the potato mixture into four equal portions.

3 Take one quarter of the potato mixture in your hands and form into a rough cake.

4 Place in the pan and flatten the mixture, using your hands or a spatula, to form a round about 1cm/½in thick. Cook for about 6 minutes until golden and crisp underneath. To cook the other side, turn over the rösti by sliding a large plate over the pan and flipping it on to the plate. Gently slide the rösti back into the pan and cook for a further 6 minutes until golden. Cook the remaining rösti in the same way, replenishing the oil when necessary and reserving 30ml/2 tbsp. Keep the rösti warm in a low oven.

5 Heat the remaining oil in the frying pan. Using a slotted spoon, remove the tofu from the marinade and reserve. Fry the tofu for 10 minutes, turning occasionally, until golden and crisp on all sides.

6 To make the sauce, heat the oil in a saucepan, add the reserved marinade and the tomatoes and cook for 2 minutes, stirring. Reduce the heat and simmer, covered, for 10 minutes, stirring occasionally, until the tomatoes break down. Press through a sieve to produce a smooth sauce.

7 To serve, place a rösti on each plate. Arrange the tofu on top. Spoon over the tomato sauce and sprinkle with sunflower seeds.

NUTRITION NOTES

Per portion:

Energy	489kcals/2498kJ
Protein	15.2g
Fat	28.7g
saturated fat	7.7g
Carbohydrate	44.9g
Fibre	3.8g
Sugars	5.9g
Calcium	567mg

HEALTH BENEFITS

Tofu, or beancurd, is made from processed soya beans and is one of nature's most nutritious foods. There is now evidence to suggest that soya can help to reduce the risk of cancer.

Stuffed Tomatoes and Peppers

Colourful peppers and tomatoes make perfect containers for various meat and vegetable stuffings. This delicious rice and herb version uses typically Greek ingredients.

INGREDIENTS

Serves 4

2 large ripe tomatoes
1 green pepper
1 yellow or orange pepper
60ml/4 tbsp olive oil, plus extra
   for sprinkling
2 onions, chopped
2 garlic cloves, crushed
50g/2oz/½ cup blanched
   almonds, chopped
75g/3oz/scant ½ cup long grain rice,
   boiled and drained
15g/½oz fresh mint, roughly chopped
15g/½oz fresh parsley, chopped
25g/1oz/2 tbsp sultanas
45ml/3 tbsp ground almonds
ground black pepper
chopped fresh herbs, to garnish

1 Preheat the oven to 190°C/375°F/ Gas 5. Cut the tomatoes in half and scoop out the insides. Drain the halves and roughly chop the insides.

NUTRITION NOTES	
Per portion:	
Energy	340Kcals/1411kJ
Protein	8.1g
Fat	25g
saturated fat	2.65g
Carbohydrate	22g
Fibre	5.1g
Sodium	19mg

2 Halve the peppers, leaving the cores intact. Scoop out the seeds and white pith. Brush the peppers with 15ml/1 tbsp of the oil and bake on a baking tray for 15 minutes. Place the peppers and tomatoes in an oven-proof dish and season with pepper.

3 Fry the onions in the remaining oil for 5 minutes. Add the garlic and chopped almonds and fry for 1 minute more.

4 Remove the pan from the heat and stir in the rice, chopped tomatoes, mint, parsley and sultanas. Season well with pepper and spoon the mixture into the tomato and pepper halves.

5 Pour 150ml/¼ pint/⅔ cup boiling water around the tomatoes and peppers and bake, uncovered, for 20 minutes. Scatter with the ground almonds and sprinkle with a little extra olive oil. Return to the oven and bake for a further 20 minutes, or until turning golden. Serve garnished with chopped fresh herbs.

Spiced Tofu Stir-fry

You could add any quickly cooked vegetable to this stir-fry – try mangetouts, sugar snap peas, leeks or thin slices of carrot. The lime juice and honey add flavour in place of high-salt sauces.

INGREDIENTS

Serves 4

10ml/2 tsp ground cumin
15ml/1 tbsp paprika
5ml/1 tsp ground ginger
a good pinch of cayenne pepper
15ml/1 tbsp caster sugar
275g/10oz firm tofu (beancurd)
60ml/4 tbsp oil
2 garlic cloves, crushed
1 bunch spring onions, sliced
1 red pepper, seeded and sliced
1 yellow pepper, seeded and sliced
225g/8oz/generous 3 cups brown-cap
    mushrooms, halved or quartered
    if necessary
1 large courgette, sliced
115g/4oz fine green beans, halved
50g/2oz/scant ½ cup pine nuts
15ml/1 tbsp lime juice
15ml/1 tbsp clear honey
ground black pepper

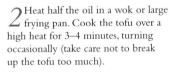

1 Mix together the cumin, paprika, ginger, cayenne and sugar with plenty of black pepper. Cut the tofu into cubes and toss them gently in the spice mixture to coat.

2 Heat half the oil in a wok or large frying pan. Cook the tofu over a high heat for 3–4 minutes, turning occasionally (take care not to break up the tofu too much).

3 Remove with a slotted spoon and set aside. Wipe out the pan with kitchen paper.

4 Add the remaining oil to the pan and cook the garlic and spring onions for 3 minutes. Add the remaining vegetables and cook over a medium heat for 6 minutes, or until beginning to soften and turn golden. Season well.

5 Return the tofu to the pan with the pine nuts, lime juice and honey. Heat through thoroughly and serve immediately.

— NUTRITION NOTES —	
Per portion:	
Energy	339Kcals/1406kJ
Protein	11.8g
Fat	24.4g
Saturated fat	2.79g
Carbohydrate	19g
Fibre	3.5g
Sodium	17mg

FREE FROM

Almost-dry Roasted Vegetables

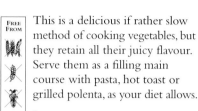

This is a delicious if rather slow method of cooking vegetables, but they retain all their juicy flavour. Serve them as a filling main course with pasta, hot toast or grilled polenta, as your diet allows.

INGREDIENTS

Serves 4
1 aubergine
2 courgettes
1 yellow pepper
1 red pepper
4 garlic cloves
1 sweet red onion
1 small fennel bulb
20 asparagus spears
10 fresh basil leaves, roughly torn
45ml/3 tbsp extra virgin olive oil
15ml/1 tbsp balsamic vinegar
salt and ground black pepper
sprigs of basil, to garnish

1 Preheat the oven to 240°C/ 475°F/Gas 9. Cut the aubergine and courgettes into 1cm/½in slices. Halve the peppers, discard the seeds and core, then cut them into chunks.

2 Finely chop the garlic and cut the onion into eight wedges.

3 Remove the root from the fennel and slice into 2.5cm/1in strips. Peel off any woody parts of the stems of the asparagus.

4 Place all the vegetables in a bowl, add the basil, then stir in the olive oil. Season with salt and pepper and mix together well.

5 Tip the vegetables into a shallow roasting dish and roast in the oven for 30–40 minutes until all the vegetables are brown on the edges. Leave to cool, then sprinkle with the balsamic vinegar and serve garnished with the sprigs of basil.

--- NUTRITION NOTES ---

Per portion:
Energy	153Kcals/634kJ
Protein	5.4g
Fat	9.6g
saturated fat	1.2g
Carbohydrate	0.0g
Fibre	5.7g
Sugar	10.2g
Sodium	0.11g

--- COOK'S TIP ---

Aubergines can soak up oil quite quickly so check on the vegetables during the cooking time.

Red Pepper Risotto

The character of this delicious risotto depends on the type of rice you use. With arborio rice, the risotto should be moist and creamy. If you use brown rice, reduce the amount of liquid for a drier dish with a nutty flavour.

INGREDIENTS

Serves 6
3 large red peppers
30ml/2 tbsp olive oil
3 large garlic cloves, thinly sliced
1½ x 400g/14oz cans chopped tomatoes
2 bay leaves
1.2–1.5 litres/2–2½ pints/5–6¼ cups
   Vegetable Stock
450g/1lb/2½ cups arborio rice (Italian
   risotto rice) or brown rice
6 fresh basil leaves, snipped
salt and ground black pepper

1 Preheat the grill. Put the peppers in a grill pan and grill until the skins are blackened and blistered all over. Put them in a bowl, cover with several layers of damp kitchen paper and leave for 10 minutes. Peel off the skins, then slice the peppers, discarding the core and seeds.

2 Heat 30ml/2 tbsp of the oil in a wide, shallow pan. Add the garlic and tomatoes and cook over a gentle heat for 5 minutes, then add the pepper slices and bay leaves. Stir well and cook for 15 minutes more.

3 Pour the stock into a saucepan and heat it to simmering point. Stir the rice into the vegetable mixture and cook for 2 minutes, then add two or three ladlefuls of the hot stock. Cook, stirring occasionally, until the stock has been absorbed.

4 Continue to add stock in this way, making sure each addition has been absorbed before pouring in the next. When the rice is tender, season with salt and pepper to taste. Remove the pan from the heat, cover and leave to stand for 10 minutes before stirring in the basil and serving.

NUTRITION NOTES

Per portion:

Energy	387kcals/1635kJ
Fat, total	10.75g
saturated fat	1.73g
polyunsaturated fat	1.3g
monounsaturated fat	6.3g
Carbohydrate	69.2g
sugar, total	7.85g
starch	60.85g
Fibre	3.2g
Sodium	645mg

Stir-fried Vegetables with Cashew Nuts

Stir-frying is the perfect way of making a delicious, colourful – and very speedy meal.

INGREDIENTS

Serves 4

900g/2lb mixed vegetables (see Cook's Tip)
30–60ml/2–4 tbsp sunflower or olive oil
2 garlic cloves, crushed
15ml/1 tbsp grated fresh root ginger
50g/2oz/½ cup cashew nuts or 60ml/4 tbsp sunflower seeds, pumpkin seeds or sesame seeds
soy sauce
salt and ground black pepper

1 Prepare the vegetables according to type. Carrots and cucumber should be cut into very fine matchsticks.

2 Heat a frying pan, then trickle the oil around the rim so that it runs down to coat the surface. When it is hot, add the garlic and ginger and cook for 2–3 minutes, stirring. Add the harder vegetables and toss over the heat for 5 minutes until they start to soften.

3 Add the softer vegetables and stir-fry all of them over a high heat for about 3–4 minutes.

<hr>

COOK'S TIP

Use a pack of stir-fry vegetables or make up your own mixture. Choose from carrots, mangetouts, baby sweetcorn, pak choi, cucumber, beansprouts, mushrooms, peppers and spring onions. Drained canned bamboo shoots and water chestnuts are delicious additions.

4 Stir in the cashew nuts or seeds. Season with soy sauce, salt and pepper to taste. Serve at once.

NUTRITION NOTES

Per portion:	
Energy	288kcals/796kJ
Fat, total	21.3g
saturated fat	2.4g
polyunsaturated fat	8.3g
monounsaturated fat	9.3g
Carbohydrate	15.76g
sugar, total	9g
starch	5.2g
Fibre	5g
Sodium	170mg

Mixed Vegetables Monk-style

Chinese monks eat neither meat nor fish, so "Monk-style" dishes are fine for vegetarians.

INGREDIENTS

Serves 4

50g/2oz dried beancurd sticks
115g/4oz fresh lotus root, or 50g/ 2oz dried
10g/¼oz dried wood ears
8 dried Chinese mushrooms
15ml/1 tbsp vegetable oil
75g/3oz/¾ cup drained, canned straw mushrooms
115g/4oz/1 cup baby corn cobs, cut in half
30ml/2 tbsp light soy sauce
15ml/1 tbsp dry sherry
10ml/2 tsp caster sugar
150ml/¼ pint/⅔ cup vegetable stock
75g/3oz/¾ cup mangetouts, trimmed and cut in half
5ml/1 tsp cornflour
15ml/1 tbsp cold water
salt, to taste

1 Put the beancurd sticks in a bowl. Cover with hot water and leave to soak for 1 hour. If using fresh lotus root, peel it and slice it; if using dried lotus root, place it in a bowl of hot water and leave to soak for 1 hour.

COOK'S TIP

The flavour of this tasty vegetable mix improves on keeping, so any leftovers would taste even better on the next day.

2 Prepare the wood ears and dried Chinese mushrooms by soaking them in separate bowls of hot water for 15 minutes. Drain the wood ears, trim off and discard the hard base from each and cut the rest into bite-size pieces. Drain the soaked mushrooms, trim off and discard the stems and chop the caps roughly.

3 Drain the beancurd sticks. Cut them into 5cm/2in long pieces, discarding any hard pieces. If using dried lotus root, drain well.

4 Heat the oil in a non-stick frying pan or wok. Stir-fry the wood ears, Chinese mushrooms and lotus root for about 30 seconds.

5 Add the pieces of beancurd sticks, straw mushrooms, baby corn cobs, soy sauce, sherry, caster sugar and stock. Bring to the boil, then cover the pan or wok, lower the heat and simmer for about 20 minutes.

6 Stir in the mangetouts, with salt to taste and cook, uncovered, for 2 minutes more. Mix the cornflour to a paste with the water. Add to the pan or wok. Cook, stirring, until the sauce thickens. Serve at once.

NUTRITION NOTES

Per portion:

Energy	118Kcals/493kJ
Protein	4.7g
Fat	3.8g
saturated fat	0.4g
Carbohydrate	15.9g
Fibre	1.3g
Sugar	9.3g
Sodium	0.67g

Braised Tofu with Mushrooms

FREE FROM

The mushrooms flavour the tofu beautifully to make this the perfect vegetarian main course.

INGREDIENTS

Serves 4

350g/12oz tofu (soya beancurd)
2.5ml/½ tsp sesame oil
10ml/2 tsp light soy sauce
15ml/1 tbsp vegetable oil
2 garlic cloves, finely chopped
2.5ml/½ tsp grated fresh root ginger
115g/4oz/1 cup fresh shiitake
  mushrooms, stalks removed
175g/6oz/1½ cups fresh
  oyster mushrooms
115g/4oz/1 cup drained, canned
  straw mushrooms
115g/4oz/1 cup button mushrooms,
  cut in half
15ml/1 tbsp dry sherry
15ml/1 tbsp dark soy sauce
90ml/6 tbsp vegetable stock
5ml/1 tsp cornflour
15ml/1 tbsp cold water
salt and freshly ground white pepper
2 spring onions, shredded

1 Put the tofu (soya beancurd) in a dish and sprinkle with the sesame oil, light soy sauce and a large pinch of pepper. Leave to marinate for 10 minutes, then drain the curd and cut into 2.5 x 1cm/1 x ½in pieces.

2 Heat the vegetable oil in a non-stick frying pan or wok. When it is very hot, fry the garlic and ginger for a few seconds. Add all the mushrooms and stir-fry for 2 minutes.

3 Stir in the sherry, dark soy sauce and stock, with salt, if needed, and pepper. Simmer for 4 minutes.

4 Mix the cornflour to a paste with the water. Stir the mixture into the wok and cook, stirring, until thickened.

5 Carefully add the pieces of tofu, toss gently to coat thoroughly and simmer for 2 minutes.

6 Scatter the shredded spring onions over the top of the mixture, transfer to a serving dish and serve.

COOK'S TIP

If fresh shiitake mushrooms are not available, use dried Chinese mushrooms soaked in hot water.

NUTRITION NOTES

Per portion:

Energy	122Kcals/510kJ
Protein	9.5g
Fat	7.4g
saturated fat	1.0g
Carbohydrate	3.6g
Fibre	1.2g
Sugar	0.3g
Sodium	0.63g

Red Cabbage and Apple Casserole

The brilliant colour and pungent flavour make this an excellent winter dish. Serve it solo, with wheat- and egg-free bread, or as a vegetable accompaniment.

INGREDIENTS

Serves 6
3 onions, chopped
2 fennel bulbs, roughly chopped
675g/1½lb red cabbage, shredded
30ml/2 tbsp caraway seeds
3 large tart eating apples or 1 large cooking apple
6 rindless streaky bacon rashers (optional)
300ml/½ pint/1¼ cups low-fat natural yogurt
15ml/1 tbsp creamed horseradish sauce
salt and ground black pepper

1 Preheat the oven to 150°C/300°F/ Gas 2. Mix the onions, fennel, red cabbage and caraway seeds in a bowl. Peel and chop the apples and the bacon rashers, if using, then stir them into the cabbage mixture. Transfer to a casserole. Mix the yogurt with the creamed horseradish sauce.

2 Stir the yogurt and horseradish mixture into the casserole, season with salt and pepper and cover tightly. Bake for 1½ hours, stirring once or twice. Serve hot.

——— NUTRITION NOTES ———	
Per portion (with bacon):	
Energy	158kcals/660kJ
Fat, total	9.7g
saturated fat	3.4g
polyunsaturated fat	1.4g
monounsaturated fat	4.05g
Carbohydrate	12.8g
sugar, total	11.6g
starch	0.2g
Fibre	4g
Sodium	378mg

Mixed Vegetables with Artichokes

Baking a vegetable medley in the oven is a wonderfully easy way of producing a quick and simple, wholesome mid-week meal.

INGREDIENTS

Serves 4
30ml/2 tbsp olive oil
675g/1½lb frozen broad beans
4 turnips, peeled and sliced
4 leeks, sliced
1 red pepper, seeded and sliced
200g/7oz fresh spinach leaves or 115g/4oz frozen spinach
2 x 400g/14oz cans artichoke hearts, drained
60ml/4 tbsp pumpkin seeds
soy sauce
salt and ground black pepper
rice, baked potatoes or wholemeal bread, to serve

1 Preheat the oven to 180°C/350°F/ Gas 4. Pour the oil into a casserole. Cook the broad beans in a saucepan of boiling lightly salted water for about 10 minutes. Drain the beans and place them with the turnips, leeks, red pepper slices, spinach and canned artichoke hearts in the casserole.

2 Cover the casserole and bake the vegetables for 30–40 minutes, or until the turnips are soft.

3 Stir in the pumpkin seeds and soy sauce to taste. Season with ground black pepper. Serve solo or with rice sprinkled with chopped fresh herbs, baked potatoes or bread.

——— NUTRITION NOTES ———	
Per portion:	
Energy	335kcals/1410kJ
Fat, total	13.4g
saturated fat	2.2g
polyunsaturated fat	3.3g
monounsaturated fat	6.5g
Carbohydrate	34.95g
sugar, total	11.4g
starch	19.4g
Fibre	16.3g
Sodium	151.5mg

Purée of Lentils with Baked Eggs

This unusual dish makes an excellent vegetarian supper. If you prefer, bake the purée and eggs in one large baking dish.

INGREDIENTS

Serves 6

450g/1lb/2 cups red lentils
3 leeks, thinly sliced
10ml/2 tsp coriander seeds,
   finely crushed
15ml/1 tbsp chopped fresh coriander
30ml/2 tbsp chopped fresh mint
15ml/1 tbsp red wine vinegar
1 litre/1³/₄ pints/4 cups Vegetable Stock
4 eggs
salt and ground black pepper
generous handful of fresh
   parsley, chopped, to garnish

1 Put the lentils in a deep saucepan. Add the leeks, coriander seeds, fresh coriander, mint, vinegar and stock. Bring to the boil, then lower the heat and simmer for 30–40 minutes or until the lentils are cooked and have absorbed all the liquid.

2 Preheat the oven to 180°C/350°F/ Gas 4. Season the lentils with salt and pepper and mix well. Spread out in four lightly greased baking dishes.

3 Using the back of a spoon, make a hollow in the lentil mixture in each dish. Break an egg into each hollow. Cover the dishes with foil and bake for 15–20 minutes or until the eggs are set. Sprinkle with plenty of chopped parsley and serve at once.

NUTRITION NOTES	
Per portion:	
Energy	470kcals/1985kJ
Fat, total	9.1g
saturated fat	2.2g
polyunsaturated fat	1.5g
monounsaturated fat	3.38g
Carbohydrate	65.8g
sugar, total	4.2g
starch	57.5g
Fibre	6.95g
Sodium	423.75mg

VARIATION
Tip a 400g/14oz can of unsweetened chestnut purée into a bowl and beat it until softened. Stir the purée into the lentil mixture, with extra stock if required. Proceed as in the main recipe.

Mushroom and Sunflower Seed Flan

Mushrooms, baby corn and spinach make a delectable filling for a flan, especially when sunflower seeds are included.

INGREDIENTS

Serves 6

175g/6oz/1½ cups wholemeal flour
75g/3oz/6 tbsp dairy-free spread
45ml/3 tbsp olive oil
175g/6oz baby corn, each cut into
  2–3 pieces
30ml/2 tbsp sunflower seeds
225g/8oz/2 cups mushrooms
75g/3oz fresh spinach leaves,
  chopped
juice of 1 lemon
salt and ground black pepper
tomato salad, to serve

1 Preheat the oven to 180°C/350°F/ Gas 4. Sift the flour into a bowl, then add the bran from the sieve. Rub in the low-fat spread until the mixture resembles breadcrumbs. Add enough water to make a firm dough.

2 Roll out the dough on a lightly floured surface and line a 23cm/9in flan dish. Prick the base, line the flan case with foil and add a layer of baking beans. Bake blind for 15 minutes, then remove the foil and beans. Return the pastry case to the oven and bake for a further 10 minutes, or until the pastry is crisp and golden brown.

— NUTRITION NOTES —	
Per portion:	
Energy	250kcals/1045kJ
Fat, total	16g
saturated fat	2.8g
polyunsaturated fat	3.85g
monounsaturated fat	8.25g
Carbohydrate	20.6g
sugar, total	1.45g
starch	19.1g
Fibre	4.05g
Sodium	434.5mg

3 Meanwhile, heat the oil in a heavy-based pan. Fry the corn with the sunflower seeds for 5–8 minutes until lightly browned all over.

— COOK'S TIP —

If the mushrooms are small, leave them whole or cut them in half or quarters.

4 Add the button mushrooms, lower the heat slightly and cook the mixture for 2–3 minutes, then stir in the chopped spinach. Cover the pan and cook for 2–3 minutes.

5 Sharpen the filling with a little lemon juice. Stir in salt and pepper to taste. Spoon into the flan case. Serve warm or cold with a tomato salad.

Wholemeal Pasta with Caraway Cabbage

FREE FROM

Crunchy cabbage and Brussels sprouts are the perfect partners for pasta in this healthy dish.

INGREDIENTS

Serves 6

90ml/6 tbsp olive or sunflower oil
3 onions, roughly chopped
350g/12oz round white cabbage, roughly chopped
350g/12oz Brussels sprouts, trimmed and halved
10ml/2 tsp caraway seeds
15ml/1 tbsp chopped fresh dill
400ml/14fl oz/1²/₃ cups Vegetable Stock
200g/7oz/1³/₄ cups fresh or dried wholewheat pasta spirals
salt and ground black pepper
dill sprigs, to garnish

1 Heat the oil in a large saucepan and fry the onions over a low heat for 10 minutes until softened.

2 Add the cabbage and Brussels sprouts and cook for 2–3 minutes, then stir in the caraway seeds and dill. Pour in the stock and season with salt and pepper to taste. Cover and simmer for 5–10 minutes until the cabbage and sprouts are crisp-tender.

───── COOK'S TIP ─────

If tiny baby Brussels sprouts are available they can be used whole for this dish.

3 Meanwhile, cook the pasta in a pan of lightly salted boiling water, following the package instructions, until just tender.

4 Drain the pasta, tip it into a bowl and add the cabbage mixture. Toss lightly, adjust the seasoning and serve.

───── NUTRITION NOTES ─────

Per portion:
Energy	227kcals/953kJ
Fat, total	9.6g
saturated fat	1.4g
polyunsaturated fat	1.5g
monounsaturated fat	5.75g
Carbohydrate	30g
sugar, total	7.65g
starch	21.6g
Fibre	6.9g
Sodium	53.5mg

Cauliflower and Broccoli with Tomato Sauce

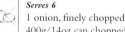

FREE FROM

A low-fat alternative to that old favourite, cauliflower cheese. The addition of broccoli to the cauliflower gives extra colour.

INGREDIENTS

Serves 6

1 onion, finely chopped
400g/14oz can chopped tomatoes
45ml/3 tbsp tomato purée
45ml/3 tbsp wholemeal flour
300ml/½ pint/1¼ cups skimmed milk
300ml/½ pint/1¼ cups water
1kg/2¼lb/6 cups mixed cauliflower and broccoli florets
salt and ground black pepper

1 Mix the onion, tomatoes and tomato purée in a small saucepan. Bring to the boil, lower the heat and simmer for 15–20 minutes.

2 Mix the flour to a paste with a little of the milk. Stir the paste into the tomato mixture, then gradually add the remaining milk and the water. Stir constantly until the mixture boils and thickens. Season to taste with salt and pepper. Keep the sauce hot.

3 Steam the cauliflower (or mixture of cauliflower and broccoli) over boiling water for 5–7 minutes or until the florets are just tender. Tip into a dish, pour over the tomato sauce and serve with extra pepper sprinkled over the top, if liked.

───── NUTRITION NOTES ─────

Per portion:
Energy	116kcals/491kJ
Fat, total	1.85g
saturated fat	0.4g
polyunsaturated fat	0.9g
monounsaturated fat	0.2g
Carbohydrate	16.1g
sugar, total	10.3g
starch	5.4g
Fibre	4.5g
Sodium	86.8mg

PIZZA AND PASTA

The Mediterranean diet, which is rich in fresh fruit and vegetables, is believed to promote good health and protect against illness. These recipes draw on the traditional dishes of Italy, pizza and pasta, using wholesome and nutritious ingredients to make wonderful healthy dishes. Enjoy Peperonata Pizza, rich with the Mediterranean flavours of red and yellow peppers, or try one of the many pasta dishes, such as creamy Penne with Chicken, Broccoli and Cheese.

Chilli, Tomato and Olive Pasta

FREE FROM

The sauce for this pasta packs a punch, thanks to the robust flavours of red chillies, anchovies and capers.

INGREDIENTS

Serves 4

45ml/3 tbsp olive oil
2 garlic cloves, crushed
2 fresh red chillies, seeded and chopped
6 drained canned anchovy fillets
675g/1½lb ripe tomatoes, peeled, seeded and chopped
2 tbsp sun-dried tomato purée
2 tbsp drained capers
115g/4oz/1 cup pitted black olives, roughly chopped
350g/12oz/3 cups egg-free penne
salt and ground black pepper
chopped fresh basil, to garnish

1 Heat the oil in a saucepan and gently fry the garlic and chilli for 2–3 minutes. Add the anchovies, mashing them with a fork, then stir in the tomatoes, sun-dried tomato purée, capers and olives. Add salt and pepper to taste. Simmer gently, uncovered, for 20 minutes, stirring occasionally.

2 Meanwhile, bring a large pan of lightly salted water to the boil and cook the penne according to the instructions on the packet, or until *al dente*. Drain the pasta well and immediately stir into the sauce. Mix thoroughly, tip into a heated serving dish, garnish with chopped fresh basil and serve at once.

— NUTRITION NOTES —	
Per portion:	
Energy	482kcals/2036kJ
Protein	16.4g
Fat	15.7g
saturated fat	1.9g
Carbohydrate	73g
Fibre	5.5g
Sugars	8.4g
Calcium	100mg

Spaghettini with Garlic and Olive Oil

FREE FROM

Fresh chilli adds a fiery touch to this simple Italian pasta dish. The cheese that is scattered over the top isn't essential, but adds a delicious salty tang. Use a hard sheep's milk cheese such as Pecorino if you're only allergic to cow's milk, or substitute a soya-based Parmesan cheese.

INGREDIENTS

Serves 4

350g/12oz egg-free spaghettini
75ml/5 tbsp extra virgin olive oil
3 garlic cloves, finely chopped
1 fresh red chilli, seeded and chopped
75g/3oz/1½ cups drained sun-dried tomatoes in oil, chopped
30ml/2 tbsp chopped fresh parsley
salt and ground black pepper
freshly grated Pecorino cheese, to serve

1 Bring a large saucepan of lightly salted water to the boil. Add the pasta and cook according to the instructions on the packet until *al dente*.

2 Towards the end of the cooking time, heat the oil in a second large pan. Add the garlic and chilli and cook gently for 2–3 minutes. Stir in the tomatoes and remove from the heat.

3 Drain the pasta thoroughly and add it to the hot oil.

4 Return the pan to the heat and cook for 2–3 minutes, tossing the pasta to coat the strands in the sauce. Season with salt and pepper, stir in the parsley and transfer to a warmed serving bowl. Scatter with grated Pecorino cheese and serve.

— NUTRITION NOTES —	
Per portion:	
Energy	554kcals/2325kJ
Protein	11.5g
Fat	28.1g
saturated fat	3.9g
Carbohydrate	68g
Fibre	3.1g
Sugars	2.5g
Calcium	38mg

Vegetable and Egg Noodle Ribbons

FREE FROM

Serve this elegant, colourful dish with stir-fried broccoli and some crusty bread as a light lunch or as a starter for six to eight people.

INGREDIENTS

Serves 4

1 large carrot, peeled
2 courgettes
50g/2oz soya margarine
15ml/1 tbsp olive oil
6 fresh shiitake mushrooms,
    finely sliced
50g/2oz frozen peas, thawed
350g/12oz broad egg ribbon noodles
10ml/2 tsp chopped mixed herbs, such
    as marjoram, chives and basil
salt and ground black pepper

1 Using a vegetable peeler, carefully slice thin strips from the carrot and from the courgettes.

2 Heat the soya margarine with the olive oil in a large frying pan. Stir in the carrot and shiitake mushrooms; fry for 2 minutes. Add the courgettes and peas and stir-fry until the courgettes are cooked, but still crisp. Season with salt and pepper.

3 Meanwhile, cook the noodles in a large saucepan of boiling water until just tender. Drain the noodles well and tip them into a bowl. Add the vegetables and toss to mix.

4 Sprinkle over the fresh herbs and season to taste. Serve at once.

NUTRITION NOTES	
Per portion:	
Energy	475kcals/2001kJ
Protein	12g
Fat	18.7g
saturated fat	7.3g
Carbohydrate	68.8g
Fibre	3.8g
Sugars	4.2g
Calcium	46mg

Pork Meatballs with Pasta

These tasty meatballs are delicious served on a bed of freshly cooked gluten-free pasta.

INGREDIENTS

Serves 6

450g/1lb lean minced pork
1 leek, finely chopped
115g/4oz mushrooms, finely chopped
15ml/1 tbsp chopped fresh thyme
15ml/1 tbsp tomato purée
1 egg, beaten
30ml/2 tbsp potato flour
15ml/1 tbsp sunflower oil
350–500g/12oz–1¼lb gluten- and
  egg-free pasta
fresh thyme sprigs, to garnish

For the tomato sauce

1 onion, finely chopped
1 carrot, finely chopped
1 celery stick, finely chopped
1 garlic clove, crushed
675g/1½lb ripe tomatoes, skinned,
  seeded and chopped
150ml/¼ pint/⅔ cup dry white wine
150ml/¼ pint/⅔ cup well-flavoured
  Vegetable Stock
15ml/1 tbsp tomato purée
15ml/1 tbsp chopped fresh basil
salt and ground black pepper

FREE
FROM

1 Preheat the oven to 180°C/350°F/ Gas 4. To make the meatballs, put the pork, leek, mushrooms, chopped thyme, tomato purée, egg and potato flour in a bowl and stir together until thoroughly mixed. Shape into small balls, place on a plate, cover and chill while making the tomato sauce.

2 Place all the sauce ingredients in a small saucepan, season to taste, then bring to the boil. Boil, uncovered, for 10 minutes until thickened.

3 Heat the oil in a frying pan, add the meatballs and cook in batches until lightly browned. Place them in a shallow, ovenproof dish and pour the tomato sauce over. Cover and bake for about 1 hour until cooked through.

4 Meanwhile, cook the pasta in a pan of lightly salted, boiling water for 8–12 minutes, or according to the packet instructions until *al dente*. Rinse under boiling water and then drain.

5 Spoon the cooked pasta into warmed bowls, spoon the meatballs and sauce over the top and serve garnished with fresh thyme sprigs.

——— NUTRITION NOTES ———	
Per portion:	
Energy	504kcals/2113kJ
Fat, total	8.8g
saturated fat	2.2g
Protein	26.5g
Carbohydrate	76.4g
sugar, total	6.9g
Fibre	2.5g
Sodium	295mg

Spinach and Hazelnut Lasagne

FREE
FROM

A vegetarian dish which is hearty enough to satisfy meat-eaters too. Use frozen spinach if you're short of time.

INGREDIENTS

Serves 4
900g/2lb fresh spinach
300ml/½ pint/1¼ cups vegetable or
  chicken stock
1 medium onion, finely chopped
1 garlic clove, crushed
75g/3oz/¾ cup hazelnuts
30ml/2 tbsp chopped fresh basil
6 sheets no pre-cook egg-free lasagne
400g/14oz can chopped tomatoes
200g/7oz/1 cup low-fat fromage frais
flaked hazelnuts and chopped parsley,
  to garnish

1 Preheat the oven to 200°C/400°F/ Gas 6. Wash the spinach and place in a pan with just the water that clings to the leaves. Cook the spinach on a fairly high heat for 2 minutes until wilted. Drain well.

2 Heat 30ml/2 tbsp of the stock in a large pan and simmer the onion and garlic until soft. Stir in the spinach, hazelnuts and basil.

3 In a large ovenproof dish, layer the spinach, lasagne and tomatoes. Season well between the layers. Pour over the remaining stock. Spread the fromage frais over the top.

4 Bake the lasagne for 45 minutes, or until golden brown. Serve hot, sprinkled with rows of flaked hazelnuts and chopped parsley.

--- COOK'S TIP ---

The flavour of hazelnuts is improved by roasting. Spread them out on a baking sheet and bake in a moderate oven at 180°C/ 350°F/Gas 4 or toast under a hot grill, until light golden.

--- NUTRITION NOTES ---

Per portion:

Energy	365Kcals/1532kJ
Fat	17g
saturated fat	1.46g
Cholesterol	0.5mg
Fibre	8.16g

Tagliatelle with Pea and Bean Sauce

A creamy pea sauce makes a wonderful combination with the crunchy young vegetables.

INGREDIENTS

Serves 4

15ml/1 tbsp olive oil
1 garlic clove, crushed
6 spring onions, sliced
115g/4oz/1 cup fresh or frozen baby
  peas, thawed
350g/12oz fresh young asparagus
30ml/2 tbsp chopped fresh sage, plus
  extra leaves, to garnish
finely grated rind of 2 lemons
400ml/14fl oz/1⅔ cups vegetable stock
  or water
225g/8oz/1½ cups fresh or frozen
  broad beans, thawed
450g/1lb egg-free tagliatelle
60ml/4 tbsp natural live yogurt

FREE FROM

——— NUTRITION NOTES ———	
Per portion:	
Energy	509Kcals/2139kJ
Fat	6.75g
saturated fat	0.95g
Cholesterol	0.6mg
Fibre	9.75g

1 Heat the oil and sauté the garlic and spring onions for 2–3 minutes.

2 Add the peas and one-third of the asparagus, together with the sage, lemon rind and vegetable stock or water. Simmer for about 10 minutes. Process in a food processor or blender until smooth.

3 Meanwhile, remove the outer skins from the broad beans and discard.

4 Cut the remaining asparagus into 5cm/2in lengths, trimming off any tough fibrous stems. Blanch the asparagus pieces in boiling water for about 2 minutes. Drain, refresh under cold water, drain again and set aside until required.

5 Cook the tagliatelle following the manufacturer's instructions until *al dente*. Drain well.

6 Add the cooked asparagus and shelled beans to the sauce and reheat. Stir in the yogurt and toss into the tagliatelle. Garnish with a few extra sage leaves and serve immediately.

——— COOK'S TIP ———
Frozen peas and beans have been suggested as an option in this recipe to cut down the preparation time, but the dish tastes even better if you use fresh young vegetables when in season.

Pasta with Passata and Chick-peas

INGREDIENTS

Serves 6

5ml/1 tsp olive oil
1 small onion, finely chopped
1 garlic clove, crushed
1 celery stick, finely chopped
425g/15oz can chick-peas, drained
250ml/8fl oz/1 cup passata
300g/10oz/2 cups egg-free pasta
salt and ground black pepper
chopped fresh parsley, to garnish

1 Heat the olive oil in a non-stick pan and fry the onion, garlic and celery until softened but not browned. Stir in the chick-peas and passata, cover and simmer for about 15 minutes.

2 Cook the pasta in a large pan of boiling, lightly salted water until just tender. Drain the pasta and add to the sauce. Toss thoroughly using two large forks, then season to taste with salt and pepper. Sprinkle with chopped fresh parsley, then serve hot.

NUTRITION NOTES

Per portion:

Energy	374Kcals/1570kJ
Fat	4.44g
saturated fat	0.32g
Cholesterol	0mg
Fibre	6.41g

Peperonata Pizza

INGREDIENTS

Makes 2 large pizzas

450g/1lb/4 cups plain flour
pinch of salt
1 sachet easy-blend yeast
about 350ml/12fl oz/1½ cups
    warm water

For the topping

1 onion, sliced
10ml/2 tsp olive oil
2 large red and 2 yellow peppers,
    seeded and sliced
1 garlic clove, crushed
400g/14oz can tomatoes
8 pitted black olives, halved
salt and ground black pepper

NUTRITION NOTES

Per portion:

Energy	965Kcals/4052kJ
Fat	9.04g
saturated fat	1.07g
Cholesterol	0mg
Fibre	14.51g

1 To make the dough, sift the flour and salt into a bowl and stir in the yeast. Stir in just enough warm water to mix to a soft dough.

2 Knead for 5 minutes, until smooth. Cover and leave in a warm place for 1 hour, or until doubled in size.

3 To make the topping, fry the onion in the oil until soft, then stir in the peppers, garlic and tomatoes. Cover and simmer for 30 minutes, until no free liquid remains. Season to taste.

4 Preheat the oven to 230°C/450°F/ Gas 8. Divide the dough in half and press out each piece on a lightly oiled baking sheet to a 28cm/11in round, turning up the edges slightly.

5 Spread over the topping, dot with olives and bake for 15–20 minutes. Serve hot or cold with salad.

Pizza with Fresh Vegetables

This pizza can be made with any combination of fresh vegetables.

INGREDIENTS

Serves 4

400g/14oz peeled plum tomatoes, fresh or canned, weighed whole, without extra juice
2 medium broccoli spears
225g/8oz asparagus
3 small courgettes
75ml/5 tbsp olive oil
50g/2oz/⅓ cup shelled peas, fresh or frozen
4 spring onions. sliced
1 quantity basic pizza dough, rolled out into 4 x 13cm/5in roundels
75g/3oz/¾ cup mozzarella cheese, cut into small dice
10 fresh basil leaves, torn into pieces
2 garlic cloves, finely chopped
ground black pepper

1 Preheat the oven to 240°C/475°F/ Gas 9 for at least 20 minutes before baking the pizza. Strain the tomatoes through the medium holes of a food mill placed over a bowl, scraping in all the pulp.

2 With a sharp knife, peel the broccoli stems and asparagus and blanch with the courgettes in a large pan of boiling water for 4–5 minutes. Drain. Cut into bite-size pieces.

3 Heat 30ml/2 tbsp of the olive oil in a small pan. Stir in the peas and spring onions and cook for about 5–6 minutes, stirring frequently. Remove from the heat.

4 Spread the puréed tomatoes all over the pizza dough, leaving just the rim uncovered. Add the other vegetables, arranging them evenly on top of the tomatoes.

5 Sprinkle with the mozzarella, basil, garlic and pepper, and the remaining olive oil. Immediately place the pizza in the oven. Bake for about 20 minutes, or until the crust is golden brown and the cheese has melted.

NUTRITION NOTES	
Per portion:	
Energy	424Kcals/1770kJ
Protein	17.2g
Fat	22.6g
saturated fat	5.05g
Carbohydrate	40g
Fibre	6.3g
Sodium	134mg

Tagliatelle with Milanese Sauce

Serve this with a green salad for a substantial, healthy supper.

INGREDIENTS

Serves 4

1 onion, finely chopped
1 celery stick, finely chopped
1 red pepper, seeded and diced
1–2 garlic cloves, crushed
150ml/¼ pint/⅔ cup homemade
  vegetable stock
400g/14oz can tomatoes
15ml/1 tbsp concentrated
  tomato purée
10ml/2 tsp caster sugar
5ml/1 tsp dried mixed herbs
350g/12oz egg-free tagliatelle
115g/4oz/1½ cups button
  mushrooms, sliced
60ml/4 tbsp white wine
115g/4oz lean cooked ham, diced
ground black pepper
chopped fresh parsley, to garnish

FREE
FROM

1 Put the onion, celery, red pepper and garlic into a non-stick pan. Add the stock, bring to the boil and cook for 5 minutes, or until tender.

NUTRITION NOTES	
Per portion:	
Energy	297Kcals/1243kJ
Protein	17.1g
Fat	3.2g
saturated fat	0.69g
Carbohydrate	51g
Fibre	5g
Sodium	414mg

2 Add the tomatoes, tomato purée, sugar and dried herbs. Season with ground pepper. Bring to the boil and simmer for 30 minutes until thick. Stir occasionally.

3 Cook the pasta in a large pan of boiling water until *al dente*. Drain thoroughly and set aside.

4 Put the mushrooms in to a pan with the white wine, cover and cook for 3–4 minutes until tender and all the wine has been absorbed.

5 Add the mushrooms and diced ham to the tomato sauce. Reheat.

6 Transfer the pasta to a warmed serving dish and spoon on the sauce. Garnish with chopped parsley.

Baked Seafood Spaghetti

In this dish, each seafood portion is baked and then served in an individual packet to be opened at the table. For best results, make the packets using aluminium foil or baking parchment.

INGREDIENTS

Serves 4

450g/1lb fresh mussels
120ml/4fl oz/½ cup dry white wine
60ml/4 tbsp olive oil
2 garlic cloves, finely chopped
450g/1lb tomatoes, fresh or canned, peeled and finely chopped
400g/14oz egg-free spaghetti or other long pasta
90g/3½oz peeled and deveined raw prawns, fresh or frozen
30ml/2 tbsp chopped fresh parsley
ground black pepper

1 Scrub the mussels well under cold running water, cutting off the "beard" with a small, sharp knife. Place the mussels and dry white wine in a large saucepan and gently heat until they open.

NUTRITION NOTES

Per portion:

Energy	530Kcals/2238kJ
Protein	22.9g
Fat	14g
saturated fat	2g
Carbohydrate	79g
Fibre	4.4g
Sodium	511mg

2 Lift out the mussels and set aside. (Discard any that have not opened.) Strain the cooking liquid through kitchen paper, and reserve. Preheat the oven to 150°C/300°F/Gas 2.

3 In a saucepan, heat the oil and garlic together for 1–2 minutes. Add the tomatoes and cook until they soften. Stir in 175ml/6fl oz/¾ cup of the cooking liquid from the mussels. Cook the pasta in boiling water until *al dente*.

4 Just before draining the pasta, add the prawns and parsley to the tomato sauce. Cook for 2 minutes. Taste for seasoning, adding pepper as desired. Remove from the heat.

5 Drain the pasta and place in a bowl. Add the tomato sauce and mix well. Stir in the mussels. Prepare four pieces of baking parchment or foil approximately 30 x 45cm (12 x 18in). Place each sheet in the centre of a shallow bowl.

6 Divide the pasta and seafood among the four pieces of paper, placing a mound in the centre of each, and twist the paper ends together to make a closed packet. (The bowl under the paper will stop the sauce from spilling while the paper parcels are being closed.)

7 Arrange on a large baking sheet and place in the centre of the oven. Bake for 8–10 minutes. Place one unopened packet on each individual serving plate.

VARIATION

Prawns naturally contain salt, so if you are following a low-salt diet, you can also substitute the prawns for cod for a dish that will be virtually salt-free.

Vegetarian Fried Noodles

Colour, texture and flavour all play a part in this quick and easy vegetarian dish.

INGREDIENTS

Serves 4
2 eggs
5ml/1 tsp chilli powder
5ml/1 tsp ground turmeric
60ml/4 tbsp vegetable oil
1 large onion, finely sliced
2 red chillies, seeded and
  finely sliced
2 medium potatoes, cubed
6 pieces fried tofu (soya beancurd),
  sliced, about 225g/8oz
225g/8oz/1 cup beansprouts
115g/4oz green beans, blanched
350g/12oz fresh thick egg noodles
ground black pepper
sliced spring onions, to garnish

1 Beat the eggs lightly, then strain them into a bowl. Heat a lightly greased omelette pan. Pour in half of the egg to cover the bottom of the pan thinly.

2 When the egg is just set, turn the omelette over and fry briefly on the other side. Slide on to a plate, blot with kitchen paper, roll up and cut into narrow strips. Make a second omelette in the same way and slice. Set aside the omelette strips to use for garnishing the finished dish.

3 In a cup, mix together the chilli powder and turmeric. Form a paste by stirring in a little water.

4 Heat the oil in a wok or large frying pan. Fry the onion until soft. Reduce the heat and add the chilli paste and sliced chillies. Fry for 2–3 minutes, stirring occasionally.

5 Add the potato cubes and fry for about 2 minutes, mixing well. Add the tofu (soya beancurd), then the beansprouts, green beans and egg noodles, stirring frequently.

6 Gently stir-fry until the noodles are evenly coated and heated through. Take care not to break up the potatoes or the tofu. Season with pepper to taste. Serve hot, garnished with the reserved omelette strips and spring onion slices.

COOK'S TIP

Always be very careful when handling chillies. Keep your hands away from your eyes as the juice from chillies will sting them, and wash your hands thoroughly after touching chillies.

NUTRITION NOTES	
Per portion:	
Energy	613Kcals/2571kJ
Protein	24.2g
Fat	27.1g
saturated fat	3.14g
Carbohydrate	73g
Fibre	2.6g
Sodium	218mg

Farfalle with Tuna

Using tuna in this quick and simple dish provides an excellent source of the cancer-fighting nutrients, omega-3 fatty acids and vitamin D.

INGREDIENTS

Serves 6

30ml/2 tbsp olive oil
1 small onion, finely chopped
1 garlic clove, finely chopped
400g/14oz can chopped Italian
    plum tomatoes
45ml/3 tbsp dry white wine
8–10 pitted black olives, cut into rings
10ml/2 tsp chopped fresh oregano or
    5ml/1 tsp dried oregano, plus extra
    fresh oregano to garnish
400g/14oz/3½ cups dried
    egg-free farfalle
175g/6oz can tuna in olive oil
salt and ground black pepper

1 Heat the olive oil in a medium skillet or saucepan, add the onion and garlic and fry gently for about 5 minutes until the onion is soft and lightly coloured.

2 Add the plum tomatoes to the pan and bring to the boil, then add the white wine and simmer for a minute or so. Stir in the olives and oregano, with salt and pepper to taste, then cover and cook for 20–25 minutes, stirring from time to time.

3 Meanwhile, cook the pasta in a large saucepan of salted boiling water according to the instructions on the packet.

4 Drain the canned tuna and flake it with a fork. Add the tuna to the sauce with 60ml/4 tbsp of the water used for cooking the pasta. Taste and adjust the seasoning.

5 Drain the cooked pasta well and tip it into a large, warmed bowl. Pour the tuna sauce over the top and toss to mix. Serve immediately, garnished with sprigs of oregano.

NUTRITION NOTES	
Per portion:	
Energy	515kcals/2181kJ
Protein	25.2g
Fat	12.7g
saturated fat	1.8g
Carbohydrate	78.2g
Fibre	4.2g
Sugars	6.9g
Calcium	54.8mg

Penne with Chicken, Broccoli and Cheese

Broccoli, with its powerful anti-cancer properties, makes a healthy addition to this dish.

INGREDIENTS

Serves 4

115g/4oz/scant 1 cup broccoli florets, divided into tiny sprigs
50g/2oz/¼ cup butter
2 skinless chicken breast fillets, cut into thin strips
2 garlic cloves, crushed
400g/14oz/3½ cups egg-free penne
120ml/4fl oz/½ cup dry white wine
200ml/7fl oz/scant 1 cup *panna da cucina* or double cream
90g/3½oz/scant 1 cup Gorgonzola cheese, rind removed and diced small
salt and ground black pepper
freshly grated Parmesan cheese, to serve

NUTRITION NOTES

Per portion:

Energy	870kcals/3646kJ
Protein	37.7g
Fat	46.1g
saturated fat	27.4g
Carbohydrate	75.9g
Fibre	3.6g
Sugars	5.1g
Calcium	135.7mg

1 Plunge the broccoli into a saucepan of boiling salted water. Bring back to the boil and boil for 2 minutes, then drain in a colander and refresh under cold running water. Shake well to remove the surplus water and set aside.

2 Melt the butter in a large skillet or saucepan, add the chicken and garlic, with salt and pepper to taste, and stir well. Fry over a medium heat for 3 minutes or until the chicken becomes white. Meanwhile, start cooking the pasta according to the instructions on the packet.

3 Pour the wine and cream over the chicken mixture in the pan, stir to mix, then simmer, stirring occasionally, for about 5 minutes until the sauce has reduced and thickened. Add the broccoli, increase the heat and toss to heat it through and mix it with the chicken. Taste for seasoning.

4 Drain the pasta and tip it into the sauce. Add the Gorgonzola and toss well. Serve with grated Parmesan.

VARIATION

Use leeks instead of broccoli, which will provide the important nutrient, allium. Fry them with the chicken.

Fresh Tomato Sauce

FREE FROM

This famous Neapolitan sauce is full of antioxidants, which can be found in its key ingredients – tomatoes, onions and olive oil. These traditional Mediterranean foods have been shown to lower the incidence of cancer.

INGREDIENTS

Serves 4

675g/1½lb ripe Italian plum tomatoes
60ml/4 tbsp olive oil
1 onion, finely chopped
350g/12oz fresh or dried
    egg-free spaghetti
1 small handful fresh basil leaves
salt and ground black pepper
coarsely shaved Parmesan cheese and
    crusty egg-free bread, to serve

1 With a sharp knife, cut a cross in the bottom (flower) end of each tomato. Bring a medium saucepan of water to the boil and remove from the heat. Plunge a few of the tomatoes into the water, leave for 30 seconds, then lift them out with a slotted spoon. Repeat with the remaining tomatoes, then peel off the skin and roughly chop the flesh.

2 Heat the oil in a large saucepan, add the onion and cook over a low heat, stirring frequently, for about 5 minutes until softened and lightly coloured. Add the tomatoes, with salt and pepper to taste, bring to a simmer, then turn the heat down to low and cover. Cook, stirring occasionally, for 30–40 minutes until thick.

3 Meanwhile, cook the pasta according to the instructions on the packet. Shred the basil leaves finely.

4 Remove the sauce from the heat, stir in the basil and taste for seasoning. Drain the pasta, tip it into a warmed bowl, pour the sauce over and toss well. Serve immediately, with shaved Parmesan handed separately.

NUTRITION NOTES	
Per portion:	
Energy	432kcals/1826kJ
Protein	11.9g
Fat	13.1g
saturated fat	1.9g
Carbohydrate	71.3g
Fibre	4.4g
Sugars	8.9g
Calcium	37.5mg

VARIATION

Some Neapolitan cooks add a little crushed garlic with the chopped onion and some use chopped fresh oregano or flat leaf parsley with the basil.

Spaghettini with Roasted Garlic

Roasted garlic and olive oil are powerful anti-cancer foods.

INGREDIENTS

Serves 4

1 whole head of garlic
400g/14oz egg-free spaghettini
120ml/4fl oz/½ cup extra virgin
   olive oil
salt and ground black pepper
coarsely shaved Parmesan cheese and
   crusty bread, to serve

1 Preheat the oven to 180°C/350°F/ Gas 4. Place the garlic in an oiled baking tin and roast for 30 minutes.

2 Cook the pasta in a saucepan of salted boiling water according to the instructions on the packet.

3 Leave the garlic to cool, then lay it on its side and slice off the top third with a sharp knife.

4 Hold the garlic over a bowl and dig out the flesh from each clove with the point of the knife. When all the flesh has been added to the bowl, pour in the oil and add plenty of black pepper. Mix well.

5 Drain the pasta and return it to the clean pan. Pour in the oil and garlic mixture and toss vigorously over a medium heat until all the strands are thoroughly coated.

6 Serve immediately, with shaved Parmesan handed separately and chunks of bread.

— NUTRITION NOTES —

Per portion:

Energy	353kcals/1502kJ
Protein	12.9g
Fat	1.8g
saturated fat	0.2g
Carbohydrate	75.7g
Fibre	3.4g
Sugars	3.5g
Calcium	27mg

— VARIATION —

For a fiery finish, sprinkle crushed, dried red chillies over the pasta when tossing it with the oil and garlic.

— COOK'S TIP —

Although you can now buy roasted garlic in supermarkets, it is essential to roast it yourself for this simple recipe, so that it melts into the olive oil and coats the strands of pasta beautifully.

FREE
FROM

Paglia e Fieno with Radicchio

FREE FROM

This light, modern pasta dish is full of wholesome ingredients that will supply the body with valuable nutrients, including antioxidants, phytochemicals, plant protein and fibre.

INGREDIENTS

Serves 4

45ml/3 tbsp pine nuts
350g/12oz dried green and white
    egg-free tagliatelle (paglia e fieno)
45ml/3 tbsp extra virgin olive oil
2 pieces drained sun-dried tomatoes in
    olive oil, cut into very thin slivers
30ml/2 tbsp sun-dried tomato paste
40g/1½oz radicchio leaves,
    finely shredded
4–6 spring onions, thinly sliced
    into rings
salt and ground black pepper

1 Put the pine nuts in a non-stick frying pan and toss over a low to medium heat for 1–2 minutes or until they are lightly toasted and golden. Remove and set aside.

2 Cook the pasta according to the packet instructions, keeping the colours separate by using two pans.

—————— NUTRITION NOTES ——————	
Per portion:	
Energy	474kcals/1994kJ
Protein	12.6g
Fat	19.6g
saturated fat	2.1g
Carbohydrate	66g
Fibre	3.1g
Sugars	3.9g
Calcium	35.5mg

3 While the pasta is cooking, heat 15ml/1 tbsp of the oil in a medium-sized skillet or saucepan. Add the sun-dried tomatoes and tomato paste, then stir in about two ladlefuls of the water used for cooking the pasta. Simmer until the sauce is slightly reduced, stirring constantly.

4 Mix in the shredded radicchio, taste and season if necessary. Keep on a low heat. Drain the tagliatelle, keeping the colours separate, and return the noodles to the pans in which they were cooked. Add about 15ml/1 tbsp oil to each pan and toss over a medium to high heat until the pasta is glistening with the oil.

5 Arrange a portion of green and white pasta in each of four warmed bowls, then spoon the sun-dried tomato and radicchio mixture in the centre. Sprinkle the spring onions and toasted pine nuts decoratively over the top and serve immediately. Before eating, each diner should toss the sauce ingredients with the pasta so that they mix together.

Prawn, Sun-dried Tomato and Basil Pizzettes

Slices of sun-dried tomatoes, with their concentrated, caramelized tomato flavour, make an excellent, easy topping for pizzas. Serve these pretty pizzettes as an appetizer or tasty snack.

INGREDIENTS

Serves 4

1 quantity basic pizza dough, rolled out
30ml/2 tbsp chilli oil
75g/3oz/¾ cup mozzarella cheese, grated
1 garlic clove, chopped
½ small red onion, thinly sliced
4–6 pieces sun-dried tomatoes, thinly sliced
115g/4oz cooked peeled prawns
30ml/2 tbsp chopped fresh basil
ground black pepper
shredded basil leaves, to garnish

1 Preheat the oven to 220°/425°F/ Gas 7. Divide the rolled out dough into eight pieces.

— NUTRITION NOTES —

Per portion:	
Energy	310Kcals/1301kJ
Protein	15.9g
Fat	13.3g
saturated fat	3.84g
Carbohydrate	34g
Fibre	1.8g
Sodium	301mg

2 Roll out each one on a lightly floured surface to a small oval about 5mm/¼in thick. Place well apart on two greased baking sheets. Prick all over with a fork.

3 Brush the bases with 15ml/1 tbsp of the chilli oil and top with the mozzarella, leaving a 1cm/½in border.

4 Divide the chopped garlic, onion, sun-dried tomatoes, prawns and chopped basil among the pizza bases. Season with pepper and drizzle the remaining chilli oil over the top. Bake for about 10 minutes until crisp and golden. Garnish with the shredded basil leaves and serve immediately.

PULSES AND GRAINS

These wholesome ingredients are an essential part of any healthy diet.

They are low in fat, high in fibre and packed with health-giving

nutrients. They are used here as the base for a range of tasty and

nutritious dishes, such as dhals and pilaffs. There is a wide choice of

dishes, such as spicy Tomato and Lentil Dhal with Toasted Almonds,

Aubergine and Chick-pea Tagine, Bulgur Wheat and Lentil Pilaff,

and Asian Rice with Fruit and Nuts.

Spicy Paella

FREE FROM

INGREDIENTS

Serves 6

2 large boneless chicken breasts
about 150g/5oz prepared squid
8–10 raw king prawns, shelled
325g/10oz cod or haddock fillets
8 scallops, trimmed and halved
350g/12oz raw mussels in shells
250g/9oz/1⅓ cups long grain rice
30ml/2 tbsp sunflower oil
bunch of spring onions, cut into strips
2 small courgettes, cut into strips
1 red pepper, cut into strips
400ml/14fl oz/1⅔ cups Chicken Stock
250ml/8fl oz/1 cup passata
salt and ground black pepper
coriander, lemon wedges, to garnish

For the marinade

2 red chillies, seeded
good handful of fresh coriander
10–15ml/2–3 tsp ground cumin
15ml/1 tbsp paprika
2 garlic cloves
45ml/3 tbsp olive oil
60ml/4 tbsp sunflower oil
juice of 1 lemon

1 First make the marinade. Blend all the ingredients in a food processor with 5ml/1 tsp salt.

2 Skin the chicken and cut into bite-size pieces. Place in a glass bowl.

3 Slice the squid into rings. Remove the heads and shell the prawns, leaving the tails intact. Skin the fish and cut into bite-size chunks. Place the fish and shellfish (apart from the mussels) in a separate bowl. Divide the marinade between the fish and chicken and stir well. Cover and marinate for 2 hours.

--- NUTRITION NOTES ---

Per portion:

Energy	613kcals/2577kJ
Protein	67.4g
Fat	11.9g
saturated fat	2.6g
Carbohydrate	58.4g
Fibre	1.9g
Sugars	5.9g
Calcium	109mg

4 Scrub the mussels, discarding any that do not close when tapped sharply, and chill until ready to use. Place the rice in a bowl, cover with boiling water and set aside for about 30 minutes. Drain the chicken and fish, and reserve the marinade separately. Heat the oil in a wok or paella pan and fry the chicken pieces for a few minutes until lightly browned.

5 Add the spring onions to the pan, fry for 1 minute and then add the courgettes and red pepper and fry for a further 3–4 minutes until slightly softened. Remove the chicken and then the vegetables to separate plates.

6 Use a spatula to scrape all the marinade into the pan and cook for 1 minute. Drain the rice, add to the pan and stir-fry for 1 minute. Add the stock, passata and reserved chicken, season with salt and pepper and stir well. Bring the mixture to the boil, then cover the pan with a large lid or foil and simmer very gently for 15–20 minutes or until the rice is almost tender.

7 Add the reserved vegetables to the pan and place all the fish and mussels on top. Cover again with a lid or foil and cook over a moderate heat for 10–12 minutes until the fish is cooked and the mussels have opened. Discard any mussels that have not opened during the cooking. Serve garnished with fresh coriander and lemon wedges.

Vegetable Couscous with Saffron and Harissa

INGREDIENTS

Serves 6

30ml/2 tbsp olive oil
450g/1lb lean lamb, cubed
2 chicken breast quarters, halved
2 onions, chopped
350g/12oz carrots, cut into chunks
225g/8oz parsnips, cut into chunks
115g/4oz turnips, cut into chunks
6 tomatoes, peeled and chopped
900ml/1½ pints/3¾ cups chicken stock
good pinch of ginger
1 cinnamon stick
425g/15oz can chick-peas, drained
400g/14oz/2 cups couscous
2 small courgettes, cut into strips
115g/4oz French beans, halved
50g/2oz/⅓ cup raisins
a little harissa
salt and ground black pepper

1 Heat half the oil in a large saucepan and fry the lamb until browned, stirring. Transfer to a plate with a slotted spoon. Brown the chicken in the same pan and transfer to the plate.

2 Heat the remaining oil, add the onions and fry over a low heat for 3 minutes, stirring, then add the carrots, parsnips and turnips. Cover and cook for 5 minutes, stirring.

3 Add the tomatoes, lamb, chicken and stock. Add the ginger and cinnamon, and season to taste. Bring to the boil and simmer gently for 35–45 minutes until the meat is tender.

4 Skin the chick-peas in a bowl of cold water, rubbing them between your fingers. Discard the skins and drain. Prepare the couscous according to the instructions on the packet.

5 Add the skinned chick-peas, courgettes, beans and raisins to the meat mixture, cover and cook over a low heat for 10–15 minutes until the vegetables are tender.

6 Transfer the chicken to a plate and remove the skin and bone. Spoon 3–4 large spoonfuls of stock into a separate saucepan. Return the chicken to the stew, add the harissa to the separate stock and heat both gently. Pile the couscous on to a serving dish and make a well in the centre. Spoon the stew over the couscous and serve with the harissa sauce.

——— NUTRITION NOTES ———	
Per portion:	
Energy	422kcals/1774kJ
Protein	16.2g
Fat	12.5g
saturated fat	1.58g
Carbohydrate	65.3g
Fibre	9.6g
Sugars	17.9g
Calcium	154mg

Tabbouleh with Fennel

A fresh salad originating in the Middle East that is perfect for a summer lunch. Serve with lettuce and pitta bread.

INGREDIENTS

Serves 4

225g/8oz/1¼ cups bulgur wheat
2 fennel bulbs
1 small red chilli, seeded and chopped
1 celery stick, thinly sliced
30ml/2 tbsp olive oil
finely grated rind and juice of 2 lemons
6–8 spring onions, chopped
90ml/6 tbsp chopped fresh mint
90ml/6 tbsp chopped fresh parsley
1 pomegranate, seeded
salt and ground black pepper

——— NUTRITION NOTES ———

Per portion:

Energy	188Kcals/791kJ
Fat	4.67g
saturated fat	0.62g
Cholesterol	0mg
Fibre	2.17g

1 Place the bulgur wheat in a bowl and pour over enough cold water to cover. Leave to stand for 30 minutes.

2 Drain the wheat through a sieve, pressing out any excess water using the back of a spoon.

3 Halve the fennel bulbs and carefully cut into very fine slices with a sharp knife.

4 Mix all the remaining ingredients together, including the soaked bulgur wheat and fennel. Season well, cover, and set aside for 30 minutes before serving.

——— COOK'S TIPS ———

Fennel has a very distinctive aniseed flavour. When you are buying fennel, choose well-rounded bulbs which are pale green to white in colour. Flat fennel is immature and you should avoid any bulbs that are deep green. With modern transportation, fennel never goes out of season, and is available all year round. It will keep for 2–3 days in the salad drawer of the fridge, but is best eaten as fresh as possible. Cut surfaces discolour quickly on exposure to air, so do not prepare fennel far in advance of using and have a bowl of water, acidulated with lemon juice, to hand. Drop in the slices as you cut them to avoid their turning brown.

Fried Rice with Mushrooms

A tasty rice dish that is almost a meal in itself. Serve with a crisp green cabbage salad.

INGREDIENTS

Serves 4

225g/8oz/1¼ cups long grain rice
15ml/1 tbsp sunflower oil
1 egg, lightly beaten
2 garlic cloves, crushed
175g/6oz/1¼ cups button
   mushrooms, sliced
15ml/1 tbsp light soy sauce
1.5ml/¼ tsp salt
2.5ml/½ tsp sesame oil
cucumber matchsticks, to garnish

1 Rinse the rice until the water runs clear, then drain thoroughly. Place it in a saucepan. Measure the depth of the rice against your index finger, then bring the finger up to just above the surface of the rice and add cold water to the same depth as the rice.

2 Bring the water to the boil. Stir, boil for a few minutes, then cover the pan. Lower the heat to a simmer and cook the rice for 5–8 minutes until all the water has been absorbed. Remove the pan from the heat and, without lifting the lid, leave for another 10 minutes before forking up the rice.

3 Heat 5ml/1 tsp of the sunflower oil in a non-stick frying pan or wok. Add the egg and cook, stirring with a chopstick or wooden spoon until scrambled. Remove and set aside.

4 Heat the remaining sunflower oil in the pan or wok. Stir-fry the garlic for a few seconds, then add the mushrooms and stir-fry for 2 minutes, adding a little water, if needed, to prevent burning.

— NUTRITION NOTES —	
Per portion:	
Energy	265kcals/1109kJ
Protein	7.4g
Fat	5.5g
saturated fat	1g
Carbohydrate	45.8g
Fibre	0.6g
Sugars	0.1g
Calcium	24mg

5 Stir in the cooked rice and cook for about 4 minutes, or until the rice is hot, stirring from time to time. Add the scrambled egg, soy sauce, salt and sesame oil. Cook for 1 minute to heat through. Serve at once, garnished with cucumber matchsticks.

COOK'S TIP

When you cook rice this way, there may be a crust at the bottom of the pan. Simply soak the crust in water for a couple of minutes to break it up, then drain and fry it with the rest of the rice.

Thai Fragrant Rice

A lovely, soft, fluffy rice dish, perfumed with delicious and fresh lemon grass.

FREE FROM

INGREDIENTS

Serves 4

1 piece lemon grass
2 limes
225g/8oz/1⅓ cups brown basmati rice
15ml/1 tbsp olive oil
1 onion, chopped
2.5cm/1in piece fresh root ginger, peeled and finely chopped
7.5ml/1½ tsp coriander seeds
7.5ml/1½ tsp cumin seeds
750ml/1¼ pints/3⅔ cups Vegetable Stock
60ml/4 tbsp chopped fresh coriander
lime wedges, to serve

COOK'S TIP

Other varieties of rice, such as white basmati or long grain, can be used for this dish but you will need to adjust the cooking times as necessary.

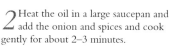

1 Finely chop the lemon grass and remove the rind from the limes. Rinse the rice in cold water. Drain through a sieve.

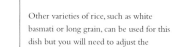

2 Heat the oil in a large saucepan and add the onion and spices and cook gently for about 2–3 minutes.

3 Add the rice and cook for a further minute, then add the stock or water and bring to the boil. Reduce the heat to very low and cover the pan. Cook for about 30 minutes, then check the rice. If it is still crunchy, cover the pan again and leave for a further 3–5 minutes. Remove from the heat.

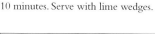

4 Stir in the fresh coriander, fluff up the grains, cover and leave for 10 minutes. Serve with lime wedges.

NUTRITION NOTES

Per portion:

Energy	259Kcals/1087kJ
Fat	5.27g
saturated fat	0.81g
Cholesterol	0mg
Fibre	1.49g

Sweet Vegetable Couscous

A wonderful combination of sweet vegetables and spices, this makes a substantial winter dish.

INGREDIENTS

Serves 4–6

generous pinch of saffron threads
45ml/3 tbsp boiling water
15ml/1 tbsp olive oil
1 red onion, sliced
2 garlic cloves
1–2 red chillies, seeded and
    finely chopped
2.5ml/½ tsp ground ginger
2.5ml/½ tsp ground cinnamon
400g/14oz can chopped tomatoes
300ml/½ pint/1¼ cups vegetable stock
    or water
4 carrots, peeled and cut into 5mm/
    ¼in slices
2 turnips, peeled and cut into 2cm/
    ¾in cubes
450g/1lb sweet potatoes, peeled and
    cut into 2cm/¾in cubes
75g/3oz/⅔ cup raisins
2 courgettes, cut into 5mm/¼in slices
400g/14oz can chick-peas, drained
    and rinsed
45ml/3 tbsp chopped fresh parsley
45ml/3 tbsp chopped fresh coriander
450g/1lb/4 cups quick-cook couscous

FREE FROM

1 Put the saffron into a small bowl, add the boiling water and set aside to infuse.

2 Heat the oil in a large saucepan or flameproof casserole. Add the onion, garlic and chillies and cook gently for about 5 minutes.

3 Add the ground ginger and cinnamon, and gently cook for a further 1–2 minutes.

4 Add the tomatoes, vegetable stock or water, saffron and soaking liquid, carrots, turnips, sweet potatoes and raisins, cover and simmer for a further 25 minutes.

5 Add the courgettes, chick-peas, parsley and coriander, and cook for a further 10 minutes.

6 Meanwhile, preheat the couscous, following the manufacturer's instructions, and then serve with the prepared vegetables.

—— NUTRITION NOTES ——

Per portion:

Energy	570Kcals/2393kJ
Fat	7.02g
saturated fat	0.83g
Cholesterol	0mg
Fibre	10.04g

—— COOK'S TIP ——

Vegetable stock can be made from a variety of uncooked vegetables. These can include the outer leaves of cabbage, lettuce and other greens, carrot peelings, leeks and parsnips. However, do not use too many green vegetables, as they have a powerful taste which can dominate the stock.

Corn Griddle Pancakes

These crisp pancakes are delicious to serve as a snack lunch or as a light supper with a crisp mixed salad.

INGREDIENTS

Serves 4, makes about 12
115g/4oz/1 cup self-raising flour
1 egg white
150ml/¼ pint/⅔ cup skimmed milk
200g/7oz can sweetcorn, drained
oil, for brushing
salt and ground black pepper
tomato chutney, to serve

1 Place the flour, egg white and skimmed milk in a food processor or blender with half the sweetcorn and process until smooth.

2 Season the batter well and add the remaining sweetcorn.

3 Heat a frying pan and brush with oil. Drop in tablespoons of batter and cook until set. Turn over the pancakes and cook the other side until golden. Serve hot with tomato chutney.

NUTRITION NOTES

Per portion:
Energy	162Kcals/680kJ
Fat	0.89g
saturated fat	0.14g
Cholesterol	0.75mg
Fibre	1.49g

Baked Polenta with Tomatoes

INGREDIENTS

Serves 4
750ml/1¼ pints/3⅔ cups Vegetable Stock
175g/6oz/1⅛ cup polenta
60ml/4 tbsp chopped fresh sage
5ml/1 tsp olive oil
2 beefsteak tomatoes, sliced
15ml/1 tbsp freshly grated
　Parmesan cheese
salt and ground black pepper

1 Bring the stock to the boil in a pan. Gradually stir in the polenta.

2 Continue stirring the polenta over a moderate heat for 5 minutes, or until the mixture begins to come away from the sides of the pan. Stir in the chopped sage and season well with salt and pepper, then spoon the mixture into a lightly oiled, shallow rectangular tin, about 23 × 33cm/9 × 13in, and spread evenly. Leave to cool.

3 Preheat the oven to 200°C/400°F/ Gas 6. Cut the cooled polenta into 24 squares using a sharp knife.

4 Arrange the polenta overlapping with tomato slices in a lightly oiled, shallow ovenproof dish. Sprinkle with Parmesan and bake for 20 minutes, or until golden brown. Serve hot.

NUTRITION NOTES

Per portion:
Energy	200Kcals/842kJ
Fat	3.8g
saturated fat	0.77g
Cholesterol	1.88mg
Fibre	1.71g

Green Lentils with Beans and Sun-dried Tomatoes

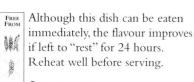

Although this dish can be eaten immediately, the flavour improves if left to "rest" for 24 hours. Reheat well before serving.

INGREDIENTS

Serves 4
60ml/4 tbsp olive oil
4 medium leeks, finely sliced
2 large courgettes, finely diced
50g/2oz sun-dried tomatoes, chopped in large pieces or, if you are on a solanacae-free diet, 50g/2oz chopped black olives
150g/5oz/¾ cup green lentils
200ml/7fl oz/scant 1 cup Retsina or dry white wine
400ml/14fl oz/1⅔ cups water
16 string beans, chopped roughly
soy sauce, which should be tamari if you are on a wheat-free diet
chopped fresh flat leaf parsley

1 Heat the oil in a pan and sweat the leeks and courgettes, covered, for 15–20 minutes or until the vegetables are well softened.

— COOK'S TIP —

This is a good dish to make in a table-top cooker or electric frying pan if you find it easier. It can be cooked in and served from the same pan.

2 Add the sun-dried tomatoes, if using, the green lentils and the wine and water.

3 Bring back to a simmer, cover and cook for 20–30 minutes or until the lentils are cooked.

4 Add the string beans and the chopped black olives, if using, to the pan and continue to cook for a further 5–10 minutes, until the beans are tender but not soft.

5 Season with soy sauce and sprinkle with parsley just before serving.

— NUTRITION NOTES —

Per portion:

Energy	338kcals/1385kJ
Fat, total	18.8g
saturated fat	2.6g
Protein	12.3g
Carbohydrate	23.3g
sugar, total	4.4g
Fibre	6.1g
Sodium	133mg

Tomato and Lentil Dhal with Toasted Almonds

Natural, live yogurt is not only the perfect accompaniment to this aromatic, antioxidant-rich dish, but is a useful source of healthy bacteria and enzymes.

INGREDIENTS

Serves 4
30ml/2 tbsp vegetable oil
25g/1oz/2 tbsp butter
1 large onion, finely chopped
3 garlic cloves, chopped
1 carrot, diced
10ml/2 tsp cumin seeds
10ml/2 tsp yellow mustard seeds
2.5cm/1in piece fresh root
    ginger, grated
10ml/2 tsp ground turmeric
5ml/1 tsp mild chilli powder
5ml/1 tsp garam masala
225g/8oz/1 cup split red lentils
400ml/14fl oz/1⅔ cups water
400ml/14fl oz/1⅔ cups coconut milk
5 tomatoes, peeled, seeded
    and chopped
juice of 2 limes
60ml/4 tbsp chopped fresh coriander
25g/1oz/¼ cup flaked almonds,
    lightly toasted
salt and ground black pepper

2 Stir in the ground turmeric, chilli powder and garam masala, and cook for 1 minute or until the flavours begin to mingle, stirring to prevent the spices burning.

3 Add the lentils, water, coconut milk and tomatoes, then season well. Bring to the boil, then reduce the heat and simmer, covered, for about 45 minutes, stirring occasionally to prevent the lentils sticking.

1 Heat the oil and butter in a large heavy-based saucepan, sauté the onion for 5 minutes until softened and lightly coloured, stirring occasionally. Add the garlic, carrot, cumin and mustard seeds and ginger, then cook for 5 minutes, stirring, until the seeds begin to pop and the carrot softens slightly.

4 Stir in the lime juice and 45ml/ 3 tbsp of the fresh coriander, then check the seasoning. Cook for a further 15 minutes until the lentils soften and become tender.

5 Sprinkle with the remaining coriander and the flaked almonds and serve.

— NUTRITION NOTES —	
Per portion:	
Energy	363kcals/1803kJ
Protein	16.1g
Fat	15.6g
saturated fat	4.7g
Carbohydrate	42.3g
Fibre	4.9g
Sugars	11.4g
Calcium	90mg

Aubergine and Chick-pea Tagine

INGREDIENTS

Serves 4

1 small aubergine, diced
2 courgettes, thickly sliced
60ml/4 tbsp olive oil
1 large onion, sliced
2 garlic cloves, chopped
150g/5oz/2 cups brown cap
   mushrooms, halved
15ml/1 tbsp ground coriander
10ml/2 tsp cumin seeds
15ml/1 tbsp ground cinnamon
10ml/2 tsp ground turmeric
225g/8oz new potatoes, quartered
600ml/1 pint/2½ cups passata
15ml/1 tbsp tomato purée
15ml/1 tbsp chilli sauce
75g/3oz/⅓ cup ready-to-eat
   unsulphured dried apricots
400g/14oz/3 cups canned chick-peas,
   drained and rinsed
salt and ground black pepper
chopped fresh coriander, to garnish
couscous, to serve

1 Sprinkle salt over the aubergine and courgettes and leave for about 30 minutes. Rinse and pat dry with kitchen paper.

2 Heat the grill to high. Arrange the courgettes and aubergine on a baking sheet and toss in 30ml/2 tbsp of the olive oil. Grill for 20 minutes, turning occasionally, until just tender and golden.

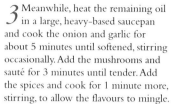

3 Meanwhile, heat the remaining oil in a large, heavy-based saucepan and cook the onion and garlic for about 5 minutes until softened, stirring occasionally. Add the mushrooms and sauté for 3 minutes until tender. Add the spices and cook for 1 minute more, stirring, to allow the flavours to mingle.

4 Add the potatoes and cook for 3 minutes, stirring. Pour in the passata, tomato purée and 150ml/ ¼ pint/⅔ cup water, cover, and cook for 10 minutes or until the sauce begins to thicken.

5 Add the aubergine, courgettes, chilli sauce, apricots and chick-peas. Season, and cook, partially covered, for 10–15 minutes until the potatoes are tender. Add a little extra water if the tagine becomes too dry. Sprinkle with chopped fresh coriander and serve with couscous.

--- NUTRITION NOTES ---

Per portion:

Energy	338kcals/1425kJ
Protein	12.5g
Fat	14.6g
saturated fat	1.9g
Carbohydrate	141.7g
Fibre	9.2g
Sugars	16.2g
Calcium	100mg

Jerusalem Artichoke Risotto

The delicious and distinctive flavour of Jerusalem artichokes makes this simple and warming risotto something special.

INGREDIENTS

Serves 4

400g/14oz Jerusalem artichokes
60ml/4 tbsp olive oil
1 onion, finely chopped or 15ml/1 tbsp
   dried onion
1 garlic clove, crushed or 5ml/1 tsp
   puréed garlic
275g/10oz/1½ cups risotto rice
120ml/4fl oz/½ cup fruity white wine
1 litre/1¾ pints/4 cups simmering
   Vegetable Stock
10ml/2 tsp chopped fresh thyme
40g/1½oz/½ cup freshly grated
   Parmesan cheese, plus extra to serve,
   or, if you are on a dairy-free diet,
   40g/1½oz chopped black olives
salt and ground black pepper
fresh thyme sprigs, to garnish

1 Peel the artichokes, cut them into pieces and steam over boiling water. Mash them with a potato masher or purée them in a bowl with a hand-held blender. Add 15ml/1 tbsp olive oil and season with salt.

COOK'S TIP

If you find the artichokes difficult to peel, scrub them well and cook them without peeling. It will be much easier to remove the nobbles when they are cooked.

2 Heat the remaining oil in a pan and fry the onion and garlic for 5–6 minutes until soft. Add the rice and cook for about 2 minutes, or until the grains are translucent around the edges.

3 Pour in the wine, stir until it has been absorbed, then add the stock, a ladleful at a time, with each quantity absorbed before adding more. When you have one ladleful of stock left, stir in the artichokes and the thyme.

4 Continue cooking until the risotto is creamy and the artichokes are hot. Stir in the Parmesan or black olives and season to taste.

5 Remove the risotto from the heat, cover the pan and leave to stand for a few minutes. Serve garnished with thyme and sprinkled with Parmesan cheese, if using.

--- NUTRITION NOTES ---
Per portion:

Energy	483kcals/1980kJ
Fat, total	16.7g
saturated fat	3.7g
Protein	13.2g
Carbohydrate	65.6g
sugar, total	3.8g
Fibre	4.2g
Sodium	701mg

FREE FROM

Rice and Beans with Avocado Salsa

INGREDIENTS

FREE FROM

Serves 4

40g/1½oz/¼ cup dried or 75g/3oz/
½ cup canned kidney beans, rinsed
and drained
4 tomatoes, halved and seeded
2 garlic cloves, chopped
1 onion, sliced
45ml/3 tbsp olive oil
225g/8oz/generous 1 cup long grain
brown rice, rinsed
600ml/1 pint/2½ cups vegetable stock
2 carrots, diced
75g/3oz/¾ cup green beans
salt and ground black pepper
4 wheat tortillas and soured cream,
to serve

For the avocado salsa

1 avocado
juice of 1 lime
1 small red onion, diced
1 small red chilli, seeded and chopped
15ml/1 tbsp chopped fresh coriander

1 If using dried kidney beans, soak overnight in cold water. Drain and rinse well. Place in a saucepan with enough water to cover and bring to the boil. Boil rapidly for 10 minutes, then simmer for about 40 minutes until tender. Drain and set aside.

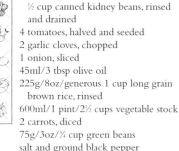

2 Heat the grill. Place the tomatoes, garlic and onion on a baking tray. Toss in 15ml/1 tbsp of the olive oil and grill for 10 minutes or until softened, turning once. Set aside to cool.

3 Heat the remaining oil in a saucepan, add the rice and cook for 2 minutes, stirring, until light golden.

4 Purée the cooled tomatoes and onions in a food processor or blender, then add the mixture to the rice and cook for a further 2 minutes, stirring frequently. Pour in the stock, then cover and cook gently for 20 minutes, stirring occasionally.

5 Reserve 30ml/2 tbsp of the kidney beans for the salsa. Add the rest to the rice mixture with the carrots and green beans and cook for 15 minutes until the vegetables are tender. Season well with salt and pepper. Remove the pan from the heat and leave to stand, covered, for 15 minutes.

6 To make the avocado salsa, cut the avocado in half and remove the stone. Peel and dice the flesh, then toss in the lime juice. Add the onion, chilli, coriander and reserved kidney beans, then season with salt.

7 To serve, spoon the hot rice and beans on to the tortillas. Hand round the salsa and soured cream.

NUTRITION NOTES

Per portion:

Energy	323kcals/1364kJ
Protein	6.8g
Fat	9.7g
saturated fat	2.0g
Carbohydrate	55.6g
Fibre	4.7g
Sugars	7.4g
Calcium	46.2mg

HEALTH BENEFITS

Brown rice contains a healthy combination of valuable nutrients, including vitamin E, and helps reduce the risk of bowel cancer.

Asian Rice with Fruit and Nuts

This colourful dish combines rice with nutrient-packed nuts and dried fruits.

INGREDIENTS

Serves 6

75g/3oz/½ cup blanched almonds
60ml/4 tbsp sunflower oil
225g/8oz carrots, cut into julienne strips
2 onions, chopped
115g/4oz/½ cup ready-to-eat unsulphured dried apricots, chopped
50g/2oz/4 tbsp raisins
375g/13oz/scant 2 cups basmati rice, soaked and drained
600ml/1 pint/2½ cups Vegetable or Chicken Stock
150ml/¼ pint/⅔ cup orange juice
grated rind of 1 orange
25g/1oz/⅓ cup pine nuts
salt and ground black pepper
1 red eating apple, cored and chopped

1 Preheat the oven to 160°C/325°F/ Gas 3. Toast the almonds in a shallow pan for 4–5 minutes until golden in colour.

2 Heat the oil in a heavy ovenproof casserole and fry the carrots and onions over a moderately high heat for 6–8 minutes until both are slightly glazed. Add the apricots, raisins and rice and cook for a few minutes, stirring all the time, until the rice is coated in the oil.

3 Add the stock, orange juice and orange rind, and season well with salt and pepper. Reserve a few almonds and pine nuts to garnish and stir in the remainder. Cover the pan with a double piece of foil and secure with the casserole lid. Cook in the oven for about 30–35 minutes until the rice is tender and all the liquid is absorbed.

4 Remove from the oven and stir in the chopped apple. Spoon on to a warmed serving dish, and then garnish with the reserved almonds and pine nuts. Serve immediately.

--- VARIATION ---

For a one-dish meal, add about 450g/1lb lamb, cut into cubes. Brown in a little oil and then transfer to a dish and cook the onion and carrots. Return the meat to the casserole with the stock and orange juice.

--- NUTRITION NOTES ---

Per portion:

Energy	689kcals/2870kJ
Protein	13.3g
Fat	26.6g
saturated fat	2.5g
Carbohydrate	9.9g
Fibre	4.5g
Sugars	22.8g
Calcium	105mg

Shellfish Risotto with Fruits of the Forest

A perfect combination of creamy Italian rice, mixed mushrooms and seafood.

INGREDIENTS

Serves 4

45ml/3 tbsp olive oil
1 medium onion, chopped
225g/8oz assorted wild and cultivated
   mushrooms such as ceps, bay boletus,
   and truffles, trimmed and sliced
450g/1lb/2¼ cups short grain arborio
   or carnaroli rice
1.2 litres/2 pints/5 cups boiling
   Chicken or Vegetable Stock
150ml/¼ pint/⅔ cup white wine
115g/4oz raw prawns, peeled
225g/8oz mussels
225g/8oz Venus or carpet shell clams
1 medium squid, cleaned, trimmed
   and sliced
3 drops truffle oil (optional)
75ml/5 tbsp chopped fresh parsley
   and chervil
cayenne pepper, to taste

1 Heat the oil in a large frying pan and fry the onion for 6–8 minutes until soft but not brown.

2 Add the mushrooms and soften until their juices begin to run. Stir in the rice and heat through.

COOK'S TIP

Before cooking, tap the shellfish with a knife. Discard any shells that do not close. After cooking, discard any unopened shells.

3 Pour in the stock and white wine. Add the raw prawns, mussels, clams and squid, stir and gently simmer for about 15 minutes.

4 Add the truffle oil, if using, stir in the herbs, cover and stand for 5–10 minutes. Season to taste with cayenne pepper and serve.

NUTRITION NOTES

Per portion:

Energy	594Kcals/2481kJ
Protein	32.6g
Fat	12g
saturated fat	1.35g
Carbohydrate	89g
Fibre	1.7g
Sodium	293mg

Thai Fried Rice

This recipe uses jasmine rice, which is sometimes known as Thai fragrant rice, adding to the dish a lovely subtle flavour.

INGREDIENTS

Serves 4

50g/2oz/½ cup coconut
   milk powder
375g/12oz/1⅔ cups jasmine rice
30ml/2 tbsp groundnut oil
2 garlic cloves, chopped
1 small onion, finely chopped
2.5cm/1in piece fresh root
   ginger, grated
225g/8oz boneless, skinless chicken
   breasts, cut into 1cm/½in dice
1 red pepper, seeded and diced
115g/4oz drained canned
   sweetcorn kernels
5ml/1 tsp chilli oil
15ml/1 tbsp hot curry powder
2 eggs, beaten
spring onion shreds, to garnish

1 In a saucepan, whisk the coconut milk powder into 475ml/16fl oz/ 2 cups water. Add the rice, bring to the boil and stir once. Lower the heat to a gentle simmer, cover and cook for 10 minutes, or until the rice is tender and the liquid has been absorbed. Spread the rice on a baking sheet and leave until completely cold.

2 Heat the oil in a wok, add the garlic, onion and ginger and stir-fry for 2 minutes.

3 Push the vegetables to the sides of the wok, add the chicken to the centre and stir-fry for 2 minutes. Add the rice and stir-fry over a high heat for 3 minutes more.

—— COOK'S TIP ——

It is important that you allow enough time for the rice to cool completely before it is fried. The oil also needs to be very hot, or the rice will absorb too much oil.

—— NUTRITION NOTES ——

Per portion:
Energy	554Kcals/2317kJ
Protein	25.9g
Fat	11.3g
saturated fat	2.15g
Carbohydrate	93g
Fibre	2.3g
Sodium	296mg

4 Stir in the red pepper, sweetcorn, chilli oil and curry powder. Toss over the heat for 1 minute. Stir in the beaten eggs and cook for 1 minute more. Garnish with spring onion shreds and serve.

FREE FROM

Lamb and Pumpkin Couscous

A traditional Moroccan-style dish marrying succulent meat, sweet vegetables and dried fruit with aromatic spices to produce a really satisfying dish.

INGREDIENTS

Serves 4–6

75g/3oz/½ cup chick-peas,
   soaked overnight
675g/1½lb lean lamb, cut into
   bite-size pieces
2 Spanish onions, sliced
a pinch of saffron
1.5ml/¼ tsp ground ginger
2.5ml/½ tsp ground turmeric
5ml/1 tsp ground black pepper
450g/1lb carrots
675g/1½lb pumpkin
75g/3oz/⅗ cup raisins
400g/14oz/2 cups couscous
fresh parsley, to garnish

1 Drain the chick-peas and cook in boiling water for 1–1½ hours until tender. Place in cold water and remove the skins by rubbing with your fingers. Discard the skins and drain.

2 Place the lamb, onions, saffron, ginger, turmeric, pepper and 1.2 litres/2 pints/5 cups water in a large saucepan. Slowly bring to the boil, then cover and simmer for about 1 hour until tender.

3 Meanwhile, prepare the vegetables. Peel the carrots and roughly cut into 6cm/2½ in pieces. Cut the pumpkin into 2.5cm/1in cubes, discarding the skin, seeds and pith.

4 Stir the carrots, pumpkin and raisins into the meat mixture, cover the pan and simmer for a further 30–35 minutes until the vegetables and meat are completely tender.

5 Prepare the couscous according to the instructions on the packet. Spoon on to a large warmed serving plate and ladle the stew on top. Garnish with parsley and serve.

— NUTRITION NOTES —	
Per portion:	
Energy	695Kcals/2911kJ
Protein	47g
Fat	16.9g
saturated fat	7.77g
Carbohydrate	93g
Fibre	7.4g
Sodium	197mg

Bulgur Wheat and Lentil Pilaff

Bulgur wheat is a useful store-cupboard ingredient. It has a nutty taste and texture and only needs soaking before serving in a salad or warming through for a hot dish.

INGREDIENTS

Serves 4

115g/4oz/½ cup green lentils
115g/4oz/⅔ cup bulgur wheat
5ml/1 tsp ground coriander
5ml/1 tsp ground cinnamon
475ml/16fl oz/2 cups water
15ml/1 tbsp olive oil
225g/8oz rindless low-salt streaky
   bacon rashers, chopped
1 red onion, chopped
1 garlic clove, crushed
5ml/1 tsp cumin seeds
30ml/2 tbsp roughly chopped
   fresh parsley
ground black pepper

1 Soak the lentils and bulgur wheat in separate clean, large bowls with plenty of cold water for about 1 hour. Drain thoroughly.

NUTRITION NOTES	
Per portion:	
Energy	357Kcals/1496kJ
Protein	20.4g
Fat	12.1g
saturated fat	3.5g
Carbohydrate	44g
Fibre	3g
Sodium	437mg

2 Tip the lentils into a pan. Stir in the coriander, cinnamon and the water. Bring to the boil and simmer until the lentils are tender and the liquid has been absorbed.

3 Meanwhile, heat the olive oil and fry the bacon until crisp. Remove and drain on kitchen paper. Add the onion and garlic to the oil remaining in the pan and fry for 10 minutes until soft and golden brown. Stir in the cumin and cook for 1 minute more. Return the bacon to the pan.

4 Stir the drained bulgur wheat into the cooked lentils, then add the mixture to the frying pan. Season with pepper and heat through. Stir in the parsley and serve.

COOK'S TIP
If possible, use Puy lentils, which have a superior flavour, aroma and texture.

FREE FROM

VEGETABLES
AND SIDE DISHES

Eating plenty of vegetables is essential for a healthy diet. This chapter

is full of delicious recipes to help you enjoy more of these valuable

ingredients. The wide selection of dishes provides the perfect choice for

any occasion, be it a weekday supper, dinner party or Sunday lunch.

Try the exotic Spiced Coconut Mushrooms and enjoy the

crisp taste of Spring Vegetable Stir-fry.

Summer Vegetable Braise

Tender, young vegetables are ideal for quick cooking in a minimum of liquid. Use any mixture of your favourite vegetables as long as they are of similar size.

INGREDIENTS

Serves 4
175g/6oz/2½ cups baby carrots
175g/6oz/2 cups sugar-snap peas
   or mangetouts
115g/4oz baby corn cobs
90ml/6 tbsp Vegetable Stock
10ml/2 tsp lime juice
salt and ground black pepper
chopped fresh parsley and snipped fresh
   chives, to garnish

3 Season the vegetables with salt and pepper to taste, then add the parsley and chives.

4 Cook the vegetables for a few seconds more, stirring them once or twice until the herbs are well mixed, then serve at once.

———— COOK'S TIP ————
You can make this dish in the winter, too, but cut larger, tougher vegetables into chunks and cook for slightly longer.

———— NUTRITION NOTES ————

Per portion:

Energy	34kcals/143kJ
Protein	2.6g
Fat	0.4g
saturated fat	0g
Carbohydrate	5.2g
Sugar	4.4g
Fibre	2.6g
Calcium	38.7mg

1 Place the carrots, peas and baby corn cobs in a large heavy-based saucepan with the vegetable stock and lime juice. Bring to the boil.

2 Cover the pan and reduce the heat, then simmer for 6–8 minutes, shaking the pan occasionally, until the vegetables are just tender.

Middle Eastern Vegetable Stew

A spiced dish of mixed vegetables that can be served as a side dish or as a vegetarian main course. Children may prefer less chilli.

INGREDIENTS

Serves 4–6

45ml/3 tbsp Vegetable or Chicken Stock
1 green pepper, seeded and sliced
2 courgettes, sliced
2 carrots, sliced
2 celery sticks, sliced
2 potatoes, diced
400g/14oz can chopped tomatoes
5ml/1 tsp chilli powder
30ml/2 tbsp chopped fresh mint
15ml/1 tbsp ground cumin
400g/14oz can chick-peas, drained
salt and ground black pepper
fresh mint leaves, to garnish

1 Heat the stock in a large flameproof casserole until boiling, then add the sliced pepper, courgettes, carrots and celery. Stir over a high heat for 2–3 minutes, until the vegetables are just beginning to soften.

— NUTRITION NOTES —

Per portion:

Energy	212–141kcals/898–598kJ
Protein	11.2–7.5g
Fat	3.6–2.4g
saturated fat	0.4–0.3g
Carbohydrate	35.7–23.8g
Sugar	7.2–4.8g
Fibre	7.7–5.1g
Calcium	90.5–60.3mg

2 Add the potatoes, tomatoes, chilli powder, mint and cumin. Add the chick-peas and bring to the boil.

— COOK'S TIP —

Chick-peas are traditional in this type of Middle Eastern dish but, if you prefer, red kidney beans or haricot beans can be used instead.

3 Reduce the heat, cover the casserole with a lid and simmer for 30 minutes, or until all the vegetables are tender.

4 Season the stew with salt and pepper to taste and serve hot, garnished with mint leaves.

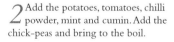

Green Beans with Tomatoes

This is a real summer favourite using the best ripe plum tomatoes and French beans.

INGREDIENTS

Serves 4

30ml/2 tbsp olive oil
1 large onion, finely sliced
2 garlic cloves, finely chopped
6 large ripe plum tomatoes, peeled, seeded and coarsely chopped
150ml/¼ pint/⅔ cup Vegetable Stock
450g/1lb French green beans, sliced in half lengthways
16 pitted black olives
10ml/2 tsp lemon juice
salt and ground black pepper

1 Heat the oil in a large frying pan. Add the onion and garlic and cook for about 5 minutes until softened.

2 Add the chopped tomatoes, stock, beans, olives and lemon juice and cook over a gentle heat for a further 20 minutes, stirring from time to time, until the sauce is thickened and the beans are tender. Season with salt and pepper to taste and serve at once.

COOK'S TIP

French beans need little preparation and now that they are grown without the string you simply top and tail them. When buying make sure that the beans snap easily – this is a good sign of freshness.

NUTRITION NOTES

Per portion:

Energy	140kcals/584kJ
Protein	3.3g
Fat	7.7g
saturated fat	1.2g
Carbohydrate	7.98g
Sugar	7.38g
Fibre	4.3g
Calcium	63mg

Potato, Broccoli and Red Pepper Stir-fry

A hot and hearty stir-fry of vegetables, with just a hint of piquancy from the fresh ginger and groundnut oil.

INGREDIENTS

Serves 2
450g/1lb potatoes
45ml/3 tbsp groundnut oil
50g/2oz/¼ cup unsalted butter
1 small onion, chopped
1 red pepper, seeded and chopped
225g/8oz broccoli, broken
    into florets
2.5cm/1in piece fresh root ginger,
    peeled and grated
ground black pepper

1 Peel the potatoes and cut them into 1cm/½in cubes.

2 Heat the oil in a large frying pan and add the potatoes. Cook for 8 minutes over a high heat, stirring and tossing occasionally, until the potatoes are browned and just tender.

3 Drain off the oil. Add the butter to the potatoes in the pan. As soon as it melts, add the onion and red pepper. Stir-fry for 2 minutes.

4 Add the broccoli florets and ginger to the pan. Stir-fry for 2–3 minutes more, taking care not to break up the potatoes. Add plenty of pepper to taste and serve at once.

NUTRITION NOTES

Per portion:

Energy	579Kcals/2421kJ
Protein	11.1g
Fat	38.9g
saturated fat	16.18g
Carbohydrate	49g
Fibre	7.6g
Sodium	31mg

COOK'S TIP

Although a wok is the preferred pan for stir-frying, for this recipe a flat frying pan is best to cook the potatoes quickly.

Cauliflower with Tomatoes and Cumin

This makes an excellent side dish to serve with barbecued or grilled meat or fish.

INGREDIENTS

Serves 4
30ml/2 tbsp sunflower or olive oil
1 onion, chopped
1 garlic clove, crushed
1 small cauliflower, broken into florets
5ml/1 tsp cumin seeds
a good pinch of ground ginger
4 tomatoes, peeled, seeded and quartered
15–30ml/1–2 tbsp lemon juice (optional)
30ml/2 tbsp chopped fresh coriander (optional)
salt and ground black pepper

1 Heat the oil in a flameproof casserole, add the onion and garlic and fry for 2–3 minutes until the onion is softened. Add the cauliflower and fry, stirring, for a further 2–3 minutes until the cauliflower is flecked with brown. Add the cumin seeds and ginger, fry briskly for 1 minute, and then add the tomatoes, 175ml/6fl oz/¾ cup water and some salt and pepper.

2 Bring to the boil and then reduce the heat, cover and simmer for 6–7 minutes, until the cauliflower is just tender.

3 Stir in a little lemon juice to sharpen the flavour, if liked, and adjust the seasoning. Scatter over the coriander, if using, and serve at once.

NUTRITION NOTES	
Per portion:	
Energy	86kcals/358kJ
Protein	2.5g
Fat	6.2g
saturated fat	0.9g
Carbohydrate	5.3g
Sugar	4.7g
Fibre	1.9g
Calcium	20mg

Roasted Vegetable Salad

Oven roasting brings out all the flavours of these classic Mediterranean vegetables. Serve them hot with grilled or roast meat or fish.

INGREDIENTS

Serves 4
2–3 courgettes
1 Spanish onion
2 red peppers
16 cherry tomatoes
2 garlic cloves, chopped
pinch of cumin seeds
5ml/1 tsp fresh thyme or 4–5 torn basil leaves
60ml/4 tbsp olive oil
juice of ½ lemon
5–10ml/1–2 tsp chilli or Tabasco sauce
fresh thyme sprigs, to garnish

1 Preheat the oven to 220°C/425°F/ Gas 7. Top and tail the courgettes and cut into long strips. Cut the onion into thin wedges then cut the red peppers into chunks, discarding the seeds and core.

2 Place the vegetables in a roasting tin, add the tomatoes, garlic, cumin and thyme. Sprinkle with the oil and toss to coat.

3 Cook in the oven for 25–30 minutes until the vegetables are very soft and slightly charred.

4 Blend the lemon juice with the chilli or Tabasco sauce and stir into the vegetables. Garnish with thyme and serve.

NUTRITION NOTES	
Per portion:	
Energy	151kcals/623kJ
Protein	2.8g
Fat	11.8g
saturated fat	1.7g
Carbohydrate	8.7g
Sugar	7.8g
Fibre	2.5g
Calcium	39mg

Glazed Sweet Potatoes with Ginger and Allspice

These delicious, candied sweet potatoes, with their succulent orange flesh, are full of the vital nutrient, betacarotene.

INGREDIENTS

Serves 6
900g/2lb sweet potatoes
50g/2oz/¼ cup butter
45ml/3 tbsp oil
2 garlic cloves, crushed
2 pieces of stem ginger, finely chopped
10ml/2 tsp ground allspice
15ml/1 tbsp syrup from ginger jar
10ml/2 tsp chopped fresh thyme, plus a few sprigs to garnish
salt and cayenne pepper

1 Peel the sweet potatoes and cut into 1cm/½in cubes. Melt the butter with the oil in a frying pan. Add the cubes and fry, stirring frequently, for about 10 minutes until just soft.

——— NUTRITION NOTES ———	
Per portion:	
Energy	373kcals/1568kJ
Protein	2.8g
Fat	19.1g
saturated fat	8.3g
Carbohydrate	50.9g
Fibre	5.4g
Sugars	15.8g
Calcium	56.4mg

2 Stir in the garlic, ginger and allspice. Cook, stirring, for 5 minutes more. Stir in the ginger syrup, salt, a generous pinch of cayenne pepper and the fresh thyme. Stir for 1–2 minutes more, then serve scattered with thyme sprigs.

Roasted Vegetables with Whole Spice Seeds

These crisp, golden vegetables are packed with goodness.

INGREDIENTS

Serves 6
3 parsnips
3 potatoes
3 carrots
3 sweet potatoes
60ml/4 tbsp olive oil
8 shallots, peeled
2 garlic cloves, sliced
10ml/2 tsp white mustard seeds
10ml/2 tsp coriander seeds, lightly crushed
5ml/1 tsp cumin seeds
2 bay leaves
salt and ground black pepper

——— VARIATION ———
Vary the selection of vegetables according to what is available. Try using swede or pumpkin instead of, or as well as, the vegetables suggested.

1 Preheat the oven to 190°C/375°F/ Gas 5. Bring a saucepan of lightly salted water to the boil. Cut the parsnips, potatoes, carrots and sweet potatoes into chunks. Add them to the pan and bring the water back to the boil. Boil for 2 minutes, then drain the vegetables thoroughly.

2 Pour the olive oil into a large, heavy roasting tin and place over a moderate heat. Add the vegetables, shallots and garlic. Fry, tossing the vegetables over the heat until they are pale golden at the edges.

3 Add the mustard seeds, coriander seeds, cumin seeds and bay leaves. Cook for 1 minute, then season with salt and pepper. Transfer the roasting tin to the oven and roast for about 45 minutes, turning occasionally, until the vegetables are crisp and golden and cooked through.

——— NUTRITION NOTES ———	
Per portion:	
Energy	190kcals/793kJ
Protein	2.3g
Fat	11.9g
saturated fat	1.77g
Carbohydrate	19.6g
Fibre	3.9g
Sugars	6.7g
Calcium	41mg

——— HEALTH BENEFITS ———
Parsnips, carrots and other root vegetables are thought to fight certain cancers.

Spring Vegetable Stir-fry

Fast, fresh and packed with nutrient-rich vegetables, this stir-fry is delicious served with rice or egg-free noodles.

INGREDIENTS

Serves 4

15ml/1 tbsp groundnut or vegetable oil
5ml/1 tsp toasted sesame oil
1 garlic clove, chopped
175g/6oz/⅓ cup asparagus tips
2.5cm/1in piece fresh root ginger, finely chopped
225g/8oz/1 cup baby carrots
350g/12oz/3 cups broccoli florets
2 spring onions, cut on the diagonal
175g/6oz/1½ cups spring greens, finely shredded
30ml/2 tbsp light soy sauce
15ml/1 tbsp apple juice
15ml/1 tbsp sesame seeds, toasted

1 Heat a wok or frying pan over a high heat. Add the groundnut or vegetable oil and sesame oil, reduce the heat and sauté the garlic for 2 minutes.

2 Add the asparagus, ginger, carrots and broccoli and stir-fry for 4 minutes. Add the spring onions and spring greens, and stir-fry for a further 2 minutes.

3 Pour over the soy sauce and apple juice and cook for 1–2 minutes until the vegetables are just tender, adding a little water if the stir-fry appears too dry.

4 Sprinkle the sesame seeds on top to serve.

NUTRITION NOTES	
Per portion:	
Energy	109kcals/592kJ
Protein	6.9g
Fat	5.8g
saturated fat	0.8g
Carbohydrate	7.7g
Fibre	5.9g
Sugars	6.9g
Calcium	174mg

Oriental Green Beans

INGREDIENTS

Serves 4

450g/1lb/3 cups green beans, trimmed
15ml/1 tbsp olive oil
5ml/1 tsp sesame oil
2 garlic cloves, crushed
2.5cm/1in piece fresh root ginger, finely chopped
30ml/2 tbsp dark soy sauce

NUTRITION NOTES	
Per portion:	
Energy	63kcals/259kJ
Protein	2.1g
Fat	4.6g
saturated fat	0.7g
Carbohydrate	3.6g
Fibre	2.5g
Sugars	2.6g
Calcium	40.7mg

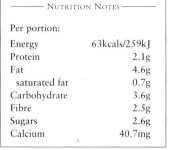

1 Steam the beans for 6 minutes or until just tender.

HEALTH BENEFITS
Green and orange vegetables are an excellent source of betacarotene, as well as vitamins C and E. When they are lightly cooked with ginger and garlic, they give the immune system a significant boost.

2 Meanwhile, heat the oils in a heavy-based saucepan, and sauté the garlic for about 2 minutes. Add the ginger and soy sauce and cook for a further 2–3 minutes until reduced, then pour over the warm beans.

3 Leave to stand for a few minutes before serving to allow all the flavours to infuse.

Courgettes Italian-style

FREE FROM

The olive oil gives this dish a delicious fragrance but does not overpower the courgettes.

INGREDIENTS

Serves 4
15ml/1 tbsp olive oil
15ml/1 tbsp sunflower oil
1 large onion, chopped
1 garlic clove, crushed
4–5 medium courgettes, sliced
150ml/¼ pint/⅔ cup hot Chicken or
   Vegetable Stock
2.5ml/½ tsp chopped fresh oregano
ground black pepper
chopped fresh parsley, to garnish

1 Heat the oils in a large frying pan and fry the onion and garlic over a moderate heat for 5–6 minutes until the onion has softened and is beginning to brown.

2 Add the courgettes slices and fry for about 4 minutes until they just begin to be flecked with brown on both sides. Stir frequently.

3 Stir in the stock, fresh oregano and pepper, and simmer gently for about 8–10 minutes until the liquid has almost evaporated. Spoon the courgettes into a serving dish, sprinkle with chopped fresh parsley and serve.

NUTRITION NOTES	
Per portion:	
Energy	82Kcals/338kJ
Protein	2.2g
Fat	5.9g
saturated fat	0.84g
Carbohydrate	5g
Fibre	1.4g
Sodium	6mg

Spiced Coconut Mushrooms

Here is a simple and delicious way to cook mushrooms. The use of groundnut oil adds a pleasant, subtle flavour. They may be served with almost any Asian meal as well as with grilled or roasted meats and poultry.

INGREDIENTS

Serves 3–4

10ml/2 tbsp groundnut oil
2 garlic cloves, finely chopped
2 red chillies, seeded and sliced
   into rings
3 shallots, finely chopped
225g/8oz/3 cups button mushrooms,
   thickly sliced
150ml/¼ pint/⅔ cup coconut milk
30ml/2 tbsp finely chopped
   fresh coriander
ground black pepper

FREE FROM

1 Heat a wok or frying pan until hot, add the oil and swirl it around, coating the sides of the wok well. When the oil is hot, add the chopped garlic and chillies, then stir-fry for a few seconds.

——— NUTRITION NOTES ———

Per portion:	
Energy	95Kcals/394kJ
Protein	2.2g
Fat	7.9g
saturated fat	1.48g
Carbohydrate	4g
Fibre	1.2g
Sodium	63mg

2 Add the chopped shallots and stir-fry for 2–3 minutes until softened. Add the sliced mushrooms and stir-fry for 3 minutes more.

3 Pour in the coconut milk and bring to the boil. Boil rapidly over high heat until the liquid is reduced by half and coats the mushrooms.

4 Taste and season as necessary. Sprinkle over the coriander and toss gently to mix. Serve at once.

Broad Beans with Mixed Herbs

Peeling the broad beans is a bit time-consuming, but well worth the effort, and this dish is so delicious that you won't want to eat broad beans any other way.

INGREDIENTS

Serves 4
375g/12oz frozen broad beans
15ml/½oz/1 tbsp soya margarine
4–5 spring onions, sliced
15ml/1 tbsp chopped fresh coriander
5ml/1 tsp chopped fresh mint
2.5–5ml/½–1 tsp ground cumin
10ml/2 tsp olive oil
salt

1 Cook the broad beans in lightly salted boiling water for about 4 minutes, or until tender.

2 Drain and, when cool enough to handle, peel away the outer skin, so you are left with the bright green seed.

3 Melt the margarine in a small pan and gently fry the spring onions for 2–3 minutes. Add the broad beans and then stir in the coriander, mint, cumin and a pinch of salt. Stir in the olive oil and serve immediately.

——— NUTRITION NOTES ———

Per portion:

Energy	122kcals/513kJ
Protein	7.7g
Fat	5.4g
saturated fat	2.4g
Carbohydrate	11.3g
Fibre	6.2g
Sugars	1.5g
Calcium	60mg

Courgettes with Moroccan Spices

This is a delicious way of cooking courgettes. Serve as an accompaniment to lamb tagines or stews, roast meats or chicken. Unless you are allergic to nuts, sprinkle with a handful of toasted sesame or sunflower seeds before serving.

INGREDIENTS

Serves 4
500g/1¼lb courgettes
lemon juice and chopped fresh
   coriander and parsley, to serve

For the spicy *charmoula*
1 onion
1–2 garlic cloves, crushed
¼ red or green chilli, seeded and
   finely sliced
2.5ml/½ tsp paprika
2.5ml/½ tsp ground cumin
45ml/3 tbsp olive oil
salt and ground black pepper

1 Preheat the oven to 180°C/350°F/ Gas 4. Cut the courgettes into quarters or eighths lengthways, depending on their size, and place in a shallow ovenproof dish or casserole.

2 Finely chop or coarsely grate the onion and blend with the other *charmoula* ingredients and 60ml/4 tbsp cold water. Pour the *charmoula* over the courgettes. Cover the dish with foil or a lid and cook in the oven for 15 minutes.

3 Baste the courgettes with the *charmoula*, and return to the oven, uncovered, for 5–10 minutes until the courgettes are tender. Sprinkle with lemon juice and fresh coriander and parsley and serve.

——— NUTRITION NOTES ———

Per portion:

Energy	95kcals/392kJ
Protein	2.4g
Fat	8g
saturated fat	1.2g
Carbohydrate	3.4g
Fibre	1.3g
Sugars	2.9g
Calcium	35mg

——— COOK'S TIP ———

Buy young courgettes with tender skin – older courgettes may need to be peeled.

SALADS

Fresh, raw salads are packed with nutrients. There is nothing like the

taste of a cool, crisp salad to complement a rich main dish.

With the addition of more substantial ingredients, such as couscous,

bulgur wheat or pasta, salads can also be enjoyed as a main meal.

Leafy salads, such as Spinach Salad with Polenta Croûtons, make

the perfect addition to any meal, while Couscous Salad and

Spanish Rice Salad make an ideal light lunch or supper.

Spanish Rice Salad

This rice salad is packed with the flavours of the Mediterranean and would make a good accompaniment to all sorts of fish, poultry and meat dishes.

INGREDIENTS

Serves 4

275g/10oz long grain rice
1 bunch spring onions, finely sliced
1 green pepper, seeded and finely diced
1 yellow pepper, seeded and finely diced
225g/8oz tomatoes, peeled, seeded and chopped
30ml/2 tbsp fresh chopped coriander

For the dressing

75ml/5 tbsp mixed sunflower and olive oil
15ml/1 tbsp rice vinegar
5ml/1 tsp gluten-free Dijon mustard
salt and ground black pepper

1 Cook the rice for 10–12 minutes until tender but still slightly firm. Do not overcook. Drain and rinse with cold water.

COOK'S TIP

Cooked garden peas, cooked diced carrot and/or canned or frozen sweetcorn could be added to this adaptable salad.

2 Allow the rice to cool completely and then place in a large serving bowl. Add the spring onions, peppers, tomatoes and coriander.

3 Make the dressing by putting all the ingredients in a jar with a tight-fitting lid and shaking vigorously until well blended. Stir the dressing into the rice and adjust the seasoning.

4 Cover and chill for about 1 hour before serving.

NUTRITION NOTES

Per portion:

Energy	275kcals/1162kJ
Protein	4.3g
Fat	11.1g
saturated fat	1.8g
Carbohydrate	42g
Sugar	2.8g
Fibre	1.6g
Calcium	37mg

Salad Niçoise

There are probably as many versions of this salad as there are cooks in Provence. This regional classic makes a wonderful lunch or starter to a main meal.

INGREDIENTS

Serves 4

225g/8oz French beans, trimmed
450g/1lb new potatoes, peeled and cut
  into 2.5cm/1in pieces
white wine vinegar and olive oil,
  for sprinkling
1 small cos or round lettuce
4 ripe plum tomatoes, quartered
1 small cucumber, peeled, seeded
  and sliced
1 green or red pepper, thinly sliced
4 eggs, hard-boiled, peeled
  and quartered
24 black olives
225g/8oz can tuna in brine, drained
50g/2oz can anchovies, drained
basil leaves, to garnish

For the dressing

15ml/1 tbsp gluten-free Dijon mustard
50g/2oz can anchovies, drained
1 garlic clove, crushed
60ml/4 tbsp lemon juice
120ml/4fl oz/½ cup sunflower oil
120ml/4fl oz/½ cup extra virgin
  olive oil
salt and ground black pepper

1 To make the dressing, place the mustard, anchovies and garlic in a bowl and blend together by pressing the garlic and anchovies against the sides of the bowl. Season generously with pepper. Using a small whisk, blend in the lemon juice or wine vinegar. Slowly whisk in the sunflower oil in a thin stream and then the olive oil, whisking until the dressing is smooth and creamy.

2 Tip the French beans into a saucepan of salted boiling water and cook for 3 minutes until tender, yet crisp. Transfer to a colander with a slotted spoon then rinse under cold running water. Drain again and set aside.

3 Add the potatoes to the same boiling water, reduce the heat and simmer for 10–15 minutes until just tender, then drain. Sprinkle with a little vinegar and olive oil and a spoonful of the dressing.

4 Arrange the lettuce on a platter, top with the tomatoes, cucumber and pepper, then add the cooked French beans and potatoes.

5 Arrange the eggs, olives, tuna and anchovies on top, distributing them evenly, and garnish with the basil leaves. Drizzle the remaining dressing over the top.

NUTRITION NOTES	
Per portion:	
Energy	319kcals/1327kJ
Protein	18.2g
Fat	25.3g
saturated fat	3.4g
Carbohydrate	4.6g
Sugar	4.3g
Fibre	2.3g
Calcium	81mg

FREE FROM

Greek Salad

Use a soya-based alternative to feta cheese if preferred.

INGREDIENTS

Serves 6

1 small cos lettuce, sliced
450g/1lb tomatoes, cut into eighths
1 cucumber, seeded and chopped
200g/7oz feta cheese, crumbled
4 spring onions, sliced
50g/2oz/½ cup black olives, pitted
   and halved

For the dressing
90ml/6 tbsp extra virgin olive oil
25ml/1½ tbsp lemon juice
salt and ground black pepper

1 Put the lettuce, tomatoes, cucumber, feta cheese, spring onions and olives into a large bowl.

2 To make the dressing, whisk together the olive oil and lemon juice, then season with salt and pepper.

3 Pour the dressing over the salad. Toss gently until the ingredients are lightly coated in the dressing, then serve immediately.

NUTRITION NOTES	
Per portion:	
Energy	215kcals/890kJ
Protein	6.6g
Fat	19.1g
saturated fat	6.4g
Carbohydrate	4.3g
Sugar	4.2g
Fibre	1.8g
Calcium	148mg

Spiced Aubergine Salad

This Middle Eastern style salad can be served either as a starter or light lunch dish or to accompany a main course rice pilaff. Choose the type of yogurt that will suit your diet, or omit it altogether.

INGREDIENTS

Serves 4

2 small aubergines, sliced
75ml/5 tbsp olive oil
50ml/2fl oz/¼ cup red wine vinegar
2 garlic cloves, crushed
15ml/1 tbsp lemon juice
2.5ml/½ tsp ground cumin
2.5ml/½ tsp ground coriander
½ cucumber, thinly sliced
2 tomatoes, thinly sliced
30ml/2 tbsp natural yogurt,
   to serve (optional)
salt and ground black pepper
chopped flat leaf parsley, to garnish

1 Preheat the grill. Brush the aubergine slices lightly with some of the oil and cook under a high heat, turning once, until golden and tender.

2 Cut the cooked aubergine slices into quarters.

3 Mix together the remaining oil, vinegar, garlic, lemon juice, cumin and coriander. Season with salt and pepper and mix thoroughly. Add the warm aubergines, stir well and chill for at least 2 hours.

4 Add the cucumber and tomatoes and mix well. Transfer to a serving dish and spoon the yogurt on top, if using.

NUTRITION NOTES	
Per portion:	
Energy	148kcals/612kJ
Protein	1.5g
Fat	14.2g
saturated fat	2.11g
Carbohydrate	3.8g
Sugar	3.6g
Fibre	1.92g
Calcium	29.7mg

Black and Orange Salad

The darkness of the olives contrasts with the brightness of the orange wedges in this attractive salad.

INGREDIENTS

Serves 4

3 oranges
115g/4oz/1 cup black olives, pitted
15ml/1 tbsp chopped fresh coriander
15ml/1 tbsp chopped fresh parsley
30ml/2 tbsp olive oil
15ml/1 tbsp lemon juice
2.5ml/½ tsp paprika
2.5ml/½ tsp ground cumin

1 Cut away the peel and pith from the oranges and cut into wedges.

2 Place the oranges in a salad bowl and add the black olives, coriander and parsley.

3 Blend together the olive oil, lemon juice, paprika and cumin. Pour the dressing over the salad and toss gently. Chill for about 30 minutes and serve.

——— NUTRITION NOTES ———	
Per portion:	
Energy	120kcals/500kJ
Protein	1.5g
Fat	8.8g
saturated fat	1.3g
Carbohydrate	9.2g
Sugar	9.2g
Fibre	2.7g
Calcium	69mg

Rocket and Coriander Salad

Rocket leaves have a wonderful, peppery flavour and, mixed with coriander, make a delicious green salad. However, unless you grow your own rocket, or have access to a plentiful supply, you may well have to use extra spinach or another green leaf in order to pad this salad out.

INGREDIENTS

Serves 4

115g/4oz or more rocket leaves
115g/4oz young spinach leaves
1 large bunch (about 25g/1oz)
   fresh coriander, chopped
2–3 fresh parsley sprigs, chopped
1 garlic clove, crushed
45ml/3 tbsp olive oil
10ml/2 tsp white wine vinegar
pinch of paprika
cayenne pepper
salt

1 Place the rocket and spinach leaves in a salad bowl. Add the chopped coriander and parsley.

2 In a small jug, blend together the garlic, olive oil, vinegar, paprika, cayenne pepper and salt.

3 Pour the dressing over the salad, toss lightly, then serve immediately.

——— NUTRITION NOTES ———	
Per portion:	
Energy	88kcals/364kJ
Protein	1.6g
Fat	8.7g
saturated fat	1.2g
Carbohydrate	0.9g
Sugar	0.8g
Fibre	1.2g
Calcium	97mg

Sweet-and-sour Artichoke Salad

FREE FROM

Agrodolce is a sweet–and–sour sauce, which works perfectly in this artichoke salad.

INGREDIENTS

Serves 4–6
6 small globe artichokes
juice of 1 lemon
30ml/2 tbsp olive oil
2 medium onions, roughly chopped
175g/6oz/1 cup fresh or frozen broad beans (shelled weight)
175g/6oz/1½ cups fresh or frozen peas (shelled weight)
ground black pepper
fresh mint leaves, to garnish

For the *salsa agrodolce*
120ml/4fl oz/½ cup white wine vinegar
15ml/1 tbsp caster sugar
a handful of fresh mint leaves, roughly torn

1 Peel the outer leaves from the artichokes and discard. Cut the artichokes into quarters and place in a bowl of water with the lemon juice.

2 Heat the oil in a large saucepan and add the onions. Cook until the onions are golden. Add the beans and stir, then drain the artichokes and add to the pan. Pour in about 300ml/½ pint/1¼ cups water and cook, covered, for 10–15 minutes.

3 Add the peas, season with pepper and cook for a further 5 minutes, stirring from time to time, until the vegetables are tender. Strain through a sieve and place all the vegetables in a bowl. Leave to cool, then chill.

4 To make the *salsa agrodolce*, mix together all the ingredients in a small pan. Heat gently for 2–3 minutes until the sugar has dissolved. Simmer gently for about 5 minutes, stirring occasionally. Leave to cool. To serve, drizzle the salsa over the vegetables and garnish with mint leaves.

NUTRITION NOTES	
Per portion:	
Energy	162Kcals/678kJ
Protein	8.2g
Fat	6.6g
saturated fat	0.96g
Carbohydrate	19g
Fibre	5.7g
Sodium	31mg

Couscous Salad

Couscous salad is popular almost everywhere nowadays. This salad has a delicate flavour and is excellent served with grilled chicken or kebabs.

INGREDIENTS

Serves 4

275g/10oz/1⅔ cups couscous
550ml/18fl oz/2½ cups boiling home-
   made vegetable stock
12 black olives in oil
2 small courgettes
25g/1oz/¼ cup flaked almonds,
   toasted
60ml/4 tbsp olive oil
15ml/1 tbsp lemon juice
15ml/1 tbsp chopped fresh coriander
15ml/1 tbsp chopped fresh parsley
a good pinch of ground cumin
a good pinch of cayenne pepper

FREE
FROM

1 Place the couscous in a large bowl and pour over the boiling stock. Stir with a fork, and then set aside for about 10 minutes for the stock to be absorbed. Fluff up with a fork.

NUTRITION NOTES	
Per portion:	
Energy	341Kcals/1418kJ
Protein	7g
Fat	19.2g
saturated fat	2.5g
Carbohydrate	37g
Fibre	1.4g
Sodium	354mg

2 Drain the olives and halve them, discarding the stones. Top and tail the courgettes and cut into small julienne strips.

3 Carefully mix the courgettes, olives and almonds into the couscous.

4 Blend together the olive oil, lemon juice, herbs and spices, and stir into the salad. Serve at room temperature.

COOK'S TIP

If you prefer, you can reconstitute the pre-cooked couscous by steaming it.

Orange and Red Onion Salad with Cumin

Cumin and mint give this lovely summer salad a Middle Eastern flavour. Choose small, seedless oranges if you can.

INGREDIENTS

Serves 6
6 oranges
2 red onions, finely sliced
15ml/1 tbsp cumin seeds
5ml/1 tsp ground black pepper
15ml/1 tbsp chopped fresh mint
90ml/6 tbsp olive oil
fresh mint sprigs and black olives
  in oil, to serve

COOK'S TIP

It is important to let the salad stand for 2 hours, so that the flavours develop and the onion softens slightly, but do not leave the salad for much longer than this.

---

1 Slice the oranges thinly, working over a bowl to catch any juice. Then, holding each orange slice in turn over the bowl, cut round with scissors to remove the peel and pith. Separate the onion slices into rings.

2 Arrange the orange slices and onion rings in layers in a shallow dish, sprinkling each layer with cumin seeds, black pepper, mint and olive oil. Pour over the orange juice saved while slicing the oranges. Leave the salad to marinate for about 2 hours.

3 Just before serving, scatter the salad with the fresh sprigs of mint and drained black olives.

NUTRITION NOTES

Per portion:

Energy	178Kcals/740kJ
Protein	2.6g
Fat	11.6g
saturated fat	1.56g
Carbohydrate	17g
Fibre	3.1g
Sodium	12mg

Spanish Salad with Capers and Olives

Sweet, ripe tomatoes are the perfect foil to the sharp tang of capers and olives.

INGREDIENTS

Serves 4
4 tomatoes, peeled and finely diced
½ cucumber, peeled and finely diced
1 bunch spring onions
1 bunch purslane or watercress, washed
8 pimiento-stuffed olives in oil
15ml/1 tbsp capers in vinegar, drained

For the dressing
30ml/2 tbsp red wine vinegar
5ml/1 tsp paprika
2.5ml/½ tsp ground cumin
1 garlic clove, crushed
75ml/5 tbsp olive oil
ground black pepper

1 Put the tomatoes and cucumber in a bowl. Trim and chop half the spring onions, add them to the salad bowl and mix lightly.

2 Break the purslane or watercress into small sprigs. Add to the tomato mixture, along with the olives and capers.

NUTRITION NOTES

Per portion:

Energy	150Kcals/615kJ
Protein	1.5g
Fat	14.8g
saturated fat	2.2g
Carbohydrate	5.8g
Fibre	1.4g
Sodium	151mg

3 Make the dressing. Mix the wine vinegar, paprika, cumin and garlic in a bowl. Whisk in the oil and add pepper to taste. Pour over the salad and toss lightly. Serve with the remaining trimmed spring onions.

Spinach Salad with Polenta Croûtons

The combination of tender baby spinach leaves, crunchy polenta croûtons and a simple lemon dressing not only makes a delicious tangy salad, but is full of cancer-fighting nutrients.

INGREDIENTS

Serves 4

1 large red onion, cut into wedges
300g/11oz/3 cups ready-made polenta, cut into 1cm/½in cubes
olive oil, for brushing
225g/8oz baby spinach leaves
1 avocado, peeled, stoned and sliced
5ml/1 tsp lemon juice

For the dressing
60ml/4 tbsp extra virgin olive oil
juice of ½ lemon
salt and ground black pepper

1 Preheat the oven to 200°C/400°F/ Gas 6. Roast the onion and polenta on lightly oiled baking sheets for about 25 minutes or until the onion is tender and the polenta is golden, turning regularly. Leave to cool slightly.

2 Meanwhile, make the dressing. Combine the olive oil, lemon juice and seasoning in a screw top jar or bowl. Shake or stir to combine.

3 Arrange the spinach leaves in a serving bowl. Toss the avocado slices in the lemon juice to prevent them browning, then add to the spinach with the roasted onions.

4 Pour over the dressing and toss with your hands to combine. Sprinkle over the polenta croûtons just before serving to retain their crunch.

NUTRITION NOTES

Per portion:

Energy	329kcals/1364kJ
Protein	6.1g
Fat	19.7g
saturated fat	3.2g
Carbohydrate	31.0g
Fibre	3.6g
Sugars	2.5g
Calcium	107.2mg

HEALTH BENEFITS

Corn, from which polenta is made, is thought to help prevent cancer of the colon, breast and prostate. Fresh spinach is a good source of the cancer-fighting nutrient, betacarotene. Extra virgin olive oil contains the antioxidant vitamin E, while lemon juice contains vitamin C – both of which have been found to help combat cancer.

Roasted Plum Tomato and Rocket Salad

This is a great side salad to accompany grilled chicken or fish and will make an excellent additional source of anti-cancer nutrients in any meal.

INGREDIENTS

Serves 4

225g/8oz/2 cups dried egg-free
  chifferini or pipe pasta
450g/1lb ripe baby plum tomatoes,
  halved lengthways
75ml/5 tbsp extra virgin olive oil
2 garlic cloves, cut into thin slivers
30ml/2 tbsp balsamic vinegar
2 pieces sun-dried tomato in olive oil,
  drained and chopped
large pinch of sugar, to taste
1 handful rocket, about 65g/2½oz
salt and ground black pepper

1 Preheat the oven to 190°C/375°F/ Gas 5. Meanwhile, cook the pasta in salted boiling water according to the instructions on the packet.

2 Arrange the halved tomatoes cut side up in a roasting tin, drizzle 30ml/2 tbsp of the oil over them and sprinkle with the slivers of garlic and salt and pepper to taste. Roast in the oven for 20 minutes, turning once.

HEALTH BENEFITS

Tomatoes contain the bioflavonoid, lycopene, which is believed to prevent some forms of cancer by reducing the harmful effects of free radicals.

3 Put the remaining oil in a large bowl with the vinegar, sun-dried tomatoes, sugar and a little salt and pepper to taste. Stir well to mix. Drain the pasta, add it to the bowl of dressing and toss to mix. Add the roasted tomatoes and mix gently.

4 Before serving, add the rocket, toss lightly and taste for seasoning. Serve at room temperature or, alternatively, chilled.

--- NUTRITION NOTES ---

Per portion:

Energy	352kcals/1480kJ
Protein	8.2g
Fat	16.6g
saturated fat	2.4g
Carbohydrate	45.4g
Fibre	3.1g
Sugars	5.5g
Calcium	54.8mg

--- VARIATIONS ---

• If you are in a hurry and don't have time to roast the tomatoes, you can leave out the roasting step and make the salad with halved raw tomatoes instead.
• If your diet permits, try adding 150g/5oz/ 1¼ cups mozzarella cheese, drained and diced, with the rocket in Step 4.

FREE
FROM

Watercress, Pear, Walnut and Roquefort Salad

Combining fresh, raw fruit and salad leaves with walnuts creates a delicious cleansing salad that is rich in antioxidants and enzymes that boost the immune system.

INGREDIENTS

Serves 6
75g/3oz/½ cup shelled walnuts, halved
2 red Williams pears
15ml/1 tbsp lemon juice
150g/5oz/1 large bunch watercress, tough stalks removed
200g/7oz/2 scant cups Roquefort, cut into chunks

For the dressing
45ml/3 tbsp extra virgin olive oil
30ml/2 tbsp lemon juice
2.5ml/½ tsp clear honey
5ml/1 tsp gluten-free Dijon mustard
salt and ground black pepper

1 Toast the walnuts in a dry frying pan for 2 minutes until golden, tossing frequently to prevent them from burning.

2 Meanwhile, make the dressing. Combine the olive oil, lemon juice, honey, mustard and seasoning in a screw-top jar or bowl. Shake or mix to combine thoroughly.

3 Halve the pears, remove the cores, then cut into slices. Toss the pear slices in the lemon juice to prevent them browning, then combine with the watercress, walnuts and Roquefort in a bowl.

4 Pour the dressing over the salad, toss well and serve immediately.

--- NUTRITION NOTES ---

Per portion:
Energy	287kcals/1189kJ
Protein	9.3g
Fat	38.0g
saturated fat	8.5g
Carbohydrate	5.9g
Fibre	1.9g
Sugars	5.8g
Calcium	237mg

Panzanella

This classic Tuscan salad brings together nutrient-packed raw vegetables with open-textured Italian bread.

INGREDIENTS

Serves 6
275g/10oz/10 slices day-old egg-free Italian-style bread, thickly sliced
1 medium cucumber, peeled and cut into chunks
5 tomatoes, seeded and diced
1 large red onion, chopped
225g/8oz/1⅓ cups good quality olives
20 basil leaves, torn

For the dressing
60ml/4 tbsp extra virgin olive oil
15ml/1 tbsp red or white wine vinegar
salt and ground black pepper

1 Soak the bread in water for about 2 minutes, then remove and squeeze gently, first with your hands and then in a dish towel to remove any excess water. Store in the fridge for 1 hour.

2 Meanwhile, make the dressing. Place the oil, vinegar and seasoning in a screw-top jar or bowl. Shake or mix to combine.

3 Mix together the cucumber, tomatoes, onion and olives in a large serving bowl. Break the bread into chunks and add to the bowl with the torn basil leaves. Pour the dressing over the salad, and toss lightly to combine. Serve immediately.

--- NUTRITION NOTES ---

Per portion:
Energy	219kcals/918kJ
Protein	4.9g
Fat	11.4g
saturated fat	1.6g
Carbohydrate	25.9g
Fibre	2.2g
Sugars	3.8g
Calcium	75.8mg

Warm Potato Salad with Herb Dressing

Many herbs are known for their medicinal qualities. The herbs suggested in this delightful salad are commonly used for cleansing and strengthening the body.

INGREDIENTS

Serves 6
1kg/2¼lb waxy or salad potatoes
90ml/6 tbsp extra virgin olive oil
juice of 1 lemon
1 garlic clove, very finely chopped
30ml/2 tbsp chopped fresh herbs, such
 as parsley, basil, thyme or oregano
salt and ground black pepper

1 Cook the potatoes in their skins in boiling salted water.

2 Meanwhile make the dressing. Mix together the olive oil, lemon juice, garlic, herbs and seasoning.

3 Drain the potatoes and leave until cool enough to handle. Peel and cut the potatoes into dice and place in a large bowl.

4 Pour the dressing over the potatoes while they are still warm and mix well. Serve at once, garnished with fresh basil leaves.

NUTRITION NOTES	
Per portion:	
Energy	217kcals/910kJ
Protein	2.9g
Fat	11.5g
saturated fat	1.7g
Carbohydrate	26.9g
Fibre	1.9g
Sugars	2.3g
Calcium	20mg

Warm Hazelnut and Pistachio Salad

INGREDIENTS

Serves 4
900g/2lb small new potatoes or
 salad potatoes
30ml/2 tbsp hazelnut or walnut oil
60ml/4 tbsp sunflower oil
juice of 1 lemon
25g/1oz/¼ cup hazelnuts
15 pistachio nuts
salt and ground black pepper
flat leaf parsley sprig, to garnish

NUTRITION NOTES	
Per portion:	
Energy	391kcals/1365kJ
Protein	6.1g
Fat	25.2g
saturated fat	2.8g
Carbohydrate	37.2g
Fibre	3.1g
Sugars	33.6g
Calcium	30.7mg

1 Cook the potatoes in their skins in boiling salted water for about 10–15 minutes until tender. Drain well and leave to cool slightly.

2 Meanwhile mix together the hazelnut or walnut oil with the sunflower oil and lemon juice and season well. Pour over the potatoes.

3 Roughly chop the nuts. Sprinkle over the potatoes. Serve garnished with flat leaf parsley.

HEALTH BENEFITS
Nuts and nut oils are a rich source of the valuable antioxidant, vitamin E, which has been associated with lowering the risks of certain types of cancer. Other vital anti-cancer nutrients contained in nuts include vitamin B, calcium and plant protein.

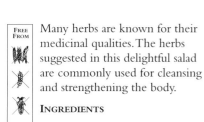

Warm Chicken Salad with Hazelnut Dressing

This simple warm salad combines pan-fried chicken and spinach with a light, nutty dressing.

INGREDIENTS

Serves 4

45ml/3 tbsp olive oil
30ml/2 tbsp hazelnut oil
15ml/1 tbsp white wine vinegar
1 garlic clove, crushed
15ml/1 tbsp chopped fresh mixed herbs
225g/8oz baby spinach leaves
250g/9oz cherry tomatoes, halved
1 bunch spring onions, chopped
2 skinless, boneless chicken breasts, cut into thin strips
salt and ground black pepper

VARIATION

Use other meat or fish such as beef or salmon in place of the chicken.

1 First make the dressing, place 30ml/2 tbsp of the olive oil, the hazelnut oil, vinegar, garlic and chopped herbs in a small bowl or jug and whisk together until thoroughly mixed. Set aside.

2 Trim any long stalks from the spinach leaves, then place in a large serving bowl with the tomatoes and spring onions and toss together to mix.

--- NUTRITION NOTES ---

Per portion:

Energy	300kcals/1250kJ
Fat, total	20.9g
saturated fat	2.7g
Protein	23.2g
Carbohydrate	4.8g
sugar, total	4.5g
Fibre	2.4g
Sodium	126mg

3 Heat the remaining 15ml/1 tbsp olive oil in a frying pan, add the chicken and stir-fry over a high heat for 7–10 minutes until the chicken is cooked, tender and lightly browned.

4 Scatter the cooked chicken pieces over the salad, give the dressing a quick whisk to blend, then drizzle it over the salad and gently toss all the ingredients together to mix. Season to taste with salt and pepper and serve immediately.

Fruit and Nut Coleslaw

A delicious and nutritious mixture of crunchy vegetables, fruit and nuts, tossed together in a light mayonnaise dressing.

INGREDIENTS

Serves 6

225g/8oz white cabbage
1 large carrot
175g/6oz/¾ cup ready-to-eat dried apricots
50g/2oz/½ cup walnuts
50g/2oz/½ cup hazelnuts
115g/4oz/1 cup raisins
30ml/2 tbsp chopped fresh parsley or chives or a mixture
105ml/7 tbsp gluten-free reduced-calorie mayonnaise
75ml/5 tbsp low-fat natural yogurt
salt and ground black pepper
fresh chives, to garnish

1 Finely shred the cabbage, coarsely grate the carrot and place both in a large mixing bowl. Roughly chop the apricots and nuts. Stir them into the cabbage and carrots with the raisins and chopped herbs.

2 In a separate bowl, mix together the mayonnaise and yogurt and season to taste with salt and pepper.

3 Add the mayonnaise to the cabbage mixture and toss together to mix.

4 Cover the bowl and set aside in a cool place for at least 30 minutes before serving, to allow the flavours to mingle. Serve the coleslaw garnished with a few fresh chives.

--- NUTRITION NOTES ---

Per portion:

Energy	283kcals/1185kJ
Fat, total	16.4g
saturated fat	0.9g
Protein	5.5g
Carbohydrate	30.1g
sugar, total	29g
Fibre	4.4g
Sodium	199mg

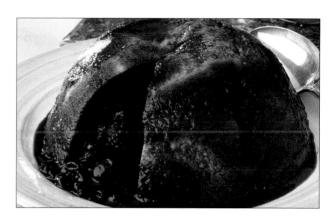

DESSERTS

This chapter shows you just how easy it is to make delicious

desserts without risking your health. Each recipe uses low-fat,

nutrient-packed ingredients to create the perfect end to a healthy meal.

Whatever your preference, there is a mouth-watering choice, such as

Dried Fruit Salad with Summer Berries, Melon Trio with Ginger

Biscuits, and Blackcurrant Sorbet, as well as traditional desserts, such

as creamy Portuguese Rice Pudding and fruity Summer Pudding.

Pears with Ginger and Star Anise

Star anise and ginger give a refreshing twist to these poached pears. Serve them chilled.

INGREDIENTS

Serves 4
75g/3oz/6 tbsp caster sugar
300ml/½ pint/1¼ cups white
   dessert wine
thinly pared rind and juice of 1 lemon
7.5cm/3in piece fresh root
   ginger, bruised
5 star anise
10 cloves
600ml/1 pint/2½ cups cold water
6 slightly unripe pears
25g/1oz/3 tbsp drained, stem ginger
   in syrup, sliced
fromage frais, to serve (optional)

1 Place the caster sugar, dessert wine, lemon rind and juice, fresh root ginger, star anise, cloves and water into a saucepan just large enough to hold the pears snugly in an upright position. Bring to the boil.

2 Meanwhile, peel the pears, leaving the stems intact. Add them to the wine mixture, making sure that they are totally immersed in the liquid.

3 Return the wine mixture to the boil, lower the heat, cover and simmer for 15–20 minutes or until the pears are tender. Lift out the pears with a slotted spoon and place them in a heatproof dish.

4 Boil the wine syrup rapidly until it is reduced by about half, then pour over the pears. Allow them to cool, then chill.

5 Cut the pears into thick slices and arrange these on four serving plates. Remove the ginger and whole spices from the wine sauce, stir in the sliced stem ginger and spoon the sauce over the pears. Serve with fromage frais, if you like.

NUTRITION NOTES	
Per portion:	
Energy	190kcals/807kJ
Protein	0.8g
Fat	0.3g
saturated fat	0g
Carbohydrate	45g
Sugar	44.7g
Fibre	5.2g
Calcium	32mg

Blackcurrant Sorbet

This luscious sorbet is easily made by hand, but it is important to alternately freeze and blend or process the mixture five or six times to get the best result. If you make lots of ice cream and sorbets, it is worth investing in an electric ice cream maker.

INGREDIENTS

Serves 6

115g/4oz/½ cup caster sugar
225g/8oz/2 cups fresh or
 frozen blackcurrants
5ml/1 tsp lemon juice
30ml/2 tbsp crème de cassis or other
 blackcurrant liqueur (optional)
2 egg whites (optional)

1 Pour 300ml/½ pint/1¼ cups water into a saucepan and add the sugar. Place over a low heat until the sugar has dissolved. Bring to the boil and boil rapidly for 10 minutes, then set the syrup aside to cool.

2 Meanwhile, cook the blackcurrants in a saucepan with 30ml/2 tbsp water over a low heat for 5–7 minutes until tender.

3 Press the cooked blackcurrants and their juice through a sieve placed over a jug. Stir the resulting blackcurrant purée into the syrup with the lemon juice and the blackcurrant liqueur, if using. Allow to cool completely, then chill for 1 hour.

4 Pour the chilled blackcurrant syrup into a freezerproof bowl; freeze until slushy, removing and whisking occasionally until it reaches this point. Whisk the egg whites, if using, in a grease-free bowl until they form soft peaks, then gently fold into the semi-frozen blackcurrant mixture.

5 Freeze the mixture again until firm, then spoon into a food processor or blender and process. Alternately freeze and process or blend until completely smooth. Serve the sorbet straight from the freezer.

NUTRITION NOTES	
Per portion:	
Energy	103kcals/438kJ
Protein	1.3g
Fat	0g
saturated fat	0g
Carbohydrate	24.2g
Sugar	24.2g
Fibre	1.3g
Calcium	25mg

Cherry Pancakes

Ingredients

Serves 4

50g/2oz/½ cup plain flour
50g/2oz/⅓ cup wholemeal flour
pinch of salt
1 egg white
150ml/¼ pint/⅔ cup skimmed milk
150ml/¼ pint/⅔ cup water
15ml/1 tbsp sunflower oil
low-fat fromage frais, to serve

For the filling

425g/14oz can black cherries in juice
7.5ml/1½ tsp arrowroot

NUTRITION NOTES

Per portion:

Energy	173Kcals/725kJ
Fat	3.33g
saturated fat	0.44g
Cholesterol	0.75mg
Fibre	2.36g

1 Sift the flours and salt into a bowl, adding any bran left in the sieve to the bowl at the end.

2 Make a well in the centre of the flour and add the egg white. Gradually beat in the skimmed milk and water, whisking hard until all the liquid is incorporated and the batter is smooth and frothy.

3 Heat a non-stick frying pan with a small amount of the oil until very hot. Pour in just enough batter to cover the base of the pan, swirling the pan to cover the base evenly.

4 Cook until set and golden, and then turn to cook the other side. Remove to a sheet of kitchen paper and then cook the remaining batter, to make about eight pancakes.

5 For the filling, drain the cherries, reserving the juice. Blend about 30ml/2 tbsp of the juice from the can of cherries with the arrowroot in a saucepan. Stir in the rest of the juice. Heat gently, stirring, until boiling. Stir over a moderate heat for 2 minutes, until thickened and clear.

6 Add the cherries to the sauce and stir until thoroughly heated. Spoon the cherries into the pancakes and fold them into quarters. Serve immediately with the fromage frais.

COOK'S TIP

If fresh cherries are in season, cook them gently in enough apple juice just to cover them, and then thicken the juice with arrowroot as in Step 5. The basic pancakes will freeze very successfully between layers of kitchen paper or greaseproof paper.

Summer Pudding

This classic pudding is made with red summer berry fruits, which are rich in antioxidants, carotenes and vitamins C and E.

INGREDIENTS

Serves 4

8 × 1cm/½in-thick slices of day-old
  egg-free white bread, crusts removed
800g/1¾lb/6–7 cups mixed berry fruit,
  such as blackberries, raspberries,
  blackcurrants, redcurrants
  and blueberries
50g/2oz/¼ cup golden caster sugar
lightly whipped double cream or crème
  fraîche, to serve

1 Trim a slice of bread to fit in the base of a 1.2 litre/2 pint/5 cup pudding basin, then trim another 5–6 slices and carefully line the sides of the basin.

2 Place all the fruit in a saucepan with the sugar. Cook gently for 4–5 minutes until the juices begin to run – it will not be necessary to add any water. Allow the mixture to cool, then spoon the berries and enough of their juices to moisten the bread into the pudding basin. Save any leftover juice to serve with the pudding.

3 Fold over the excess bread, then cover the fruit with the remaining bread slices, trimming them to fit. Place a small plate or saucer directly on top of the pudding, fitting it inside the basin. Weight it down with a 900g/2lb weight if you have one, or use a couple of full cans as weights.

4 Leave the pudding in the fridge for at least 8 hours or overnight. To serve, run a knife between the pudding and the basin and turn it out on to a plate. Spoon any reserved juices over the top and serve with whipped cream or crème fraîche.

HEALTH BENEFITS

Berries and currants are rich in antioxidant nutrients that can inhibit the growth of cancer cells and protect against cell damage by carcinogens.

NUTRITION NOTES

Per portion:

Energy	266kcals/1125kJ
Protein	7.4g
Fat	1.5g
saturated fat	0.25g
Carbohydrate	59.3g
Fibre	3.2g
Sugars	26.9g
Calcium	110mg

Melon Trio with Ginger Biscuits

Fresh melon and ginger are both powerful anti-cancer foods, brimming with goodness, which makes this eye-catching dessert a refreshing and healthy choice.

INGREDIENTS

Serves 4

¼ watermelon
½ honeydew melon
½ Charentais melon
60ml/4 tbsp stem ginger syrup

For the biscuits

25g/1oz/2 tbsp unsalted butter
25g/1oz/2 tbsp caster sugar
5ml/1 tsp clear honey
25g/1oz/¼ cup plain flour
25g/1oz/¼ cup mixed glacé fruit,
    finely chopped
1 piece of stem ginger in syrup,
    drained and finely chopped
30ml/2 tbsp flaked almonds

1 Remove the seeds from the melons, cut them into wedges, then slice off the rind. Cut all the flesh into chunks and mix in a bowl. Stir in the ginger syrup, cover and chill until ready to serve.

2 Meanwhile, make the biscuits. Preheat the oven to 180°C/350°F/ Gas 4. Melt the butter, sugar and honey in a saucepan. Remove from the heat and stir in the remaining ingredients.

3 Line a baking sheet with non-stick baking paper. Space four spoonfuls of the mixture on the paper at regular intervals, leaving plenty of room for spreading. Flatten the mixture slightly into rounds and bake for 15 minutes or until the tops are golden.

4 Let the biscuits cool on the baking sheet for 1 minute, then lift each one in turn, using a fish slice, and drape over a rolling pin to cool and harden. Repeat with the remaining ginger mixture to make eight biscuits in all.

5 Serve the melon chunks with some of the syrup and the ginger biscuits.

NUTRITION NOTES

Per portion:

Energy	219kcals/919kJ
Protein	2.6g
Fat	9.5g
saturated fat	3.7g
Carbohydrate	32.5g
Fibre	1.3g
Sugars	27.5g
Calcium	45mg

COOK'S TIP

For an even prettier effect, scoop the melon flesh into balls with the large end of a melon baller.

Portuguese Rice Pudding

This recipe uses egg yolks that are only very lightly cooked. Omit them, if you wish, and use soya milk in place of cow's milk.

INGREDIENTS

Serves 4–6
175g/6oz pudding rice
600ml/1 pint/2½ cups creamy milk
65g/2½oz/5 tbsp butter or pure
    vegetable margarine
2–3 strips pared lemon rind
115g/4oz/½ cup caster sugar
4 egg yolks (optional)
salt
ground cinnamon, for sprinkling

1 Cook the rice in plenty of lightly salted water for about 5 minutes so that it is still uncooked but has lost its brittleness.

2 Drain well and then place in a saucepan with the milk, butter or margarine and lemon rind. Very slowly bring to the boil, then cover and simmer over a low heat for about 20 minutes until the rice is thick and creamy.

3 Turn off the heat and allow the rice mixture to cool a little. Remove and discard the lemon rind and then stir in the sugar and egg yolks, if using.

4 Divide among four to six serving bowls and dust with ground cinnamon. Cool and serve.

— NUTRITION NOTES —	
Per portion:	
Energy 568–378kcals/2375–1583kJ	
Protein	12.1–8g
Fat	27–18g
saturated fat	15.4–10.2g
Carbohydrate	70–47g
Sugar	37–24g
Fibre	0g
Calcium	230–154mg

FREE FROM

Fresh Fruit Salad

FREE FROM

When peaches and strawberries are out of season, use bananas and grapes, or any other fruits.

INGREDIENTS

Serves 6
2 peaches
2 eating apples
2 oranges
16–20 strawberries
30ml/2 tbsp lemon juice
15–30ml/1–2 tbsp orange
    flower water
icing sugar, to taste
a few fresh mint leaves, to decorate

1 Blanch the peaches for 1 minute in boiling water, then peel away the skin and cut the flesh into thick slices. Discard the stone.

2 Peel and core the apples and cut into thin slices. Peel the oranges with a sharp knife, removing all the pith, and segment them, catching any juice in a bowl.

3 Hull the strawberries and halve or quarter if large. Place all the fruit in a large serving bowl.

4 Blend together the lemon juice, orange flower water and any orange juice. Taste and add a little icing sugar to sweeten, if liked.

5 Pour the fruit juice mixture over the salad and serve decorated with a few fresh mint leaves.

--- NUTRITION NOTES ---

Per portion:

Energy	79kcals/338kJ
Protein	1.9g
Fat	0.2g
saturated fat	0
Carbohydrate	18.5g
Fibre	3.4g
Sugars	18.5g
Calcium	47mg

Dried Fruit Salad with Summer Berries

FREE FROM

This is a wonderful combination of fresh and dried fruit and, if you use frozen raspberries or blackberries in the out-of-season winter months, the salad can be made throughout the year. It makes a delicious breakfast dish, served with a cereal that suits your diet.

INGREDIENTS

Serves 4
115g/4oz/½ cup dried apricots
115g/4oz/½ cup dried peaches
1 fresh pear
1 fresh apple
1 fresh orange
115g/4oz/⅔ cup mixed raspberries
    and blackberries
1 cinnamon stick
50g/2oz/¼ cup caster sugar
15ml/1 tbsp clear honey
30ml/2 tbsp lemon juice

1 Soak the apricots and peaches in water for 1–2 hours until plump, then drain and halve or quarter.

2 Peel and core the pear and apple and cut into cubes. Peel the orange with a sharp knife, removing all the pith, and cut into wedges. Place all the fruit in a large saucepan with the raspberries and blackberries.

3 Add 600ml/1 pint/2½ cups water, the cinnamon, sugar and honey.

4 Bring to the boil, then cover the pan and and simmer very gently for 10–12 minutes until the fruit is just tender, stirring occasionally.

5 Remove the pan from the heat and stir in the lemon juice. Allow to cool, then pour the fruit salad into a serving bowl and chill for 1–2 hours before serving.

--- NUTRITION NOTES ---

Per portion:

Energy	190kcals/811kJ
Protein	2.1g
Fat	0.4g
saturated fat	0
Carbohydrate	47.4g
Fibre	5.1g
Sugars	47.4g
Calcium	50mg

Apple and Banana Crumble

An old favourite, this crumble is naturally sweet with a crisp topping contrasting beautifully with the soft fruit. Bananas are delicious in a crumble and serve with low-fat yogurt.

INGREDIENTS

Serves 6

2 large cooking apples
2 large bananas
60ml/4 tbsp water
50g/2oz/¼ cup low-fat spread
30–45ml/2–3 tbsp pear and
   apple spread
25g/1oz/¼ cup wholemeal flour
115g/4oz/1 cup porridge oats
30ml/2 tbsp sunflower seeds
low-fat yogurt, to serve (optional)

1 Preheat the oven to 180°C/350°F/ Gas 4. Cut the apples in quarters, remove the cores, then chop them into small pieces, leaving the skin on. Peel and slice the bananas. Mix the apples, bananas and water in a saucepan and cook until soft and pulpy.

2 Melt the low-fat spread with the pear and apple spread in a separate pan. Stir in the flour, oats and sunflower seeds and mix well.

3 Transfer the apple and banana mixture to an 18cm/7in baking dish and spread the oat crumble over the top. Bake for about 20 minutes or until the topping is golden brown. Serve warm or at room temperature, alone or with low-fat yogurt.

NUTRITION NOTES	
Per portion:	
Energy	181kcals/806kJ
Fat, total	7.36g
saturated fat	1.5g
polyunsaturated fat	2.9g
monounsaturated fat	2.5g
Carbohydrate	28.5g
sugar, total	12g
starch	16.3g
Fibre	3.2g
Sodium	58mg

Chocolate and Orange Mousse

There's no hint of deprivation in this divine dessert! It makes a great occasional treat, but eat with a high fibre main course.

INGREDIENTS

Serves 8

175g/6oz good-quality dark chocolate, broken into squares
grated rind and juice of 1½ large oranges, plus extra pared rind for decoration
5ml/1 tsp powdered gelatine
4 size 2 eggs, separated
90ml/6 tbsp unsweetened soya cream
60ml/4 tbsp brandy
chopped pistachio nuts, to decorate

1 Melt the chocolate in a heatproof bowl over a pan of hot water. Put 30ml/2 tbsp of the orange juice in a heatproof bowl and sprinkle the gelatine on top. When the gelatine is spongy, stand the bowl over a pan of hot water and stir until it has dissolved.

NUTRITION NOTES	
Per portion:	
Energy	230kcals/966kJ
Fat, total	12.4g
saturated fat	4.6g
polyunsaturated fat	0.6g
monounsaturated fat	3.4g
Carbohydrate	17.3g
sugar, total	17g
Starch	0.2g
Fibre	0.55g
Sodium	113mg

2 Let the chocolate cool slightly, then beat in the orange rind, egg yolks, soya cream and brandy, followed by the gelatine mixture and the remaining orange juice. Set aside.

3 Whisk the egg whites in a grease-free bowl until they form soft peaks, then gently fold them into the chocolate and orange mixture.

4 Spoon or pour the mixture into six sundae dishes or glasses, or into a single glass bowl. Cover and chill until the mousse sets. Decorate with the chopped pistachio nuts and extra pared orange rind before serving.

CAKES AND BAKES

A slice of rich, moist cake is seen by many as the ultimate treat. This chapter is devoted to those people who don't want to miss out on the odd slice of cake, but who want to look after their health as well. Spicy Sultana Muffins and Apple and Date Balls are perfect for diabetics as they rely on the natural sweetness of the ingredients, whilst Victoria Sandwich Cake and Country Apple Cake are great for those suffering from coeliac disease as they are gluten-free.

Chocolate Brownies

Dark and full of flavour, these brownies are irresistible. They make a good tea-time treat, or are perfect for accompanying a cup of coffee with friends.

INGREDIENTS

Makes 20
150g/5oz/²/₃ cup dairy-free spread
150g/5oz/scant 1 cup stoned dates, softened in boiling water, then drained and finely chopped
150g/5oz/1¼ cups self-raising wholemeal flour
10ml/2 tsp baking powder
60ml/4 tbsp cocoa powder dissolved in 30ml/2 tbsp hot water
60ml/4 tbsp apple and pear spread
90ml/6 tbsp unsweetened coconut milk
50g/2oz/½ cup walnuts or pecan nuts, roughly broken

1 Preheat the oven to 160°C/325°F/ Gas 3 and grease a 28 x 18cm/ 11 x 7in shallow baking tin. Cream the low-fat spread with the dates. Sift the flour with the baking powder, then fold into the creamed mixture, alternately with the cocoa, apple and pear spread and coconut milk. Stir in the nuts.

2 Spoon the mixture into the prepared tin, smooth the surface and bake for about 45 minutes or until a fine skewer inserted in the centre comes out clean. Cool for a few minutes in the tin, then cut into bars or squares. Cool on a wire rack.

——— NUTRITION NOTES ———	
Per brownie:	
Energy	91kcals/382kJ
Fat, total	5.6g
saturated fat	1.4g
polyunsaturated fat	2g
monounsaturated fat	2g
Carbohydrate	8.3g
sugar, total	3.12g
starch	5.15g
Fibre	1.3g
Sodium	142mg

Spicy Sultana Muffins

Sunday breakfasts will never be the same again, once you have tried these delicious muffins! They are easy to prepare and take only a short time to bake.

INGREDIENTS

Makes 6
75g/3oz/6 tbsp dairy-free spread
1 small egg
120ml/4fl oz/½ cup unsweetened coconut milk
150g/5oz/1¼ cups wholemeal flour
7.5ml/1½ tsp baking powder
5ml/1 tsp ground cinnamon
generous pinch of salt
115g/4oz/²/₃ cup sultanas

1 Preheat the oven to 190°C/375°F/ Gas 5. Grease six muffin or deep bun tins. Beat the low-fat spread, egg and coconut milk in a bowl.

2 Sift the flour, baking powder, cinnamon and salt over the beaten mixture. Fold in, then beat well. Fold in the sultanas. Divide among the tins.

3 Bake for 20 minutes or until the muffins have risen well and are firm to the touch. Cool slightly on a wire rack before serving.

——— COOK'S TIP ———
These muffins taste equally good cold. They also freeze well, packed in freezer bags. To serve, leave them to thaw overnight, or defrost in a microwave, then warm them briefly in the oven.

——— NUTRITION NOTES ———	
Per muffin:	
Energy	123kcals/514kJ
Fat, total	6.3g
saturated fat	1.75g
polyunsaturated fat	1.35g
monounsaturated fat	2.65g
Carbohydrate	14.85g
sugar, total	14.35g
starch	0.5g
Fibre	0.4g
Sodium	278.5mg

Country Apple Cake

FREE FROM

INGREDIENTS

Makes one 18cm/7in cake

115g/4oz/½ cup soft margarine
115g/4oz/½ cup light soft brown sugar
2 eggs, beaten
115g/4oz/1 cup gluten-free self-raising
   flour, sifted
50g/2oz/½ cup rice flour
5ml/1 tsp gluten-free baking powder
10ml/2 tsp mixed spice
1 medium cooking apple, peeled, cored
   and chopped
115g/4oz/1 cup raisins
about 60ml/4 tbsp semi-skimmed milk
15g/½oz/2 tbsp flaked almonds
custard or ice cream, to serve
   (optional)

1 Preheat the oven to 160°C/325°F/
Gas 3. Lightly grease and line a
deep 18cm/7in round, loose-bottomed
cake tin.

2 Place the margarine and sugar in a
bowl and cream together until pale
and fluffy. Gradually add the eggs,
beating well after each addition. Fold in
the flour, rice flour, baking powder and
mixed spice and mix well.

— VARIATIONS —

Use sultanas or chopped ready-to-eat dried
apricots or pears instead of the raisins.

3 Fold in the chopped apple, raisins
and enough milk to make a soft,
dropping consistency.

4 Turn the mixture into the prepared
tin and level the surface. Sprinkle
the flaked almonds over the top. Bake
for 1–1¼ hours until risen, firm to the
touch and golden brown.

5 Cool in the tin for about
10 minutes, then turn out on to a
wire rack to cool. Cut into slices when
cold. Alternatively, serve warm, in slices,
with custard or ice cream. Store the
cold cake in an airtight container or
wrapped in foil.

— NUTRITION NOTES —

Per cake:
Energy	2506kcals/10483kJ
Fat, total	120g
saturated fat	25g
Protein	35g
Carbohydrate	340g
sugar, total	214g
Fibre	6g
Sodium	1695mg

Chocolate and Prune Cake

This delicious cake is high in soluble fibre although it is also quite high in sugar, so enjoy it as an occasional treat.

INGREDIENTS

Makes a 20cm/8in cake

300g/11oz dark chocolate
150g/5oz/²/₃ cup dairy-free spread
200g/7oz/generous 1 cup ready-to-eat stoned prunes, quartered
3 eggs, beaten
150g/5oz/1¼ cups gram flour, sifted with 10ml/2 tsp gluten-free baking powder
120ml/4fl oz/½ cup coconut milk, rice milk or soya milk

1 Preheat the oven to 180°C/350°F/ Gas 4. Grease and base-line a deep 20cm/8in round cake tin. Melt the chocolate in a heatproof bowl over a saucepan of hot water.

2 Mix the low-fat spread and prunes in a food processor. Process until light and fluffy, then scrape into a bowl.

3 Gradually fold in the melted chocolate and eggs, alternately with the flour mixture. Beat in the coconut milk, rice milk or soya milk.

COOK'S TIP

Use dark chocolate with a high proportion of cocoa solids (70%) for this cake.

4 Spoon the mixture into the cake tin, level the surface with a spoon, then bake for 20–30 minutes or until the cake is firm to the touch. A fine skewer inserted in the cake should come out clean. Leave to cool on a wire rack before serving.

— NUTRITION NOTES —	
Per cake:	
Energy	3178kcals/13315kJ
Fat, total	174g
saturated fat	74g
polyunsaturated fat	24g
monounsaturated fat	63g
Carbohydrate	340g
sugar, total	260g
starch	72g
Fibre	35g
Sodium	2640mg

Sunflower Sultana Scones

INGREDIENTS

Makes 10–12
225g/8oz/2 cups self-raising flour
5ml/1 tsp baking powder
25g/1oz/2 tbsp soft margarine
30ml/2 tbsp golden caster sugar
50g/2oz/⅓ cup sultanas
30ml/2 tbsp sunflower seeds
150ml/¼ pint/⅔ cup natural yogurt
about 30–45ml/2–3 tbsp skimmed milk

1 Preheat the oven to 230°C/450°F/
Gas 8. Lightly oil a baking sheet.
Sift the flour and baking powder into a
bowl and rub in the margarine evenly.

2 Stir in the sugar, sultanas and half
the sunflower seeds, then mix in
the yogurt, with just enough milk to
make a fairly soft, but not sticky dough.

3 Roll out on a lightly floured
surface to about 2cm/¾in thickness.
Cut into 6cm/2½in flower shapes or
rounds with a biscuit cutter and lift on
to the baking sheet.

4 Brush with milk and sprinkle with
the rest of the seeds. Bake for
10–12 minutes, until risen and golden.

5 Cool the scones on a wire rack.
Serve split and spread with jam or
low-fat soya-free spread.

NUTRITION NOTES	
Per portion:	
Energy	176Kcals/742kJ
Fat	5.32g
saturated fat	0.81g
Cholesterol	0.84mg
Fibre	1.26g

Prune and Peel Rock Buns

INGREDIENTS

Makes 12
225g/8oz/2 cups plain flour
10ml/2 tsp baking powder
50g/2oz/½ cup ready-to-eat prunes
75g/3oz/⅜ cup demerara sugar
50g/2oz/⅓ cup chopped mixed peel
finely grated rind of 1 lemon
50ml/2fl oz/¼ cup sunflower oil
75ml/5 tbsp skimmed milk

NUTRITION NOTES	
Per portion:	
Energy	135Kcals/570kJ
Fat	3.35g
saturated fat	0.44g
Cholesterol	0.13mg
Fibre	0.86g

1 Preheat the oven to 200°C/400°F/
Gas 6. Lightly oil a baking sheet.
Chop the prunes. Sift together the
flour and baking powder and stir in
the sugar, prunes, peel and lemon rind.

2 Mix together the sunflower oil and
skimmed milk, then stir into the
mixture, to make a dough which just
binds together.

3 Spoon into heaps on the baking
sheet and bake for 20 minutes, until
golden. Cool on a wire rack.

Victoria Sandwich Cake

Serve this light, gluten-free equivalent of the classic sponge cake sandwiched together with your favourite jam. For special occasions, fill the cake with prepared fresh fruit, such as raspberries or sliced peaches, as well as jam and whipped dairy cream or fromage frais.

INGREDIENTS

Makes one 18cm/7in cake
175g/6oz/¾ cup soft margarine
175g/6oz/¾ cup caster sugar
3 eggs, beaten
175g/6oz/1½ cups gluten-free self-raising flour, sifted
60ml/4 tbsp jam
150ml/¼ pint/⅔ cup whipped cream or fromage frais
15–30ml/1–2 tbsp icing sugar, for dusting

1 Preheat the oven to 180°C/350°F/Gas 4. Lightly grease and base-line two 18cm/7in sandwich tins.

2 Place the margarine and caster sugar in a bowl and cream together until pale and fluffy.

3 Add the eggs, a little at a time, beating well after each addition. Fold in half the flour, using a metal spoon, then fold in the rest.

4 Divide the mixture evenly between the two sandwich tins and level the surface with the back of a spoon.

5 Bake for 25–30 minutes until the cakes have risen, feel just firm to the touch and are golden brown. Turn out and cool on a wire rack.

6 When the cakes are cool, sandwich them with the jam and whipped cream or fromage frais. Dust the top of the cake with sifted icing sugar and serve cut into slices. Store the cake in the fridge in an airtight container or wrapped in foil.

NUTRITION NOTES	
Per cake:	
Energy	3140kcals/13110kJ
Fat, total	166g
saturated fat	36g
Protein	35g
Carbohydrate	391g
sugar, total	263g
Fibre	0g
Sodium	1486mg

VARIATION

Replace 30ml/2 tbsp of the flour with sifted gluten-free cocoa powder. Sandwich the cakes with chocolate butter icing.

Fruit and Nut Chocolates

When beautifully boxed, these make perfect presents.

INGREDIENTS

Makes 20

50g/2oz ready-to-eat stoned prunes or dried apricots
50g/2oz/⅓ cup sultanas or raisins
25g/1oz/2 tbsp ready-to-eat dried apples, figs or dates
25g/1oz/⅓ cup flaked almonds
25g/1oz/¼ cup hazelnuts or walnuts
30–60ml/2–4 tbsp lemon juice
50g/2oz good-quality dark chocolate

1 Chop the fruit and nuts in a food processor or blender until fairly small. Add 30ml/2 tbsp lemon juice and process again to mix. Scrape the mixture into a bowl, taste and add more lemon juice if needed.

2 Melt the chocolate in a heatproof bowl over simmering water. Roll the fruit mixture into small balls. Using tongs or two forks, roll the balls in the melted chocolate, then place them on oiled foil to cool and set. If the chocolate becomes too solid to work with, reheat it gently.

NUTRITION NOTES	
Per chocolate:	
Energy	42kcals/176kJ
Fat, total	2.3g
saturated fat	0.55g
polyunsaturated fat	0.8g
monounsaturated fat	0.8g
Carbohydrate	4.95g
sugar, total	4.85g
starch	0.05g
Fibre	0.5g
Sodium	1.9mg

Apple and Date Balls

INGREDIENTS

Makes 20

1kg/2¼lb cooking apples or pears
115g/4oz/⅔ cup dried, stoned dates
250ml/8fl oz/1 cup apple juice
5ml/1 tsp ground cinnamon
50g/2oz/½ cup finely chopped walnuts

NUTRITION NOTES	
Per ball:	
Energy	47kcals/198kJ
Fat, total	1.8g
saturated fat	0.15g
polyunsaturated fat	1.25g
monounsaturated fat	0.3g
Carbohydrate	7.6g
sugar, total	7.6g
starch	0g
Fibre	1g
Sodium	1.9mg

1 Halve the unpeeled fruit and place in a large heavy-based saucepan. Add the dates, apple juice and ground cinnamon. Cook over a very low heat, stirring occasionally, for 4–6 hours or until the mixture forms a dry paste. Scrape into a bowl and cool, then roll into bite-sized balls. Toast the nuts under the grill until golden.

2 Coat the balls in the nut mixture. Twist each ball in a sweet wrapper or cellophane; store in an airtight box.

VARIATION
Use half-and-half ground cinnamon and ginger instead of the 5ml/1 tsp cinnamon.

BREADS

There is nothing like the smell of freshly baked bread to make the mouth water. It is wonderful at any time of day, whether toasted for breakfast, served with soup or spread thick with butter and jam. This chapter offers a selection of healthy bread recipes, which are ideal for those on special diets, including a selection that have been specially designed for those with a sensitivity to wheat or gluten, such as Rice, Buckwheat and Corn Bread and Fruit, Nut and Seed Teabread.

Tuscan No-salt Bread

This bread from Tuscany is made without salt and probably originates from the days when salt was heavily taxed.

INGREDIENTS

Makes 1 loaf

500g/1¼lb/5 cups strong unbleached white bread flour
350ml/12fl oz/1½ cups boiling water
15g/½oz fresh yeast
60ml/4 tbsp lukewarm water

——— Nutrition Notes ———	
Per loaf:	
Energy	1883Kcals/8014kJ
Protein	65g
Fat	7.8g
Saturated fat	1.08g
Carbohydrate	414g
Fibre	17g
Sodium	34mg

1 First make the starter. Sift 175g/6oz/1½ cups of the flour into a large bowl. Pour over the boiling water, leave for a couple of minutes, then mix well. Cover with a damp dish towel and leave for 10 hours.

2 Lightly flour a baking sheet. Cream the yeast with the lukewarm water. Stir into the starter.

3 Gradually add the remaining flour and mix to form a dough. Turn out on to a lightly floured surface and knead for 5–8 minutes until elastic.

4 Place in a lightly oiled bowl, cover with lightly oiled clear film and leave to rise, in a warm place, for 1–1½ hours, or until doubled in bulk.

5 Turn out the dough on to a lightly floured surface, knock back and shape into a round.

6 Fold the sides of the round into the centre and seal. Place seam side up on the prepared baking sheet. Cover with lightly oiled clear film and leave to rise, in a warm place, for 30–45 minutes, or until doubled in size.

7 Flatten the loaf to about half its risen size and flip over. Cover with a large upturned bowl and leave to rise, in a warm place, for 30 minutes.

8 Meanwhile, preheat the oven to 220°C/425°F/Gas 7. Slash the top of the loaf, using a sharp knife, if wished. Bake for 30–35 minutes or until a light golden colour. Transfer to a wire rack to cool.

Spiced Naan Bread

The many seeds and the yogurt used in this recipe provide ample flavour, allowing you to avoid using salt. Traditionally baked in a fiercely hot tandoori oven, good results can also be achieved by using a hot oven and a grill.

INGREDIENTS

Makes 6
450g/1lb/4 cups plain flour
5ml/1 tsp baking powder
1 sachet easy-blend dried yeast
5ml/1 tsp caster sugar
5ml/1 tsp fennel seeds
10ml/2 tsp black onion seeds
5ml/1 tsp cumin seeds
150ml/¼ pint/⅔ cup hand-hot milk
30ml/2 tbsp oil, plus extra
    for brushing
150ml/¼ pint/⅔ cup plain yogurt
1 egg, beaten

1 Sift the flour and baking powder into a mixing bowl. Stir in the yeast, sugar, fennel seeds, black onion seeds and cumin seeds. Make a well in the centre. Stir the hand-hot milk into the flour mixture, then add the oil, yogurt and beaten egg. Mix to form a ball of dough.

2 Turn out the dough on to a lightly floured surface and knead it for 10 minutes until smooth. Return to the clean, lightly oiled bowl and roll to coat with oil. Cover the bowl with clear film and set aside until the dough has doubled in bulk.

3 Put a heavy baking sheet in the oven and preheat the oven to 240°C/475°F/Gas 9. Knead the dough again lightly and divide it into six pieces. Keep five pieces covered while working with the sixth.

4 Quickly roll the piece of dough out to a tear-drop shape, brush lightly with oil and slap the naan on to the hot baking sheet. Repeat with the remaining dough.

5 Preheat the grill. Bake the naan in the oven for 3 minutes until puffed up, then place the baking sheet under the grill for about 30 seconds, or until lightly browned. Serve the naan hot or warm as an accompaniment to an Indian curry.

NUTRITION NOTES

Per portion:

Energy	355Kcals/1500kJ
Protein	11.2g
Fat	8g
Saturated fat	1.67g
Carbohydrate	64g
Fibre	2.3g
Sodium	150mg

VARIATION

Vary the spices used by adding chopped chilli to the mixture, or sprinkling the naan with poppy seeds before baking.

FREE FROM

Sun-dried Tomato Bread

A delicious bread from the south of Italy. The combination of tomatoes and milk produce a lovely sweet bread that does not require the addition of salt.

INGREDIENTS

Makes 4 small loaves

675g/1½lb/6 cups strong white
   bread flour
25g/1oz/2 tbsp caster sugar
25g/1oz fresh yeast
400–475ml/14–16fl oz/1⅔–2 cups
   warm milk
15ml/1 tbsp tomato purée
75ml/5 tbsp oil from the jar of
   sun-dried tomatoes
75ml/5 tbsp extra virgin olive oil
75g/3oz/¾ cup drained sun-dried
   tomatoes in oil, chopped
1 large onion, chopped

1 Sift the flour and sugar into a bowl and make a well in the centre. Crumble the yeast, mix with 150ml/¼ pint/⅔ cup of the warm milk and add to the flour.

2 Mix the tomato purée into the remaining milk until evenly blended, then add to the flour with the tomato oil and olive oil.

3 Gradually mix the flour into the liquid ingredients until you have a dough. Turn out on to a floured surface and knead for about 10 minutes until smooth and elastic. Return to the clean bowl, cover with a cloth and leave to rise in a warm place for about 2 hours.

4 Knock the dough back and add the tomatoes and onion. Knead until evenly distributed through the dough. Shape into four rounds and place on a greased baking sheet. Cover with a dish towel and leave to rise again for about 45 minutes.

5 Preheat the oven to 190°C/375°F/ Gas 5. Bake the bread for 45 minutes, or until the loaves sound hollow when you tap them underneath with your fingers. Leave to cool for a few minutes on a wire rack before eating warm.

NUTRITION NOTES	
Per loaf:	
Energy	971Kcals/4087kJ
Protein	24.9g
Fat	36.5g
Saturated fat	6.85g
Carbohydrate	145g
Fibre	7.3g
Sodium	353mg

Olive and Oregano Bread

This is a great accompaniment to salads and is good served warm.

INGREDIENTS

Serves 8–10

300ml/10fl oz/1¼ cups warm water
5ml/1 tsp active dried yeast
pinch of sugar
15ml/1 tbsp olive oil
1 onion, chopped
450g/1lb/4 cups strong white flour
5ml/1 tsp salt
1.5ml/¼ tsp ground black pepper
50g/2oz/¼ cup black olives
15ml/1 tbsp black olive paste
15ml/1 tbsp chopped fresh oregano
15ml/1 tbsp chopped fresh parsley

1 Put half the water in a jug. Sprinkle the yeast on top. Mix in the sugar and leave in a warm place for about 10 minutes until frothy.

2 Heat the olive oil in a frying pan, add the chopped onion and fry gently until it has softened and turned golden brown.

— NUTRITION NOTES —

Per loaf:	
Energy	1920kcals/8130kJ
Protein	63g
Fat	41g
saturated Fat	9g
Carbohydrate	345g
Fibre	15g
Sugars	15g
Calcium	97mg

3 Sift the flour with the salt and pepper. Make a well in the centre. Add the yeast mixture, the fried onion (with the oil), the olives, olive paste, herbs and remaining water. Gradually incorporate the flour and mix, adding a little water if necessary.

4 Turn the dough on to a floured surface and knead until smooth and elastic. Place the dough in a mixing bowl, cover with a damp cloth and leave in a warm place to rise until doubled in bulk. Lightly grease a baking sheet with soya margarine.

5 Turn the dough on to a floured surface and knead again. Shape into a 20cm/8in round and place on the baking sheet. Make criss-cross cuts over the top, cover and leave in a warm place for 30 minutes until well risen. Preheat the oven to 220°C/425°F/Gas 7.

6 Dust the loaf with flour. Bake for 10 minutes, then lower the temperature to 200°C/400°F/Gas 6. Bake for 20 minutes more or until the loaf sounds hollow when it is tapped underneath. Transfer to a wire rack to cool before serving.

Fruit Malt Bread

INGREDIENTS

Makes 1 loaf
250g/9oz/2¼ cups self-raising
   wholemeal flour
pinch of salt
2.5ml/½ tsp bicarbonate of soda
175g/6oz/1 cup dried fruit
15ml/1 tbsp malt extract
250ml/8fl oz/1 cup skimmed milk
low-fat spread, to serve (optional)

--- COOK'S TIP ---

Use any combination of dried fruit you
like for this bread. Choose from sultanas,
raisins and currants, or include chopped
dried pears, apricots, peaches or mangoes.

1 Preheat the oven to 160°C/325°F/
Gas 3. Grease a 23 x 13cm/9 x 5in
loaf tin. Line the base with non-stick
baking paper. Sift the flour, salt and
bicarbonate of soda into a bowl. Stir in
the dried fruit.

2 Heat the malt extract and milk in a
small saucepan, stirring until the
malt extract has dissolved. Tip it into
the dry ingredients and mix well.

3 Spoon the mixture into the
prepared tin. Bake for 45 minutes
or until a fine skewer inserted in the
loaf comes out clean. Cool on a wire
rack. Serve in slices, alone or with a
low-fat spread.

--- NUTRITION NOTES ---

Per loaf:	
Energy	1330kcals/5670kJ
Fat, total	6.5g
saturated fat	1g
polyunsaturated fat	2.5g
monounsaturated fat	7.5g
Carbohydrate	295g
sugar, total	138g
starch	155g
Fibre	26g
Sodium	1015mg

Banana Bread

The very ripe bananas that are often sold off cheaply in supermarkets are perfect for this tried and trusted favourite.

INGREDIENTS

Makes 1 loaf
115g/4oz/ ½ cup dairy-free spread, plus extra for greasing
5ml/1 tsp bicarbonate of soda
225g/8oz/2 cups wholemeal flour
2 eggs, beaten
3 very ripe bananas
30−45ml/2−3 tbsp unsweetened soya milk

1 Preheat the oven to 180°C/350°F/ Gas 4. Grease and base line a 23 x 13cm/9 x 5in loaf tin. Cream the low-fat spread in a bowl until it is fluffy. Sift the bicarbonate of soda with the flour, then add to the creamed low-fat spread, alternately with the eggs.

2 Peel the bananas and slice them into a bowl. Mash them well, then stir them into the cake mixture. Mix in the coconut milk or soya milk.

3 Spoon the mixture into the loaf tin and level the surface with a spoon. Bake for about 1¼ hours or until a fine skewer inserted in the centre comes out clean. Cool on a wire rack.

VARIATION

Sunflower seeds make a good addition to banana cake. Add about 50g/2oz/ ½ cup to the mixture just before baking.

NUTRITION NOTES

Per loaf:	
Energy	1616kcals/5090kJ
Fat, total	66g
saturated fat	17.5g
polyunsaturated fat	15.2g
monounsaturated fat	26.5g
Carbohydrate	215g
sugar, total	70g
starch	145g
Fibre	23.5g
Sodium	2320mg

Rice, Buckwheat and Corn Bread

Freshly baked, this wonderful bread is delicious served straight from the oven. Cut into thick slices and serve with fruit conserve or honey for breakfast.

INGREDIENTS

Makes one 900g/2lb loaf

200ml/7fl oz/scant 1 cup tepid semi-skimmed milk
200ml/7fl oz/scant 1 cup tepid water
350g/12oz/3 cups brown rice flour
50g/2oz/½ cup buckwheat flour or soya flour
50g/2oz/½ cup gluten-free cornmeal
5ml/1 tsp caster sugar
5ml/1 tsp salt
7g/¼oz sachet easy-blend dried yeast
40g/1½oz/3 tbsp soft margarine
1 medium egg, beaten, plus extra for glazing
30ml/2 tbsp sesame seeds

--- COOK'S TIP ---

You can bake the bread in a different-shaped tin, such as a deep round or square cake tin, if preferred.

--- NUTRITION NOTES ---

Per loaf:

Energy	2200kcals/9188kJ
Fat, total	59g
saturated fat	12g
Protein	62g
Carbohydrate	344g
sugar, total	21g
Fibre	14g
Sodium	493mg

1 Lightly grease a 900g/2lb loaf tin. Mix the milk and water together in a measuring jug.

2 Place the rice flour, buckwheat or soya flour, cornmeal, sugar and salt in a bowl and stir in the dried yeast. Mix well until all the ingredients are combined, then lightly rub in the margarine until the mixture resembles fine breadcrumbs.

3 Add the milk and water mixture and the egg and beat together to form a smooth, thick consistency.

4 Spoon the mixture into the prepared tin, then cover and leave in a warm place until it has risen to the top of the tin.

5 Preheat the oven to 200°C/400°F/Gas 6. Brush the top of the bread with a little beaten egg and scatter the sesame seeds over it. Bake for about 30 minutes until lightly browned. Run a knife all round the edge of the tin to loosen the loaf.

6 Turn out the bread on to a wire rack to cool slightly and serve warm. Alternatively, leave on the rack until completely cold, then cut into slices. To store, wrap the loaf in foil or seal in a plastic bag.

Cheese and Onion Cornbread

Full of flavour, this gluten-free cornbread is delicious served freshly baked, warm or cold in slices, either on its own or spread with a little low-fat spread. It makes an ideal accompaniment to soups, stews and chillies.

INGREDIENTS

Makes one 900g/2lb loaf
15ml/1 tbsp sunflower oil
1 onion, thinly sliced
175g/6oz/1½ cups gluten-free cornmeal
75g/3oz/¾ cup rice flour
25g/1oz/¼ cup soya flour
15ml/1 tbsp gluten-free baking powder
5ml/1 tsp caster sugar
5ml/1 tsp salt
115g/4oz/1 cup coarsely grated mature Cheddar cheese
200ml/7fl oz/scant 1 cup tepid milk
2 eggs
40g/1½oz/3 tbsp soft margarine, melted

--- COOK'S TIP ---

Reserve a little of the grated cheese and cooked onion and scatter it over the top of the bread before baking.

1 Preheat the oven to 190°C/375°F/ Gas 5. Lightly grease a 900g/2lb loaf tin. Heat the oil in a frying pan, add the onion and cook gently for 10–15 minutes until softened, stirring occasionally. Remove from the heat and set aside to cool.

2 Place the cornmeal, rice flour, soya flour, baking powder, sugar and salt in a bowl and combine thoroughly. Stir in the cheese, mixing well.

3 Beat together the milk, eggs and melted margarine. Add to the flour mixture and mix well.

4 Stir in the cooled, cooked onions and mix again.

5 Spoon the onion mixture into the prepared tin, level the surface and bake for about 30 minutes until the bread has risen and is golden brown.

6 Run a knife around the edge to loosen the loaf. Turn out on to a wire rack to cool slightly and serve warm. Alternatively, leave it on the rack until completely cold, then cut into slices. To store the loaf, wrap it in foil or seal in a plastic bag.

--- NUTRITION NOTES ---

Per loaf:
Energy	2314kcals/9631kJ
Fat, total	121g
saturated fat	42g
Protein	83g
Carbohydrate	220g
sugar, total	21.2g
Fibre	9g
Sodium	3100mg

Fruit, Nut and Seed Teabread

Cut into slices and spread with a little low-fat spread, jam or honey, this teabread makes an ideal breakfast bread.

INGREDIENTS

Makes one 900g/2lb loaf

115g/4oz/⅔ cup dried dates, chopped
115g/4oz/½ cup ready-to-eat dried
   apricots, chopped
115g/4oz/1 cup sultanas
115g/4oz/½ cup light soft brown sugar
225g/8oz/2 cups gluten-free self-
   raising flour
5ml/1 tsp gluten-free baking powder
10ml/2 tsp mixed spice
75g/3oz/¾ cup chopped mixed nuts,
   such as walnuts and hazelnuts
75g/3oz/¾ cup mixed seeds, such as
   millet, sunflower and sesame seeds
2 eggs, beaten
150ml/¼ pint/⅔ cup semi-
   skimmed milk

— NUTRITION NOTES —	
Per loaf:	
Energy	3022kcals/12686kJ
Fat, total	107g
saturated fat	14g
Protein	70.4g
Carbohydrate	470g
sugar, total	294g
Fibre	20g
Sodium	944mg

1 Preheat the oven to 180°C/350°F/ Gas 4. Lightly grease a 900g/2lb loaf tin. Place the chopped dates and apricots and sultanas in a large mixing bowl and stir in the sugar.

2 Place the flour, baking powder, spice, mixed nuts and seeds in a separate bowl and mix well.

3 Stir the eggs and milk into the fruit, then add the flour mixture and beat together until well mixed.

4 Spoon into the prepared tin and level the surface. Bake for about 1 hour until the teabread is firm to the touch and lightly browned.

5 Allow to cool in the tin for a few minutes, then turn out on to a wire rack to cool completely. Serve warm or cold, cut into slices, either on its own or spread with low-fat spread and jam. Wrap the teabread in foil to store.

INFORMATION FILE

USEFUL ADDRESSES

AUSTRALIA

Allergy and Environmental Sensitivity Support and Research Association
PO Box 298
Ringwood VIC 3134
Tel: (61) 39888 1282

Australian Cancer Society
PO Box 4708
Sydney NSW 2001
Tel: (01) 2267 1944

The Biological Farmers of Australia Cooperative Ltd (BFA)
Level 1
T & G Arcade Building
477 Ruthven Street
Toowoomba QLD 4350
Tel: (07) 6393299

The Brain Foundation
PO Box 579
Suite 21, Regent House
Alexander Street
Crow's Nest
Sydney NSW 2065
Tel: (61) 29437 5967

The Coeliac Society of Australia
PO Box 271
Wahroonga NSW 2076
Tel: (61) 29411 4100

Diabetes Australia
National Office
5–7 Phipps Place
Deakin ACT 2615
Tel: 1 (800) 640 862

Hyperactivity Association
15/29 Bertram Street
Chatswood NSW 2067
Tel: (61) 29441 2186

Organic Herb Growers of Australia (OHGA)
PO Box 6171
South Lismore NSW 2480
Tel: (02) 6622 0100

CANADA

Canadian Cancer Society
10 Alcorn Avenue
Toronto
Ontario M4V 3B1

Canadian Coeliac Association
6519B Mississauga Road
Ontario L5N 1A6
Tel: (1) 905 567 7195

Canadian Diabetic Association
15 Toronto Street
Suite 800
Toronto
Ontario M5C 2E3

NEW ZEALAND

Cancer Society of New Zealand
PO Box 1724
Auckland
New Zealand
Tel: (09) 524 2628

SOUTH AFRICA

The Coeliac Society of South Africa
Box No 64203
Highland North 2073
Johannesburg
Tel: (27) 11 440 3431

South African Diabetes Association
PO Box 1715
Saxonwold 21342
Tel: (27) 11 788 4595

UNITED KINGDOM

Action Against Allergy
PO Box 278
Twickenham
Middlesex TW1 4QQ
Tel: 020 8892 2711

The Anaphylaxis Campaign
PO Box 149
Fleet
Hampshire GU13 0FA
Tel: 01252 542029

Arthritic Association
2 Hyde Gardens
Eastbourne
East Sussex BN21 4PN
Tel: 01323 416 550

Arthritis Care
18 Stephenson Way
London NW1 2HD
Tel: 020 7916 500

Arthritis Research Campaign
41 Eagle Street
London
WC1R 4AR
Tel: 01246 558033

Bacup
3 Bath Place
Rivington Street
London EC2A 3JR
Tel: 020 7613 2121

**British Association for
Counselling**
1 Regent Place
Rugby
Warwickshire CV21 2PJ
www.counselling.co.uk
Tel: 01788 578 323

The British Allergy Foundation
Deepdene House
30 Bellegrove Road
Welling
Kent DA16 3PY
Tel: 020 8303 8525/8583

British Cancer Help Centre
Grove House
Cornwallis Grove
Clifton
Bristol BS8 4PG
Tel: 0117 980 9505

British Diabetic Association
10 Queen Anne's Street
London W1M 0BD
Tel: 020 7323 1531

The British Goat Society
34–36 Fore Street
Bovey Tracey
Newton Abbott
Devon TQ13 9AD

British Heart Foundation
14 Fitzhardinge Street
London W1H 4DH
Tel: 020 7935 0185

**The British Nutrition
Foundation**
High Holborn House
52–54 High Holborn
London WC1V 6RQ
Tel: 020 7404 6504
Fax: 020 7404 6747

Cancer Research Campaign
10 Cambridge Terrace
London NW1 4JL
Tel: 020 72241333

**The Coeliac Society of
Great Britain**
PO Box 220
High Wycombe
Bucks HP11 2HY
Tel: 01494 437 278

**Council for Complementary
and Alternative Medicine**
Suite 1
19a Cavendish Square
London W1M 9AD
Tel: 020 7409 1440

Department of Health
Richmond House
79 Whitehall
London SW1A 2NS
Tel: 020 7210 3000

Gerson Therapy Information
(The Debra Shepherd Trust)
Chapel Farm
West Humble
Dorking
Surrey RH5 6AY

**The Hyperactive Children's
Support Group**
71 Whyke Lane
Chichester
Sussex PO19 2LD
Tel: 01903 725182

**Imperial Cancer
Research Fund**
PO Box 123
Lincoln's Inn Fields
London WC2A 3PX
Tel: 020 7242 0200

**Infant and Dietetic Foods
Association**
6 Catherine Street
London WC2B 5JJ
Tel: 020 78362460

**Institute for Complementary
Medicine**
PO Box 194
London SE16 1QZ
Tel: 020 7237 5165

**Institute for Optimum
Nutrition**
13 Blades Court
Deodar Road
London SW15 2NU
Tel: 020 8877 9993

Medic Alert Foundation
1 Bridge Wharf
156 Caledonian Road
London N1 9UU
Tel: 020 7833 3034

The Migraine Trust
45 Great Ormond Street
London WC1N 3HZ
Tel: 020 7831 4818

**Ministry of Agriculture,
Fisheries and Food**
Room 306 C
Ergon House, c/o Nobel House
17 Smith Square
London SW1P 3JR
Tel: 0345 573012

**The National Asthma
Campaign**
Providence House
Providence Place
London N1 0NT
Tel: 020 7226 2260

The National Dairy Council
5–7 John Princes Street
London W1M 0AP
Tel: 020 7499 7822

The National Eczema Society
163 Eversholt Street
London NW1 1BU
Tel: 020 7388 3444

**The National Osteoporosis
Society**
PO Box 10
Bath BA3 3YB
Tel: 01761 471 771

**Royal Society for the
Promotion of Health**
38a St George's Drive
London SW1V 4BH
Tel: 020 7630 0121

Ryton Organic Gardens
Ryton-on-Dunsmore
Coventry CV8 3LG
Tel: 01203 303517

The Soil Association
40–56 Victoria Street
Bristol BS1 6LB
Tel: 01179 290661

FURTHER READING

100% Health
by Patrick Holford – Piatkus

The Allergy Connection
by John Mansfield MD – Thorsons
Publishing Group

An Alternative Approach to Allergies
by Theron G. Randolph and
Ralph W. Moss – Harper & Row

The Antioxidants
by Richard Passwater – Keats
Publishing Inc

Arthritis
by John Mansfield – Thorsons
Publishing Group

Caduceus (Healing into Wholeness)
38 Russell Terrace
Leamington Spa
Warwickshire CV31 1HE
Tel: 01926 451897

*The Complete Guide to Food Allergy
and Intolerance*
by Professor Jonathan Brostoff and
Linda Gamlin – Bloomsbury

The Complete Guide to Food Allergy and Intolerance
by Dr Jonathan Brostoff and Linda Gamlin – Crown Publishers, Inc.

A Consumer's Guide to Medicines in Food
by Ruth Winter – Crown Trade Paperbacks

Dr Mandell's 5-day Allergy Relief System
by Marshall Mandell and Lynne Waller Scanlon – Thomas Crowell

Fighting Cancer – A Survival Guide
by Jonathan Chamberlain – Headline

Food for Life
by Neal Barnard – Crown Trade Paperbacks

The Food Pharmacy
by Jean Carper – Bantam Books

The Healing Foods
by Patricia and Judith Benn Hurley – Dell Publishing

The Inside Story on Food and Health
Berrydale Publishers
5 Lawn Road
London NW3 2XS
Tel: 020 7722 2866

Journal of Alternative and Complementary Medicine
Green Library
9 Rickett Street
London SW6 1RU
Tel: 020 7385 4566

Nutrition and Cancer
by Sandra Goodman – Green Library Publications

Positive Health
51 Queen Square
Bristol BS1 4LH
Tel: 0117 983 8851

Super Healing Foods
by Frances Sheridan Goulart – Parker Publishing Company

A Time to Heal
by Beata Bishop – Hodder & Stoughton

The Whole Way to Allergy Relief & Prevention
by Jacqueline Krohn – Hartley & Marks

ORGANIC FOODS, WHOLEFOODS AND REMEDIES

Abel & Cole
8–13 Milkwood Road
London SE24 0FJ
Tel: 0800 376 4040

Bushwacker Wholefoods
132 King Street
Hammersmith
London W6 0QU

Demeter Wholefoods
12 Welles Street
Sandbach
Cheshire CW11 1GT

Dove's Farm Foods Ltd
Salisbury Road
Hungerford
Berkshire RG17 0RF

The Fresh Food Company
326 Portobello Road
London W10 5RU
Tel: 020 89690351

Good Nature
2 The Esplanade
Fowey
Cornwall PL23 1HY
Tel: 01726 832110

Graig's Farm Free-range Organic and Additive-free Meats
Graig Farm
Dolau
Llandrindod Wells
Powys LD1 5TL
Tel: 01597 851655

Harvest Natural Foods
224 Cheltenham Road
Bristol BS6 5QU
Tel: 0117 9425997

Hobbs House Bakery
39 High Street
Chipping Sodbury
Gloucestershire BS37 6BA
Tel: 01454 321629

C. Lidgate
110 Holland Park Avenue
London W11 4UA
Tel: 020 7727 8243

Living Earth Produce
Ruskin Mill
Old Bristol Road
Nailsworth
Gloucestershire GL6 0LA
Tel: 01453 837510

Millstone Wholefoods
15 High Street
Oban
Argyll PA24 4BG

Nature's Harvest
19 North Street
Leighton Buzzard
Bedfordshire LU7 7EF
Tel: 01525 371378

Nature's Trail
665 Ecclesall Road
Hunters Bar
Sheffield S11 8PT
Tel: 0114 266 5984

Naturally Yours
The Horse and Gate Farm
Witcham Toll
Ely
Cambridgeshire CB6 2AB
Tel: 01353 778723

Neal's Yard Remedies
Neal's Yard
London WC2H 9DP
Tel: 020 7379 7662

The Organic Food Shop
45 Broughton Street
Edinburgh EH1 3JU

Organic Meat and Products
Jamesfield Farm
Newburgh
Fife KY14 6EW
Tel: 01738 850498

Organic Roots
Crabtree Farm
Dark Lane
King's Norton
Birmingham B38 0BS
Tel: 01564 822294

The Organic Shop
3 Sett Close
New Mills
High Peak
Derbyshire SK22 4DW
Tel: 01663 747550

Out of this World
Gosforth Shopping Centre
High Street
Newcastle-upon-Tyne
NE3 1JZ
Tel: 0191 2130421

Planet Organic
42 Westbourne Grove
London W2 5SH
Tel: 020 7221 7171

Seasons Forest Row Ltd
10 Hartfield Road
Forest Row
East Sussex RH18 5DN
Tel: 01342 824673

Stoneybridge Farm Shop
Stoneybridge Organic
  Nursery
Tywardreath
Par
Cornwall PL24 2TY
Tel: 01726 813858

Wholefoods Ltd
24 Paddington Street
London W1M 4DR
Tel: 020 7935 3924

Wild Oats
210 Westbourne Grove
London W11 2RH
Tel: 020 7229 1063

MAIL ORDER FOODS

Doves Farm Foods Ltd
(Specialist flours)
Salisbury Road
Hungerford
Berkshire RG17 0RF
Tel: 01488 684880

Gluten-free Foods Ltd
Unit 270
Centennial Park
Elsee
Borhamwood
Hertfordshire WD6 3SS
Tel: 020 8953 4444

Health Screening Ltd
1 Church Square
Taunton
Somerset TA1 1SA

Lifestyle Healthcare Ltd
(Gluten-free foods)
Centenary Business Park
Henley-on-Thames
Oxfordshire RG9 1DS
Tel: 01491 411767

Nutricia Dietary Products Ltd
Newmarket Avenue
White Horse Business Park
Trowbridge
Wiltshire BA14 0XQ
Tel: 01225 711801

Trufree Foods
(Mail order gluten- and wheat-free flours)
225 Putney Bridge Road
London SW15 2PY
Tel: 020 8874 1130

INDEX OF RECIPES FOR SPECIAL DIETS

CANCER PREVENTION

HEALTHY HEART

INDEX

ACKNOWLEDGEMENTS

The following photographs have been reproduced with the
kind permission of those listed: p6, p9, p12, p15, p22, p33,
p35t, p35b, p59, p62, p67, p68, p82, p83, p91, p94, p95, p115t,
p115b, p124, p133t, p133b and p134, Tony Stone Images;
and p56, Superstock.